# Lecture Notes in Computer Science  10537

*Commenced Publication in 1973*
Founding and Former Series Editors:
Gerhard Goos, Juris Hartmanis, and Jan van Leeuwen

## Editorial Board

More information about this series at http://www.springer.com/series/7411

Congduc Pham · Jörn Altmann
José Ángel Bañares (Eds.)

# Economics of Grids, Clouds, Systems, and Services

14th International Conference, GECON 2017
Biarritz, France, September 19–21, 2017
Proceedings

 Springer

*Editors*
Congduc Pham
UPPA, LIUPPA laboratory,
  UFR Sciences et Techniques
Pau
France

José Ángel Bañares 🆔
Department of Computer Science
Universidad de Zaragoza
Zaragoza
Spain

Jörn Altmann
Seoul National University
Seoul
South Korea

ISSN 0302-9743          ISSN 1611-3349  (electronic)
Lecture Notes in Computer Science
ISBN 978-3-319-68065-1          ISBN 978-3-319-68066-8  (eBook)
DOI 10.1007/978-3-319-68066-8

Library of Congress Control Number: 2017955086

LNCS Sublibrary: SL5 – Computer Communication Networks and Telecommunications

Printed on acid-free paper

This Springer imprint is published by Springer Nature
The registered company is Springer International Publishing AG
The registered company address is: Gewerbestrasse 11, 6330 Cham, Switzerland

# Preface

This volume constitutes the proceedings of the 14th International Conference on the Economics of Grids, Clouds, Systems, and Services (GECON 2017). This series of conferences serves as an annual meeting place, to bring together distributed systems expertise (e.g., in resource allocation, quality of service management, and energy consumption) with economics expertise (focusing on both micro- and macro-economic modelling and analysis) for creating effective solutions in this space. The conviction that we need to adopt a multidisciplinary approach and build links between ICT technical expertise and economics expertise has been the main leitmotif of GECON conferences.

The intertwinement of economy and technology is more and more present, and complexity is gaining momentum. Now more than ever, it is necessary to understand the interdependencies between the economy and ICT as a discipline. Only then it is possible to deal with the complexity. The cloud is the best exponent of this approach. As it is not possible to isolate the economy from other disciplines, such as politics or sociology, economics should be considered in the development of cloud systems and cloud services. Moreover, the impact of ICT is becoming so significant compared with other disciplines that the economy itself is transforming into an information and knowledge economy.

GECON 2017 was held during September 19–21, 2017, by the Laboratoire d'Informatique de l'Université de Pau et des Pays de l'Adour (LIUPPA) in the exceptional Biarritz city located in the heart of the French Basque Country. The conference took place at the Municipal Casino of Biarritz offering both high-level conference facilities and an incredible view of the ocean! We would like to express our deepest thanks to the Organizing Committee chaired by Congduc Pham.

For this year's edition, we received 38 submissions. Each submission was assessed by three to five reviewers of the international Program Committee. Ten of these 38 submissions were selected as full papers, for an acceptance rate of 26%. Additionally, shorter work-in-progress papers were integrated in the volume. This combination of full and work-in-progress papers fulfills the twofold aim of gathering original work and building a strong multidisciplinary community in this increasingly important area of a future information and knowledge economy. It enables open and informed dialogue between presenters and the audience. Our intention in accepting work-in-progress papers is underpinned by our conviction that the GECON conference is the best framework for presenters to better position their work for future events and to get an improved understanding of the impact their work is likely to have on the research community. The schedule for the conference this year was structured, to encourage discussions and debates with enough discussion time included in each paper presentation session, led by the session chair.

We would like to wholeheartedly thank the reviewers and Program Committee members for completing their reviews on time and giving insightful and valuable feedback to the authors. Furthermore, we would like to thank Alfred Hofmann of Springer for his support in publishing the proceedings of GECON 2017. The collaboration with Alfred Hofmann and his team was, as in the past years, efficient and effective. We are also grateful to the invited speakers for their contributions:

- Bruno Tuffin, Inria Campus Universitaire de Beaulieu, Rennes, France, who delivered a talk about "Network Neutrality: Modeling and Challenges and Its Impact on Clouds"
- Abdur Rahim, Fondazione Bruno Kessler (FBK)/Create-Net, Trento, Italy, who delivered a talk on "IoT and Data Analytics for Developing Countries from Research to Business Transformation"
- Corentin Dupont, Tomas Bures, Mehdi Sheikhalishahi, Congduc Pham, and Abdur Rahim, who discussed their invited paper "Low-cost IoT, Big Data, and Cloud Platform for Developing Countries"

This volume of the GECON 2017 proceedings has been structured in sections following the sessions that comprised the conference program:

Section 1: Pricing in Cloud and Quality of Service
Session 2: Work in Progress on Service Management
Session 3: Work in Progress on Business Models and Community Cooperation
Session 4: Work in Progress on Energy Efficiency and Resource Management
Session 5: Resource Management
Session 6: Edge Computing
Session 7: Cloud Federation
Session 8: Work in Progress on Service Selection and Coordination

September 2017                                              Congduc Pham
                                                           Jörn Altmann
                                                      José Ángel Bañares

# Organization

GECON 2017 was organized by the Laboratoire d'Information de l'Université de Pau et des Pays de l'Adour (http://liuppa.univ-pau.fr).

## Executive Committee

### Chairs

| | |
|---|---|
| Congduc Pham | Pau and Adour University, France |
| Jörn Altmann | Seoul National University, South Korea |
| José Ángel Bañares | University of Zaragoza, Spain |
| Richard Chbeir | Pau and Adour University, France |
| Ernesto Exposito | Pau and Adour University, France |

## Program Committee

| | |
|---|---|
| Alvaro Arenas | IE University, Spain |
| Ashraf Bany Mohammed | The University of Jordan, Jordan |
| Georg Garle | Technische Universität München, Germany |
| Emanuele Carlini | ISTI-CNR, Italy |
| Jeremy Cohen | Imperial College London, UK |
| Costas Courcoubetis | SUTD, Singapore |
| Massimo Coppola | Institute of Information Science and Technologies, Italy |
| Patrizio Dazzi | ISTI-CNR, Italy |
| Alex Delis | National and Kapodistrian University of Athens, Greece |
| Javier Diaz-Montes | Rutgers University, USA |
| Karim Djemame | University of Leeds, UK |
| Patricio Domingues | Polytechnic Institute of Leiria, Portugal |
| Giancarlo Fortino | University of Calabria, Italy |
| Felix Freitag | Universitat Politècnica de Catalunya, Spain |
| Marc Frincu | University of Southern California, USA |
| Netsanet Haile | Seoul National University, South Korea |
| Chun-Hsi Huang | University of Connecticut, USA |
| Bahman Javadi | Western Sydney University, Australia |
| Odej Kao | Technische Universität Berlin, Germany |
| Kibae Kim | Seoul National University, South Korea |
| Stefan Kirn | University of Hohenheim, Germany |
| Bastian Koller | HLRS, University of Stuttgart, Germany |
| Somayeh Koohborfardhaghighi | University of Amsterdam, The Netherlands |
| George Kousiouris | National Technical University of Athens, Greece |
| Dieter Kranzlmüller | Ludwig-Maximilians-Universität München, Germany |

| | |
|---|---|
| Dimosthenis Kyriazis | National Technical University of Athens, Greece |
| Renato Lo Cigno | University of Trento, Italy |
| Dan Ma | Singapore Management University, Singapore |
| Richard Ma | National University of Singapore, Singapore |
| Roc Meseguer | Universitat Politècnica de Catalunya, Spain |
| Mircea Moca | Babes-Bolyai University of Cluj-Napoca, Romania |
| Maurizio Naldi | Università di Roma Tor Vergata, Italy |
| Leandro Navarro | Universitat Politècnica de Catalunya, Spain |
| Marco Netto | IBM Research, Brazil |
| Frank Pallas | Technische Universität Berlin, Germany |
| George Pallis | University of Cyprus, Cyprus |
| Dana Petcu | West University of Timisoara, Romania |
| Ioan Petri | Cardiff University, UK |
| Radu Prodan | University of Innsbruck, Austria |
| Ivan Rodero | Rutgers, The State University of New Jersey, USA |
| Rizos Sakellariou | University of Manchester, UK |
| Lutz Schubert | OMI, University of Ulm, Germany |
| Mathias Slawik | Technische Universität Berlin, Germany |
| Burkhard Stiller | University of Zurich, Switzerland |
| Stefan Tai | Technische Universität Berlin, Germany |
| Rafael Tolosana-Calasanz | University of Zaragoza, Spain |
| Bruno Tuffin | Inria Rennes Bretagne Atlantique, France |
| Iraklis Varlamis | Harokopio University of Athens, Greece |
| Claudiu Vinte | Bucharest University of Economic Studies, Romania |
| Gabriel von Voigt | Leibniz Universität Hannover, Germany |
| Rüdiger Zarnekow | Technische Universität Berlin, Germany |
| Dimitrios Zissis | University of the Aegean, Greece |

## Steering Committee

| | |
|---|---|
| Jörn Altmann | Seoul National University, South Korea |
| José Ángel Bañares | University of Zaragoza, Spain |
| Steven Miller | Singapore Management University, Singapore |
| Maria Nikolaidou | Harokopio University of Athens, Greece |
| Omer F. Rana | Cardiff University, UK |
| Gheorghe Cosmin Silaghi | Babes-Bolyai University, Romania |
| Konstantinos Tserpes | Harokopio University of Athens, Greece |

## Sponsoring Institutions and Companies

Seoul National University, Seoul, South Korea
University of Zaragoza, Spain
Université de Pau et des Pays de l'Adour, France
Springer LNCS, Heidelberg, Germany
Future Generation Computer Systems Journal
Electronic Markets Journal

# Contents

**Work in Progress on Service Selection and Coordination**

**Keynote Topics**

# Pricing in Cloud and Quality of Service

# Insurance Pricing and Refund Sustainability for Cloud Outages

Loretta Mastroeni[1] and Maurizio Naldi[2(✉)]

[1] Department of Economics, Roma Tre University of Rome,
Via Silvio d'Amico 77, 00154 Rome, Italy
[2] Department of Civil Engineering and Computer Science, University of Rome
Tor Vergata, Via del Politecnico 1, 00133 Roma, Italy
maurizio.naldi@uniroma2.it

**Abstract.** Cloud outages may cause heavy economic losses for customers, who may ask the cloud provider for compensation. Cloud providers may therefore wish to insure themselves against that risk. Considering a scenario where outages take place according to a Poisson process and their duration follows a generalized Pareto model, we provide formulas to properly set the insurance premium under three measures of outage severity: number of outages, number of long outages, unavailability. We also assess the sustainability of refunds, by setting thresholds on unit refund per damaging events.

**Keywords:** Cloud · Service level agreement · Outages · Insurance · Pricing · Pareto distribution

## 1 Introduction

Cloud services are gaining acceptance as a storage and computing resource for both individual and corporate customers [37], especially replacing corporate storage facilities [19,32]. Though the quality of cloud services is typically guaranteed in Service Level Agreements (SLA) attached to contracts [3,38], their performance is often far from the expected [5].

In particular, cloud services are subject to outages, when the service suddenly drops. Models have been proposed to evaluate the availability of a large-scale cloud ex-ante [8,9,14], also over multiple clouds [34]. At the same time, campaign measurements have been conducted to describe the extent of outages [10,16].

Though rare, such outages may be more frequent than network outages (adding a layer of proneness to failures) [25,27,29]. A relevant consequence of service disruption is the economic loss due to the interruption of activities relying on the cloud (ever more important for many businesses) [11,30]. The Value-at-Risk for customers in the case of outages has been evaluated in [28]. In the case that outages are not explicitly covered in the SLA or exceed the provisions agreed on in the SLA, the cloud customer may act against the cloud provider to be compensated for the losses it incurs, respectively through a legal action or the enforcement of SLA provisions [22,31]. Since outages may affect all the

© Springer International Publishing AG 2017
C. Pham et al. (Eds.): GECON 2017, LNCS 10537, pp. 3–17, 2017.
DOI: 10.1007/978-3-319-68066-8_1

customers, the scale of compensation obligations may be so large as to spur the risk of financial failure for the cloud service provider [2].

In turn, the cloud provider may protect against such compensation requests through an insurance policy. Such insurance policies have been investigated in the case of network failures for the network connectivity service [20], against price rises in the context of clouds [21], and for the case of double homing in clouds [26].

In this paper, we wish to provide a method to set the insurance premium that a cloud provider may pay against cloud outages. After describing a statistical model for cloud outages in Sect. 2 and briefly reviewing the economic consequences of outages in Sect. 3, we provide the following contributions:

- we introduce the expected utility paradigm to derive a general formula for the insurance premium in Sect. 4;
- we define three performance metrics that cover most situations considered in SLAs (number of outages, number of long outages, unavailability) in Sect. 5;
- we derive formulas for the insurance premium for all three performance metrics in Sect. 6;
- for the case of compensations linked to the cloud service fee, we set limits for the refund factor so that it is sustainable in Sect. 7.

## 2    A Model for Service Status

The interruption of cloud services blocks all the activities of the company that rely on the cloud. In many cases, the whole company may depend on the use of the cloud, so that an outage can be really blocking for the customer company. Since the appearance and duration of cloud outages determine the extent of the interruption, in this section we review the major measurement campaigns of cloud outages and provide a probability model for both the frequency of outages and their duration. Though models have been provided to evaluate the availability of a cloud on the basis of its service architecture (see, e.g., [1, 17, 24]), we prefer to rely on measurement campaign, which describe the availability as actually observed by customers.

The availability of the service offered by the cloud provider to its customers may be modelled as a simple ON-OFF process, where the service alternates between two states, respectively providing the full service or no service at all. We do not consider here the case of a graceful degradation, where some service features are available and some are not, or the quality parameters are degraded from normal operating conditions (e.g. a service time exceeding the normal values). The service state jumps from the ON to the OFF value whenever an outage occurs, and reverts to the ON state when the outage ends and the service is fully restored. Marking the passage from each state to the other requires a careful identification of the time when the triggering event takes place. Since alternative definitions of such events lead to different measures of the duration of the ON and OFF states, some care must be exercised, at least to achieve an internal consistency of the measurement process; the dangers involved in this procedure have been outlined in [15]. In this paper, we do not enter into the details of the measurement process and assume that a valid and consistent measurement of the outages has been carried out. In the following we refer to the analysis of cloud outages carried out in [25], which relies on an extensive period of observations of a wide variety of cloud providers by customers. We provide a statistical model for the outage frequency and duration.

For the number $N$ of outages over a time $T$, we adopt a Poisson model, as already done in [13]:

$$\mathbb{P}[N = k] = e^{-\lambda T} \frac{(\lambda T)^k}{k!} \tag{1}$$

The expected value $\mathbb{E}[N] = \lambda T$ can be estimated from the sampling frequency, which is reported in Table 1 for the cloud providers analysed in [25], assuming that the time period $T$ is measured in year units.

As to the statistical characteristics of the duration $D$ of outages, in [25] a Generalized Pareto distribution (GPD) has been proposed after a comparison with other distributions based on the mean excess function. Its cumulative distribution function is

$$\mathbb{P}[D < x] = G_{\xi,\beta}(x) = \begin{cases} 1 - (1 + \xi x/\beta)^{-1/\xi} & \text{if } \xi \neq 0 \\ 1 - e^{-x/\beta} & \text{if } \xi = 0 \end{cases}, \tag{2}$$

where $\beta$ is the scale parameter and $\xi$ is the shape parameter. For the case where durations are expressed in minutes, the estimates for the two parameters are reported in Table 2 [25].

**Table 1.** Frequency of outages.

| Provider | Outages per year | Inter-outage times [days] |
|---|---|---|
| Google | 13.48 | 27.53 |
| Amazon | 4.48 | 85.6 |
| Rackspace | 47.53 | 7.78 |
| Salesforce | 46.4 | 8.56 |
| Windows Azure | 11.06 | 36.67 |

**Table 2.** Estimated parameters of the Generalized Pareto distribution.

| Company | Scale parameter $\beta$ | Shape parameter $\xi$ |
|---|---|---|
| Google | 405.29 | 0.39 |
| Amazon | 276.43 | −0.12 |
| Rackspace | 381.19 | 0.3 |
| Salesforce | 192.47 | −0.64 |
| Windows Azure | 312.32 | −0.35 |

The first two moments are respectively

$$\mathbb{E}[D] = \frac{\beta}{1 - \xi}$$

$$\mathbb{V}[D] = \frac{\beta^2}{(1 - \xi)^2(1 - 2\xi)}$$

(3)

The generalized Pareto distribution lends itself to fit a variety of distributions. Though in Eq. (2) two forms have been defined, depending on whether the shape parameter is either zero or nonzero, in all the cases examined in [25] a distinctly non-zero value has been estimated, though the sign is positive for some providers and negative for others. In the following, we assume that $\xi \neq 0$. The influence of the sign of the shape parameter on the GPD tail is summarized as follows:

1. if the shape parameter is positive, the tail decreases as a polynomial;
2. if the shape parameter is negative, the tail is finite.

We may consider a number of metrics to define the degradation of service quality. In the following we consider three such metrics, which cover most of the cases that can be met in practice. Namely, we consider the economic loss to be proportional to one of the following quantities as measured over a period $T$:

- Number of outages;
- Number of outages lasting more that a prescribed threshold (long outages);
- Cumulative outage duration (unavailability).

## 3    Economic Consequences of Service Interruptions

When an outage takes place, the service provider suffers an economic loss, which stems from a number of components. In [12] the structure of such loss has been described for the case of outages due to large scale Internet attacks. It is anyway mostly valid for outages due to unintentional reasons as well. In this section, we review the loss categories and relate them to the performance metrics introduced in Sect. 2.

According to that model, the economic loss includes four basic components:

1. Downtime Loss;
2. Disaster Recovery;
3. Liability;
4. Loss od customers.

There are two major contributors to downtime losses: the decrease in productivity, especially when operations heavily rely on the cloud (employees can no longer operate as usual), and the loss of revenues due to discontinued services. In addition to what is suffered during the outage, Disaster Recovery Costs have

**Table 3.** Typical losses for service interruption.

| Business sector | Loss [k$/minute] |
|-----------------|------------------|
| Brokerage       | 100–200          |
| Manufacturing   | 50–100           |
| Point-of-aale   | 20–100           |
| Travel agency   | 1–10             |

to be considered, since restarting the service requires the effort (and time) of employees and external staff. Since both downtime losses and disaster recovery are incurred by customers as well as by the cloud provider itself, the cloud provider may be held liable for what is suffered by its customers and be compelled to pay compensation. Finally, the reputation of the cloud provider may be damaged due to the dissatisfaction of customers for service degradation or interruption, which may lead to a reduced rate of new subscriptions and an increased churn rate.

Of the four contributions listed above, the first and the second one concern both the cloud provider and its customers, while the third and the fourth one affect just the cloud provider, but their intensity is a direct consequence of the severity of the first and second. The Downtime Loss may be quite relevant. For example, in [33] the estimated downtime losses reported in Table 3 are given, depending on the business sector of the company suffering the service interruption. For example, if we take the largest reported value, the losses for a single customer over a month are 86.4 k$ even with a 99.999% availability.

When considering insurance as a protection means for the cloud provider against the economic loss due to outages, we have to check whether the cloud provider is held responsible for those losses suffered by its customers or by other service providers relying on the cloud. In the following, though the derivation is quite general, we refer mainly to liability losses, where the loss is the compensation paid to customers.

In order to account for such economic losses, we must understand how each loss item may be captured by a specific performance metric. For example, the downtime loss is typically proportional to the outage duration, as Table 3 suggests, since the losses are expressed per minute of outage. The same can be said for the Disaster Recovery component, since the cost is proportional to the time employed by the repair team. Instead, the parameter most suitable to describe the Liability component depends on the formulation of the contractual obligations. In general, we may even consider the overall loss as the sum of terms depending on different service degradation metrics. Several cases have been considered in the literature. In [7], the penalty for SLA violations is set as a multiple of the revenues pertaining to the traffic flow that is affected by service degradation. In [39] a sample refund scheme is provided that sets refunds as a stairwise

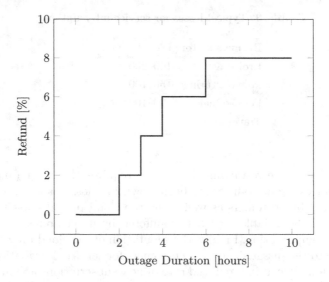

**Fig. 1.** Refund as a percentage of the annual service fee.

function of the outage duration (see Fig. 1): as long as the outage duration is shorter than 6 h, the refund is approximately proportional to the outage duration. In [40] the penalty is set as a reduction of the fees plus some additional compensation, and is computed on the basis of the number of violations. In the following, we consider the three metrics introduced at the end of Sect. 2, which cover most cases defined in SLAs.

## 4   The Expected Utility Paradigm

As hinted in the Introduction, the customer may ask for compensation when it suffers economic losses due to a cloud outages. Independently of whether it does so within the provisions of an SLA or through legal action, the compensation becomes an additional economic loss for the cloud provider. In order to hedge against the risk deriving from uncertain economic losses, the cloud provider may subscribe an insurance policy. In this section, we derive the fair price of such a policy. We adopt the pricing methodology based on the expected utility approach as described in [18].

We consider a cloud provider, whose assets are worth $\omega$, which faces a possible monetary loss $X$. On the other hand, the cloud provider may buy an insurance policy and pay just the insurance premium $P$ to be covered against that risk.

We assume that the cloud provider perceives the loss of the amount of money $x$ through the utility function $u(x)$. Actually, losing the same amount of money may be perceived differently, depending on the conditions of the insured cloud provider: even a small amount of money may have a significant impact for a cloud provider if it changes the overall economic balance from a profit condition to a loss one, while the same amount of money may be irrelevant for a company that is making anyway a large profit, since it represents just a small change in its return on investment.

Since the loss $X$ is a random variable, we have rather to consider the expected utility of the residual value of the company's assets when the loss $X$ is suffered. We then obtain the maximum tolerable premium $P$ when the perceived value under the uncertain loss and the perceived value under the payment of the insurance policy are held equal, i.e., when the following equilibrium equation is satisfied:

$$\mathbb{E}[u(\omega - X)] = u(\omega - P). \tag{4}$$

We can find an approximate solution of the equilibrium equation by expanding both terms through a Taylor series in the neighbourhood of $\omega - \mathbb{E}[X]$:

$$
\begin{aligned}
u(\omega - P^+) &\simeq u(\omega - \mathbb{E}[X]) + (\mathbb{E}[X] - P^+)u'(\omega - \mathbb{E}[X]) \\
u(\omega - X) &\simeq u(\omega - \mathbb{E}[X]) + (\mathbb{E}[X] - X)u'(\omega - \mathbb{E}[X]) \\
&\quad + \frac{(\mathbb{E}[X] - X)^2}{2}u''(\omega - \mathbb{E}[X])
\end{aligned} \tag{5}
$$

By employing the second of these Taylor expansions we get

$$
\begin{aligned}
\mathbb{E}[u(\omega - X)] &\simeq u(\omega - \mathbb{E}[X]) + (\mathbb{E}[X] - \mathbb{E}[X])u'(\omega - \mathbb{E}[X]) + \frac{\mathbb{V}[X]}{2}u''(\omega - \mathbb{E}[X]) \\
&= u(\omega - \mathbb{E}[X]) + \frac{\mathbb{V}[X]}{2}u''(\omega - \mathbb{E}[X])
\end{aligned} \tag{6}
$$

Finally, by replacing those expressions in the equilibrium Eq. (4) we obtain the maximum tolerable premium

$$P \simeq \mathbb{E}[X] + \frac{\mathbb{V}[X]}{2}r(\omega - \mathbb{E}[X]), \tag{7}$$

where we have introduced the risk aversion coefficient $r$, which takes into account the effect of the utility function:

$$r(x) = -\frac{u''(x)}{u'(x)}. \tag{8}$$

Though several options are possible for the utility function (see, e.g., Sect. 1.3 in [18]), the assumption of a constant risk aversion coefficient has been adopted for cloud customers in [23]:

$$r(x) = \alpha > 0. \tag{9}$$

In that case, the utility function exhibits the Constant Absolute Risk Aversion (CARA) property [36], and the only function that satisfies the CARA property is the exponential function $u(x) = 1 - e^{-\alpha x}$, which leads to the maximum tolerable premium

$$P \simeq \mathbb{E}[X] + \alpha \frac{\mathbb{V}[X]}{2}. \tag{10}$$

Under the CARA property the premium formulation is therefore of the mean-variance type, where the risk-aversion coefficient is to be defined to obtain the premium: higher values of $\alpha$ are associated to a growing aversion for risk and then to the willingness to pay a higher premium: in [6] the risk-aversion coefficient is assumed to take values in the [0.5,4] range.

## 5   Loss Statistics

As stated at the end of Sect. 2, we consider three metrics to describe the cloud performance degradation: number of outages, number of long outages, and unavailability. Following the model described in Sect. 2, in this section we derive the main statistics concerning those metrics and the resulting economic loss. Though we mainly refer to the economic loss suffered by customers, for which integral compensation is sought, in the following we keep the formulation general, so that the economic loss $X$ may represent the overall economic loss suffered by the cloud provider (included the losses directly suffered by the cloud provider as well as those due to its liability).

### 5.1   Number of Outages

The occurrence of failures is described by a Poisson model as per Eq. (1). If each outage causes an economic loss $k_f$, the overall economic loss is

$$X_f = k_f N \tag{11}$$

Over the time $T$ its expected value and variance are respectively

$$\begin{aligned} \mathbb{E}[X] &= k_f \lambda T \\ \mathbb{V}[X] &= k_f^2 \lambda T. \end{aligned} \tag{12}$$

### 5.2   Number of Long Outages

By long outages we mean outages whose duration exceeds a given threshold $W$. If the economic loss $X$ is proportional to the number of long outages, we have

$$X_{lf} = k_{lf} N_{lf} = k_{lf} \sum_{i=1}^{N_T} I_{[D_i > W]}, \tag{13}$$

where $I_{[y]}$ is the indicator function, which takes the value 1 if the condition $y$ is satisfied, and the value 0 otherwise, and $k_{lf}$ is the unit loss per long outage.

The indicator function is actually a random variable with a Bernoulli distribution, so that its first two moments are

$$\mathbb{E}[I_{[D_i>W]}] = \mathbb{P}\left[I_{[D_i>W]} = 1\right] = 1 - \mathbb{P}[D_i < W]$$

$$= 1 - \left[1 - \left(1 + \frac{\xi W}{\beta}\right)^{-\frac{1}{\xi}}\right] = \left(1 + \frac{\xi W}{\beta}\right)^{-\frac{1}{\xi}} \qquad (14)$$

$$\mathbb{V}[I_{[D_i>W]}] = \mathbb{P}\left[I_{[D_i>W]} = 1\right]\left(1 - \mathbb{P}\left[I_{[D_i>W]} = 1\right]\right)$$

$$= \left(1 + \frac{\xi W}{\beta}\right)^{-\frac{1}{\xi}}\left[1 - \left(1 + \frac{\xi W}{\beta}\right)^{-\frac{1}{\xi}}\right] \qquad (15)$$

Since Eq. (13) is a random sum of independent Bernoulli variables, we can obtain the probability distribution of the economic loss (which is now a discrete variable whose possible values are multiples of the unit loss per long outage $k_{lf}$):

$$\mathbb{P}[X_{lf} = jk_{lf}] = \sum_{n=1}^{\infty} \mathbb{P}\left[\sum_{i=0}^{n} I_{[D_i>W]} = j \middle| N_T = n\right] \mathbb{P}[N_T = n]$$

$$= \sum_{n=1}^{\infty} \binom{n}{j}\left(1 + \frac{\xi W}{\beta}\right)^{-\frac{j}{\xi}}\left[1 - \left(1 + \frac{\xi W}{\beta}\right)^{-\frac{1}{\xi}}\right]^{n-j} \frac{(\lambda T)^n}{n!} e^{-\lambda T}.$$

$$(16)$$

By resorting to Wald's identities (see, e.g., Sect. 34.14.2.11 of [35] or Sect. 1.7.3 of [4]), we can compute the mean and the variance of the economic loss

$$\mathbb{E}[X_{lf}] = k_{lf}\mathbb{E}[N_T]\mathbb{E}\left[I_{[D_i>W]}\right] = k_{lf}\lambda T\left(1 + \frac{\xi W}{\beta}\right)^{-\frac{1}{\xi}},$$

$$\mathbb{V}[X_{lf}] = k_{lf}^2\left\{\mathbb{E}^2\left[I_{[D_i>W]}\right]\mathbb{V}[N_T] + \mathbb{V}\left[I_{[D_i>W]}\right]\mathbb{E}[N_T]\right\}$$

$$= k_{lf}^2\left\{\left(1 + \frac{\xi W}{\beta}\right)^{-\frac{2}{\xi}}\lambda T + \left(1 + \frac{\xi W}{\beta}\right)^{-\frac{1}{\xi}}\left[1 - \left(1 + \frac{\xi W}{\beta}\right)^{-\frac{1}{\xi}}\right]\lambda T\right\}$$

$$= k_{lf}^2\lambda T\left(1 + \frac{\xi W}{\beta}\right)^{-\frac{1}{\xi}}\left\{\left(1 + \frac{\xi W}{\beta}\right)^{-\frac{1}{\xi}} + \left[1 - \left(1 + \frac{\xi W}{\beta}\right)^{-\frac{1}{\xi}}\right]\right\}$$

$$= k_{lf}^2\lambda T\left(1 + \frac{\xi W}{\beta}\right)^{-\frac{1}{\xi}}$$

$$(17)$$

We can use Wald's identities since there is only a weak correlation among the number of summands in the sum (13) and each of the summands: the duration of an outage (e.g., its exceeding $W$) is independent of the number of outages, while the number of outages is very weakly correlated with the outage duration, as long as we consider services with high availability.

## 5.3  Unavailability

Now the economic loss is proportional to the cumulative unavailability time $U$ over the period $T$:

$$X_u = k_u U = k_u \sum_{i=1}^{N_T} D_i, \qquad (18)$$

where $k_u$ is the loss per unit time.

We have again a random sum, for which we can apply the Wald's identities, following the same considerations introduced in Sect. 5.2. The mean economic loss and its variance are respectively

$$\mathbb{E}[X_u] = k_u \mathbb{E}[U] = k_u \mathbb{E}[D_i]\mathbb{E}[N_T]$$
$$= k_u \frac{\beta}{1-\xi}\lambda T \qquad (19)$$

$$\mathbb{V}[X_u] = k_u^2 \mathbb{V}[U_T] = k_u^2 \left\{ \mathbb{E}^2[D_i]\mathbb{V}[N_T] + \mathbb{V}[D_i]\mathbb{E}[N_T] \right\}$$
$$= k_u^2 \left[ \frac{\beta^2}{(1-\xi)^2}\lambda T + \lambda T \frac{\beta^2}{(1-\xi)^2(1-2\xi)} \right]$$
$$= k_u^2 \frac{\beta^2}{(1-\xi)^2}\lambda T \left( 1 + \frac{1}{1-2\xi} \right) = k_u^2 \frac{\beta^2}{(1-\xi)^2}\lambda T \frac{2-2\xi}{1-2\xi} \qquad (20)$$
$$= \frac{2k_u^2\beta^2\lambda T}{(1-\xi)(1-2\xi)}$$

# 6  Premium Setting

After deriving the first two moments of the economic loss in Sect. 5, in this section we now employ the mean-variance model of Eq. (10) to obtain the insurance premium, again for the three performance measures separately.

## 6.1  Number of Outages

Replacing the results of Eq. (12) in Eq. (10) we get the premium (actually the maximum tolerable premium) over a period $T$:

$$P_f = k_f\lambda T + \frac{\alpha k_f^2\lambda}{2}T = k_f\lambda T \left( 1 + \frac{\alpha k_f}{2} \right). \qquad (21)$$

## 6.2  Number of Long Outages

Recalling Eq. (17) the premium is

$$P_{lf} = k_{lf}\lambda T \left( 1 + \frac{\xi W}{\beta} \right)^{-\frac{1}{\xi}} + \frac{\alpha}{2}k_{lf}^2\lambda T \left( 1 + \frac{\xi W}{\beta} \right)^{-\frac{1}{\xi}}$$
$$= k_{lf}\lambda T \left( 1 + \frac{\xi W}{\beta} \right)^{-\frac{1}{\xi}} \left( 1 + \frac{\alpha k_{lf}}{2} \right) \qquad (22)$$

### 6.3  Unavailability

After recalling Eqs. (19) and (20), we have

$$P_{\mathrm{u}} = k_{\mathrm{u}} \frac{\beta}{1-\xi} \lambda T + \frac{\alpha}{2} \frac{2 k_{\mathrm{u}}^2 \beta^2 \lambda T}{(1-\xi)(1-2\xi)}$$

$$= \frac{k_{\mathrm{u}} \beta \lambda T}{1-\xi} \left( 1 + \frac{\alpha k_{\mathrm{u}} \beta}{1-2\xi} \right) \tag{23}$$

## 7  Refund Sustainability

In Sect. 6, we have seen that the premium is anyway related to the unit refund that the cloud provider has vowed to pay the customer in the case of service disruptions: a higher refund leads to higher economic losses for the cloud provider and therefore to a higher premium. The refund value has therefore to be set so as not to have too large a premium. Typically SLAs set a compensation as a fraction of the periodic service fee $F$. In this section, we introduce a constraint on the compensation parameters so that the refund procedure is sustainable.

If we consider the periodic (annual or monthly) fee $F$ paid by the customer to the cloud provider, that fee is eroded by the insurance premium. We wish that erosion to be minimal, so that the cloud provider retains a significant net revenue from cloud operations. We wish therefore to have

$$P_* < \rho F \qquad \rho \in (0, 1), \tag{24}$$

where the asterisk is a jolly character so that the expression may be applied to any of the three performance parameters, and $\rho$ sets the fraction of the fee that the cloud provider may accept to lose due to compensation.

On the other hand, the unit refund per damaging event (i.e., either $k_{\mathrm{f}}$, $k_{\mathrm{lf}}$ or $k_{\mathrm{u}}$, according to the performance parameter considered for refund setting) is typically expressed as a fraction of the fee, as shown in Fig. 1. We can therefore write

$$k_* = \gamma F \qquad \gamma \in (0, 1). \tag{25}$$

Since the economic loss $X_*$ is proportional to the loss statistics $L$ (which is either $N_{\mathrm{f}}$, $N_{\mathrm{lf}}$ or $U$), as embodied by Eqs. (11), (13), and (18), we have the general constraint

$$P_* = \mathbb{E}[X_*] + \alpha \frac{\mathbb{V}[X_*]}{2} = k_* \mathbb{E}[L] + k_*^2 \alpha \frac{\mathbb{V}[L]}{2} = \gamma F \mathbb{E}[L] + \gamma^2 F^2 \alpha \frac{\mathbb{V}[L]}{2} < \rho F \tag{26}$$

from which we obtain a quadratic inequality in the coefficient $\gamma$

$$F \alpha \frac{\mathbb{V}[L]}{2} \gamma^2 + \mathbb{E}[L]\gamma - \rho < 0, \tag{27}$$

Since the discriminant associated to the quadratic form is

$$\Delta = \left( \frac{\mathbb{E}[L]}{2} \right)^2 + \frac{\alpha}{2} F \rho \mathbb{V}[L] \tag{28}$$

and $\gamma > 0$, we get the following constraint on the refund factor $\gamma$ to be sustainable

$$\gamma < \frac{2\sqrt{\Delta} - \mathbb{E}[L]}{\alpha F \mathbb{V}[L]} = \frac{\sqrt{1 + 2\alpha F \rho \frac{\mathbb{V}[L]}{\mathbb{E}^2[L]}} - 1}{\alpha F \frac{\mathbb{V}[L]}{\mathbb{E}[L]}} \tag{29}$$

From this general expression we can now obtain the specific constraints on the refund factor for the three performance parameters. In order to get a numerical feeling for the values at hand, we will apply the formulas to the case of Google (see Tables 1 and 2), assuming a fee $F = 100$, a premium not larger than 5% of the fee ($\rho = 0.05$), and a risk aversion factor $\alpha = 2$.

## 7.1  Number of Outages

In this case the loss statistics is the number of outages $N_f$, so that $\mathbb{E}[L] = \lambda T$ and $\mathbb{V}[L] = \lambda T$ and

$$\frac{\mathbb{V}[L]}{\mathbb{E}[L]} = 1 \qquad \frac{\mathbb{V}[L]}{\mathbb{E}^2[L]} = \frac{1}{\lambda T} \tag{30}$$

From Eq. (29) the constraint on the refund factor is then

$$\gamma < \frac{\sqrt{1 + \frac{2\alpha F \rho}{\lambda T}} - 1}{\alpha F}. \tag{31}$$

For the numeric case defined at the beginning of the section, we obtain $\gamma < 0.00287$, so that the maximum sustainable refund for an outage is 2.87‰ of the fee.

## 7.2  Number of Long Outages

Here $L = N_{lf}$, and

$$\frac{\mathbb{V}[L]}{\mathbb{E}[L]} = 1 \qquad \frac{\mathbb{V}[L]}{\mathbb{E}^2[L]} = \frac{1}{\lambda T}\left(1 + \frac{\xi W}{\beta}\right)^{\frac{1}{\xi}} \tag{32}$$

so that Eq. (29) becomes

$$\gamma < \frac{\sqrt{1 + \frac{2\alpha F \rho}{\lambda T}\left(1 + \frac{\xi W}{\beta}\right)^{\frac{1}{\xi}}} - 1}{\alpha F} \tag{33}$$

For the numeric case defined at the beginning of the section, considering a duration threshold $W = 120$ (2 h), we obtain $\gamma < 0.0036$, so that the maximum sustainable refund for any outage exceeding 2 h is 3.6‰ of the fee.

### 7.3  Unavailability

Here $L = U$, and

$$\frac{\mathbb{V}[L]}{\mathbb{E}[L]} = \frac{2\beta}{1 - 2\xi} \qquad \frac{\mathbb{V}[L]}{\mathbb{E}^2[L]} = \frac{2}{\lambda T}\frac{1 - \xi}{1 - 2\xi} \tag{34}$$

so that Eq. (29) becomes

$$\gamma < \frac{1 - 2\xi}{2\alpha\beta F}\left[\sqrt{1 + \frac{4\alpha F \rho}{\lambda T}\frac{1 - \xi}{1 - 2\xi}} - 1\right] \tag{35}$$

For the numeric case defined at the beginning of the section, we obtain $\gamma <$ $2.77 \cdot 10^{-6}$, so that the maximum sustainable refund for an hour of unavailability is 0.166‰ of the fee.

## 8  Conclusions

Relying on a statistical model for the occurrence of outages and their duration, we have derived formulas for the insurance premium that a cloud provider should pay to protect itself against the compensation claims that may arrive from its customers. The formulas can be employed as well to cover against economic losses directly suffered by the cloud provider. The selection of performance parameters adopted to set the premium is wide enough to cover for most compensation definitions found in SLAs. At the same time we have set a constraint of the refund factor so that the compensation promised to customers is sustainable.

This set of premium formulas and refund constraints allow any cloud provider to delimit the risk associated to outages so that its business proposition is sustainable. In the absence of this risk hedging, the cloud provider would be vulnerable to the risk of excessive compensations due to SLA provisions.

## References

1. Bala, A., Chana, I.: Fault tolerance-challenges, techniques and implementation in cloud computing. IJCSI Int. J. Comput. Sci. Issues 9(1), 288–293 (2012)
2. Bartolini, C., El Kateb, D., Le Traon, Y., Hagen, D.: Cloud providers viability: how to address it from an IT and legal perspective? In: Altmann, J., Silaghi, G.C., Rana, O.F. (eds.) GECON 2015. LNCS, vol. 9512, pp. 281–295. Springer, Cham (2016). doi:10.1007/978-3-319-43177-2_19
3. Baset, S.A.: Cloud SLAs: present and future. ACM SIGOPS Operating Syst. Rev. 46(2), 57–66 (2012)
4. Beichelt, F.: Stochastic Processes in Science, Engineering and Finance. Chapman & Hall/CRC, Boca Raton (2006)
5. Bermbach, D.: Quality of cloud services: Expect the unexpected. IEEE Internet Comput. 21(1), 68–72 (2017)
6. Böhme, R., Kataria, G.: Models and Measures for Correlation in Cyber-Insurance. In: DIMACS Workshop on Information Security Economics, 18–19 January 2007

7. Bouillet, E., Mitra, D., Ramakrishnan, K.: The structure and management of service level agreements in networks. IEEE J. Sel. Areas. Commun. **20**(4), 691–699 (2002)
8. Bruneo, D.: A stochastic model to investigate data center performance and QoS in IaaS cloud computing systems. IEEE Trans. Parallel Distrib. Syst. **25**(3), 560–569 (2014)
9. Buyya, R., Ranjan, R., Calheiros, R.N.: Modeling and simulation of scalable cloud computing environments and the cloudsim toolkit: Challenges and opportunities. In: International Conference on High Performance Computing & Simulation, HPCS 2009, pp. 1–11. IEEE (2009)
10. Cheng, X., Bounfour, A.: Performance analysis of public cloud computing providers. In: Tenth Mediterranean Conference on Information Systems (MCIS) (2016)
11. Cholda, P., Følstad, E.L., Helvik, B.E., Kuusela, P., Naldi, M., Norros, I.: Towards risk-aware communications networking. Rel. Eng. Sys. Safety **109**, 160–174 (2013)
12. Dübendorfer, T., Wagner, A., Plattner, B.: An economic damage model for large-scale internet attacks. In: 13th IEEE International Workshops on Enabling Technologies (WETICE 2004), pp. 223–228, 14–16 June 2004
13. Franke, U., Buschle, M., Österlind, M.: An experiment in SLA decision-making. In: Altmann, J., Vanmechelen, K., Rana, O.F. (eds.) GECON 2013. LNCS, vol. 8193, pp. 256–267. Springer, Cham (2013). doi:10.1007/978-3-319-02414-1_19
14. Ghosh, R., Longo, F., Frattini, F., Russo, S., Trivedi, K.S.: Scalable analytics for IaaS cloud availability. IEEE Trans. Cloud Comput. **2**(1), 57–70 (2014)
15. Hogben, G., Pannetrat, A.: Mutant apples: a critical examination of cloud SLA availability definitions. In: 2013 IEEE 5th International Conference on Cloud Computing Technology and Science (CloudCom), vol. 1, pp. 379–386. IEEE (2013)
16. Hu, Z., Zhu, L., Ardi, C., Katz-Bassett, E., Madhyastha, H.V., Heidemann, J., Yu, M.: The need for end-to-end evaluation of cloud availability. In: Faloutsos, M., Kuzmanovic, A. (eds.) PAM 2014. LNCS, vol. 8362, pp. 119–130. Springer, Cham (2014). doi:10.1007/978-3-319-04918-2_12
17. Jhawar, R., Piuri, V., Santambrogio, M.: Fault tolerance management in cloud computing: a system-level perspective. IEEE Syst. J. **7**(2), 288–297 (2013)
18. Kaas, R., Goovaerts, M., Dhaene, J., Denuit, M.: Modern Actuarial Risk Theory. Springer, Heidelberg (2004)
19. Mansouri, Y., Buyya, R.: To move or not to move: Cost optimization in a dual cloud-based storage architecture. J. Netw. Comput. Appl. **75**, 223–235 (2016)
20. Mastroeni, L., Naldi, M.: Network protection through insurance: premium computation for the on-off service model. In: 8th International Workshop on the Design of Reliable Communication Networks DRCN, Krakow, Poland, pp. 46–53, 10–12 October 2011
21. Mastroeni, L., Naldi, M.: Pricing of insurance policies against cloud storage price rises. SIGMETRICS Perform. Eval. Rev. **40**(2), 42–45 (2012)
22. Mastroeni, L., Naldi, M.: Compensation policies and risk in service level agreements: a value-at-risk approach under the ON-OFF service model. In: Cohen, J., Maillé, P., Stiller, B. (eds.) ICQT 2011. LNCS, vol. 6995, pp. 2–13. Springer, Heidelberg (2011). doi:10.1007/978-3-642-24547-3_2
23. Morshedlou, H., Meybodi, M.R.: Decreasing impact of SLA violations: a proactive resource allocation approach for cloud computing environments. IEEE Trans. Cloud Comput. **2**(2), 156–167 (2014)
24. Nabi, M., Toeroe, M., Khendek, F.: Availability in the cloud: state of the art. J. Netw. Comput. Appl. **60**, 54–67 (2016)

25. Naldi, M.: The availability of cloud-based services: is it living up to its promise? In: 9th International Conference on the Design of Reliable Communication Networks, DRCN 2013, Budapest, Hungary, pp. 282–289 (2013)
26. Naldi, M.: Balancing leasing and insurance costs to achieve total risk coverage in cloud storage multi-homing. In: Altmann, J., Vanmechelen, K., Rana, O.F. (eds.) GECON 2014. LNCS, vol. 8914, pp. 146–158. Springer, Cham (2014). doi:10.1007/978-3-319-14609-6_10
27. Naldi, M.: Accuracy of third-party cloud availability estimation through ICMP. In: 39th International Conference on Telecommunications and Signal Processing (TSP), pp. 40–43. IEEE, Vienna (2016)
28. Naldi, M.: Evaluation of customers losses and value-at-risk under cloud outages. In: 2017 40th International Conference on Telecommunications and Signal Processing (TSP). IEEE (2017)
29. Naldi, M.: ICMP-based third-party estimation of cloud availability. Int. J. Adv. Telecommun. Electrotechnics Signals Syst. **6**(1), 11–18 (2017)
30. Naldi, M., D'Acquisto, G.: A normal copula model for the economic risk analysis of correlated failures in communications networks. J. UCS **14**(5), 786–799 (2008)
31. Naldi, M., Mastroeni, L.: Violation of service availability targets in service level agreements. In: Federated Conference on Computer Science and Information Systems - FedCSIS 2011, Szczecin, Poland. pp. 537–540, 18–21 September 2011
32. Naldi, M., Mastroeni, L.: Economic decision criteria for the migration to cloud storage. Eur. J. Inf. Syst. **25**(1), 16–28 (2016)
33. Pesola, M.: Network protection is a key stroke. Financial Times, FT Business Continuity, 9 March 2004
34. Petcu, D.: Service quality assurance in multi-clouds. In: Altmann, J., Silaghi, G.C., Rana, O.F. (eds.) GECON 2015. LNCS, vol. 9512, pp. 81–97. Springer, Cham (2016). doi:10.1007/978-3-319-43177-2_6
35. Poularikas, A.D.: Probability and stochastic processes. In: Poularikas, A.D. (ed.) The Handbook of Formulas and Tables for Signal Processing. CRC Press (1999)
36. Pratt, J.W.: Risk aversion in the small and in the large. Econometrica **32**(1–2), 122–136 (1964)
37. Rittinghouse, J.W., Ransome, J.F.: Cloud Computing: Implementation, Management, and Security. CRC Press (2016)
38. Serrano, D., Bouchenak, S., Kouki, Y., de Oliveira Jr., F.A., Ledoux, T., Lejeune, J., Sopena, J., Arantes, L., Sens, P.: Sla guarantees for cloud services. Future Gener. Comput. Syst. **54**, 233–246 (2016)
39. Sherif, M.H.: Managing Projects in Telecommunication Services. Wiley, New York (2006)
40. Wustenhoff, E.: Service Level Agreement in the Data Center. Sun BluePrints OnLine, April 2002

# Pricing IaaS: A Hedonic Price Index Approach

Persefoni Mitropoulou, Evangelia Filiopoulou, Mara Nikolaidou,
and Christos Michalakelis[✉]

Department of Informatics and Telematics, Harokopio University,
Tavros, 177 78 Athens, Greece
{persam, evangelf, mara, michalak}@hua.gr

**Abstract.** Infrastructure as a Service (IaaS) is a rapidly expanding model of cloud computing. It includes control of computing resources, such as memory, computing power and storage capacity, satisfying the most fundamental IT needs for businesses on a usage-based payment model. Currently, there is an increased demand for IaaS services, which in turn feeds competition among cloud providers. As the price of cloud services depends on the supported characteristics and cloud providers do not adopt the same pricing model, the study of continuously evolving pricing schemes for such an innovative business model is a challenge. The work presented in this paper focuses on the construction of a price index based on a hedonic pricing model, emphasizing, besides basic functionality features, additional qualitative and quantitative attributes defined the Quality of Services provided. The aim of the study is to determine the importance of each feature and its effect on the final price. This is achieved by constructing the price index with data from 23 well-known IaaS cloud providers taking into account both functional and non-functional attributes of cloud computing services. In addition, a comparison of results between the present findings and our previous work is made, to assess the differences in estimates of each attribute contributory value to the shaping of IaaS pricing function.

**Keywords:** Cloud computing · Non-functional requirements · Infrastructure-as-a-Service · Pricing models · Hedonic price indices

## 1 Introduction

In recent years cloud computing has transformed ICT industry and has been established as a significant driver for cost saving and agility. Cloud services have rapidly evolved and have a profound impact on global economy and society. Cloud computing has become a popular computing architecture in IT market and it is composed of three service models:

- Infrastructure as a Service (IaaS), which includes control of fundamental computing resources, such as memory, computing power and storage capacity.
- Platform as a Service (PaaS) that provides control over the deployed applications and possibly configuration settings for developer platforms.
- Software as a Service (SaaS), which includes the use of software services accessed through a web browser or a program interface [1].

© Springer International Publishing AG 2017
C. Pham et al. (Eds.): GECON 2017, LNCS 10537, pp. 18–28, 2017.
DOI: 10.1007/978-3-319-68066-8_2

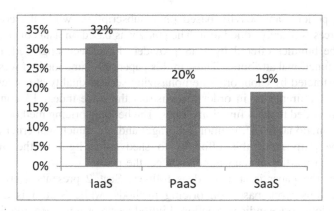

**Fig. 1.** Worldwide public cloud services forecast (2016–2020) [3].

This paper focuses on IaaS service, since according to Gartner Inc it is expected to present the highest growth in 2018, as shown in Fig. 1. Some key benefits of IaaS are high flexibility, usage-based payment scheme, allowing users to pay what they use as they use it, and the fact that the latest technology is always employed. This way customers can achieve a much faster service delivery [2]. Analytically, IaaS service is expected to grow up to 31.5% and it is estimated to reach $45,5 billion. On the contrary, SaaS service is expected to grow 19%, reaching $55,14 billion and PaaS service will develop 19% reaching 16,6 billion [3].

Commercial success of cloud computing is based on pricing models, provided that pricing models are transparent for both providers and clients. However, pricing schemes usually veil the prices of resources such as CPU, Memory and Storage [4]. Most cloud providers such as IBM, Amazon and Microsoft charge a prominent set of predefined packages, known as pricing bundling strategy [5]. For example Amazon offers compute optimized bundle with 16 CPUs, 122 GB of memory and 320 GB of storage for $1.33 per hour [5]. Consequently, cloud clients having specific requirements are driven to select from the predefined cloud bundles.

Customers' requirements are categorized into functional and non-functional [6]. As far as IaaS is concerned, functional requirements prescribe basic properties as computing power, memory, storage and network access speed. In addition, the Quality of Service (QoS) provided to clients is defined by non-functional requirements related to availability, security, elasticity and usability of cloud computing [7]. Both functional and non-functional features are prescribed in cloud service bundles and priced as an integrated service. However, it is important to estimate the impact of each feature, functional or non-functional, on the cloud bundle price.

Pricing efforts in existing literature often neglect the impact of non-functional client requirements, related to QoS of IaaS cloud bundles. The authors have proposed to use a hedonic pricing model for constructing a price index of IaaS, based on basic functional properties, such as CPUs, memory, storage and OS [8, 9]. Data from 23 cloud providers were collected and processed, based on information provided by Cloudorado cloud comparison engine (https://www.cloudorado.com). The study indicated that cloud pricing policies are heavily based on a subscription, while the cost of using specific resources is usually added to it. The study was based on data collected in 2014. Since then, the bundles offered by IaaS providers have been upgraded and heavily based on non-functional attributes. Thus, in this paper, the same method was applied in current data extracted by Cloudorado, emphasizing service quality attributes related to non-functional requirements, in order to construct the price index. 13 non-functional properties were added to the 4 functional ones. The hedonic pricing method indicates to which extent functional (CPU, memory, storage) and non-functional criteria affect the price [4]. The purpose of this effort is to shed some light in the manner that non-functional properties of IaaS bundles affect the price.

The rest of the paper is structured as follows: Sect. 2 presents a brief literature review of previous work based on pricing methods, while Sect. 3 is a theoretical approach of hedonic price indices. Section 4 introduces non-functional requirements on IaaS service and Sect. 5 describes price index construction by presenting the data collection process of cloud bundles, the methodology and the results. Finally Sect. 6 presents the final conclusions.

## 2 Literature Review

Nowadays IaaS cloud computing services demand has been increased creating in turn high competition among cloud providers who are not all pursuing the same pricing model. The study of continuously evolving pricing schemes for such an innovative business model is a really interesting task, as there are several cloud services with comparable functionality but usually available to customers at different prices.

The "pay-as-you-go" pricing scheme is commonly used to charge the users only for the services they need, paying for the required computing instances and just for the time they use them and not for what the resources value. If more IaaS resources are required during a task, customers simply ask the provider [10]. Another quite static pricing method is based on the period of subscription, meaning that a fixed price is set for a specific bundle of IaaS cloud services according to a longer period of subscription. As a consequence, users may underpay for the required resources if they use them extensively, but they might overpay if they barely need them [11]. One of the rarest fixed pricing models of cloud services is the one that is totally based on cost, but it is hard to implement. Users are offered the maximum utilization of the provider's resources and pay for what the resources really value [12].

Although these static pricing schemes of IaaS cloud services have been used from many cloud providers in order to guarantee service level agreement, it is still inevitable to satisfy equally both the cloud vendors' and cloud users' requirements. This is the reason why dynamic pricing methods have been widely developed and used. In [13] an optimized fine-grained and fair pricing scheme is studied in order to derive an optimal price that satisfies both customers and providers simultaneously and also find a best-fit billing cycle to maximize social welfare. Rohitratana and Altmann [14] proposed an agent-based simulation of four different pricing models that indicated that the Demand-Driven (DD) pricing scheme was the best approach in ideal cases. A real-time pricing algorithm for cloud computing resources was introduced in [15] that analyzed some history utilization data and found the final price that was mostly beneficial for the provider because it reduced its costs, allowing at the same time resources to be used more effectively. Furthermore, there are some pricing methods that are mostly driven by competitors' prices [16] and some others based on the amount of money customers are ready to pay [17].

Apart from fixed and dynamic pricing of IaaS cloud computing services, another approach that describes price as the result of a multidimensional function shaped by the service's characteristics is the construction of price indices. Especially a price index which is based on a hedonic pricing method, takes into consideration different factors of IaaS cloud computing services trying to estimate the contributory value of each characteristic to the shaping of the total price of a service bundle. Price indices were primarily developed seeking to capture the effect of different attributes to the final pricing in the context of other areas than the cloud computing, such as the environment, the housing market or automobiles and then they have been widely used to more technological areas [18]. The hedonic pricing method has been proposed in [19] to make pricing plans more transparent among cloud providers by analyzing two price comparison methods and in [8, 9] to estimate the importance of each IaaS resource and its effect on the final price.

## 3 Hedonic Price Indices

Hedonic methods are regression models in which a product price is related to its characteristics, considered as a function of them, linear or non-linear. The main assumption is that a product is a bundle of characteristics and that consumers just buy bundles of characteristics instead of the product itself. A hedonic method decomposes the studied product into its characteristics obtaining estimates of the contributory value of each one.

According to the definition of [19]: "*A hedonic price index is any price index that makes use of a hedonic function. A hedonic function is a relation between the prices of different varieties of a product, such as the various models of personal computers, and the quantities of characteristics in them*". The importance of a price index is that it can be used to determine suggested prices for combinations of the characteristics that were not included, or they were not available, when the index was constructed.

These methods can be used to construct a quality-adjusted price index of a service. An informative overview of the hedonic methods and how they are constructed can be found in [18, 19].

The advantage of this method is that the necessary calculations are easy to implement. Hedonic methods are also very fast to apply but the disadvantage is that index price can change even if no new products exist, or if all prices remain the same. Among the strengths of a hedonic pricing method are that it can be used to estimate values based on actual choices and its versatility, since it can be adapted to consider several possible interactions between market goods and environmental quality.

A hedonic function, which relates a number of the product's characteristics with the corresponding price is:

$$P_i = f(X_i) \tag{1}$$

where $P_i$ is the price of a variety (or a model) $i$ of the considered product and $X_i$ is a vector of characteristics associated with the specific variety. Characteristics may correspond to dummy variables, according to the concept of the study. The hedonic function is then used, for a number of different characteristics among the varieties of the product and the price index is calculated. As soon as the characteristics to be considered are determined then, for $N$ varieties of the product (or service) the following equations must be evaluated:

$$\begin{aligned} P_i &= b_0 + b_1 \cdot X_{1i} + b_2 \cdot X_{2i} + e_i, \\ i &= 1, \dots, N \end{aligned} \tag{2}$$

In this paper, the vector of characteristics $X_i$, corresponds to the configuration of the IaaS cloud services, including characteristics such as RAM size, number of CPUs, memory size, bandwidth etc., while in the second formulation met in the paper includes the non-functional parameters, participating as dummy variables. The description of these parameters is given in the corresponding section.

## 4   Non-functional Requirements of IaaS Cloud Services

This section describes all the qualitative characteristics of IaaS cloud bundles which were not considered before in the previous findings in [8, 9] and are now included in the collected price bundles in order to find their effect on the final price. There has been a growing demand and need for a more detailed IaaS cloud services selection process by considering several non-functional and functional criteria.

In general, it is commonly acceptable that non-functional requirements are very important and can be critical for the selection of an IaaS cloud computing bundle of services. This type of requirements usually specifies criteria that can be used to judge some operations of a cloud bundle, rather than specific behaviors. Cloud services selection is an important purchasing activity for many providers and nowadays consumers demand not only cheaper and fully functional services, but also high quality products, on-time delivery and excellent after-sale services. This is the reason why finding a cloud provider with the right quality services at the right price, at the right quantities and at the right time is a very difficult and challenging task. Selection of IaaS cloud services is a multiple criteria decision making (MCDM) problem involving multiple criteria that can be both qualitative and quantitative [7, 20].

Every non-functional requirement is actually an attribute of an IaaS cloud bundle. The required overall non-functional parameters of the IaaS cloud computing services include security, availability, portability, scalability and usability and each one of them constitutes a different category with corresponding attributes, as shown in Table 1. The hedonic price index of this study is constructed with data collected from the Cloudorado platform for 13 non-functional requirements [20].

**Table 1.** Non-functional requirements.

| Requirement | Attributes | Description |
| --- | --- | --- |
| Security | Encrypted Storage | *The storage volume is encrypted* |
| | Safe Harbor/EU Directive 95/46/EC | *The provider is compliant with EU Directive 95/46/EC on the protection of personal data. For US companies' compliance with Safe Harbor principles is checked* |
| Availability | Service Level Agreement (SLA) Level | *The SLA level expressed (regardless of past performance), in percentage points of availability.* |
| | Backup Storage | *Storage-based backup is available* |
| | Free Support | *Support cost is included in the price of the basic plan; any other additional support beyond the basic plan is paid* |
| Elasticity/scalability | Burstable CPU | *The CPU allocation can be either fixed or can burst to a higher capacity if current conditions allow it* |
| | Auto-scaling | *Vertical: adding more resources to a server, such as disk space, RAM or processing units. Horizontal: adding more servers* |
| | Resource usage Monitoring | *There are integrated monitoring solutions offered by cloud providers, so that users can monitor current resource utilization (i.e. CPU, RAM, disk, network etc.) in their cloud servers for no additional cost* |
| Usability/Portability | Web Interface | *A web management interface is available.* |
| | API | *An API management is available for automating cloud servers and interacting with them* |
| | One Account for All Locations | *There is one account and single interface to manage all different locations or a separate account for each location* |
| | Image from Cloud Server | *A provider supports creating an image from an existing VM and then deploying it to other cloud servers* |
| | Limited Free Trial | *A free trial of cloud services is offered for a limited period of time or for a certain amount of credit to be spent on cloud services, so that customers can use it to run tests* |

## 5   Price Index Construction

Data collection is based on Infrastructure as a Service (IaaS) which is the most straightforward service of the service models for delivering cloud services. Cloudorado [21], a cloud computing platform that offers cloud computing comparison service was used for data collection. Cloudorado accepts customers' functional requirements of cloud computing such as compute power, storage, memory, operating system and returns a comparison of different but equivalent cloud services. In addition, the platform has been updated and supports non-functional requirements such as security, reliability and cloud management features.

The collection of cloud bundles is specified by functional and non-functional criteria, meaning that each bundle of IaaS services includes resources such as memory (RAM), storage, compute power (CPU) and operating system (OS) that constitute the functional attributes and 13 non-functional features, as described in Sect. 4. The considered values of all these features are shown in Table 2.

**Table 2.** The values of functional and non-functional attributes of IaaS bundles.

| Requirements category | Attributes | Values |
|---|---|---|
| Functional requirements | CPU (v cores) | 1x, 2x, 4x, 8x, 16x, 32x |
| | RAM (GB) | 2, 4, 8, 16, 32, 64, 128, 256 |
| | Storage (GB) | 50, 100, 200, 500, 1000, 2000, 5000, 10000 |
| | OS | Linux/Windows |
| Non-functional requirements | Encrypted Storage | Yes/No |
| | Safe Harbor/EU Directive 95/46/EC | Yes/No |
| | SLA | 99.90%/99.95%/99.98%/99.99%/100% |
| | Backup Storage | Yes/No |
| | Free Support | Yes/No |
| | Burstable CPU | Burstable/Fixed |
| | Auto-scaling | None/Vertical/Horizontal/Both |
| | Resource usage Monitoring | Yes/No |
| | Web Interface | Yes/No |
| | API | Yes/No |
| | One Account for All Locations | Yes/No |
| | Image from Cloud Server | Yes/No |
| | Limited Free Trial | Yes/No |

The total number of collected price instances is 806 and bundles are derived from 23 providers, shown in Table 3. The dataset was collected by selecting specific computing requirements (e.g. 2xCPU, 4 GB RAM, 50 GB Storage, Linux etc.) but these criteria were not fulfilled by all cloud providers, therefore the number of the collected price bundles of each provider may vary.

At first the price index construction is based on cloud bundles that include only functional parameters. Then, the dataset was enlarged by adding non-functional features, in order to examine and highlight the influence of non-functional requirements on

**Table 3.** Cloud IaaS providers.

| Providers | |
|---|---|
| Microsoft Azure | Stratogen |
| Amazon | eApps |
| Google | Data Dimension |
| CloudSigma | CloudWare |
| Atlantic.net | ZippyCloud |
| M5 | Exoscale |
| Elastichosts | Vps.net |
| Bitrefinery1 | Dreamhost |
| Storm | Zettagrid |
| RackSpace | CloudSolutions |
| e24cloud.com | Gigenet |
| Joynet | |

the price. The hedonic model's parameters were estimated by the use of the ordinary least squares (OLS).

## 5.1 Price Index Construction Based on Functional Requirements

IaaS characteristics (CPU, RAM, STORAGE and Operating System - OS) participate as independent variables in the hedonic pricing model. The operating system parameter (OS) participates as a dummy variable having the value of 0 for Linux based systems and 1 for Windows.

The price index construction estimated the following parameters and equation and the corresponding results of the hedonic pricing method are summarized in Table 4:

**Table 4.** The contributory value of each functional attribute.

| Coefficients | Values |
|---|---|
| Constant | 242,04*** |
| CPU | 21,37*** |
| RAM | 16,32*** |
| Storage | 0,09* |
| OS | 15,12*** |

***p < .01, **p < .05,
*p < .1, n.s. not
significant.

$$\text{Price (\$)} = 242,04 + 21,27 * \text{CPU} + 16,32 * \text{RAM} + 0.09 * \text{STORAGE} + 15,12 * \text{OS} \quad (3)$$

The regression model accounts for a 37,1% value of $R^2$ indicating that the model does not succeed in describing the variance of the mode and construct an effective price index, According to the model results, the Constant, which corresponds to a fixed annually fee, contributes more to the price index, followed by the CPU and the RAM size. The operating system selection is also of importance and, finally, the storage size presents the lowest contribution to the price index, therefore it does not particularly affect the price.

## 5.2 Price Index Construction Based on Functional and Non-functional Requirements

In this analysis, IaaS resources (CPU, RAM, STORAGE) and the operating system (OS) attribute are the functional characteristics which participate as variables in the hedonic pricing model in combination with all the other aforementioned non-functional parameters that take part as dummy or discrete variables. The Subscription characteristic is considered to have a fixed value, meaning 'Annual Subscription' like before and the 'Web Interface' attribute is also checked but is always equal to 'Yes' since all cloud companies provide it. The estimated parameters of the price index construction are presented in descending order, as shown in Table 5.

**Table 5.** The contributory value of each functional and non-functional attribute.

| Coefficients | Values |
|---|---|
| Constant | 165,5*** |
| Safe Harbor/EU Directive 95/46/EC | 50,62*** |
| Image from cloud server | 28,28** |
| Burstable CPU | 27,09*** |
| One Account For All Locations | 25,68*** |
| Encrypted storage | 17,30*** |
| OS | 14,24*** |
| RAM | 13,45*** |
| CPU | 11,98* |
| Support included | 8,71* |
| Auto-scaling | 4,07*** |
| API | 2,95* |
| SLA Level | 1,33** |
| Back-up storage | 1,29* |
| Resource usage monitoring | 0,84* |
| Storage | 0,12*** |
| Limited free trial | 0,06* |

***$p < .01$, **$p < .05$, *$p < .1$, n.s. not significant.

The calculated $R^2$ value equals 73,8%, meaning that a much higher percentage of variance is described by this model. It is known that the more variance that is accounted for by the regression model the closer the data points will fall to the fitted regression line [18]. More specifically, in this case all parameters are significant and they contribute to the shaping of the price. The requirement that decides whether a cloud provider is compliant or not with EU Directive 95/46/EC on the protection of personal data or with Safe Harbor principles for US companies seems to be a crucial non-functional parameter, that justifies why security is one of the most important user concerns in the context of cloud computing. Storage does not affect the price very much, which also supports the finding of the previous price index, which was based only on functional parameters. Furthermore, the requirement of portability, in other terms the possibility to create an image from an existing VM and then deploy it to another and the existence of one account to manage all different locations, affects pricing at a high level resulting in reduction of price of the bundles by a factor of more than 25.

## 6 Conclusions

The work performed in this paper focuses on the construction of a price index based on a hedonic pricing model, following and updating the findings of our previous work [8, 9] focused on functional features, such as CPU, memory and storage space, by including non-functional characteristics describing the Quality of IaaS cloud computing model. The hedonic pricing method was evaluated using data from 23 IaaS cloud providers, corresponding to more than 800 price bundles taking into account 4 functional and 13 non-functional properties of cloud computing services.

The aim of this empirical study was to estimate the importance of each feature and its effect on the final price. According to the derived results and the construction of the corresponding index, apart from the constant parameter, which indicates the importance of the subscription in the pricing scheme, the high values of non-functional features indicate that they affect the price more than functional ones. Security, being represented from 'compliance with Safe Harbor/EU Directive 95/46/EC' and 'encrypted storage' attributes, and portability, consisting of 'Image from cloud server' and 'One account for all locations' are of substantial importance. In addition, the possibility of whether the CPU allocation can burst to a higher capacity or not is quite significant. However, the storage and limited free trial parameters seem to affect less the final pricing of cloud bundles of services. As a next step, we plan to investigate further the importance of non-functional features in constructing cloud bundles of service and the contribution of each of them in determining the cost for the providers themselves. It seams that non-functional features, as for example security and portability, are more costly for the providers, that functional ones, as for example storage.

The existence of a price index for the IaaS cloud services, as highlighted in this work, can provide very useful information, not only about business plans and pricing methods but also regarding the market of cloud itself and helping to guide investment. Several qualitative features of IaaS cloud bundles were included the price index construction in order to find their importance and effect on the final price. The results indicate that non-functional requirements are very important and considered critical by clients for the selection of an IaaS bundle of services. Finding a cloud provider with the right quality services at the right price, at the right quantities and at the right time is a very difficult and challenging task involving multiple criteria that can be both qualitative and quantitative.

# References

1. Mell, P., Grance, T.: The NIST definition of cloud computing (2011)
2. Rimal, B.P., Choi, E., Lumb, I.: A taxonomy and survey of cloud computing systems. In: INC, IMS and IDC, pp. 44–51 (2009)
3. Pettey, C., Goasduff, L.: Gartner Says Worldwide Public Cloud Services Market to Grow 18 Percent in 2017 (2017). http://www.gartner.com/newsroom/id/3616417
4. El Kihal, S., Schlereth, S., Skiera, B.: Price comparison for Infrastructure-as-a-Service. In: European Conference on Information Systems, p. 12 (2012)
5. Venkatesh, R.V.M.: The design and pricing of bundles: a review of normative guidelines and practical approaches (2009). Handbook of pricing research in marketing. 232. Amazon EC2 Instance Types (2017). https://aws.amazon.com/ec2/instance-types/. Accessed 13 June 2017
6. Glinz, M.: On non-functional requirements. In: 15th IEEE International Requirements Engineering Conference, 2007, RE 2007. IEEE (2007)
7. Grossman, R.L.: The case for cloud computing. IT Prof. **11**(2), 23–27 (2009)
8. Mitropoulou, P., et al.: A hedonic price index for cloud computing services. In: CLOSER 2015, 5th International Conference on Cloud Computing and Services Science, Lisbon, Portugal (2015)
9. Mitropoulou, P., et al.: Pricing cloud IaaS services based on a hedonic price index. Computing **98**(11), 1075–1089 (2016)
10. Al-Roomi, M., et al.: Cloud computing pricing models: a survey. Int. J. Grid Distrib. Comput. **6**(5), 93–106 (2013)
11. Jin, H., et al.: Towards optimized fine-grained pricing of IaaS cloud platform. IEEE Trans. cloud Comput. **3**(4), 436–448 (2015)
12. Rohitratana, J., Altmann, J.: Impact of pricing schemes on a market for Software-as-a-Service and perpetual software. Future Gener. Comput. Syst. **28**(8), 1328–1339 (2012)
13. Li, H., Liu, J., Tang, G.: A pricing algorithm for cloud computing resources. In: 2011 International Conference on Network Computing and Information Security (NCIS). IEEE (2011)
14. Rohitratana, J., Altmann, J.: Agent-based simulations of the software market under different pricing schemes for software-as-a-service and perpetual software. In: Altmann, J., Rana, O.F. (eds.) GECON 2010. LNCS, vol. 6296, pp. 62–77. Springer, Heidelberg (2010). doi:10.1007/978-3-642-15681-6_5
15. Ruiz-Agundez, I., Penya, Y.K., Bringas, P.G.: A flexible accounting model for cloud computing. In: 2011 Annual SRII Global Conference (SRII). IEEE (2011)
16. Siham, E.K., Schlereth, C., Skiera, B.: Price comparison for Infrastructure-as-a-Service (2012)
17. Berndt, E.R.: The Practice of Econometrics: Classic and Contemporary. Addison-Wesley Publishing, Reading (1991)
18. Sonmez, M.: Review and critique of supplier selection process and practices. © Loughborough University (2006)
19. Triplett, J.E.: Handbook on Hedonic Indexes and Quality Adjustments in Price Indexes. Science, Technology and Industry Working Papers, ed. OECD. OECD Publishing (2004)
20. Cloud Computing Price Comparison Engine

# Non-neutrality Pushed by Big Content Providers

Patrick Maillé[1](✉) and Bruno Tuffin[2]

[1] IMT Atlantique,
2, rue de la Châtaigneraie, 35576 Cesson-Sévigné Cedex, France
patrick.maille@imt.fr
[2] Inria Campus Universitaire de Beaulieu,
35042 Rennes Cedex, France
bruno.tuffin@inria.fr

**Abstract.** Major content/service providers are publishing grades they give to Internet Service Providers (ISPs) about the quality of delivery of their content. The goal is to inform customers about the "best" ISPs. But this could be an incentive for, or even a pressure on, ISPs to differentiate service and provide a better quality to those big content providers in order to be more attractive. This fits the network neutrality debate, but instead of the traditional vision of ISPs pressing content providers, we face here the opposite situation, still possibly at the expense of small content providers though. This paper designs a model describing the various actors and their strategies, analyzes it using non-cooperative game theory tools, and quantifies the impact of those advertised grades with respect to the situation where no grade is published. We illustrate that a non-neutral behavior, differentiating traffic, is not leading to a desirable situation.

**Keywords:** Network economics · Competition · Net neutrality

## 1 Introduction

Internet traffic has considerably increased in volume in recent years [5], but a large proportion of it is actually due to a very small number of content providers. As of 2013 in North America for example, Netflix and YouTube were accounting for 50% of all traffic[1]. Such big service or content providers (CPs) are becoming omnipresent in our daily life and as a consequence are part of the attractiveness of the subscription to Internet Service Providers (ISPs). On the other hand they have strong quality requirements to be themselves attractive to customers, wishing to propose high definition video services that ISPs need to comply with. To ensure the right service to their customers, those CPs report the quality provided by the various ISPs for their service. Google (owner of YouTube) on its web page https://www.google.com/get/videoqualityreport/ is grading ISPs, depending on

---

[1] https://www.cnet.com/news/netflix-youtube-gobble-up-half-of-internet-traffic/.

© Springer International Publishing AG 2017
C. Pham et al. (Eds.): GECON 2017, LNCS 10537, pp. 29–39, 2017.
DOI: 10.1007/978-3-319-68066-8_3

your location, based on how well they are able to stream YouTube videos, providing badges "YouTube HD Verified", "standard definition" or "lower definition". Here, Google joined Netflix who were using the so-called *ISP speed index* (see https://ispspeedindex.netflix.com/) to measure Netflix performance on the different ISPs. That information indeed helps customers to choose the "best" ISP if they are interested in finding the one optimizing the considered service. It can also put some relevant competitive pressure on ISPs to upgrade their network. But on the down side, it can also be seen as an incentive for ISPs to differentiate service between sources and favor such big providers in order to receive the best grades, at the expense of small providers.

This differentiation threat is highly related to the *network neutrality debate* [1,3,4,10]. This debate has been vivid for around 20 years, with laws passed worldwide by governments. It comes from ISPs complaining that distant but heavy resource-consuming content providers use their network without financial compensation. As a retaliation if no payment was made, ISPs threatened to block or slow down the traffic of those content providers. This created a lot of protests from user associations and content providers. Interestingly, the threat we imagine in the present work is somewhat the opposite one: ISPs incentivized to favor big CPs to obtain better grades hence more customers, to the benefits of those big providers.

Our goal is to model and analyze ISPs' best strategies in terms of quality offered to a big CP in a competitive context. End users are assumed heterogeneous in terms of interest in the big CP whose quality is publicized. ISPs have to decide how much of their capacity they assign to the big CP. This is to our knowledge the first model trying to tackle this problem. The game is analyzed as a Stackelberg game [8] where:

1. first, ISPs competitively decide how much weight they give to the big CP;
2. then, users decide what ISP to subscribe to, given that more subscribers also leads to more congestion.

The game is solved by backward induction meaning that, in their decision, ISPs anticipate the subsequent choices of users. We then compare the results with the case where ISPs are neutral, i.e., when they do not favor the big CP. Our results show that a non-neutral scenario may be prejudicial to everybody because no equilibrium in the capacity assignment game between ISPs may exist. Surprisingly also, we highlight situations where such an equilibrium exists with full capacity assigned to the big CP, which leads to the same user repartition between ISPs as in the neutral case.

The rest of this paper is organized as follows. Section 2 presents the model and the notations. Section 3 explains the two levels of the game solved by backward induction. The repartition game between users is solved analytically, while the capacity assignment game between ISPs is analyzed numerically, illustrating among other things that there is not necessarily a Nash equilibrium. Section 4 finally discusses the results and the comparison with a neutral situation in order to decide whether scrutiny and regulation should be imposed, and Sect. 5 presents the most interesting extensions of the model.

## 2    Model

We define the model in this section. We consider two ISPs in competition for users. Users are heterogeneous in their preferences between a good quality for a big CP and for other content (seen as aggregated into a second CP). ISPs have to decide the level of capacity they devote to the big CP, in order to be either more attractive to this CP or more focused on other CPs. User choices are based on the average level of quality they experience, weighted by their preferences among CPs.

### 2.1    Content Providers

To simplify the analysis, we therefore consider two competing CPs, indexed by 1 and 2. CP 1 is assumed to be the big CP, while the other represents the aggregated competitors.

Let $\alpha_1 = \alpha$ and $\alpha_2 = 1 - \alpha$ be the (aggregated) volume of traffic requested from CP 1 and CP 2, respectively, by users. The total volume is normalized to 1 without loss of generality; it is then a proportion. Note that we assume that consumption is constant and independent of the CP attractiveness; user attractiveness to the ISP is with respect to the grade publicized by the CPs.

### 2.2    ISPs and Quality

We consider two ISPs, named $A$ and $B$, competing for customers. ISP $i$ has a capacity (that is, throughput) $C_i$, for $i \in \{A, B\}$, and allocates a proportion $\beta_{i,j}$ ($j \in \{1, 2\}$) of this capacity for the traffic of CP $j$, with $\beta_{i,1} + \beta_{i,2} = 1$. A neutral behavior corresponds to $\beta_{i,j} = \alpha_j$: the capacity allocated to each CP corresponds to its actual usage, i.e., there is no service differentiation for any CP.

Let $m_A$ (resp. $m_B$) be the mass of users associated with ISP $A$ (resp. $B$). We define the quality offered to CP $j$ by ISP $i$ as

$$Q_{i,j} := \frac{C_i \beta_{i,j}}{\alpha_j m_i}.$$

In other words, the quality (for CP $j$ with ISP $i$) is the average capacity (reserved by ISP $i$ for CP $j$ traffic) per unit of (this specific) traffic: in particular, it is inversely proportional to the traffic load of CP $j$ at ISP $i$. A neutral behavior with $\beta_{i,j} = \alpha_j$ leads to $Q_{i,j} = C_j/m_i$.

### 2.3    End Users

End users are assumed heterogeneous in their sensitivity to the ISPs' grades (publicized by CPs), even if not reflected in their actual consumption. A user is characterized by a parameter $\theta \in [0, 1]$ representing the relative weight associated to the quality offered to CP 1. Formally, the felt quality of a user $\theta$ at ISP $i$ is

$$\theta Q_{i,1} + (1 - \theta) Q_{i,2}.$$

A user $\theta$ will then choose an ISP providing the largest quality, i.e., ISP

$$i_\theta \in \text{argmax}_{k \in \{A,B\}} \theta Q_{k,1} + (1-\theta) Q_{k,2}. \tag{1}$$

Let $F$ be the cumulative distribution of $\theta \in [0,1]$ and $f$ its density, so that user choices give

$$m_i = \int \mathbb{1}_{\{i=\text{argmax}_{k \in \{A,B\}} \theta Q_{k,1} + (1-\theta) Q_{k,2}\}} f(\theta) d\theta$$

where $\mathbb{1}_{\{C\}}$ is the indicator function that condition $C$ is satisfied.

In what follows, we will assume $\theta$ uniformly distributed over $[0,1]$ for sake of simplicity. But it can be easily generalized by a change of variable.

## 3    Multilevel Game

The notations being introduced, we now define the game between all actors.

### 3.1    Game Definition

In our model, ISPs and end users make decisions: each ISP chooses the fraction of capacity to allocate to each CP, given that its decision as well as that of its competitor both impact its market share, since end users choose their ISP in terms of the felt (weighted average) quality according to (1).

But decisions are not taken at the same time scale. Actually ISPs play first and then users make their own choice. The framework is therefore that of a so-called Stackelberg game [8].

We thus end up with a multilevel game where:

1. Each ISP $i$ plays with its capacity repartition $\beta_{i,1}$ allocated to CP 1 (the other being allocated $1 - \beta_{i,1}$) in order to maximize its market share.
2. Given the allocated qualities, users choose their ISP.

Note that we do not consider pricing strategies of ISPs. This would complicate the analysis and blur the conclusions; we rather assume here that competition has led to ISPs offering similar prices and trying to gain market shares by improving the user perceived quality.

The game is a leader-follower game, meaning that even if ISPs play first, they will make their decision strategically, by anticipating the subsequent decision of users. Hence, to make their decisions, ISPs are assumed able to compute the end users' repartition for any combination $(\beta_{i,j})_{i,j}$. Similarly, in our analysis we apply the *backward induction* method, i.e., perform optimizations on capacity repartitions anticipating the reactions of users.

## 3.2   Repartition of Users Among ISPs

Consider the values $\beta_{i,j}$ as fixed. How do users distribute themselves according to ISPs?

Define

$$C'_{i,j} := \frac{C_i \beta_{i,j}}{\alpha_j}$$

as the available capacity per unit of users for CP $j$ at ISP $i$, so that $Q_{i,j} = \frac{C'_{i,j}}{m_i}$.

A user $\theta$ will choose ISP $A$, and ISP $B$ otherwise, if the (weighted) felt quality at ISP $A$ is larger than that at ISP $B$, i.e., if

$$\theta Q_{A,1} + (1 - \theta)Q_{A,2} > \theta Q_{B,1} + (1 - \theta)Q_{B,2},$$

or equivalently

$$\theta \left( Q_{A,1} - Q_{A,2} - Q_{B,1} + Q_{B,2} \right) > Q_{B,2} - Q_{A,2}. \tag{2}$$

From this inequality, we can get the following existence and uniqueness result about the repartition of users among ISPs.

**Proposition 1.** *Assume a uniform distribution of user sensitivities $\theta$ over the interval $[0,1]$ and any profile of ISP strategies without blocking (i.e., with $\beta_{j,i} > 0$ for all $j$ and $i$). Then, there exists a unique user repartition equilibrium $(m_A, m_B)$. Moreover,*

- *If $C'_{A,1}/C'_{A,2} = C'_{B,1}/C'_{B,2}$, all users are indifferent between $A$ and $B$, but the repartition is such that*

$$\left( m_A = \frac{C'_{A,2}}{C'_{A,2} + C'_{B,2}} \quad , \quad m_B = \frac{C'_{B,2}}{(C'_{A,2} + C'_{B,2})} \right). \tag{3}$$

- *Otherwise, there exists a value $\theta^*$ such that all users with $\theta < \theta^*$ choose one ISP, and users with $\theta > \theta^*$ choose the other.*
  - *If $C'_{A,1}/C'_{A,2} > C'_{B,1}/C'_{B,2}$ values of $\theta > \theta^*$ choose $A$ and values of $\theta < \theta^*$ choose $B$,*
  - *We are in the opposite situation if $C'_{A,1}/C'_{A,2} < C'_{B,1}/C'_{B,2}$.*

*Proof.* The proof is provided in Appendix A.

Note that the same arguments of the proof can be used, with simplified settings, to express unique solutions if some $\beta_{i,j}$ are zero. But we did not display those particular cases to avoid overloading the proposition.

### 3.3  Game Between ISPs on the Quality Offered to CPs

ISPs $A$ and $B$ play respectively on $\beta_{A,1} \in [0,1]$ and $\beta_{B,1} \in [0,1]$ to maximize $m_A$ and $m_B = 1 - m_A$, respectively, using the values determined in the previous subsection. Given that we do not have any useful closed-form solution for $(m_A, m_B)$ in terms of $(\beta_{A,1}, \beta_{B,1})$ (actually they are solutions of second degree polynomials involving several conditions, and do not yield an exploitable expression), we resort to numerical evaluations to solve the game between ISPs.

We first draw the best responses of each ISP in terms of the strategy of its competitor. A Nash equilibrium is a point which is a best response for each ISP, that is an intersection of best-response curves: no one has an interest to unilaterally move from it.

**Best Responses.** Figure 1(a) describes the market shares of ISPs in terms of their strategy $\beta_{i,1}$ when the strategy $\beta_{j,1}$ of the opponent is fixed. The value where it is maximized gives the best response $\mathrm{BR}_i(\beta_{j,1})$ of ISP $i$ in terms of $\beta_{j,1}$. The parameters values in Fig. 1(a) are $\alpha_1 = 0.3$, $\alpha_2 = 1 - \alpha_1 = 0.7$, $C_A = 5$, $C_B = 4$. Here it is optimal to choose $\alpha_i = 1$. We have also checked that when $\alpha_1$ is large, we have the opposite situation and decreasing masses $m_A$ and $m_B$, resulting in optimal values $\alpha_i = 0$. Though, the functions are not always monotonous, even if it is the case in many situations. Choose for example $\alpha_1 = 0.5$ (still with $\alpha_2 = 1 - \alpha_1$). Figure 1(b) describes the corresponding market shares of ISPs, with an interior value $\beta_{A,1}$ maximizing $m_A$ for $\beta_{B,1} = 0.4$.

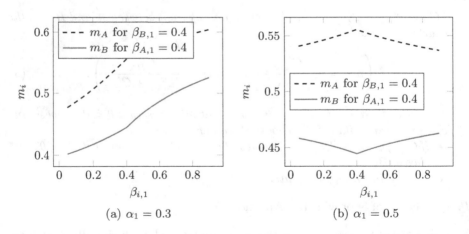

(a) $\alpha_1 = 0.3$                    (b) $\alpha_1 = 0.5$

**Fig. 1.** Market shares $m_i$ of ISPs in terms of the strategy $\beta_{i,1}$ for given $\beta_{j,1}$ when $\alpha_1 = 0.3, \alpha_2 = 0.7$ (a), and $\alpha_1 = \alpha_2 = 0.5$ (b).

**Nash Equilibrium.** Figures 2(a) and (b) display, respectively for $\alpha_1 = 0.3$ and $\alpha_1 = 0.5$, the best responses of $A$ and $B$ on the same graph to determine graphically the Nash equilibria.

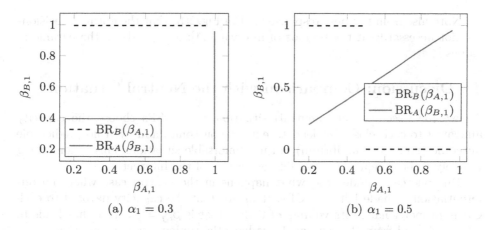

(a) $\alpha_1 = 0.3$                    (b) $\alpha_1 = 0.5$

**Fig. 2.** Best responses in the repartition game when $\alpha_1 = 0.3, \alpha_2 = 0.7$ (a) and $\alpha_1 = \alpha_2 = 0.5$ (b).

When $\alpha_1 = 0.3$ (and $\alpha_2 = 0.7$), since best responses of players are always 1, the Nash equilibrium is $(1,1)$. In other words, ISPs give all capacity to a single CP, CP 1. On the other hand, when $\alpha_1 = 0.5$ and $\alpha_2 = 0.5$ as in Fig. 2(b), while the best response of $A$ is linearly increasing with $\beta_{B,1}$, there is a discontinuity in the best response of $B$ and we actually end up with no Nash equilibrium, i.e., no point where each ISP would want to maintain its strategy.

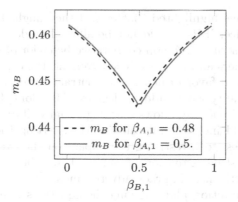

**Fig. 3.** Market shares $m_B$ in terms of $\beta_{B,1}$ for given $\beta_{A,1}$ when $\alpha_1 = 0.5$ and $\alpha_2 = 0.5$.

To understand the discontinuity, in Fig. 3 we plot $m_B$ in terms of $\beta_{B,1}$ for two close values of $\beta_{A,1}$ where the jump arises: 0.48 and 0.5. The maximal values are at the extreme points of the interval $[0, 1]$ and give very close market shares. For $\beta_{A,1} = 0.48$ the optimal value is at 1, but it is at 0 for $\beta_{A,1} = 0.5$.

Note also from the best response of $A$ in Fig. 2(b) that the optimal decisions are not necessarily at the bounds of interval $[0, 1]$; it depends on the parameter values.

## 4   Discussion: Comparison with the Neutral Situation

As we have seen, a (non-neutral) situation where ISPs choose the capacity allocated to each class can lead to extreme outcomes and even no predictable outcome (no Nash equilibrium), an uncomfortable situation. This is something unlikely to be accepted by the different actors of the Internet.

But one can wonder too what happens in the neutral case where no differentiation is made between CPs. It means that the capacity devoted to each CP is proportional to its volume of traffic, that is $\beta_{i,j} = \alpha_j$. But that leads to $C'_{i,j} = C_i$, and from Proposition 1, we have the (unique) user repartition

$$(m_A = C_A/(C_A + C_B), m_B = C_B/(C_A + C_B)).$$

No comparison can be made with the case $\alpha_1 = \alpha_2 = 0.5$ where there is no Nash equilibrium, but going back to the non-neutral scenario where $\alpha_1 = 0.3$ and $\alpha_2 = 0.7$, for which we have obtained at equilibrium $\beta_{A,1} = \beta_{B,1} = 1$, we are again from Proposition 1 in the situation where $C'_{A,1}/C'_{A,2} = C'_{B,1}/C'_{B,2}$, so surprisingly the same user repartition as in the neutral case. This would mean no change of behavior from the user point of view, but far less content diversity.

## 5   Conclusions and Perspectives

In this paper, we have highlighted that even if they might have some pressure to differentiate service, ISPs should not be allowed to do so and their behavior should be under scrutiny. A non-cooperative behavior of ISPs would lead to unpredictable behaviors and potentially less content. Hence, this model provides economic arguments in favor of neutrality, contrary to most of the existing literature on net neutrality where adding degrees of freedom (for ISPs to manage traffic as they want) generally allows reaching social welfare [2,6,7,9].

Future work could include dimensioning (i.e., setting the capacity) among ISP decision variables, to investigate the impact on the overall quality of service. Another interesting extension of our work will be to consider not only heterogeneous attractiveness in grade advertisements, but a similar (correlated) heterogeneous consumption plan. Solving the equations is much more difficult though, and the present model is, at least to our knowledge, the first one trying to analyze such a problem.

## A   Proof of Proposition 1

*Proof.* A user $\theta$ strictly prefers ISP $A$ over $B$ if and only if

$$\frac{\theta C'_{A,1} + (1 - \theta)C'_{A,2}}{m_A} > \frac{\theta C'_{B,1} + (1 - \theta)C'_{B,2}}{m_B},$$

or equivalently $\theta\Delta > \delta$ with
$$\begin{cases} \Delta := \dfrac{C'_{A,1}-C'_{A,2}}{m_A} - \dfrac{C'_{B,1}-C'_{B,2}}{m_B} \\ \delta := \dfrac{C'_{B,2}}{m_B} - \dfrac{C'_{A,1}}{m_A}. \end{cases}$$

Therefore, we can distinguish three possible types of equilibria.

(a) In an equilibrium with $\Delta > 0$, all users with $\theta > \delta/\Delta$ select ISP $A$, all users with $\theta < \delta/\Delta$ prefer ISP $B$, and the set of users indifferent between $A$ and $B$ is of measure zero. Hence, for a type-$a$ equilibrium the masses of users with each ISP are of the form $m_A = 1 - F(\theta_a^*)$ and $m_B = F(\theta_a^*)$ with $F$ the cdf of user-specific values $\theta$, and $\theta_a^*$ the corresponding value of $\delta/\Delta$ at this equilibrium. A user with sensitivity $\theta_a^*$ should be indifferent between both ISPs, i.e.,

$$\frac{\theta_a^* C'_{A,1} + (1-\theta_a^*)C'_{A,2}}{1-F(\theta_a^*)} - \frac{\theta_a^* C'_{B,1} + (1-\theta_a^*)C'_{B,2}}{F(\theta_a^*)} = 0.$$

When $\theta$ follows a uniform distribution over $[0,1]$, then $F(x) = x$ and the previous equality becomes

$$\frac{\theta_a^*}{1-\theta_a^*}(C'_{A,1} - C'_{A,2}) + C'_{B,2} - C'_{B,1} - \frac{C'_{B,2}}{\theta_a^*} + \frac{C'_{A,2}}{1-\theta_a^*} = 0. \tag{4}$$

With non-blocking ISP strategies, $C'_{A,1}$ and $C'_{B,2}$ are strictly positive, and (4) has a unique solution in $(0,1)$.

Summarizing, we have a type-$a$ equilibrium if the corresponding $\Delta$ is strictly positive, i.e., if in addition to (4) we have

$$\frac{C'_{A,1} - C'_{A,2}}{1-\theta_a^*} > \frac{C'_{B,1} - C'_{B,2}}{\theta_a^*}. \tag{5}$$

In particular, (5) implies that $(C'_{A,2} - C'_{A,1})\frac{\theta_a^*}{1-\theta_a^*} < C'_{B,2} - C'_{B,1}$, which plugged into (4) gives

$$\frac{\theta_a^*}{1-\theta_a^*} > \frac{C'_{B,2}}{C'_{A,2}}, \tag{6}$$

or equivalently

$$\frac{1}{\theta_a^*} < 1 + \frac{C'_{A,2}}{C'_{B,2}}. \tag{7}$$

Finally, re-writing (4) as

$$C'_{A,1}\frac{\theta_a^*}{1-\theta_a^*} - C'_{B,2}\frac{1}{\theta_a^*} + C'_{A,2} + C'_{B,2} - C'_{B,1} = 0 \tag{8}$$

and plugging (6) and (7), we get

$$0 < C'_{A,1}\frac{C'_{B,2}}{C'_{A,2}} - C'_{B,2}\left(1 + \frac{C'_{A,2}}{C'_{B,2}}\right) + C'_{A,2} + C'_{B,2} - C'_{B,1}$$

$$= C'_{A,1}\frac{C'_{B,2}}{C'_{A,2}} - C'_{B,1}$$

or $\frac{C'_{A,1}}{C'_{A,2}} > \frac{C'_{B,1}}{C'_{B,2}}$. As a result, a type-$a$ equilibrium, which is unique from (4) can only exist when $\frac{C'_{A,1}}{C'_{A,2}} > \frac{C'_{B,1}}{C'_{B,2}}$.

(b) We can treat similarly the case when $\Delta < 0$, by exchanging the roles of ISPs $A$ and $B$ with respect to the previous case. Hence, such an equilibrium is of the form $m_A = \theta_b^*, m_B = 1 - \theta_b^*$ with $\theta_b^*$ the unique solution in $(0,1)$ of

$$\frac{\theta_b^* C'_{B,1}}{1 - \theta_b^*} - \frac{(1 - \theta_b^*)C'_{A,2}}{\theta_b^*} + C'_{B,2} - C'_{A,1} = 0, \tag{9}$$

and such a (unique) equilibrium can only exist when $\frac{C'_{A,1}}{C'_{A,2}} < \frac{C'_{B,1}}{C'_{B,2}}$.

(c) Finally, at an equilibrium with $\Delta = 0$, all users must be indifferent between the ISPs (otherwise they all prefer the same, while its competitor has no demand (no congestion) and thus infinite quality, a contradiction). Therefore, for all $\theta$ we have $\frac{\theta C'_{A,1} + (1-\theta)C'_{A,2}}{m_A} = \frac{\theta C'_{B,1} + (1-\theta)C'_{B,2}}{m_B}$, which implies, using $m_A + m_B = 1$, that we have

$$\begin{cases} \frac{C'_{A,1}}{m_A} = \frac{C'_{B,1}}{1 - m_A} \\ \frac{C'_{A,2}}{m_A} = \frac{C'_{B,2}}{1 - m_A} \end{cases}$$

In particular, such an equilibrium can only exist when $\frac{C'_{A,1}}{C'_{A,2}} = \frac{C'_{B,1}}{C'_{B,2}}$ (by looking at ratios of left-hand sides and right-hand sides in the above system of equations), and while the specific user choices are not unique, solving the equation(s) leads to unique values of $m_A$ and $m_B$, given as in (3).

Regrouping the three cases establishes the uniqueness of a user equilibrium as stated in the proposition. To establish existence, we reason on the relative values of $\frac{C'_{A,1}}{C'_{A,2}}$ and $\frac{C'_{B,1}}{C'_{B,2}}$.

- First, if $\frac{C'_{A,1}}{C'_{A,2}} = \frac{C'_{B,1}}{C'_{B,2}}$ then one can check that $m_A$ and $m_B$ given as in (3) is indeed an equilibrium.
- Second, if $\frac{C'_{A,1}}{C'_{A,2}} > \frac{C'_{B,1}}{C'_{B,2}}$, assume that we do not have a type-$a$ equilibrium, i.e., that the solution $\theta_a^*$ of (4) does not give a strictly positive $\Delta$ (or in other words, (5) is not satisfied). We prove below that this leads to a contradiction, following steps close to those of the uniqueness proof. Indeed, (5) not being satisfied means $\frac{\theta_a^*}{1-\theta_a^*}(C'_{A,1} - C'_{A,2}) \leq C'_{B,1} - C'_{B,2}$, which when plugged into (4) gives

$$\frac{\theta_a^*}{1 - \theta_a^*} \leq \frac{C'_{B,2}}{C'_{A,2}} \qquad \text{and} \qquad \frac{1}{\theta_a^*} \geq 1 + \frac{C'_{A,2}}{C'_{B,2}}.$$

Like for the uniqueness proof, plugging those inequalities into (8) leads to $\frac{C'_{A,1}}{C'_{A,2}} \leq \frac{C'_{B,1}}{C'_{B,2}}$, a contradiction with our starting assumption. Hence, when $\frac{C'_{A,1}}{C'_{A,2}} > \frac{C'_{B,1}}{C'_{B,2}}$ there exists a type-$a$ equilibrium.

– Third, if $\frac{C'_{A,1}}{C'_{A,2}} < \frac{C'_{B,1}}{C'_{B,2}}$, by exchanging the roles of $A$ and $B$ we also have existence, of a type-$b$ equilibrium.

# References

1. Crocioni, P.: Net neutrality in Europe: desperately seeking a market failure. Telecommun. Policy **35**(1), 1–11 (2011). http://www.sciencedirect.com/science/article/pii/S0308596110001461
2. Economides, N., Tåg, J.: Network neutrality on the internet: a two-sided market analysis. Inf. Econ. Policy **24**(2), 91–104 (2012). http://www.sciencedirect.com/science/article/pii/S0167624512000029
3. Lenard, T.M., May, R.J. (eds.): Net Neutrality or Net Neutering: Should Broadband Internet Services be Regulated. Springer, New York (2006)
4. Maillé, P., Reichl, P., Tuffin, B.: Internet governance and economics of network neutrality. In: Hadjiantonis, A.M., Stiller, B. (eds.) Telecommunication Economics. LNCS, vol. 7216, pp. 108–116. Springer, Heidelberg (2012). doi:10.1007/978-3-642-30382-1_15
5. Maillé, P., Tuffin, B.: Telecommunication Network Economics: From Theory to Applications. Cambridge University Press, Cambridge (2014)
6. Musacchio, J., Schwartz, G., Walrand, J.: A two-sided market analysis of provider investment incentives with an application to the net neutrality issue. Rev. Netw. Econ. **8**(1), 22–39 (2009)
7. Njoroge, P., Ozdaglar, A., Stier-Moses, N.E., Weintraub, G.Y.: Investment in two-sided markets and the net neutrality debate. Rev. Netw. Econ. **12**(4), 355–402 (2013)
8. Osborne, M., Rubinstein, A.: A Course in Game theory. MIT Press (1994)
9. Schwartz, G., Musacchio, J., Felegyhazi, M., Walrand, J.C.: Network regulations and market entry. In: Jain, R., Kannan, R. (eds.) GameNets 2011. LNICSSITE, vol. 75, pp. 108–123. Springer, Heidelberg (2012). doi:10.1007/978-3-642-30373-9_8
10. Wu, T.: Network neutrality, broadband discrimination. J. Telecommun. High Technol. **2**(1), 141–176 (2003)

# Work in Progress on Service Management

# Risk Cost Accounting and Bottom Price Calculation – A Risk Management Information System

Markus Siepermann[✉] [iD]

Technische Universität Dortmund, 44221 Dortmund, Germany
markus.siepermann@tu-dortmund.de

**Abstract.** Due to legal regulations, most firms have installed risk management systems that monitor existence-threatening risks. Minor risks are usually not in their focus so that these systems are often not adequate for an effective operational risk management as they lack of a consistent quantification, valuation, and handling of risks. In particular for service providers who offer services at different levels, considering risks and their potential costs is crucial for the pricing scheme. Therefore, this paper presents a new kind of a risk management information system that extends the traditional cost accounting by introducing the concept of risk costs. This allows a consistent and uniform valuation and comparison of risks as well as an easy integration into existing enterprise IS. Besides the provision of detailed overviews of the risk situation of cost centers, cost units, business units, business areas etc., different levels of risk adjusted bottom prices for products and services can be calculated.

**Keywords:** Managerial accounting · Risk information system · Risk management · Risk cost accounting · Bottom price calculation

## 1 Introduction

For nearly two decades, governments oblige companies [3, 15] by law (e.g. US: Sarbanes-Oxley Act, Germany: KonTraG) to install a risk management system (RMS) that enables them to monitor their risk situation. The exact implementation itself is not regulated by law. Instead, firms can choose how to "live" their risk management (RM). Usually, strategically oriented RMS are used that monitor only such risks that threaten the very existence of a firm. As a matter of fact, minor risks are therefore neglected. Empirical studies underline that such risk information systems (RIS) commonly used in business are not adequate for an effective RM [21]. Although it should be possible to integrate a RIS into an existing enterprise information system [6] and although a RIS should be based on a single consistent measurement [8] both requirements are mostly not fulfilled [21].

In particular, when RM is done on an operational instead of the strategic level, using a consistent quantification of risks is crucial. Otherwise, risks can hardly be compared and therefore not controlled and handled adequately. Hence, this paper presents a new concept for a RIS that is based on a consistent quantification of risks.

© Springer International Publishing AG 2017
C. Pham et al. (Eds.): GECON 2017, LNCS 10537, pp. 43–55, 2017.
DOI: 10.1007/978-3-319-68066-8_4

For this, it extends the classic managerial cost accounting (MCA) with a sample accounting that assigns risk costs to products or services, cost centers, business areas etc. Such a risk oriented sample accounting provides several advantages. First of all, it can easily be integrated into existing information systems (IS) without any changes in classic calculations. Secondly, decision makers get an IS that provides risk information about different business areas in several detail levels. Thirdly, the sample accounting allows for computing costs under risk so that it is possible to calculate more realistic (bottom) prices. This, in particular, is important for service providers as services costs depend on many different parameters like contracted volume, performance, failure rate, response time etc. that all are subject to risks and therefore to uncertainty [27].

The remainder of this paper is organized as follows. The next section gives a short overview about existing risk information concepts. Section 3 deals with the fundamental definitions and the concept of risk costs. In Sect. 4, the RIS itself is presented that consists of two parts: The risk cost center accounting and the product risk cost accounting. This concept is illustrated by an example in Sect. 5 before the paper closes with a summary and an outlook.

## 2 Research Background

As legislation does not define risk and especially RM [2] but the area of application [15], the RM literature provides numerous suggestions for the information supply of RM. Because of the complexity of risks, many authors recommend a so-called risk map [11] where important risks are put into a coordinate system according to their potential harm and incidence rate. Its advantage is the aggregate and therefore management appropriate visualization of a firm's risk situation. Additionally, risks do not need to be quantified exactly. A rough estimate is often sufficient because potential harm as well as the incidence rate are not measured exactly but in fuzzy categories. But because of the aggregate presentation, information about the risks, i.e. their exact harm and incidence rate, the relations between causes and effects are getting lost [11].

Many authors try to overcome this deficit by using the Balanced Scorecard (BSC) (e.g. [13]) that provides a holistic management view on different heterogeneous information. The BSC is usually used in strategic fields where its strength is to present complex situations clearly and in a concentrated form. Especially the usage of cause-effect chains is advantageous in comparison to simple approaches like the risk map. But as those interdependencies are quite difficult to identify and to quantify, authors usually resign to quantify them [19] with only a few exceptions (e.g. [19, 24, 28]). Siepermann [28] gives an extensive overview about different approaches. This overview shows that there is no silver bullet using the BSC. Instead, the BSC provides many degrees of freedom so that different approaches do not necessarily lead to the same results. In a strategic field of application, this is acceptable. But in an operational field, an exact and consistent quantification cannot be renounced. For this, several authors propose risk costs but resign to define them exactly [17]. In addition, they do not show how to continue processing the risk costs consistently. In this paper, such a consistent processing is shown.

The MCA already copes with risks and their costs in four different ways [18, 20]: First of all, during the planned cost accounting, planned prices are forecasted as precisely as possible. If necessary, different prices are used during one period. Secondly, quantities are planned according to the optimal consumption, but waste is constantly examined so that over-consumption finds its way into the planning. Thirdly, imputed risks are also considered within the cost accounting. And fourthly, for cost control purposes, post calculations regularly take place in order to discover the appearance and quantity of risks and imputed risks so that they can be considered in future calculations. But a comprehensive consideration of all enterprise risks does not take place within the MCA. Costs for RM are reported not specifically and scattered among the whole accounting. Costs for the risk analysis can be found within administration costs. Costs for risk reducing measures (except insurances) cannot be identified at all (e.g. costs for material of higher quality in order to improve the product quality and to reduce warranty claims). An explicit disclosure of such risk costs in cost centers is highly recommended for RM purposes because only in this case RM becomes visible concerning the cost aspect. This improves the whole view on a firm's risk situation.

## 3  Risk and Risk Costs

### 3.1  Risk

The usual meaning of risk represents a venture, a danger or the possibility of a loss, as well as the possibility that a negative occurrence of some sort will occur [12, 23]. The risk manifests itself – in the case of occurrence – as property loss, loss of profits, etc. [1]. The main characteristic of risk consists of the uncertainty which will occur in the future. For the quantitative determination, the possible developments are set in relation to a reference value. Since risks are of a forward-looking nature which is highly dependent on business decisions in firms, almost all recent scientific publications define risk as the possibility that, due to uncertainty about future events, the realized value and the plan size of a firm's economic key figure differ negatively [5, 25]. Thus, the value of a risk $R_T$ in period $T = [t,t']$ concerning key figure K is the potential difference between the key figure's realized value $K_t^{I(t')}$ at the end of the period (t') and its planned target value $K_t^{P(t')}$:

$$R_T(K) = K_t^{I(t')} - K_t^{P(t')} \tag{1}$$

During planning, the value $K_t^{I(t')}$ is an anticipated value that has to be calculated with the help of the plan size and the risk value. For the determination of risk value several approaches exist like the maximum possible loss, the value at risk or the lower partial moments. Which of these metrics are used depends on the purpose. The banking sector usually uses the value at risk. In order to determine the maximum risk, the maximum possible loss is used. For an averaged view on the risk situation the lower partial moments of the first order should be used. This metric indicates the averaged risk if the plan size is missed [29].

## 3.2    Risk Costs

A closed and commonly accepted definition of risk costs does not exist in literature. The MCA uses imputed risks which are extraordinary expenses that are unusual for the business and occur suddenly, sporadically and unexpectedly, i.e. haphazardly [22]. But they do not cover all possible risks [9], are distributed among several periods, and are mostly summed up in one calculatory cost type so that they cannot distinguish unwanted over-consumption and price deviations [7]. For cost accounting matters this is reasonable, but for risk management, risk costs should be reported on an accrual basis [7]. Besides, not only (unexpected) deviations but also expenses for the risk management process itself should be considered as risk costs [16, 26].

As a result, *risk costs* comprise two kinds of costs: *Risk management costs* and *risk following costs*. *Risk management costs* encompass all costs that arise for the risk management process, i.e. for analysis, control, and monitoring of risks as well as counter measures in order to ensure a firm's continued existence [25]. These costs are already considered within the MCA but scattered among the whole accounting. *Risk following costs* are monetarily valuated negative deviations from a planned target value that occur because a potential risk strikes in reality. If these deviations result in out-payments, we are usually facing cost overruns. Otherwise, we talk about some kind of opportunity costs like lost profit [16]. If we understand the wasted time that was not used well as a good, we are facing costs in the common sense [4] even if these costs are not considered in the classic cost accounting.

Missing a target value can accrue due to three kinds of deviations: price, quantity, and quality. Any other deviation can be explained by one of these three deviations. Therefore, risk costs can be subdivided into price risk costs, quantity risk costs and quality risk costs. However, these factors are intertwined: The higher the quality of a good is, the higher is its price. The less (higher) the quality is, the more (less) of the good is needed. The lower the quality of the good is, the lower is the quality of the end product/service resulting in less output. Thus, when calculating the risk values and a good cannot be procured with the planned quality, the price respectively the risk value of the price must be lower. Therefore, before calculating the price risk value, the quantity and the quality risk value have to be calculated in advance. Not until then and under consideration of this quality risk value the price risk value can be calculated correctly. A suitable process is as follows: Price and quality are subject to a 3D density function. If the quality is determined, the 3D-density function is cut by a vertical plane onto which the 2D price density function is projected. With the help of this 2D density function, the price risk value can be determined. This process can also be applied for calculating services risks. Different service levels imply different cutting planes so that different risk values can be obtained.

# 4    Risk Information System

The MCA is the central IS for decision makers. There, all relevant data is collected and analyzed. It is the basis for planning, control and monitoring of all processes in a firm. It consists of the cost type accounting, cost center accounting and the cost-unit accounting

[7, 18]. In analogy to this, we introduce a RIS, i.e. the *risk cost accounting* with the same structure. As seen in Sect. 3, risk costs are of three types: price risk costs, quantity risk costs and quality risk costs. But although many risk classifications exist (e.g. [5, 9, 10, 12]), a universal risk categorization is said to be unobtainable so that each firm has to categorize its risks on its own [12, 14]. Even if this situation is not satisfactory, it is sufficient for our purpose. For this, we will focus on a risk cost center accounting and a risk cost-unit accounting in the following chapters.

## 4.1   Risk Cost Centre Accounting

While the classic cost center accounting records which costs occur in each area of a firm during a period [7, 18, 20], the risk cost center accounting records the risks and their risk costs that due to uncertainty can but do not necessarily have to occur. The formation of centers should be oriented to the classic MCA. Only if the allocation of risks and risk costs is not clearly possible, sub or aggregated centers should be built.

First of all, all risks (causes as well as effects) have to be determined and recorded in that risk cost center where they occur. That means if there is the risk of hard disc crash (effect) in the risk cost center Computing, then this risk should be recorded there even if the reason for the risk (cause) is a low quality of hard discs for which the risk cost center procurement is responsible. Risks that occur in several centers and cannot clearly be assigned to one center are recorded in an aggregated risk cost center. After the risks, the risk costs are determined and recorded. Risk management costs for administration and risk measures are already part of the classic MCA so that they just have to be clearly accentuated as risk costs. In contrast, risk following costs have to be calculated explicitly according to the risks and their risk values of a risk cost center: The recorded risks have an effect on the firm's key figures that are already part of the classic cost accounting, i.e. quantities and prices. Additionally, within a risk cost accounting the quality of goods may also matter. These effects are recorded in each risk cost center. Then, the risk costs can be calculated in a sample accounting in addition to the classic cost calculation. The allocation bases of the risk cost centers remain the same as in the classic accounting. Also for sub centers the allocation bases of the superior centers can be used. Only for additional aggregated centers, new suitable allocation bases have to be found.

Cost deviations result from deviations concerning price, quantity and quality where quality can mostly be transferred into quantity. Thus, for each cost position of the classic accounting we are facing two risk positions in the risk accounting: price risk costs and quantity risk costs where the latter one can be subdivided into quality risk costs. The distinction between variable and fixed costs remains even if variable risk costs usually will be higher than fixed risk costs. This is because fixed costs are less dependent on processes and decisions and therefore fluctuate less and can be predicted better. For each cost type, there are additional risk price costs and quantity price costs so that the variable costs per unit as well as the fixed costs increase. Figure 1 illustrates the increase in costs when risk costs are considered.

Akin to the cost deviations of second order in the classic cost accounting [18, 20], there are risk cost deviations that can be added to one single deviation cause (price risk or quantity risk) or recorded as cumulative deviations. Because these second order

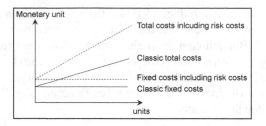

**Fig. 1.** Cost changes under consideration of risk costs.

deviations result from two different risks and therefore possibly two different parties are responsible for these costs, an explicit recording as cumulative deviation should be used. The classic planned costs $C_{T,s}^P$ in period $T = [t,t']$ of a risk cost center s is the sum of all single costs $c_{T,s,i}^P$ that can be divided into fixed and variable costs with $p_{T,i}^P$ being the planned price for good i and $m_{T,s,i}^P$ being the planned quantity. In the case of variable costs, the quantity $m_{T,s,i}^P$ as a rule is a linear function of the allocation base AB $(m_{T,S,i}^{P\,variable} = f(AB_{T,S}^P))$ [18, 20]:

$$C_{T,s}^P = \sum_{i=1}^n c_{T,s,i}^P = \sum_{i=1}^n \left( c_{T,s,i}^{P\,variable} + c_{T,s,i}^{P\,fixed} \right) = \sum_{i=1}^n p_{T,i}^P \cdot \left( m_{T,s,i}^{P\,variable} + m_{T,s,i}^{P\,fixed} \right) \quad (2)$$

Due to risks, prices and quantities can deviate from the planned size with a price risk value $R_T^P(p_{T,i}^P)$ and a quantity risk value $R_T^P(m_{T,s,i}^P)$ so that the realized costs $C_{t,s}^{I(t')}$ at t' (the end of period T) and predicted at t (the beginning of period T) will exceed the planned costs and risk cost will occur:

$$C_{t,s}^{I(t')} = \sum_{i=1}^n \left( \left( p_{T,i}^P + R_T^P(p_{T,i}^P) \right) \cdot \left( m_{T,s,i}^{P\,variable} + R_T^P(m_{T,s,i}^{P\,variable}) + m_{T,s,i}^{P\,fixed} + R_T^P(m_{T,s,i}^{P\,fixed}) \right) \right) \quad (3)$$

Then, the risk following costs $RC_{T,s}^P = RC_{T,s}^{P\,variable} + RC_{T,s}^{P\,fixed}$ of risk cost center s are composed of price risk costs, quantity risk costs and the combination of both:

$$\begin{aligned}
RC_{T,s}^P = \sum_{i=1}^n \Big( & p_{T,i}^P \cdot \left( R_T^P(m_{T,S,i}^{P\,variable}) + R_T^P(m_{T,S,i}^{P\,fixed}) \right) && \text{price risk costs} \\
& + R_T^P(p_{T,i}^P) \cdot \left( m_{T,S,i}^{P\,variable} + m_{T,S,i}^{P\,fixed} \right) && \text{quantity risk costs} \\
& + R_T^P(p_{T,i}^P) \cdot \left( R_T^P(m_{T,S,i}^{P\,variable}) + R_T^P(m_{T,S,i}^{P\,fixed}) \right) \Big) && \text{price/quantity risk costs}
\end{aligned} \quad (4)$$

Given the allocation base $AB_{T,s}^P$ we get a new risk adjusted calculation rate in addition to the classic calculation rate of cost center s:

$$RCR_{T,s}^{P} = RC_{T,s}^{P\,variable} / AB_{T,s}^{P} \qquad (5)$$

## 4.2 Risk Cost-Unit Accounting

The classic cost-unit accounting consists of two parts: the product costing and the period costing. The latter one can be extended to a short-term profit and loss account. The purpose of the product costing is the calculation of cost prices in order to determine quotation prices, the bottom prices, the value of stock and prices for advertised bidding [7, 18, 20]. With the help of the cost center accounting, the overhead costs then are allocated source-related to the cost units.

Also for a risk cost accounting the risk costs should be allocated source-related to the cost units in order to see which products bear more what kind of risks. Additionally, quotation prices and bottom prices should be calculated according to a firm's risk situation. Prices lower than risk oriented bottom prices do not reflect the firm's risk situation because if risks occur the firm will probably not be able to cover these risks within the limits of the planned business concern. The basis for a risk oriented cost-unit accounting is the classic cost-unit accounting with the classic costs and their parameters. With the help of the risk values of the cost parameters, it is then again possible, like in the risk cost center accounting, to calculate the risk costs of a firm's cost units. The structure as well as the cost structure of the risk cost-unit accounting is similar to the classic accounting. There are direct risk costs that can directly be allocated to a cost unit. Variable overhead risk costs come from the risk cost center accounting and can be allocated easily to the cost units according to the stress of a cost center by cost units. Fixed overhead risk costs as well as risk costs that cannot be allocated directly to cost units because they belong to a set of similar units and it is not possible to distinguish which cost unit is the originator (e.g. law risks when rights are violated), have to be taken into account during contribution margin accounting.

Risk management costs as well as imputed risks are already part of the cost unit accounting and just have to be accentuated as risk costs. They must not be allocated to cost units twice. Thus, only the risk following costs need a special consideration. The total risk costs of a cost unit i $RCUC_{T,i}^{P}$ are composed of the clearly assignable direct risk costs $DRC_{T,i}^{P}$ and the overhead risk costs $ORC_{T,i}^{P}$ that are allocated to the cost units according to the stress of a cost center:

$$RCUC_{T,i}^{P} = DRC_{T,i}^{P} + ORC_{T,i}^{P} \qquad (6)$$

Let $x_i$ be the production quantity of cost unit i. Then, direct risk costs are composed of the nv variable direct risk costs multiplied with $x_i$ and the nf fixed direct risk costs:

$$DRC_{T,i}^{P} = \sum_{j=1}^{nv} x_{T,i}^{P} \cdot vDRC_{T,ij}^{P} + \sum_{j=1}^{nf} fDRC_{T,ij}^{P} \qquad (7)$$

Let $S_P$ be the number of procurement, $S_M$ the number of main (production or services), and $S_A$ the number of administration and distribution cost centers, $mdc_{T,i}^P$ the direct material costs of cost unit i, $q_{T,s,i}^P$ the stress of cost center s by cost unit i, $h_{T,i}^P$ the direct costs of production and $rh_{T,i}^P$ the risk oriented direct costs of production. Then, the total overhead risk costs of a risk cost unit i are:

$$ORC_{T,i}^P = x_{T,i}^P \cdot \left( \sum_{s=1}^{S_P} mdc_{T,i}^P \cdot RCR_{T,s}^P + \sum_{s=1}^{S_M} q_{T,s,i}^P \cdot RCR_{T,s}^P + \sum_{s=1}^{S_A} (h_{T,i}^P + rh_{T,i}^P) \cdot RCR_{T,s}^P \right) \quad (8)$$

The risk oriented direct costs of production $rh_{T,i}^P$ are the sum of all variable direct and the overhead risk costs that are allocated according to the stress of the cost centers:

$$rh_{T,i}^P = \sum_{j=1}^{n} vDRC_{T,ij}^P + \sum_{s=1}^{S_P} mdc_{T,i}^P \cdot RCR_{T,s}^P + \sum_{s=1}^{S_M} q_{T,si}^P \cdot RCR_{T,s}^P \quad (9)$$

Then, the risk cost price $rs_{T,i}^P$ of a risk cost unit i is:

$$rs_{T,i}^P = \sum_{j=1}^{n} vERK_{T,ij}^P + \sum_{s=1}^{S_P} mdc_{T,i}^P \cdot RCR_{T,s}^P + \sum_{s=1}^{S_M} q_{T,si}^P \cdot RCR_{T,s}^P + \sum_{s=1}^{S_A} (h_{T,i}^P + rh_{T,i}^P) \cdot RCR_{T,s}^P \quad (10)$$

The total risk costs of a cost unit that reflect the complete risk potential of the cost unit are as follows:

$$RCUC_{T,i}^P = x_{T,i}^P \cdot rs_{T,i}^P + \sum_{j=1}^{m} fDRC_{T,ij}^P \quad (11)$$

Usually, costs will be higher when risks are considered because of the surplus of risk costs. That means that if prices remain the same, the profit margin is shrinking. For this, instead of the classic cost price $s_{T,i}^P$ the cost price under risk $s_{T,i}^P + rs_{T,i}^P$ should be used as bottom price because the risk cost price comprises the averaged cost deviations that result from risks. These cost deviations will quite likely occur in the planning period so that prices below $s_{T,i}^P + rs_{T,i}^P$ mean that the costs of the cost unit will not be covered at an averaged occurrence of risks.

Beside variable (risk) costs also fixed direct (risk) costs should be taken into account. While the (risk) cost price tells what price to claim for each additional unit, the (risk) cost price with fixed direct (risk) costs tells what price to claim when the product is produced for the first time in the planning period assuming that the fixed costs are periodically degradable. Thus, the fixed (risk) costs must be made proportional to the planned sales volume $sv_{T,i}^P$. Let F be the number of different fixed direct costs. Then, the classic proportionalized direct costs $pfDC_{T,i}^P$ are calculated as follows:

$$\text{pfDC}^P_{T,i} = \sum_{j=1}^{F} \text{DirectFixedCosts}^P_{T,i,j}/\text{sv}^P_{T,i} \qquad (12)$$

The fixed direct risk costs can be made proportional in the same way using the sales volume under risk. But note that the denominator is different then. In comparison to the proportionalized direct fixed risk costs, the classic one distributes the fixed costs among a bigger quantity. That means that the proportionalized direct fixed risk costs are not the risk value of the classic proportionalized direct fixed costs. Therefore, the risk costs that are allocated to the sales volume under risk have to be considered in the calculation:

$$\text{pfDRC}^P_{T,i} = \left( \sum_{j=1}^{F} R^P_T(\text{DirectFixedCosts}^P_{T,i,j}) - R^P_T(\text{sv}^P_{T,i}) \cdot \text{pfDC}^P_{T,i} \right) / \left( \text{sv}^P_{T,i} + R^P_T(\text{sv}^P_{T,i}) \right) \quad (13)$$

Then, we get four kinds of bottom prices: The lowest one remains the cost price $s^P_{T,i}$. Above this, the next bottom price is the cost price under risk $s^P_{T,i} + \text{rs}^P_{T,i}$. These are the costs that will quite likely be realized during the planning period so that this bottom price is much more realistic. In order to consider also the fixed direct costs, the proportionalized fixed direct costs $\text{pfDC}^P_{T,i}$ are the next bottom price. The last bottom price are the proportionalized direct fixed risk costs $\text{pfDRC}^P_{T,i}$ that takes all direct costs and direct risk costs into account. For sure, these bottom prices can be undercut in the case of price war or below capacity employment. But a permanent lower price than the cost price under risk is dangerous because then the variable costs that will be realized with quite high probability cannot be covered during the period.

## 5    Example

In this section, the risk cost accounting is illustrated by an example for each calculation. A Cloud Service Provider provides a computing service with the help of 100 computers running 24/7. Energy production is in-house as well as maintenance. The first calculation is the (risk) cost center accounting for the cost center "Maintenance & Repair". On the left side of Fig. 2 we can see the classic cost center accounting.

The right side depicts the risk cost center accounting. The column "Risk" contains the risk value of each parameter that can be found in the first column. The wages are subject to a price risk with a risk value of 2 monetary units (MU) but not to a quantity risk. Concerning the overtime, there is a risk of 90 additional hours. The operating/auxiliary material is subject to all types of risk: Price risk of 6 MU, quantity risk of 12 kg and quality risk of a 10% lower quality. The cost center uses electricity produced by cost center Power. This cost center has a risk adjusted calculation rate of 0.05 so that there is a price risk accordingly. Beyond that, there is a quantity risk of 500 kWh needed additionally. Summing all up, we get a classic calculation rate of 61.10 MU and a risk adjusted calculation rate of 2.69 MU in addition. This risk adjusted

**Fig. 2 — Classic cost center accounting: Maintenance & Repair** (Allocation base 8760 h)

| | | Quantity | Price | Total | Variable | Fixed |
|---|---|---|---|---|---|---|
| Employees | | | | | | |
| Wages | h | 8760 | 55.00 | 481,800.00 | 481,800.00 | 0.00 |
| variable | | 8760 | | | | |
| fix | | 0.00 | | | | |
| Overtime | h | 920.00 | 55.00 | 50,600.00 | 50,600.00 | 0.00 |
| variable | | 920.00 | | | | |
| fix | | 0.00 | | | | |
| Operating/Auxiliary material | | | | | | |
| Lubricants | kg | 100.00 | 35.00 | 3,500.00 | 2,625.00 | 875.00 |
| variable | | 75.00 | | | | |
| fix | | 25.00 | | | | |
| Subtotal | | | | 535,900.00 | 535,025.00 | 875.00 |
| Power | | | | | | |
| Electricity | kWh | 4,000.00 | 0.2370 | 948.00 | 237.00 | 711.00 |
| variable | | 1,000.00 | | | | |
| fix | | 3,000.00 | | | | |
| Total | | | | 536,848.00 | 535,262.00 | 1,586.00 |
| Calculation Rate | | | | | 61.10 | |

**Fig. 2 — Risk cost center accounting: Maintenance & Repair** (Allocation base 8760.00 h)

| | | Risk type | Plan | Risk | Total | Variable | Fixed |
|---|---|---|---|---|---|---|---|
| Employees | | | | | | | |
| Wages | h | Price | 55.00 | 2.00 | 17,520.00 | 17,520.00 | 0.00 |
| | | Quantity | 8,760 | 0.00 | 0.00 | | |
| | | variable | 8,760 | 0.00 | | 0.00 | |
| | | fixed | 0.00 | 0.00 | | | 0.00 |
| | | Price/Quantity | | | 0.00 | 0.00 | 0.00 |
| Overtime | h | Price | 55.00 | 0.00 | 0.00 | 0.00 | 0.00 |
| | | Quantity | 920.00 | 90.00 | 4,950.00 | | |
| | | variable | 920.00 | 90.00 | | 4,950.00 | |
| | | fixed | 0.00 | 0.00 | | | 0.00 |
| | | Price/Quantity | | | 0.00 | 0.00 | 0.00 |
| Operating/Auxiliary material | | | | | | | |
| Lubricants | kg | Price | 35.00 | 6.00 | 600.00 | 450.00 | 150.00 |
| | | Quantity | 100.00 | 12.00 | 420.00 | | |
| | | variable | 75.00 | 2.00 | | 70.00 | |
| | | fixed | 25.00 | 10.00 | | | 350.00 |
| | | Quality | 1.00 | 0.10 | 388.89 | | |
| | | variable | | 8.33 | | 291.67 | |
| | | fixed | | 2.78 | | | 97.22 |
| | | Price/Quantity | | | 72.00 | 12.00 | 60.00 |
| | | Price/Quality | | | 66.67 | 50.00 | 16.67 |
| Subtotal | | | | | 24,017.56 | 23,343.67 | 673.89 |
| Power | | | | | | | |
| Electricity | kWh | Price | 0.2370 | 0.0500 | 200.00 | 50.00 | 150.00 |
| | | Quantity | 4,000.00 | 500.00 | 118.50 | | |
| | | variable | 1000.00 | 500.00 | | 118.50 | |
| | | fixed | 3000.00 | 0.00 | | | 0.00 |
| | | Price/Quantity | | | 25.00 | 25.00 | 0.00 |
| Total | | | | | 24,361.06 | 23,537.17 | 823.89 |
| Risk adjusted calculation rate | | | | | | 2.69 | |

**Fig. 2.** Classic and risk cost center accounting for cost center maintenance and repair.

**Fig. 3 — Classic cost-unit accounting: Computing Service** (Planned output 876,000 h)

| | ME | Quantity | Price | Total | Variable | Fixed |
|---|---|---|---|---|---|---|
| Operating Material | | | | | | |
| Prod. Coeff. | | 0.400 | | | | |
| Energy | kWh | 350,400 | 0.237 | 83,044.80 | 83,044.80 | 0.00 |
| Cooling | kWh | 321,408 | 0.24 | 76,173.70 | 0.00 | 76,173.70 |
| Total | | | | 159,218.50 | 83,044.80 | 76,173.70 |
| Direct costs | | | | 0.09480 | | |
| Computing center overhead costs | | | | 0.05000 | | |
| Costs of service provided | | | | 0.14480 | | |
| Administration overhead costs | | | 1.78% | 0.00258 | | |
| Cost price | | | | 0.14738 | | |

**Fig. 3 — Risk cost-unit accounting: Computing Service** (Planned output 876,000 h)

| | | Risk type | Plan | Risk | Total | Variable | Fixed |
|---|---|---|---|---|---|---|---|
| Operating Material | | | | | | | |
| Prod. Coeff. | | Quantity | 0.400 | 0.075 | | | |
| Energy | kWh | | | | | | |
| | | Price | 0.237 | 0.050 | 17,520.00 | 17,520.00 | 0.00 |
| | | Quantity | 350,400 | 65,700.90 | 15,570.90 | 15,570.90 | 0.00 |
| | | Price/Quantity | | | 3,285.00 | 3,285.00 | 0.00 |
| Cooling | piece | Price | 0.24 | 0.05 | 16,070.40 | 0.00 | 16,070.40 |
| Total | | | | | 52,446.30 | 36,375.90 | 16,070.40 |
| Direct risk costs | | | | | 0.04153 | | |
| Computing center overhead costs | | | | | 0.03000 | | |
| Costs of service provided | | | | | 0.07153 | | |
| Administration overhead risk costs | | | | | 0.20% | | |
| on costs of services provided | | | | | 0.1448 | 0.00028 | |
| on risk costs of services provided | | | | | 0.0715 | 0.00014 | |
| Cost price under risk | | | | | 0.07195 | | |

**Fig. 3.** Classic and risk cost-unit accounting for the service computing.

calculation rate is then used as a price risk in other risk cost centers like Power or the Computing center that make use of cost center Maintenance & Repair.

The (risk) cost-unit accounting calculates the cost price of a service. The pricing of the computing service is based on hours. The calculation of the direct costs resembles the one of the (risk) cost center accounting (see Fig. 3). Overhead costs for the cost center that generates the service (here: computing center) are added to the direct costs. Administrative overhead costs calculated within the (risk) cost center accounting for the cost center Administration are added on a percental basis (1.78% and 0.20%).

Using the fixed direct (risk) costs in addition to cost prices and their risk values, four bottom prices can be calculated. The lowest bottom price is the classic cost price of 0.147 MU per h (see Fig. 4). If the selling price is lower, the firm incurs losses. But

| | Computing Service | | |
|---|---|---|---|
| | classic | Risk value | under risk |
| Planned volume | 876,000.00 | -52,560.00 | 823,440.00 |
| Planned price | 0.490 | -0.050 | 0.440 |
| Cost price | 0.147 | 0.072 | 0.219 |
| Profit margin I | 0.343 | 0.122 | 0.221 |
| Fixed Direct costs | 76,173.70 | 16,070.40 | 92,244.10 |
| Proportional | 0.087 | 0.025 | 0.112 |
| Bottom price | 0.234 | 0.097 | 0.331 |
| Profit margin II | 0.256 | 0.147 | 0.109 |

**Fig. 4.** Classic and risk cost price and bottom prices for the service computing.

even if the selling price is below 0.219 MU (the second bottom price), the probability of losses is high because this bottom price comprises the quite probable risk that will occur in the planning period. The last two bottom prices of 0.234 MU and 0.331 MU under risk also consider the fixed costs. Usually, the selling prices should be greater than the last bottom price under risk because only then all probable risks are covered.

# 6 Conclusion

The MCA is the most important IS of an enterprise. It provides a detailed overview about the costly structure of all business areas. The only deficit is that it does not handle risks and risk costs in detail, only averaged costs of several periods are considered by imputed risks. Therefore, this paper extended the classic cost accounting with a risk cost accounting. This new accounting system provides a detailed view about a firm's risk situation. The risk situation of cost centers as well as the risk contribution of cost-units can be analyzed in detail. The integration into existing IS can easily be done because the risk cost accounting is designed as a sample accounting that can be done alongside. If the risk accounting is introduced in a firm, it is only necessary to determine the risk values of different cost parameters. The calculation itself can be done automatically.

Further research must be done concerning the risk values themselves. It is evident to calculate them. But the calculation is also difficult. Risks and risk measures are embedded in a highly complex risk cause and effect network that influences the risk values. One change in this network can affect several other risks and therefore different parameters. What is needed is an additional IS with which such a risk cause effect chain can be stored, analyzed and risk values calculated.

# References

1. Aven, T., Renn, O.: On risk defined as an event where the outcome is uncertain. J. Risk Res. **12**(1), 1–11 (2009)
2. Bainbridge, S.M.: Caremark and enterprise risk management (2009)
3. Bakar, B.A., Rasid, S.Z.A., Rizal, A.M.: Performance measures use, government regulation, risk management and accountability. In: 2014 Proceedings of the 3rd International Congress on Interdisciplinary Behavior and Social Science (ICIBSoS 2014), Bali, Indonesia. CRC Press (2015)

4. Bishop, R.C., Heberlein, T.A.: Measuring values of extramarket goods: Are indirect measures biased? Am. J. Agric. Econ. **61**(5), 926–930 (1979)
5. Bitz, H.: Risikomanagement nach KonTraG. Stuttgart (2000)
6. Boyko, V., Rudnichenko, N., Kramskoy, S., Hrechukha, Y., Shibaeva, N.: Concept implementation of decision support software for the risk management of complex technical system. In: Shakhovska, N. (ed.) Advances in Intelligent Systems and Computing. AISC, vol. 512, pp. 255–269. Springer, Cham (2017). doi:10.1007/978-3-319-45991-2_17
7. Braun, K.W., Tietz, W.M., Harrison, W.T., Bamber, L.S., Horngren, C.T.: Managerial Accounting. Pearson, Boston (2014)
8. Bromiley, P., McShane, M., Nair, A., Rustambekov, E.: Enterprise risk management: Review, critique, and research directions. Long Range Plan. **48**(4), 265–276 (2015)
9. Bussmann, K.F.: Das betriebswirtschaftlicher Risiko. Meisenheim am Glan (1955)
10. Carter, R.L., Crockford, G.N.: The development and scope of risk management. In: Pountney, B. (ed.) Handbook of Risk Management, Supplement 55, Kingston upon Thames 1999, 1.1-01–1.1-21 (1999)
11. Colletaz, G., Christophe, H., Pérignon, C.: The risk map: A new tool for validating risk models. J. Bank. Finance **37**(10), 3843–3854 (2013)
12. Collier, P.M., Berry, A.J., Burke, G.T.: Risk and Management Accounting: Best Practice Guidelines for Enterprise-Wide Internal Control Procedures, vol. 2(11). Elsevier, Oxford (2007)
13. Cooper, D.J., Ezzamel, M., Qu, S.: Popularizing a management accounting idea: the case of the balanced scorecard (2016)
14. Dickinson, G.: Enterprise risk management its origins and conceptual foundation. Geneva Pap. Risk Insur. - Issues Pract. **26**(3), 360–366 (2001)
15. Dionne, G.: Risk management: history, definition, and critique. Risk Manage. Insur. Rev. **16** (2), 147–166 (2013)
16. Fatemi, A., Luft, C.: Corporate risk management: costs and benefits. Glob. Finance J. **13**(1), 29–38 (2002)
17. Gleißner, W., Romeike, F.: Anforderungen an die Softwareunterstützung für das Risikomanagement. Zeitschrift für Controlling Manage. **2**, 154–164 (2005)
18. Horngren, C.T., Bhimani, A., Datar, S.M., Foster, G., Horngren, C.T.: Management and cost accounting. Financial Times/Prentice Hall, Harlow (2002)
19. Kaplan, R.S., Norton, D.P.: The Balanced Scorecard: Translating Strategy into Action. Harvard Business Press, Boston (1996)
20. Kaplan, R.S., Atkinson, A.A., Morris, D.J.: Advanced Management Accounting, vol. 3. Prentice Hall, Upper Saddle River (1998)
21. Lackes, R., Siepermann, M., Springwald, S.: Risk Management information systems as possibility to meet with the global risk situation. In: Enterprise and Competitive Environment, Bučovice 2011, pp. 457–472 (2011)
22. McNeil, J.A., Frey, R., Embrechts, P.: Quantative Risk Management: Concepts, Techniques and Tools. Princeton University Press, Princeton (2015)
23. Miller, K.D.: A framework for integrated risk management in international business. J. Int. Bus. Stud. **23**(2), 311–331 (1992)
24. Perramon, J., Rocafort, A., Bagur-Femenias, L., Llach, J.: Learning to create value through the 'balanced scorecard' model an empirical study. Total Qual. Manag. Bus. Excellence **27** (9), 1121–1139 (2016)
25. Rücker, U.-C.: Finanzierung von Umweltrisiken im Rahmen eines systematischen Risikomanagements. Sternenfels (1999)
26. Schmit, J.T., Roth, K.: Cost effectiveness of risk management practices. J. Risk Insur. **57**(3), 455–470 (1990)

27. Selviaridis, K., Norrman, A.: Performance-based contracting in service supply chains: a service provider risk perspective. Supply Chain Manage. Int. J. **19**(2), 153–172 (2014)
28. Siepermann, C.: Risk management in logistics with the balanced scorecard. In: Grzybowska, K., Golinska, P. (eds.): Selected Logistics Problems and Solutions, Posen, pp. 243–265 (2011)
29. Unser, M.: Lower partial moments as measures of perceived risk: An experimental study. J. Econ. Psychol. **21**(3), 253–280 (2000). doi:10.1016/S0167-4870(00)00004-0

# BASMATI: An Architecture for Managing Cloud and Edge Resources for Mobile Users

Jörn Altmann[1], Baseem Al-Athwari[1], Emanuele Carlini[2], Massimo Coppola[2],
Patrizio Dazzi[2], Ana Juan Ferrer[6], Netsanet Haile[1], Young-Woo Jung[5],
Jamie Marshall[4], Enric Pages[6], Evangelos Psomakelis[3,7], Ganis Zulfa Santoso[5],
Konstantinos Tserpes[3,7(✉)], and John Violos[3]

[1] College of Engineering, Seoul National University, Seoul, Republic of Korea
jorn.altmann@acm.org, {baseem,netsaneth}@snu.ac.kr
[2] ISTI-CNR, Pisa, Italy
{e.carlini,m.coppola,p.dazzi}@isti.cnr.it
[3] ICCS-NTUA, Athens, Greece
{psomakelis,tserpes,violos}@mail.ntua.gr
[4] Amenesik SARL, St Pierre Les Nemours, France
ijm@amenesik.com
[5] Cloud Computing Research Department, ETRI, Daejeon, Republic of Korea
{jungyw,ganis}@etri.re.kr
[6] Atos Origin, Barcelona, Spain
{ana.juanf,enric.pages}@atos.net
[7] HUA, Athens, Greece

**Abstract.** The BASMATI architecture is designed to improve the service quality perceived by end-users. In particular, it focuses on the support of applications that offer services to mobile end-users, ranging from those crossing national borders to those roaming around locally and who both need access to widely dispersed cloud resources. To achieve this, the architecture of BASMATI is built around the concepts of cloud federation and offloading, embodying both heterogeneous resources of different cloud providers and various computational devices located at the edge of the network with different access policies. The BASMATI architecture leverages intelligent decision support for brokering resources, user mobility modeling, a highly reactive management of applications, and a business-oriented cloud federation logic, to drive the efficient and proactive allocation of services onto proper cloud resources. Within this paper, we describe the architectural requirements and the architecture, overview.

**Keywords:** Cloud computing · Cloud federation · Distributed computing · Quality of Service · Service level agreement · Resource brokering · Mobile computing · Cloud architecture design

## 1 Introduction

The cloud computing paradigm is rapidly changing the landscape of information technology. It offers to most end-users and application providers a close

© Springer International Publishing AG 2017
C. Pham et al. (Eds.): GECON 2017, LNCS 10537, pp. 56–66, 2017.
DOI: 10.1007/978-3-319-68066-8_5

approximation of unlimited scalability with virtually zero fixed costs for infrastructure by allowing to rent computing resources and services as pay-per-use [1].

Furthermore, the adoption of the service oriented architecture (SOA) approach for exploiting cloud resources allows easy use of externalized resources and services. In order to safeguard the integrity of the business, cloud service rentals need to be coupled with contracts (i.e., Service Level Agreements), specifying the expected quality of service (QoS). Elastic and dynamic service provisioning also mandates that service level agreements (SLA) are supported by automatic contract re-negotiation, enforcement, and monitoring of the QoS [2].

With the rising of cloud computing technology, the mobile computing paradigm has also grown widespread. Customized apps on end-user's mobile devices are more and more the primary front-end to a plethora of back-end application services hosted on clouds (e.g., storage services, calendar services, email services, social networking services).

While a single marketplace for cloud services can be highly beneficial to both end-users and application service providers, the lack of universal cloud standards and technologies results in poor interoperability between data-centers. It also increases the user lock-in to specific service providers. This collides with the core requirement of mobile cloud applications, i.e. the swift resource relocation within heterogeneous infrastructures.

To address this lack of interoperability, academia and industry have given shape to cloud federations, in which various cloud service providers join their resources to collaboratively increase their market share [3]. Nowadays, the original cloud federation concept is further evolving into more complex, heterogeneous and functionality-rich paradigms [4].

However, existing cloud federations do not realize inter-cloud interoperability. They do not allow heterogeneous services to be represented in a directory of services. They also do not provide a single access point for application service providers to control their application services for supporting the needs of mobile users, who require cross-border access to geographically spread cloud services.

To solve this shortcoming, within the framework of the South-Korea and EU Horizon 2020 joint research project BASMATI – *Cloud Brokerage Across Borders for Mobile Users and Applications*, a federated cloud platform with intelligent decision support for brokering resources has been developed [5]. To this point, the BASMATI federated cloud platform comprises already several optimization algorithms and a cloud federation architecture. The basis for the global design of the BASMATI architecture builds on a wide range of recent projects and technologies, including CompatibleOne [6], OPTIMIS [7], PaaSport, and Broker@Cloud, Easiclouds [8], Contrail [9], and AnyBroker.

The contributions with respect to the cloud federation architecture, which are presented in this article, are: first, a detailed description of the way that the different architecture layers and modules interact with each other; second, intelligent decision support for exploiting cloud services, edge resources, knowledge about users, and application behavior. The contributions allow the platform to forecast the expected load and latencies imposed on specific service instances and allow foreseeing the utilization of allocated resources across multiple clouds.

The remainder of this article is organized as follows: Sect. 2 gives a quick overview about the state-of-the-art in cloud federation architectures. Section 3 discusses the assumptions and sets out the requirements for the cloud federation architecture. The BASMATI architecture is introduced in Sect. 4. Section 5 concludes the paper with brief summary and a discussion.

## 2 Related Work

### 2.1 Cloud Federation

Various research works have defined cloud federation. Haile and Altmann (2015) described cloud federation as a strategic alliance between cloud providers, in which cloud providers have reached a cross-site agreement for cooperating regarding the deployment of service components and the use of capacity from each other to cope with demand variations of clients [3]. Another definition is offered by Altmann and Kashief (2014) as a model for enabling convenient, on-demand network access to a shared pool of configurable computing resources (e.g., networks, servers, storage, applications, and services) that can be rapidly provisioned and released with minimal management effort or service provider interaction [8].

As part of a cloud federation, even a small service provider can offer a truly global service without spending a dime building new infrastructure. For companies with spare capacity in the data center, the federation also provides a simple way to monetize that capacity by submitting it to the marketplace for other providers to buy, creating an additional source of revenue.

There are immediate benefits for end users, too. The federated cloud means that end users can host apps with their federated cloud provider of choice, instead of choosing from a handful of global cloud providers on the market today and making do with whatever pricing, app support and SLAs they happen to impose. Cloud users can choose a local host with the exact pricing, expertise and support package that fits their need, while still receiving instant access to as much local or global IT resources as theyd like. They get global scalability without restricted choice, and without having to manage multiple providers and invoices. This is an extension of the concept of federation as defined previously (e.g. [10,11]) and which assumed that the federation should be comprised solely from cloud providers rather than cloud service providers who manage a limited number of cloud resources.

### 2.2 Existing Cloud Architectures

Among the many cloud architectures that exists, this overview on the state-of-the-art focuses on the ad-hoc mobile cloud platforms. These platforms follow design patterns that are of interesting to BASMATI.

The ad-hoc mobile cloud approach organizes the collective resources of the various mobile devices in the local vicinity, in order to create a virtual-cloud. In such context, a mobile device will use the resources of other close devices (the virtual cloud) instead of its own, in the same way, it would do with a remote datacenter. In principle, this approach can support high user mobility and create virtual clouds on demand according to the necessity. Several ad-hoc mobile cloud platforms try to recreate typical cluster computation (such as MapReduce) in a virtual cloud composed of mobile devices. The approach presented by Huerta-Canepa and Lee realize a Hadoop ([12]) computation on top of a virtual cloud [13]. Hyrax supports a distributed computation based on Hadoop on a virtual cloud as well [14], also including the Hadoop Distributed File System (HDFS) for the storage. Ghasemi-Falavarjani et al. developed a context-aware offloading middleware for mobile cloud (OMMC) to collect contextual information of mobile devices [15]. By considering neighboring mobile devices as service providers, they investigated the resource allocation problem to select service providers that minimizes the completion time of the offloading along maximizing lifetime of mobile devices satisfying deadline constraint [15]. Pu et al. proposed device-to-device (D2D) Fogging framework for mobile task offloading based on network-assisted D2D collaboration, where mobile users can dynamically and beneficially share the computation and communication resources among each other via the control assistance by the network operators. The purpose of their D2D Fogging is to achieve energy efficient task executions for network wide users [16].

## 3   Basic Assumptions and Challenges

The architecture of the BASMATI platform makes a few assumptions with respect to the type of the applications, the off-loading, and quality of service management. Based on those assumptions, the requirements for BASMATI architecture are derived.

A mobile application is typically split into two parts, the front-end (FE), which is executed on a mobile device, and the back-end (BE), which is a composition of services deployed in the Cloud. It is assumed that it is mainly the BE that poses the hardest limitations on the mobile app in terms of performance. A basic tool to tackle those limitations and ensure that the application will perform according to its promised levels is offloading, i.e. the delegation of some computational task from a resource to another with the purpose to optimize the overall system operation. Commonly, this delegation is directed from the core of the computing infrastructure (i.e. cloud) to the *edge* of the network hierarchy and is supported by dedicated, low power devices such as Raspberry Pi and Banana Pi. This sort of service shuffling across clouds, is in some cases is also called *Cloudbursting*.

The key to performing efficient offloading of this sort, is to carefully monitor the resource utilization against its promised thresholds and apply optimization techniques that consider the state of the whole system rather than a part of it, including the application context. As such, apart from SLA objectives, violation history [17,18] and resource availability BASMATI seeks for correlations between user characteristics -including mobility patterns- and resource utilization. By ingesting those factors (resource requirements, availability and application context) in a single complex, performance analysis module, BASMATI achieves to intelligently offload tasks by leveraging on the edge infrastructure's characteristics.

The BASMATI architecture provides specific support for offloading by providing a combined brokering support that encompasses Clouds and Edges. The optimization function of the cloud brokering support for the offloading can deal with services and resources from very distinct Clouds with different cost, federation memberships, SLA metrics, and types of network constraints (bandwidth, latency, access policies). The optimization function of the brokering support can consider the proximity of appropriate edge and Cloudlet resources for offloading.

In order to support a seamless mobile experience, the BASMATI architecture not only needs to address SLAs but also targets Quality of Experience (QoE) for the end-user. QoE perception is linked to parameters akin to both latencies (network, back-end server startup) and bandwidths (network and compute bandwidth, and access to Cloud-stored content). Based on a suitable metrics of user QoE, BASMATI can provide resources that match the user needs in term of QoE (e.g., allocate additional servers to services when needed). It can be performed by anticipating users' behavior in the short term (e.g., by tracking and analyzing aggregated user activities). This task of the BASMATI architecture is performed by modules for analyzing the patterns of user mobility and by exploit models for analyzing the application behavior with respect to its environment.

## 4    The BASMATI Architecture

The platform governing the BASMATI ecosystem is organized according to a layered architecture composed of three layers (Fig. 1). The lowest layer is the *Providers Management Layer* for managing cloud providers and for edge providers. The middle layer is the *Federation Management Layer*, which provides to the federation of cloud providers. The upper layer is the *Application Management Layer* for managing application back-end and application front-end. Each of the these three layers is comprised of a number of modules.

### 4.1    Providers Management Layer

The providers management (PM) layer deals with the resources that are offered by providers in the context of the federation and can be exploited by the application. It provides an abstraction for the different kinds of resources involved in BASMATI. For example, the two main resource types (i.e., cloud resources and edge resources) do not require different types of mechanisms for resource accounting, user identity management, and for the actual deployment of applications onto the provider resources. However, the restrictions that come with the low-capacity of edge resources.

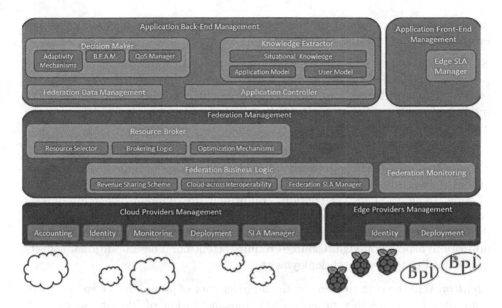

**Fig. 1.** BASMATI architecture.

**Cloud Providers Management.** The cloud providers management (CPM) includes all those mechanisms and components aimed at easing the exploitation of distinct cloud providers of the cloud federations. Adapters, stubs or partial re-implementation of common services depend on the API provided by the underlying cloud providers.

*Identity.* Each partner member of the federation exposes the identity API, which allows other members of the federation to make use of the offered services so long as the terms of the federation agreement governing the offer is respected. This is an essential part of the federation, as it is the backbone for the resource and service pricing schemes. It will be used for security, the identification of the financial transactions required for invoicing, federation member management, and for revenue and cost sharing across the cloud federation.

*Accounting.* The accounting module records all transaction using the information from the identity module and the monitoring module. It provides the raw resource usage data needed for charging according to the service level agreement.

*Deployment.* After joining a cloud federation, cloud providers expose deployment APIs for the use by customers and other members of the federation. Cloud providers also expose APIs for monitoring the deployed services. From an operative point of view, the deployment module accesses the services of the cloud provider.

*Monitoring.* The monitoring module collects monitoring data from the cloud provider and aggregates and filters this information before forwarding the information to modules of the federation management layer, including the federated SLA manager and accounting.

*SLA Manager.* The SLA manager organizes the SLA templates offered by cloud providers and maintains a list of SLAs that have been established between customers (or cloud federation) with a cloud provider. It also checks whether the quality of service satisfy the established SLAs and reports this violation to the application controller.

**Edge Providers Management (EPM).** The edge providers management (EPM) comprises modules that address the restrictions that come with the use of edge resources. Those restrictions comprise many different ownership of edge resources, large number of providers of edge resources, and restricted functionality of resources. Besides the aspects that are considered for cloud resources, some additional aspects of edge resources require attention. These additional aspects are related to identity and deployment.

*Identity.* With respect to identity, the large number of providers of edge resources mandates for a possibly decentralized implementation of identity services. It would allow not only to deal with the large number of providers of edge resources but also with the mobility of users as different locations offer different edge resources.

*Deployment.* The deployment service will support front-end-offloading, which is a variation of computation offloading and requires different protocols than those of the CPM deployment.

### 4.2    Federation Management (FM) Layer

FM layer is aimed at providing the mechanisms for achieving an efficient mapping of applications onto the clouds of providers participating in the BASMATI federation. This layer comprises three modules: *federation business logic, federation monitoring, and resource broker.*

**Federation Business Logic.** This module embodies the logic and mechanisms to face three key duties: *(i)* enabling the effective deployment and execution of applications across different cloud providers; a feature of paramount importance in the context of BASMATI, in which final users are expected to be highly nomadic, thus accessing cloud resources from many different locations; *(ii)* orchestrating and managing the SLAs of applications for the federation; *(iii)* setting proper revenue sharing schema, defined and implemented within the federation and implemented.

**Federation Monitoring.** The federation monitoring acts as the collector of data sources from various resources belonging to the federation and applications. To realize that, the federation monitoring (1) has a tight relationship with the monitoring components at the cloud providers management level and (2) needs to coordinate and integrate seamlessly with applications running in the BASMATI environment.

**Resource Broker.** The resource broker role in the BASMATI architecture is to provide tools and mechanisms for selecting resources fulfilling the minimum performance requirements of applications (e.g., capacity constraints, availability of resources). To this end, it exploits mechanisms for heuristically provide a range of resources with different values of attributes. For this, the brokering logic organizes the indexing and retrieval of the list of cloud resources available for placement and offloading.

## 4.3   Application Management (AM) Layer

The AM layer is the architectural layer devoted to the management of BASMATI applications. It is composed of two parts: application back-end management and application front-end management. The former dealing with the governance of the cloud-side subset of applications, whereas the latter focuses on the front-end of applications (e.g., smart-phone apps), which run on mobile devices. The AM layer comprises 7 modules.

**Federation Data Management.** This modules provides the mechanisms enabling the efficient management of application-related data. In addition, the mechanisms are able to work both with structured and unstructured data sources, while providing access to the information to the application as well to the decision maker.

**Knowledge Extractor.** One of the key features of the BASMATI approach are the advanced solutions for the characterization of the behavior of applications, the mobility of users, and the combination of such analyses to generate a more complex situational knowledge (i.e., the information associated to a certain kind of user when interacting with a given type of application). The models built by Knowledge Extractor are exploited by the decision maker to drive the mapping of application onto resources.

**Decision Maker.** In order to perform a proper allocation of BASMATI applications into the resources belonging to the cloud federation, BASMATI relies on the interplay of three modules: decision maker, application controller, and resource broker. The decision maker is the component analyzing the requirements of applications, represented by means of the BASMATI Enhanced Application Model (BEAM), a TOSCA[1] dialect. BEAM describes the structure of applications along with (non) functional requirements. The information provided by the knowledge extractor can be used to drive the eventual composition and replication of the modules of the applications. By interacting with the resource broker about the available resources (requiring the minimum requirements), a ranked list of deployment plans are derived and eventually passed to the Application Controller. To this end, the decision maker exploits optimization mechanisms that consider feedback on past allocations to perform resource classification and prediction on the behavior of applications.

**Application Controller.** The application controller, which performs the actual deployment, takes the deployment plans provided by the decision maker and uses one of those for the actual deployment and keeps the remaining one for alternative deployments that might be needed in case of a SLA violation.

**Edge SLA Manager.** The Edge SLA Manager is the module, running on mobile devices, aimed at identifying potential edge devices, with which service level agreements could be established for supporting the application. This is the module driving workload offloading from smart-phones and tablets to the devices located at the edge of federation.

## 5   Conclusion

Our paper reflects the architecture design of the BASMATI multi-cloud brokering platform and a descriptions of its modules. It highlights the emphasis on the challenges infused by the nature of mobile cloud services but also by the cloud marketplace as it is shaped in EU and Korea, which is dominated by small cloud service providers who manage a limited amount of cloud resources to support applications. The same market is also characterized by the lack of cloud vendors.

The paper addresses all the issues that stem from the requirements analysis based on the abovementioned characteristics. The emphasis is put on the support of cloud service providers' federations and task offloading towards the edge of the computing and network infrastructure. It remains to validate the platform using real use cases and a reference implementation in order to check the platform interplay with advanced mechanisms on (1) user and application behavior and on (2) offloading.

**Acknowledgements.** This research has been carried on with support of the BAS-MATI project. BASMATI (http://basmati.cloud) has received funding from the European Unions Horizon 2020 research and innovation programme under grant agreement no. 723131 and from ICT R&D program of Korean Ministry of Science, ICT and Future Planning no. R0115-16-0001.

---

[1] https://www.oasis-open.org/committees/tosca/.

# References

1. Rohitratana, J., Altmann, J.: Impact of pricing schemes on a market for software-as-a-service and perpetual software. Future Gener. Comput. Syst. **28**(8), 1328–1339 (2012)
2. Breskovic, I., Altmann, J., Brandic, I.: Cost model based service placement in federated hybrid clouds. Future Gener. Comput. Syst. **29**(4), 1000–1011 (2014)
3. Haile, N., Altmann, J.: Risk-benefit-mediated impact of determinants on the adoption of cloud federation. In: 19th Pacific Asia Conference on Information Systems (PACIS 2015). AIS (2015)
4. Carlini, E., Dazzi, P., Mordacchini, M.: A holistic approach for high-level programming of next-generation data-intensive applications targeting distributed heterogeneous computing environment. Procedia Comput. Sci. **97**, 131–134 (2016)
5. Altmann, J., Carlini, E., Coppola, M., Dazzi, P., Ferrer, A.J., Haile, N., Jung, Y.W., Kang, D.J., Marshall, I.J., Tserpes, K., Varvarigou, T.: A brokerage architecture on federated clouds for mobile applications. In: Bubak, M., Turaa, M., Kasztelnik, M. (eds.) CGW16 Proceedings, ACC CYFRONET AGH, Krakw, pp. 59–60 (2016)
6. Yangui, S., Marshall, I.J., Laisne, J.P., Tata, S.: Compatibleone: the open source cloud broker. J. Grid Comput. **12**(1), 93–109 (2014)
7. Ferrer, A.J., Hernndez, F., Tordsson, J., Elmroth, E., Ali-Eldin, A., Zsigri, C., Sirvent, R., Guitart, J., Badia, R.M., Djemame, K., Ziegler, W., Dimitrakos, T., Nair, S.K., Kousiouris, G., Konstanteli, K., Varvarigou, T., Hudzia, B., Kipp, A., Wesner, S., Corrales, M., Forg, N., Sharif, T., Sheridan, C.: Optimis: a holistic approach to cloud service provisioning. Future Gener. Comput. Syst. **28**(1), 66–77 (2012)
8. Altmann, J., Kashef, M.M.: Cost model based service placement in federated hybrid clouds. Future Gener. Comput. Syst. **41**, 79–90 (2014)
9. Carlini, E., Coppola, M., Dazzi, P., Ricci, L., Righetti, G.: Cloud federations in contrail. In: European Conference on Parallel Processing, pp. 159–168. Springer, Berlin, Heidelberg (2011)
10. Rochwerger, B., Breitgand, D., Levy, E., Galis, A., Nagin, K., Llorente, I.M., Montero, R., Wolfsthal, Y., Elmroth, E., Caceres, J., et al.: The reservoir model and architecture for open federated cloud computing. IBM J. Res. Dev. **53**(4), 1–4 (2009)
11. Celesti, A., Tusa, F., Villari, M., Puliafito, A.: How to enhance cloud architectures to enable cross-federation. In: 2010 IEEE 3rd International Conference on Cloud Computing (CLOUD), pp. 337–345. IEEE (2010)
12. Shvachko, K., Kuang, H., Radia, S., Chansler, R.: The hadoop distributed file system. In: 26th Symposium on Mass Storage Systems and Technologies (MSST), pp. 1–10. IEEE (2010)
13. Huerta-Canepa, G., Lee, D.: A virtual cloud computing provider for mobile devices. In: 1st ACM Workshop on Mobile Cloud Computing and Services: Social Networks and Beyond. ACM (2010)
14. Marinelli, E.E.: Hyrax: cloud computing on mobile devices using mapreduce. In: No. CMU-CS-09-164, Carnegie-Mellon University Pittsburgh PA School of Computer Science, pp. 1–10 (2009)
15. Ghasemi-Falavarjani, S., Nematbakhsh, M., Ghahfarokhi, B.S.: Context-aware multi-objective resource allocation in mobile cloud. Comput. Electr. Eng. **44**, 218–240 (2015)

16. Pu, L., Chen, X., Xu, J., Fu, X.: 2d fogging: an energy-efficient and incentive-aware task offloading framework via network-assisted d2d collaboration. J. Sel. Areas Commun. **34**(12), 3887–3901 (2016)
17. Tserpes, K., Aisopos, F., Kyriazis, D., Varvarigou, T.: A recommender mechanism for service selection in service-oriented environments. Future Gener. Comput. Syst. **28**(8), 1285–1294 (2012)
18. Tserpes, K., Aisopos, F., Kyriazis, D., Varvarigou, T.: Service selection decision support in the internet of services. In: Altmann, J., Rana, O.F. (eds.) GECON 2010. LNCS, vol. 6296, pp. 16–33. Springer, Heidelberg (2010). doi:10.1007/978-3-642-15681-6_2

# A Comparative Study of Classification Techniques for Managing IoT Devices of Common Specifications

Argyro Mavrogiorgou[✉], Athanasios Kiourtis,
and Dimosthenis Kyriazis

Department of Digital Systems, University of Piraeus, Piraeus, Greece
{margy,kiourtis,dimos}@unipi.gr

**Abstract.** As information technology and telecommunication systems continue to grow in size and complexity, especially with the Internet of Things (IoT) domain that is being hailed as the next industrial revolution, emerging technologies have to anticipate this dramatic increase of heterogeneous connected devices. This paper proposes a solution that can be used to manage this huge number of devices, by classifying them and predicting their device's type, based on their specifications. Four (4) classification algorithms are being applied on a dataset containing the specifications of known devices (in terms of known device type), which is being used for predicting the unknown devices' types. These algorithms are analyzed using the WEKA data mining tool and a comparative study is undertaken to find the classifier that performs the best analysis on the dataset obtained, using a set of predefined performance metrics to compare the results of each classifier.

**Keywords:** IoT devices · Heterogeneous devices · Device specification · Device type · Classification · Classification algorithms

## 1 Introduction

Today's Internet of Things (IoT) domain is increasing rapidly, with billions of smart devices being invisibly interconnected, leading to the connectivity for everything [1]. According to Machina Research [2], 27 billion of connected devices are expected by 2024, while according to Cisco's report [3], there will belong nearly 1.5 mobile devices per capita by 2020, and more than 601 million wearable devices will be in use. Thus, it becomes clear that the number of devices is growing rapidly, resulting in a myriad of heterogeneous devices that will be connected to the IoT world in the near future. However, IoT devices are typically characterized by a high degree of heterogeneity, in terms of having different specifications, capabilities, and functionalities. In such a scenario, it is necessary to manage the interoperability between such heterogeneous elements [4]. Therefore, the problem that arises is the difficulty of managing the enormous number of heterogeneous devices that include their own specifications, and interfaces [5]. In that case, the IoT promises to cope with this challenge by facilitating automatic identification, interaction and access to all of these devices.

© Springer International Publishing AG 2017
C. Pham et al. (Eds.): GECON 2017, LNCS 10537, pp. 67–77, 2017.
DOI: 10.1007/978-3-319-68066-8_6

To address this challenge, in this paper a solution is proposed for managing the huge amounts of heterogeneous devices that exist. In more details, our solution proposes the facilitation of the identification of different IoT devices and the prediction of their type, based on their specifications (i.e. software and hardware specifications). To achieve this, a series of different classification algorithms are being followed so as to identify the various devices' types and classify them according to their type, resulting into the best matching solution. In each one of these algorithms, a training dataset is being given as an input, containing details and specifications of several devices of a known type, in order to efficiently train the proposed classifier. Then, the classifier is being tested along with a specific number of devices of unknown type that are being included into a test dataset, and probabilistically categorizes the devices of the unknown type, according to the common specifications that they may have with the devices of the known type. In our case, a scenario is presented using multiple heterogeneous IoT medical devices, which are classified based on their specifications, and are being grouped so as to identify all of the chosen unknown devices' types.

This paper is organized as follows. Section 2 describes the related work regarding the era of classification, while it also explores the classification algorithms that will be used in this study. Section 3 describes the proposed solution for grouping IoT devices based on their specifications, Sect. 4 outlines a use case of the proposed solution, while Sect. 5 analyzes our conclusions and future plans.

## 2 Related Work

### 2.1 Classification Approaches

Classification can be considered as the most important supervised learning technique, where objects with common properties are grouped into classes [6–8]. It is one of the most frequently tasks carried out in the IT world, that is why various classification techniques have been proposed in the literature, putting their efforts on the extraction and the prediction of useful either structured or unstructured data insights. In this domain, in [10] classification algorithms have been implemented for heart disease prediction, while in [12] classification approaches have been presented for diagnosis and prognosis of cancer. The proposed study in [11] has been designed to determine how data mining classification algorithms perform with increased input data sizes, using the Decision Tree, the Multi-Layer Perceptron Neural Network, and the Naïve Bayes classification algorithms. What is more, in [13] assorted classification algorithms are being applied on a talent dataset, so as to judge the performance of the individuals, while the researchers in [14] focus on the application of various classification techniques over the public healthcare dataset for analyzing the healthcare system [9]. In [15] the Naïve Bayes, the Support Vector Machines (SVM), as well as the Random Forest algorithms are being applied for classifying Android malwares, while in [16] the classification techniques of K-Nearest Neighbor, Naïve Bayes, SVM, and Random Forest are used for device classification, based on the devices' connectivity. Finally, in [17] a collaborative classification is defined for recognizing daily activities with a smartwatch, whose evaluation is conducted through the J48 Decision Tree, Random Forest, Bayesian Network, and SVM algorithms.

Considering the aforementioned related work and the current trends of the rich digital environment, in this paper we are using a series of existing machine learning techniques for classifying different types of IoT devices based on their specifications (i.e. software and hardware specifications). More specifically, in order to obtain more effective and accurate results, four (4) different classification algorithms are being explored, whose performance is being compared in terms of accuracy, for predicting the devices' type according to the given specifications.

## 2.2 Classification Algorithms

**K-Nearest Neighbor (KNN).** K-Nearest Neighbor (KNN) is one of the simplest machine learning algorithms that does not make any generalized assumptions either based on the underlying data distribution or the training data itself. It is a versatile algorithm, as its applications range from vision of proteins to computational geometry of graphs. Due to its characteristics, KNN can be used for both classification and regression predictive problems [18]. In more details, KNN stores feature vectors and class labels associated with them, for all the training samples, whilst a number K is responsible for deciding how many neighbors influence the classification process. To predict the class of a test set, the closest K neighbors from the training set are selected, and the final prediction is made based on the distance between the training samples and the given test set [19, 20].

**Naïve Bayes (NB).** Naïve Bayes (NB) is a simple probabilistic based supervised machine learning classifier based on applying Bayes' theorem with an assumption of independence among features [21–23]. Its model is easy to build and particularly useful for very large datasets, while along with its simplicity, NB is known to outperform even highly sophisticated classification methods, as it is easy and fast to predict the class of a test dataset [24]. Therefore, it is an eager and fast learning classifier that can be used for making predictions in real time, being mostly used in text classification. More specifically, NB generates a model by calculating the posterior probability of each possible class given the attributes while "naively" assuming independence between attributes, having as an outcome the class with the highest posterior probability [22].

**Support Vector Machine (SVM).** Support Vector Machine (SVM) is a set of supervised learning methods used mostly for classification or regression tasks [26]. Given labeled training data, SVM outputs an optimal hyperplane which categorizes new examples, based on the concept of decision planes [25]. Due to its nature, it uses a subset of training points in the decision function, thus being memory efficient, while it is also considered versatile. More specifically, SVM is implemented in practice using a kernel. The training of the hyperplane is done by transforming the problem using linear algebra, while it can be rephrased using the inner product of any two (2) given observations, rather than the observations themselves [26]. It performs classification by finding the hyperplane that maximizes the margin between the two (2) classes, while the vectors that define the hyperplane are the support vectors.

**Random Forest (RF).** Random Forest (RF) is a machine learning method for classification and regression that is based on constructing decision trees at training time [29]. RF is being mainly used for text classification, and image recognition, whilst it can run efficiently on large datasets, handle thousands of input variables without variable deletion [27, 29], and estimate missing data. In more details, RF uses a modified tree-learning algorithm that selects, at each candidate split in the learning process, a random subset of the features [28]. When the training set for the current tree is drawn, about one-third of the cases are left out of the sample. After each tree is built, all of the data is run down the tree, and proximities are computed for each pair of cases. If two cases occupy the same terminal node, their proximity is increased by one, whilst at the end of the run, these proximities are being divided by the number of the trees [27].

## 3   Proposed Solution

Our solution proposes the identification and classification of different IoT devices and prediction of their device's type, based on their specifications, extending the initial steps of our previous work [30]. In more details, in order to achieve this, a series of different classification algorithms will be performed so as to identify the various devices' types and classify them according to their type, resulting into the best matching solution. As depicted in Fig. 1, our solution consists of three (3) stages:

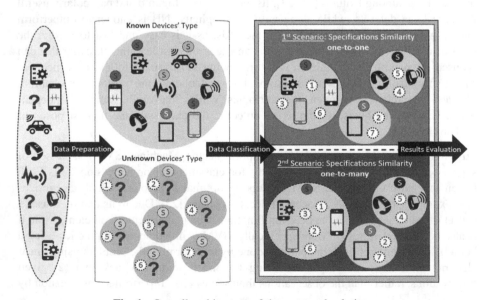

**Fig. 1.** Overall architecture of the proposed solution.

In the first stage, the *Data Preparation* takes place, where after capturing the specifications of the different devices (either with a known or with an unknown device type) and storing them into the corresponding datasets, their preprocessing occurs. In the first place, the recognized devices are being separated into two (2) different groups, the one that contains all the devices with known type of device (i.e. labeled data), and the other one that contains all the devices with unknown type of device (i.e. unlabeled data). In the second place, all this captured data is being transformed and cleaned manually into a single and understandable format, as such kind of data derives from different sources, thus having their own different formats. Thus, we ensure data reliability, removing redundancies, delivering accuracy, as well as assuring the completeness of the data. It must be noted that in this stage, it is required prior knowledge of the devices' specifications (i.e. hardware and software specifications).

In the second stage, the *Data Classification* takes place, which is the most important stage of the proposed solution. During this stage, the preprocessed datasets are being loaded into the data mining tool, where the implementation of the classification algorithms is performed, in order to classify the different IoT devices and predict their device's type, based on their specifications. Thus, by knowing the device type of some known devices (e.g. mobile phones, sensors), as well as their specifications (e.g. brand, dimensions, etc.), we can classify them, considering the known devices' types and the similar specifications that all these devices may have. Consequently, based on the classification's outcomes, it is possible to identify the unknown devices' types, assuming that the devices with the same specifications will be of the same type (e.g. all the sensors will have the same specifications). To this end, as depicted in the overall architecture of the proposed solution (Fig. 1), two (2) potential scenarios arise:

*1st Scenario:* The available devices of both known and unknown type may have exactly the same specifications (one-to-one scenario). For example, as shown in Fig. 2, it is supposed that we have prior knowledge of the type of device A, but we do not have prior knowledge of the type of device C, whilst both devices have the same specifications. By classifying their specifications, it is observed that these devices belong to the same classification group, as they have exactly the same specifications, and as a result, they have the same device type (e.g. both are activity trackers).

*2nd Scenario:* The available devices may have partial specifications in common. (one-to-many scenario). For example, as shown in Fig. 2, it is supposed that we have prior knowledge of the type of device A and B, having different specifications, while there is no prior knowledge of the type of device C, which has some common specifications with device A and device B. By classifying their specifications, it is observed that device C belongs both to the same classification group with device A and to the same classification group with device B, as device C has some partial specifications of the same nature with the two devices. Thus, device C may have the same type of device either with device B (e.g. smartwatch) or with device A (e.g. activity tracker).

In order to achieve the aforementioned classification, in the chosen classifier, a training dataset is being given as an input, containing the specifications of several devices of known type, to efficiently train its model. Then, the classifier receives as an input a test dataset containing an amount of devices' specifications of unknown type,

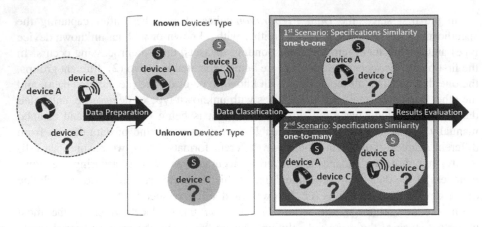

**Fig. 2.** Example of possible scenarios of the proposed solution.

and probabilistically categorizes the devices of the unknown type according to the similar specifications that they may have, based on the devices of the known type.

In the third stage, the *Results Evaluation* occurs, by evaluating the classifier's results, based on some predefined performance metrics, like the precision, recall, etc.

## 4   Use Case

### 4.1   Dataset Description

The training dataset used for this experimental classification consists of 100 manually selected instances of 100 known medical IoT devices. These instances contain information about six (6) different types of specifications (i.e. measurement units, length, width, height, weight, and type) of the devices, outlining the type of the device that each one of them belongs to (i.e. blood pressure monitor, glucometer, thermometer, body weight scale, oximeter, and activity tracker). The file format of the dataset used is Attribute-Relation File Format (ARFF), so as to be directly uploaded to the data mining tool. It should be noted that all the chosen specifications contain the same semantics in terms of descriptions and measurement units (e.g. all the devices' weight is measured into grams (g)), whilst each specification can be measured only through a single measurement unit (e.g. a blood pressure monitor may produce both mmHg and bpm measurement units – in our scenario we will keep only one of them). With regards to the test dataset, it contains the same attributes as the training dataset, with the only difference that the value of the class instance (i.e. type) is undefined.

### 4.2   Working Environment

Current study uses a processing environment with 16 GB RAM, Intel i7-4790 @ 3.60 GHz × 8 CPU Cores, 2 TB Storage, and Windows 10 operating system. This experiment is carried out in WEKA tool [31], which is an open source data mining tool, used for classifying the accuracy of datasets, by applying different algorithmic approaches, including data preprocessing, clustering, classification, regression, visualization, as well as feature selection. However, as mentioned above, in our study we will investigate the KNN, the NB, the SVM, and the RF classification algorithms.

## 4.3 Performance Metrics

The performance metrics are used to evaluate and interpret the classifiers' results. In WEKA, there exist eight (8) different performance metrics:

- *Confusion Matrix*: It contains information about the classifications' results.
- *True Positive Rate (TPR)*: It is the percentage of correct predictions.
- *False Positive Rate (FPR)*: It is the proportion of instances classified in class x, but belong to a different class, along with all the instances that are not in class x.
- *Recall*: It is the proportion of instances that are correctly predicted as positive.
- *Precision*: It estimates the probability that a positive prediction is correct.
- *Training Time (TT)*: It is the time taken by the classifier to build dataset's model.
- *Receiver Operating Characteristics Curve (ROC)*: It is used to design the curve between TPR and FPR, where the area under the curve gives the value of ROC.
- *F-Measure*: It is the average mean of Precision and Recall.

## 4.4 Experimental Results

In the first place, before uploading the datasets (both training and test dataset) into WEKA, their preparation occurs. To this end, the received data is assumed that it was both cleaned and interoperable, thus no further transformation was needed. Hence, two (2) different ARFF files were constructed, one for the training dataset and one for the test dataset. Both datasets contained the same six (6) attributes (i.e. measurement unit, length, width, height, weight, and type) and had the same prediction class (i.e. type), where the training dataset contained instances of 100 different devices of known device type, and the test dataset contained 1 instance of a device of unknown type. An instance of the chosen attributes is shown in Fig. 3.

After the datasets preparation, the latter were uploaded into WEKA. As mentioned in Sect. 3, the classification algorithms that will be used are the: (i) KNN, (ii) NB, (iii) SVM, and (iv) RF. Firstly, different experiments of these algorithms were performed upon the training dataset, having as a common part that all of them used "10-fold cross-validation" as a test mode and "full training set" as classifier model [32]. A snapshot of the first ten (10) devices of the training dataset is being shown in Fig. 4.

```
1   @relation specs_training
2   @attribute measurements {mmHg, mg/dL, kg, SpO2, C, steps}
3   @attribute length real
4   @attribute width real
5   @attribute height real
6   @attribute weight real
7   @attribute type {blood_pressure_monitor, glucometer, thermometer, body_weight_scale, oximeter, activity_tracker}
```

**Fig. 3.** Attributes of the datasets.

```
10   @data
11   mmHg, 141, 121, 72, 350, blood_pressure_monitor
12   mg/dL, 96, 61, 26, 67.2, glucometer
13   C, 164.8, 32.4, 38.7, 85.5, thermometer
14   kg, 340, 400, 25, 2000, body_weight_scale
15   SpO2, 37.8, 32.3, 64, 60, oximeter
16   mg/dL, 96, 34.5, 19, 50, glucometer
17   kg, 325, 325, 23, 2100, body_weight_scale
18   mmHg, 139.7, 68.58, 38.1, 305, blood_pressure_monitor
19   kg, 317.5, 317.5, 21.84, 1800, body_weight_scale
20   mmHg, 150, 140, 100, 600, blood_pressure_monitor
21   SpO2, 28, 33, 62, 272.16, oximeter
```

**Fig. 4.** Snapshot of the training dataset.

After training the four (4) different classifiers, the re-evaluation of their models took place. For that reason, the constructed test dataset was used, which contained the specifications of 1 device of unknown type. In more details, the value of the class instance (i.e. type) of this device was undefined, thus by implementing the trained classifiers into this dataset, the unknown device would be classified into one of the existing devices' types. The data of the test dataset are being shown in Fig. 5.

```
10   @data
11   mmHg, 140, 100, 48, 270, ?
```

**Fig. 5.** Snapshot of the test dataset.

As a result, by applying the aforementioned classification algorithms into the constructed training and test dataset, the prediction of the class of the instance of the device with the unknown type takes place. More specifically, all the algorithms correctly predicted that this device possibly belongs to the group of the blood pressure monitors, as its specifications have many similarities with the specifications of the classified blood pressure monitors. Indeed, comparing the specifications of the unknown instance with those of the blood pressure monitors, it is observed that the specifications are pretty much the same. However, this conclusion is not sufficient for our study, as it is needed to decide which of the four (4) applied classification algorithms have the most efficient, and accurate results. For that reason, to compare these algorithms, the classification's results in combination with the predefined performance metrics of WEKA are analyzed and compared to each other, as shown in Table 1.

**Table 1.** Comparative summary of the classifiers' performance metrics.

| Classifier | TPR | FPR | Precision | Recall | F-Measure | ROC | TT (secs) |
|---|---|---|---|---|---|---|---|
| KNN | 1,000 | 0,000 | 1,000 | 1,000 | 1,000 | 0,999 | 0,005 |
| NB | 0,990 | 0,002 | 0,991 | 0,990 | 0,990 | 0,998 | 0,005 |
| SVM | 1,000 | 0,000 | 1,000 | 1,000 | 1,000 | 0,999 | 0,03 |
| RF | 1,000 | 0,000 | 1,000 | 1,000 | 1,000 | 0,998 | 0,01 |

In our case, according to Table 1, KNN is the best classifier for the devices' specifications datasets used in this study, as it has the highest percentage rates of the performance metrics and took the least time for its results to be made.

# 5    Conclusions

In this paper, we have studied the challenging topic of classifying and identifying heterogeneous IoT devices. We have considered data coming from devices of both known and unknown types, and proposed a solution for facilitating the identification of different IoT devices and prediction of their device's type, based on their specifications. In this solution, a series of different classification algorithms was followed to identify the devices' types and classify them according to their type, resulting into the best matching solution. In each one of these algorithms, the same training dataset was given as an input containing the specifications of several devices of a known type, to efficiently train each classifier. Then, the classifier was tested along with a device of unknown type included into a test dataset, and probabilistically categorized it based on the common specifications that it had with the devices of the known type.

Currently, we are working on the evaluation of the proposed solution, by testing it with more classification algorithms and more heterogeneous IoT devices, considering more valuable and characteristic specifications of the devices. Our future work includes the development of a mechanism that will not require prior knowledge of the devices' specifications, while this mechanism will be able to translate the devices' individual specifications into a common format, thus not being necessary for the specifications to contain the same semantics in terms of specifications descriptions and measurement units. To this end, it is within our future plans to parameterize our mechanism so as to be able to accept and process multiple values with a plethora of parameters in different attributes – instead of a single parameter.

**Acknowledgements.** The CrowdHEALTH project has received funding from the European Union's Horizon 2020 research and innovation programme under grant agreement No 727560. Athanasios Kiourtis would also like to acknowledge the financial support from the "Foundation for Education and European Culture (IPEP)".

# References

1. Oweis, N.E., Aracenay, C., George, W., Oweis, M., Soori, H., Snasel, V.: Internet of Things: overview, sources, applications and challenges. In: Second International Afro-European Conference for Industrial Advancement, AECIA, pp. 57–67 (2016)
2. Global M2 M market. https://machinaresearch.com/news/global-m2m-market-to-grow-to-27-billion-devices-generating-usd16-trillion-revenue-in-2024. Accessed 13 July 2017
3. Cisco: Cisco visual networking index: global mobile data traffic forecast update. White Paper (2015)
4. Pires, F. et al.: A platform for integrating physical devices in the Internet of Things. In: Embedded and Ubiquitous Computing, EUC, pp. 23–241. IEEE (2014)
5. Pham, C., Lim, Y., Tan, Y.: Management architecture for heterogeneous IoT devices in home network. In: Consumer Electronics, pp. 1–5. IEEE (2016)
6. Han, J., Cai, Y., Cercone, N.: Concept-based data classification in relational databases. In: 1991 AAAI Workshop Knowledge Discovery in Databases, pp. 77–94 (1991)
7. Witten, I.H., Frank, E., Hall, M.A., Pal, C.J.: Data Mining: Practical Machine Learning Tools and Techniques. Morgan Kaufmann, San Francisco (2016)

8. Giusti, A., Ritter, G., Vichi, M. (eds.): Classification and Data Mining. Springer Science & Business Media, Heidelberg (2012)
9. Gorade, S.M., Deo, A., Purohit, P.: A Study of Some Data Mining Classification Techniques (2017)
10. Jabbar, M.A., Chandrab, P.: Heart disease prediction system using associative classification and genetic algorithm. In: International Conference on Emerging Trends in Electrical, Electronics and Communication Technologies, ICECIT (2012)
11. Akinola, S.O., Oyabugbe, O.J.: Accuracies and training times of data mining classification algorithms: an empirical comparative study. J. Softw. Eng. Appl. **8**, 470–477 (2015)
12. Majali, J., Niranjan, R., Phatak, V.: Data mining techniques for diagnosis and prognosis of cancer. Int. J. Adv. Res. Comput. Commun. Eng. **4**(3), 613–616 (2015)
13. Salvithal, N.N.: Appraisal management system using data mining. Int. J. Comput. Appl. **135** (12), 45–50 (2016). ISSN: 0975-8887
14. Sharma, T., Sharma, A., Mansotra, V.: Performance analysis of data mining classification techniques on public health care data. Int. J. Innov. Res. Comput. Commun. Eng. **4**(6), 155–169 (2016)
15. Li, Y., Shen, T., Sun, X., Pan, X., Mao, B.: Detection, classification and characterization of android malware using API data dependency. In: Thuraisingham, B., Wang, X., Yegneswaran, V. (eds.) SecureComm 2015. LNICSSITE, vol. 164, pp. 23–40. Springer, Cham (2015). doi:10.1007/978-3-319-28865-9_2
16. Arora, D., Li, K.F., Loffler, A.: Big data analytics for classification of network enabled devices. In: 2016 30th International Conference on Advanced Information Networking and Applications Workshops, WAINA. IEEE (2016)
17. Kim, H., et al.: Collaborative classification for daily activity recognition with a smartwatch. In: 2016 IEEE International Conference on Systems, Man, and Cybernetics, SMC. IEEE (2016)
18. Introduction to k-nearest neighbors: simplified. https://www.analyticsvidhya.com/blog/2014/10/introduction-k-neighbours-algorithm-clustering/. Accessed 13 July 2017
19. A Detailed Introduction to K-Nearest Neighbor (KNN) Algorithm. https://saravananthirumuruganathan.wordpress.com/2010/05/17/a-detailed-introduction-to-k-nearest-neighbor-knn-algorithm/. Accessed 13 July 2017
20. K Nearest Neighbors – Classification. http://www.saedsayad.com/k_nearest_neighbors.htm. Accessed 13 July 2017
21. Kłopotek, M.A.: Very large Bayesian multinets for text classification. Futur. Gener. Comput. Syst. **21**, 1068–1082 (2015)
22. Rish, I.: An empirical study of the naive Bayes classifier. In: IJCAI 2001 Workshop on Empirical Methods in Artificial Intelligence, vol. 3, no. 22. IBM (2001)
23. Naive Bayes. http://scikit-learn.org/stable/modules/naive_bayes.html. Accessed 13 July 2017
24. Naive Bayesian. http://www.saedsayad.com/naive_bayesian.htm. Accessed 13 July 2017
25. Support Vector Machine - Classification (SVM). http://www.saedsayad.com/support_vector_machine.htm. Accessed 13 July 2017
26. Chau, A.L., Li, X., Yu, W.: Support vector machine classification for large datasets using decision tree and Fisher linear discriminant. Futur. Gener. Comput. Syst. **36**, 57–65 (2014)
27. Random Forests. https://www.stat.berkeley.edu/~breiman/RandomForests/cc_home.htm. Accessed 13 July 2017
28. Ho, T.K.: A data complexity analysis of comparative advantages of decision forest constructors. Pattern Anal. Appl. **5**(2), 102–112 (2002)
29. Zakariah, M.: Classification of large datasets using Random Forest Algorithm in various applications: Survey. Money **4**(3), 189–198 (2014)

30. Mavrogiorgou, A., Kiourtis, A., Kyriazis, D.: Plug'n'play IoT devices: an approach for dynamic data acquisition from unknown heterogeneous devices. In: Barolli, L., Terzo, O. (eds.) Complex, Intelligent, and Software Intensive Systems, CISIS 2017. Advances in Intelligent Systems and Computing, vol. 611, pp. 885–895. Springer, Cham (2018)
31. Weka 3: Data Mining Software in Java. http://www.cs.waikato.ac.nz/ml/weka/, Accessed 13 July 2017
32. Kawade, D.R., Oza, K.S.: SMS spam classification using WEKA. Int. J. Electron. Commun. Comput. Technol. 5 (2015)

# Work in Progress on Business Models and Community Cooperation

# Agency Monitoring Patterns
# for Value Networks

Patrício de Alencar Silva[1]([✉]), Faiza Allah Bukhsh[2],
Jefferson da Silva Reis[1], and Angélica Félix de Castro[1]

[1] Programa de Pós-Graduação em Ciência da Computação, Universidade
Federal Rural do Semi-Árido, Rio Grande do Norte, Brazil
{patricio.alencar,angelica}@ufersa.edu.br,
sreis.jefferson@gmail.com
[2] Department of Computer Science, University of Twente,
7500 AE, Enschede, The Netherlands
f.a.bukhsh@utwente.nl

**Abstract.** Value network models represent an arrangement of actors, activities and objects of business value configured to satisfy a market segment's need. As some actors might act unreliably due to unpredicted weaknesses, opportunism that threat value co-creation, monitoring becomes an issue necessary for designing a realistic value model. The research question addressed in this paper is how value network models could be designed with a preventive monitoring organization. We therefore propose a monitoring task ontology and five agency communication patterns for this end. The ontology blends principles of Multiple Agency, Speech Acts, Enterprise Ontology and Value Modeling. We demonstrate the utility of the ontology with a case-based scenario from the Smart Metering markets, and a conformity-test supported by the $e^3$value tool. The case scenario comes from the Directive 2009/72/EC of the European Parliament.

**Keywords:** Agency theory · Ontology · Smart metering · Value networks

## 1 Introduction

Value networks aggregate economically responsible actors exchanging objects of business value to satisfy a market segment's need [1]. Value models describe the economic communication underlying this type of information system, which is driven by a shared interest in positive profit [2]. However, realistic value models should account for unreliable behavior of its constituencies. This scenario can be analyzed from an Agency viewpoint, whereby consumers might act as principals, who need to control back-end suppliers acting as third-parties, and to cooperate with intermediaries acting as agents or regulators [3–5]. Yet from this perspective, monitoring becomes an intrinsic issue of the initial configuration of a value network, and the search for core business objects and proof of performance becomes one.

Adopting a Design Science perspective [6], the question addressed here is *how value models could be designed with a preventive monitoring organization*. From an organizational perspective [7], this question splits into: *Whose perspective, or which*

C. Pham et al. (Eds.): GECON 2017, LNCS 10537, pp. 81–93, 2017.
DOI: 10.1007/978-3-319-68066-8_7

*constituency's point of view, is the dominant? What domain of activity is focused on? What level of analysis is used? What time frame is employed? What type of information are to be used? What referent is employed?* To cope with these issues, we propose a monitoring task ontology and five Agency communication patterns for value network modeling. Ontologies are evaluated with specific frameworks that define requirements for verification, validation and assessment [8]. In this paper, the ontology is partially validated via demonstration of a case scenario in Smart Metering for Renewables [9].

The following sections are organized as follows: in Sect. 2, a brief theoretical background is presented, covering some of the fundamental concepts of Value Network Modeling, Enterprise Ontology and Speech Acts; in Sect. 3, the monitoring task ontology and the Agency monitoring patterns for value network modeling are descri-bed in detail; in Sect. 4, we elaborate on the theoretical validation of the ontology via case-based scenarios of a Smart Energy Metering value network; and we discuss the research results achieved thus far in Sect. 5.

## 2  Theoretical Background

*Value Modeling* is a young discipline of Information Systems and Software Engi-neering. The e³value tool [2] is a framework for analysis of networked businesses, supported by a tool for profitability analysis. The tool is based on an ontology describing economic concepts such as actors, market segments, business activities and objects of economic value. However, the concept of a *value transfer* is ambiguous, as value is perceptual, and therefore cannot be transferred, but only communicated. This conceptual issue is somehow treated in e³value with the assumption that senders and receivers of value propositions share the same perception on valuation. As a decision support system, e³value models are *predictive*, expressing only promises, but not assurances of value creation.

On a process viewpoint, the *Enterprise Ontology* proposed by Dietz [10] deepens the structure of an individual organization by describing its constituent processes with communication patterns adapted from Searle's Speech Acts Theory [11]. The ontology assumes that internal Enterprise actors engage on production acts (i.e. *p-acts*, e.g. production, use and consumption of resources) and coordination acts (i.e. *c-acts*, e.g. request, offering and acceptance). Production acts are communicated through coordi-nation acts among pairs of actors, which comprises the *operational axiom* of the theory. The *transactional axiom* defines transactions as combinations of operations organized as communication pattern involving two actors. The *composition axiom* specifies how transactions are organized as business processes. Finally, the *distinction axiom* describes the role of human actors on interpreting business intra-organizational pro-cesses with ontological, datalogical and infological acts.

Searle's work on *Speech Acts* has inspired many applications of Artificial Intelli-gence, specially the design of multi-agent communication protocols, whereby rational agents express the meaning of their actions and plans. Speech Acts can be used to profile behavior through communication. For instance, Searle and Vanderveken's classification of illocutionary acts can be combined with the Role-Based Access Control (RBAC) model [12] to classify Agents' behavior. We take this direction on classifying Agency monitoring behavior in value networks, as described in the following section.

## 3   Agency Monitoring Patterns for Value Networks

### 3.1   Monitoring Task Ontology

A *business need* is the starting point to configure a value network. The dominant *Agency viewpoint* is the monitor's: a role played by the final consumer, according to the Service-Dominant Logic [13]. A business need has a *monitoring rationale*, which is the cause of monitoring, dependent on the nature of the business, e.g. business opportunity, weakness or threat [14]. The *monitored domain* is the back-end value activity assigned to the suppliers. A *monitoring plan* is represented by a policy, further elaborated as patterns. The *status* of a business need is assessed with a measure of value (an enumerated class of disjoint value partitions including *value surplus*, *value balance* and *value shortage*) (Fig. 1).

A *policy* is defined as a composition of roles performed by *actors*, *activities* and *objects*, resembling the Role-Based Access Control (RBAC) metamodel [12]. Actors relate to activities via coordination acts, and activities relate to objects via production acts. A *core object* is what satisfy a consumer's need (e.g. energy, water, or a hotel service); a *proof-of-performance object* (PoP) is an image of a core object produced by witnessing or experience (e.g. metering reports or consumers' rating); a *certification and accreditation object* (CnA) is the key to unlock access to private proof-of-performance objects (e.g. responsible party accreditations); and a *counter-object* is the price paid in exchange of any kind of object [15]. Activities are defined by production acts changing the nature of business objects (e.g. produce, consume, bundle, distribute, grant or transfer). The definition of a policy is polymorphic, deriving the five Agency monitoring patterns described later. The patterns represent plans whereby the monitor could obtain core objects and corresponding proof. Nonetheless, a selection mechanism is necessary to differentiate similar value propositions, which leads to a discussion on subjective valuation of objects.

The *value* of a business object splits into classes of *objective* and *subjective values*. The former is described as a quadruple of *time*, *location*, *quantity* and *quality*, accounting for how production acts transform the intrinsic nature of value objects. The latter is perceptual, defined by communication acts uttered by actor-roles. Examples of subjective values relevant to businesses include *reliability*, *responsiveness* and *trust* [16–18]. Subjective values are enumerated with five value partitions extracted from the SERVQUAL model: *ideal*, *forecasted*, *equitable*, *deserved* and *minimum tolerable performance* [16]. A subjective value has two roles, the definition of which depends on who communicates the valuation [19]. A monitor declares his *expected value*, whereas a monitoring agent testifies (i.e. by experience or witnessing) or reports (i.e. via second-hand proofs) his *perceived value*. The logic behind the roles of subjective values is that the monitor relies preventively on monitoring agents' evaluation of the perceived value of a product or a service. For instance, trip planners such as Trivago and TripAdvisor, rank hotel services based on consumers' rating [20]. Finally, a value proposition is a composite association of

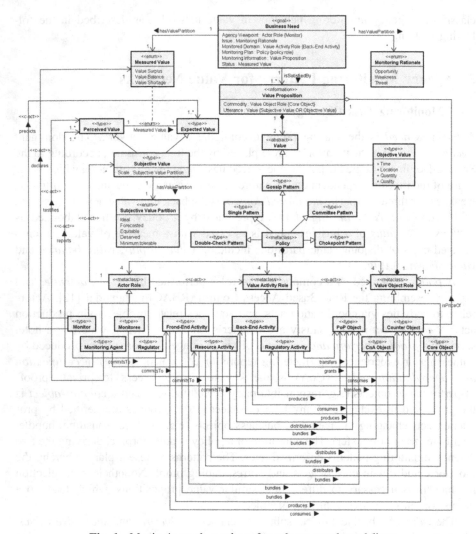

**Fig. 1.** Monitoring task ontology for value network modeling.

a core object, and respective objective and subjective values. The OR-restriction is based on Description Logics, as object values and subjective values are distinct, admitting no common instances. The value proposition of a core object might satisfy a business need. To close the cycle, the monitor declares the *status* of a business need as a *measured value*, which is represented as an association class for subjective assessment of the difference between expected and perceived values.

## 3.2    Agency Monitoring Patterns

### Single Monitoring Pattern

*Context:* whenever the monitor delegates no monitoring responsibility (vide Fig. 2).

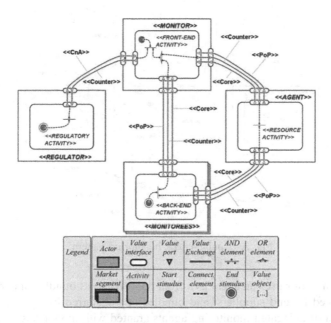

**Fig. 2.** Single monitoring pattern.

*Solution:* The monitor consumes core business objects produced by back-end suppliers, bundled by an agent, or from both. To validate core objects, the monitor bundles a CnA object granted by the regulator to access proofs produced by agents or *monitorees*. The strategy is selfish, as the monitor must monitor both agents and third-parties.

*Economic effectiveness:* the monitoring price ranges from two to three counter-objects produced by the monitor, consumed by the regulator and bundled by agents or *monitorees*.

## Double-Check Monitoring Pattern

*Context:* when the monitor *partially* delegates his monitoring responsibility (vide Fig. 3).

*Solution:* this pattern is based on proof triangulation. The monitor consumes core objects produced by *monitorees* (or bundled by agents), bundles a monitoring certification granted by the regulator, and bundles proofs produced by *monitorees* (or bundled by agents). The agents are also granted with a monitoring certification.

*Economic effectiveness:* is the same as for the single pattern, but the monitor has an option to bundle proofs produced by *monitorees* and bundled by agents.

## Chokepoint Monitoring Pattern

*Context:* whenever the monitor *fully* delegates his monitoring responsibility for not engaging in direct economic exchange with back-end suppliers.

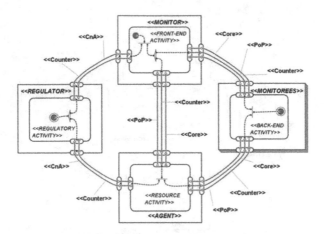

**Fig. 3.** Double-check monitoring pattern.

*Solution:* the monitor uses an agent as a front door to access bundles of core and proof objects produced by end suppliers, and bundled or transferred by agents. The pattern creates a chain of delegated monitoring agents granted with monitoring accreditations. The bottom agent is granted with a CnA object to monitor end suppliers while being monitored by a certified chokepoint agent (vide Fig. 4).

*Economic effectiveness:* the monitoring price is simplified into one counter-object produced by the monitor and bundled or distributed by the entry agent, with the advantages of the double-check pattern for bundling core and proof objects.

**Committee Monitoring Pattern**

*Context:* whenever the monitor partially delegates his monitoring responsibility to at least two agents, assembling a committee to monitor back-end suppliers.

*Solution:* the monitor consumes core objects produced by back-end suppliers, or bundled by the agents. The monitor also bundles proofs produced directly by back-end suppliers, or bundled by agents. All the members of the monitoring committee formed by the monitor and the two agents are certified by a regulator. The monitor operates as a dashboard, whereby all kinds of objects flow throughout the value network (vide Fig. 5).

*Economic effectiveness:* the monitoring price ranges from two to four counter-objects produced by the monitor, consumed by the regulator or the *monitorees*, and bundled, transferred or distributed by the agents.

**Gossip Monitoring Pattern**

*Context:* whenever the monitor fully delegates his monitoring responsibility to an agent, obtaining core and valid proof objects from distinct paths within the network.

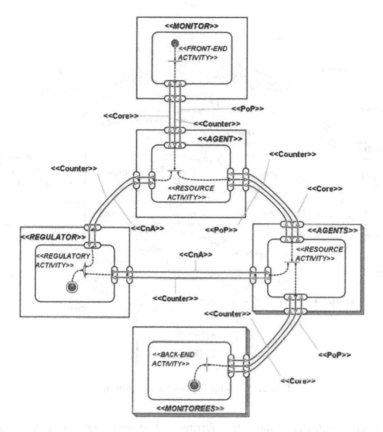

**Fig. 4.** Chokepoint monitoring pattern

*Solution:* this pattern evolves on the chokepoint pattern by considering a direct exchange between the monitor and back-end suppliers, and a triangle of regulated monitoring agents. The monitor consumes a core object produced by the back-end suppliers, and a corresponding proof bundled by a chokepoint agent. A market segment of agents has direct access to core and corresponding proof objects produced by the *monitorees.* The proof object flows within a circuit of certified agents throughout, which explains the name of the pattern (vide Fig. 6).

*Economic effectiveness:* the monitoring price comprehends exactly two counter-objects produced by the monitor, respectively consumed by the final end-suppliers and bundled or distributed by an agent.

## 4    Theoretical Validation: A Case Scenario in Smart Metering

The Directive 2009/72/EC [9] normalizes common rules for liberalized European energy markets. This liberalization transforms the top-down energy supply chain into a peer-to-peer value network of actors operating with accredited and certified roles of

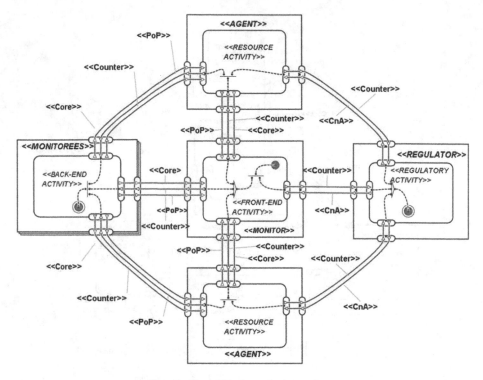

**Fig. 5.** Committee monitoring pattern.

producing, bundling, distributing, transferring and metering energy. Due to environmental drivers, however, these value networks shall most rely on renewables (e.g. wind, solar and biomass energy). The intermittency of renewables makes energy production activities unreliable by weakness, described in the monitoring task ontology as a monitoring rationale of a consumer willing to consume this type of commodity. However, renewables represent also a business opportunity for smart metering operators. Among many services, smart meters provide decision support for energy trade based on market price signals. Still, European reports on smart metering initiatives have uncovered barriers to the adoption of the technology by the population. Householders are specially concerned about security of private consumption information when choosing a metering operator. Privacy is a subjective value, and can only be assessed by experience. The case question is *how a householder could choose among metering operators whose services ever experienced.* Assuming the householders' viewpoint as service-dominant, the case question is translated into *how a smart metering value model could be designed with a preventive monitoring organization.* We use this problem to demonstrate the modeling utility of our monitoring task ontology based on a narrative analysis of three concepts: goal, policy and value proposition.

**Goal Analysis.** The self-monitored value model for the case is illustrated in Fig. 7. A householder operates as a Balance Responsible Party (BRP) in the Energy market, by consuming less or selling unused energy via demand-response control supported by

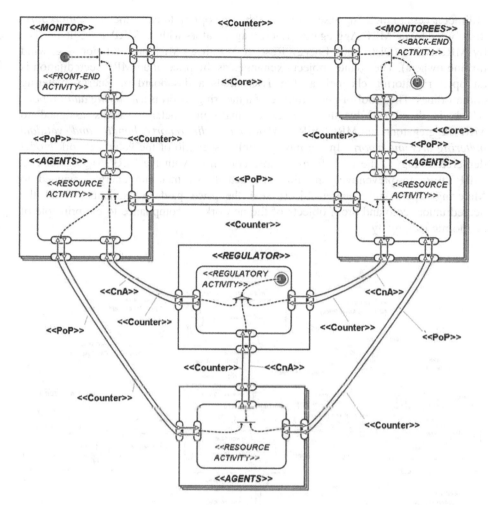

**Fig. 6.** Gossip monitoring pattern.

smart meters. The BRP has the dominant viewpoint as a monitor, and is motivated by the opportunity to create value surplus out of smart metering assets produced as core objects by a market segment of Metering Operators. The BRP needs metering assets with best value propositions not only for objective value, i.e. time, location, quantity and quality of measurement, but also for subjective value of service, such as privacy. To demonstrate how the BRP could achieve this goal, his monitoring plan is organized as a committee monitoring pattern described as follows.

**Policy Analysis.** The BRP's business need can be filled through alternative pathways. To have direct access to *metering assets*, the BRP needs a Metering Responsible Party (MRP) *accreditation* granted by the Transmission System Operator (TSO), who is committed to manage metering reports. The proof-of-performance of a metering asset is a *metering account report*, which describes objective measurement values. To have indirect access to metering assets, the BRP has the option to consume *metering reports* distributed by an MRP-Aggregator (Energy aggregators with an MRP accreditation) or by MRP-DERs (Distributed Energy Resources with an MRP accreditation, e.g. wind turbine owners). The counter-object exchanged as the price of an MRP accreditation is an open monitoring channel, as the TSO needs a dashboard of Energy metering commodities. The proof-of-performance of a metering report is a *metering audit report*, which is distributed by the activity of managing metering assets assigned to MRP-Aggregators or MRP-DERs. *Metering audit reports bundle and validate metering account reports*. In the most complete scenario of the value network model depicted in Fig. 7, the BRP form a triple *committee* with the MRP-Aggregator and MRP-DERs to preventively monitor the activity of metering energy assigned to Metering Operators. Counter-objects seal the price paid in exchange of all the accreditation, core and proof objects of the network, in compliance to the principle of economic reciprocity.

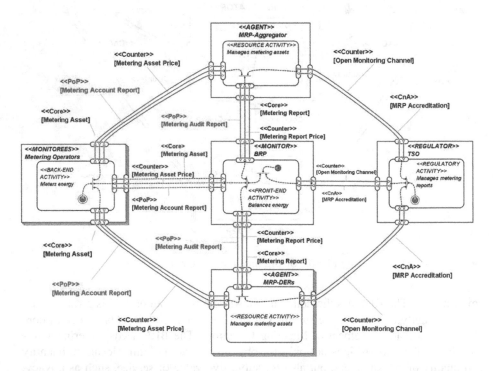

**Fig. 7.** Smart metering value network model organized by the *committee monitoring pattern.*

**Value Proposition Analysis.** a policy pattern answers the monitor's questions of *what, who* and *how* to monitor within a value network, but not *why*, which points to the monitor's *goal status* of *value surplus*. All the Agency monitoring patterns described in Sect. 3 are *effective* in describing plans to satisfy a monitor's need with core business objects. However, Business and Economics research have demonstrated that value surplus depends not only on objective values, but also on subjective ones [17–20]. In a value network, objective values are necessary, but insufficient for the monitor to *declare* value surplus. In our case scenario, it is not the cheapest metering asset that might satisfy a householder's need, but instead, the prospective value surplus generated by this technology. The question now shifts to how a householder operating as a BRP could choose a Metering Operator, based on subjective values to be returned by the metering asset, which leads to an *economic efficiency* issue internal to the monitoring pattern organization.

The *committee pattern* favors delegated monitoring. The core object subject to value proposition analysis is the *metering asset* owned by Metering Operators, and its corresponding proof is the *metering account report* produced by Metering Operators, bundled by MRP-Aggregators or MRP-DERs, and distributed back to BRPs as *metering audit reports*. Both DERs and Aggregators use the metering asset technology, thereby acquiring *experience* to assess the level of *privacy* offered by the smart metering assets. The agents have the option to transfer this subjective value assessment to BRPs upon accreditation. The rest of the value proposition analysis is summarized in Table 1.

**Table 1.** Value proposition analysis based on the committee monitoring pattern.

|  | MRP-aggregator (agent) | MRP-DERs (agent) | BRP (monitor) |
|---|---|---|---|
| Core Object | Metering asset | Metering asset | Metering asset |
| Proof Object | Metering audit report | Metering audit report | Metering account report |
| Objective value | (15 min, national, GWh, 0.75) | (15 min, national, MWh, 0.85) | (15 min, local, kWh, 0,90) |
| Subjective value | Forecasted privacy | Equitable privacy | Equitable privacy |
| Measured value | *Value surplus* | *Value balance* | **Value surplus** |

As an image of the core object, the proof object can be used to prospect the value of monitoring. In our example, the *objective value* of a metering report can be assessed by its monitorability, i.e. *time*, *location*, *quantity* and *quality* of energy measurement. For instance, the *metering audit reports* distributed by Aggregators are published every 15 min, nationwide, in the order of GWh, with a predictability factor for renewables around 75%. Equivalent measurement attributes apply to assets managed by the other members of the committee. However, choosing a meter based on subjective values is different: the BRP has the option to delegate this task to the agents. According to the monitoring ontology, the BRP could prospect the *expected value* of privacy offered by the meter asset as *equitable*, whereas DERs could report or testify the same value *perceived* as *equitable*, and the Aggregators, as *forecasted*. The difference between monitors' expected value and agents' perceived value is defined in the ontology as *measured value*: an enumerated class of partitions for value surplus, shortage or balance.

Hence, comparing the *equitable privacy* expected by BRPs with the *forecasted* and *equitable* perceptions of value reported by the agents leads to a value surplus and a value balance, respectively. If the BRP considers the Agents' evaluation as valid, then a *value surplus* is set as the *status* of the *business need*, closing the ontology interpretation.

## 5   Conclusions and Future Research

The main contributions of this work are threefold: (1) the Agency monitoring patterns simplify the design of realistic value network models; (2) the semi-formal logic of delegated Agency monitoring emphasizes the business relevance of subjective values and supports the economic efficiency analysis of the monitoring patterns, which is an aspect missed by fellow researchers [2]; and (3) the case demonstration opens a discussion about the modeling utility of the ontology on describing socially relevant case scenarios, such as the search for privacy-preserving smart metering assets. The actors and activities described in the value network model designed for the case are regulated, and the communication channels for the monitoring objects can be supported by e-Commerce and e-Government solutions for social feedback on private and public infrastructure services. At least three immediate research directions will extend this work. First, the formalization of the ontology in Web Ontology Language (OWL) will support automatic model checking of the Agency monitoring patterns within a value network model, besides enabling querying and reasoning of specific model properties. Second, the library of patterns might be extended with unexplored classes of patterns, e.g. anti-patterns, green value patterns or adaptation patterns. Third, the ontology shall be evaluated regarding its users' acceptance, ease of use and perceived modeling utility.

## References

1. Normann, R., Ramírez, R.: From value chain to value constellation: designing interactive strategy. Harvard Bus. Rev. **71**(4), 65–77 (1993)
2. Gordijn, J., Akkermans, J.M.: Value-based requirements engineering: exploring innovative e-commerce ideas. Requirements Eng. **8**(2), 114–134 (2003)
3. Eisenhardt, K.M.: Agency theory: an assessment and review. Acad. Manag. Rev. **14**(1), 57–74 (1969)
4. Jacobides, M.G., Croson, D.C.: Information policy: shaping the value of agency rela-tionships. Acad. Manag. Rev. **26**(2), 202–223 (2001)
5. Freeman, J., Rossi, J.: Agency coordination in shared regulatory space. Harvard Law Rev. **125**(5), 1134–1209 (2012)
6. Wieringa, R.J.: Design Science Methodology for Information Systems and Software Engineering. Springer, Heidelberg (2014)
7. Cameron, K.: Critical Questions in Assessing Organizational Effectiveness. Org. Dyn. **9**(2), 66–80 (1980)
8. Gómez-Pérez, A.: Ontology evaluation. In: Staab, S., et al. (eds.) Handbook on Ontologies, pp. 251–273. Springer, Heidelberg (2004)

9. European Parliament, Council of the European Union: Directive 2009/72/EC of the European Parliament and of the Council of 13 July 2009 concerning common rules for the internal market in electricity and repealing Directive 2003/54/EC (Text with EEA relevance). Official Journal of the European Union, L 211, 14 August 2009

10. Dietz, J.L.G.: Enterprise Ontology: Theory and Methodology. Springer, Heidelberg (2006)

11. Searle, J.R., Vanderveken, D.: Foundations of Illocutionary Logic. Cambridge University Press (1985)

12. Ferraiolo, D.F., Sandhu, R., Gavrila, S., Kuhn, D.R., Chandramouli, R.: Proposed NIST standard for role-based access control. ACM Trans. Inf. Syst. Secur. 4(3), 224–274 (2001)

13. Vargo, S.L., Akaka, M.A.: A service-dominant logic as a foundation for service science: clarifications. Serv. Sci. 1(1), 32–41 (2009)

14. Loucopoulos, P., Kavakli, V.: Enterprise knowledge management and conceptual modelling. In: Goos, G., Hartmanis, J., van Leeuwen, J., Chen, Peter P., Akoka, J., Kangassalu, H., Thalheim, B. (eds.) Conceptual Modeling. LNCS, vol. 1565, pp. 123–143. Springer, Heidelberg (1999). doi:10.1007/3-540-48854-5_11

15. Mankiw, N.G.: Principles of Economics, 7th edn. Cengage Learning, Stamford (2014)

16. Parasuraman, A., Berry, L.L., Zeithaml, V.A.: Refinement and reassessment of the SERVQUAL scale. J. Retail. 67(4), 420–450 (1991)

17. Lapierre, J.: Customer-perceived value in industrial contexts. J. Bus. Ind. Mark. 15(2–3), 122–145 (2000)

18. Biggemann, S., Buttle, F.: Intrinsic value of business-to-business relationships: an empirical taxonomy. J. Bus. Res. 65(8), 1132–1138 (2012)

19. Steedman, I.: Positive profits with negative surplus value. Econ. J. 85(337), 114–123 (1975)

20. Kesting, P., Günzel-Jensen, F.: SMEs and new ventures need business model sophistication. Bus. Horiz. 58(3), 285–293 (2015)

# Active Contributors in Online Social Networks – An Empirical Study on German Gen Y's Facebook Usage

Richard Lackes, Markus Siepermann[✉][iD], and Arbnesh Stadelhoff

Technische Universität Dortmund, 44221 Dortmund, Germany
{richard.lackes,markus.siepermann,
arbnesh.stadelhoff}@tu-dortmund.de

**Abstract.** Every day, millions of users especially from the generation Y visit Facebook. They do not only read the contributions and shared data of friends and other community members in a passive way but many of them generate own content in an active way. Active users upload private photos and reports as well as they post status updates and create comments to other contributions. Although Facebook's handling of private data has often been criticised, the intensity of user generated content seems to be uninfluenced. Therefore the question arises what are the determining factors of active use in Online Social Networks and how important is the influence of trust and risks in social network providers. Do own negative experiences influence the kind of usage of OSN? To answer these questions we conducted an empirical study on Generation Y's use of Facebook in Germany and analysed the impact of motivation, trust, risks and negative consequences on the usage behaviour. Results show that Generation Y largely mistrusts Facebook and its security functions. Therefore, the active use is low in comparison to the passive use. But, as we could show that passive use is a strong driver of active use, the improvement of passive usage leads to active usage over time and explains Facebook's success.

**Keywords:** Online Social Networks · Facebook · Active usage · Usage behaviour

## 1 Introduction

In 2014, 890 million people worldwide logged in and visited just Facebook each day [11], not counting the billions of people visiting other social networks and social media sites. As those sites are free of charge, business models apply that are based on advertising, data mining, and information selling [8]. Therefore, OSN are reliant on recurrent users who regularly perform actions in the OSN so that advertisements can be sold and usage data can be collected. This only happens if users are attracted by new content and interaction with other users [8, 19]. In particular, so-called Generation Y (Gen Y), people born between 1981 and 1999, made this success of online social networks possible. This group of digital natives is said to be more active and create therefore more personal information due to online interaction [38]. Obviously, Gen Y is a key for analyses of social media usage as they are early adopters that influence the

© Springer International Publishing AG 2017
C. Pham et al. (Eds.): GECON 2017, LNCS 10537, pp. 94–105, 2017.
DOI: 10.1007/978-3-319-68066-8_8

success of such sites and are interesting as marketing target group. For OSN providers it is therefore crucial to know what enhances and inhibits their use of OSN.

In particular, this question holds in front of the numerous data leaks of the past years (i.e. Sony 2011, ebay 2014, yahoo 2016). One can ask to what extent these data leaks affect the users' future behaviour because these events severely harm the integrity of and therefore the users' trust in the firms [6, 23]. If users fear that their personal data are not secure, they may reduce frequency and duration of their visits up to a complete migration to other sites [8]. Because the fund model of OSN is dependent on continuous activities their providers must be interested in building and maintaining a trustful relation to their users [6]. While much research was done investigating who participates in social media sites and why, literature analyzing the role of privacy and data risk aspects as well as the characteristics of OSN for the usage behaviour is scarce. In this paper, we therefore aim to answer the following research questions:

1. *What influences users to participate actively in OSN?*
2. *Which role does the data risk play for the usage of OSN?*

We focus on Facebook as the most important representative of OSN in our analysis because it is very popular in Gen Y and has become a steady part of many people's daily life. We conducted a survey among Gen Y users of Facebook that analysed their different kinds of usage and the influence of motivational aspects and perceived risk and trust on it. Previous research was mainly restricted on personal traits of OSN users. In contrast, this paper focuses on the characteristics of the OSN Facebook itself. We analyse how these characteristics are perceived by users and how this perception influences their usage behaviour. We aim to shed light on the role of data risk aspects and the reputation of the network provider influence and how they impact the behaviour of OSN users. In particular, we have a look at the experience of users. In our study we investigate how the perceived data risk impacts the usage behaviour of Gen Y members and what factors drive them to actively participate in OSN.

The remainder of this paper is organised as follows: In the next section, we give an overview of the related literature in the field of OSN usage identifying four different streams of research in this field. Then, in Sect. 3, we develop the research that is analysed in Sect. 4 with the help of a survey conducted in 2015. The results are discussed in Sect. 5 where we derive managerial implications, point to some limitations and give an outlook on future work.

## 2  Literature Review

Online Social Networks are web-based services that offer users the possibility of building and managing a personal profile, administering a list of other users with whom they are in relationship, and to communicate with other users. Then, the set of users and their connections build a (social) network. In addition, OSN usually offer the possibility to build groups, share multimedia resources and comment postings or shared resources of others. During the past years, several authors investigated the reasons why and which people join OSN and what makes them actively participate in those networks. Within this field, four different streams can be distinguished.

## 2.1  Lurking

The first stream of research deals with reasons why people lurk on social media sites [28, 29, 31]. Lurking means that mem-bers of the network or the community do not actively participate and do not post, share photos etc. They maintained the following reasons for lurking: Beneath some people like just only reading and browsing there are a lot of users that still learn about the group and are too shy to actively participate. That implies that lurking/non-lurking is not a fixed intention but may alter during time. This is underlined by results of [31] who found a significant positive relationship between the level of perceived intimacy and posting.

## 2.2  Personality Traits

The second stream of research analyses which personality traits of people influence the usage of OSN [1, 27, 34, 36]. All papers have in common that they use the Five-Factor-Model (FFM) with its five personality traits [24]. Due to different research methods like self-reporting questionnaires [34] versus observed behavior [1] some contradictory results occur (e.g. neurotics posting photos versus non-posting). Moore and McElroy [27] are the only ones that do not only examine the impact of personality traits on usage but also on regrets. Seidman [36] extends this research stream by examining how personality traits influence the motivation (belongingness and self-presentation) to use OSN and is therefore also related to the third research stream.

## 2.3  Personal Needs

The third research stream investigates the motivation of people for using OSN due to their personal needs (emotional, cognitive, social or habitual) [2, 30, 39]. Quan-Haase and Young [30] analyzed the motivations to use Facebook and Twitter and found only little differences. Main gratifications of both media are entertainment, relaxation, and escape. While Cheung et al. [2] identified social presence, meaning the presence of peers in the OSN, as the main factor for usage, Wang et al. [39] found solitude and interpersonal support the main drivers for using OSN.

## 2.4  Characteristics of OSN

This paper is most related to the fourth stream of research that focuses on the characteristics of the OSN itself as factors for the usage and trust [17, 18, 20, 32]. Kwon and Wen [18] combine personality traits (altruism), motivational factors (social identity and encouragement) with properties of the OSN (telepresence) and classic constructs of the Technology Acceptance Model (TAM) [7]. Their results confirm the TAM and show that the perceived encouragement that users experience in OSN influences the usefulness as well as the usage while altruism and telepresence do not affect the usefulness. Lin and Lu [20] focus their research on network externalities and benefits that users of OSN perceive. Their results indicate that the sheer number of OSN members is less relevant than the number of peers within the network confirming the results of Cheung et al. [2]. Also Rauniar et al. [32] examine and confirm the influence of peers in the network. Krasnova et al. [17] focus on motivational factors influencing the disclosure of information in OSN. They found that the convenience of cultivating relationships and enjoyment mainly push users to disclose information but that the perceived risk concerning privacy violations can lower this effect. If people trust the OSN and its provider, the perception of risks is reduced.

### 2.5 Scope of Paper

In contrast to the above mentioned papers, we will mainly concentrate on the usage behaviour of Gen Y. On the basis of users' perception of risks and implicitly suspected negative consequences users judge OSN as dangerous if safety functions are not perceived as useful. In addition, we will have a look at the role of lurking. As previous results show [29, 31], lurkers can be switched to active members indicating that the lurking may have a positive relation to active usage.

## 3  Research Model

### 3.1  Usage and Motivation

The use of OSN can be either active or passive. *Passive use* is often termed lurking meaning that persons officially are members of the site but do not contribute to the community by any own content, i.e. sharing photos or posting messages [28]. While reading of posts, watching photos or videos, or just browsing friend lists is a typical lurking behaviour, OSN offer actions that lie between lurking and *Active use*: liking and sharing of posts, photos, brands etc. We understand these functions also as *Passive use* because it doesn't create new content but replicate already existing content. In contrast, *Active use* of OSN means actively creating new content [38], i.e. uploading of own photos and videos, posting of current activities, writing own posts or commenting other posts as well as sending messages to others and chatting. Only a minority of passive users are online with the intention to lurk [29]. As a consequence, passive users can turn to active users over time [9]. Therefore, we hypothesise:

$H_1$:   *Passive use of OSN positively influences the Active use of OSN*

One important reason to join OSN is peer pressure [30]. Most people use OSN because their peers are also in the OSN [32] so that they can communicate with [2] and get information about them [30]. OSN are used to connect with peers and to maintain existing offline relationships [10]. Other reasons are self-presen-tation [41], to find new friends [5], or because it is fashionable [30]. We subsume all these reasons to participate in OSN under the term *Motivational aspects*. Therefore we hypothesise:

$H_2$:   *The Motivational aspects of users positively influence the Passive use of OSN.*
$H_3$:   *The Motivational aspects of users positively influence the Active use of OSN*

## 3.2   Risk and Trust

Users of OSN are exposed to a variety of threats like identity theft, cyber-bullying, cross-profiling etc. Therefore, people attach importance to privacy and safety in OSN [22]. That means when users participate in OSN, create own content, and disclose information about themselves, they expect others not to abuse these information. Thus, if users perceive a high level of intimacy in the OSN, they are more willing to create own content, post photos etc. [8, 31]. In that way the *Perceived risk* can destroy this intimacy and restrict the OSN usage. In sum, we hypothesise:

$H_4$:    The Perceived risk in OSN negatively influences the Passive use of OSN.
$H_5$:    The Perceived risk in OSN negatively influences the Active use of OSN

If the perceived risks come true and the data privacy is violated, OSN users usually face *Negative consequences* that we define as negative outcomes in the private or job-related field whose cause lie in the usage of OSN. We hypothesise:

$H_6$:    The Perceived risk in OSN positively influences the perceived Negative consequences in OSN

The fear of negative consequences may change the behaviour and users create less content [6, 27]. That means:

$H_7$:    The Negative consequences in OSN negatively influence the Active use of OSN

Trust is a multidimensional concept [23, 25] Menon et al. [26] see trust as the belief of the trusting person in attributes of the trustee while Fung and Lee [13] understand trust as the truster's willingness to believe the trustee. In other words, trust is "the willingness of a party to be vulnerable to the action of another party [...] irrespective of the ability to monitor or control the other party" [23, p. 712]. Thus, in the case of OSN, trust exhibits two facets: The involved parties and the control mechanisms [37]. In general, three parties are involved: The truster, the OSN provider, and other OSN users [17, 37]. The second facet is the control of personal information and self-created information [17]. We define *Perceived control* as the belief of users to what extent they are able to protect their private information. As a result, the better the safety functions are perceived by OSN users, the less they will perceive the risk of OSN and the more they will trust its provider [8]. In sum, *Trust in the OSN and its providers* as well as the *Perceived control* over the personal data decreases the *perceived risk* in OSN [16]. Therefore, we hypothesise:

$H_8$:    Perceived control negatively influences the Perceived risk in OSN.
$H_9$:    Perceived control positively influences the Trust in networks and providers.
$H_{10}$:    Trust in networks/providers negatively influences the Perceived risk in OSN

The resulting research model is depicted in Fig. 1.

# 4  Analysis

## 4.1  Data Collection

We conducted a survey among members of Gen Y in Germany for testing the research model described in the previous section. The questionnaire, consisting of 27 questions for the model measured in a 5-point-Likert-Scale and 20 demographics, was deployed via the Internet and answered by 564 persons belonging to our target group Gen Y. All observations have less than 15% missing values [15], so that the sample size is beyond the recommended sample size of Chin [4] for receiving stable results of the model estimation. Females (males) account for 66% (34%) of the participants. The participants' age was between 18 and 33 years and about 82% of them use Facebook for more than 3 years. More than 95% enters Facebook at least one time a day.

To accomplish the target of proving the theoretical evaluated relationships between unobserved constructs on the basis of the questionnaire, we used a structural equation model (SEM). Smart PLS [33] is used for a variance-based analysis of the collected empirical data and the evaluated theoretical SEM [15]. In addition to the PLS algorithm, a bootstrapping is used for the determination of the significance of weights, loadings and path coefficients with 5000 samples and 564 cases [14, 15, 35]. SPSS was used for the regression analysis for tests on multicollinearity. For missing values case wise replacement was applied.

## 4.2  Measurement Model

In our model, the two constructs *Perceived control* and *Trust in networks and provider* are reflective constructs. In order to assess the reliability and the validity of a reflective construct, the indicator reliability, the convergence criteria, and the discriminant validity are to be considered [14, 15]. The indicator reliability is composed of the t-statistic and the loading [3]. In our model, all t-statistics exceed the value of 2.57 implying a significance level of 1%. All reflective indicators are significant. As the convergence criterion - consisting of the average variance extracted (AVE), the composite reliability and the Cronbach's alpha [40] - and the discriminant validity - consisting of the Fornell-Larcker criterion [12] and the cross loadings - were in the allowed range, a prediction of the latent variable is obtained through its indicators [4].

The residual five constructs are formative. To analyse the significance of the indicators, the weights have to be greater than 0.1 [4] or smaller than −0.1 [35]. The t-statistics have to comply with the same constraints as reflective constructs. In the constructs *Active use*, *Passive use* and *Perceived risk* the t-statistic of all indicators exceed the limit of 2.57 with a significant level of 1% and have a positive influence on the construct. Concerning the construct *Motivational aspects*, two indicators are significant with a significance level of 1% and one accomplishes a significant level of 10%. Regarding the construct *Negative experiences*, the t-statistics of two indicators are beyond the limit of 2.57, at which one weight is below −0.1 and the other beyond 0.1. One indicator satisfies the limit of 1.96 as well as the weight limit of 0.1. Considering the discriminant validity for the formative constructs, the highest latent variable correlation is between *Active use* and *Passive use* (0.7523) and is below the allowed maximum of 0.9. The investigation regarding multicollinearity [40] is done with SPSS.

We calculated the variance inflation factor (VIF) for all indicators [35]. All values are in the allowed range [14, 15] and fulfil the condition index [15] so that all indicators are sufficiently different and independent.

## 4.3   Structural Model

For calculating the significance level of the relationship between the constructs, a regression analysis is performed. Thereby, the explanatory power of the model is determined by the coefficient of determination $R^2$ of the latent variables. 62.2% of the variance of the target construct *Active use* is explained due to the dependent constructs. The $R^2$ value is moderate for *Active use. Passive use* ($R^2 = 0.220$), *Negative consequences* ($R^2 = 0.253$) and *Perceived risk* ($R^2 = 0.227$) achieve a weak level. The $R^2$ value of the construct *Trust in networks and providers* exceeds as well as *Active use* the threshold of 0.33 and is therefore moderate [4]. The variance inflation factor, VIF, regarding the constructs indicates that there is no multicollinearity [15] so that the regression analysis is performable [40].

The accuracy of our hypotheses is determined by the path coefficients and by the t-statistics. The path coefficients have to exceed the limit of 0.1 [21] ([3] claims a limit of 0.2). To confirm a negative relation between the constructs, the path coefficient has to be less than −0.1 [35, 40]. Figure 1 shows the path coefficients and the significance levels of the hypotheses and the $R^2$ of all constructs. Seven ($H_1$, $H_2$, $H_3$, $H_4$, $H_6$, $H_8$, $H_9$ and $H_{10}$) of ten hypotheses are confirmed with a significance level of 1% and $H_8$ could be confirmed with a significance level of 5%. Hypotheses $H_5$ and $H_7$ could be rejected because the path coefficients do not fulfil the given requirement.

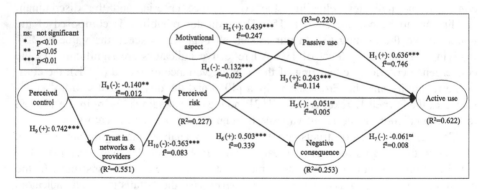

**Fig. 1.**  Research model and results of PLS Algorithm.

## 5   Results and Discussion

The results of the survey are very satisfactory. Eight of ten hypotheses could be confirmed with high confidence while only two hypotheses ($H_5$ and $H_7$) could not. Our key target *Active use* can be explained at a medium level (in the upper range), *Trust in networks and providers* also at a medium level and *Passive use* as well as *Negative consequences* and *Perceived risk* still at a weak level.

## 5.1 Active Usage of Online Social Networks and the Influence of Risks

The aim of this paper was to investigate the active usage of Gen Y members in OSN and to identify the influencing factors on it. For a provider the user activities are essential for his economic success. Members using the OSN actively generate new content and initiate communication processes ("the community is living"). By that, user specific data can be collected, analysed and used for marketing purposes.

If we have a look at our key construct *Active use*, the construct *Passive use* has the highest effect with an effect size of $f^2 = 0.746$ ($H_1$). That means that an intensive passive usage leads mostly to an active usage, possibly after a time users had entered an OSN. 93% of the interviewees answered that they read status notifications multiple times each day. But only 2.3% publish own posts, 1.06% upload photos, 7.8% comment on posts often or very often. This gap together with the confirmed strong relationship between passive and active use implies that if users are not already active users they will very likely become active soon. This is underlined by the *Motivational aspects* to use OSN. The wish to let others participate in one's life has the strongest effect followed by communication with friends and the wish to find new friends. The *Motivational aspects* as a whole show a much stronger effect on *Passive use* ($H_2$, $f^2 = 0.247$) than on *Active use* ($H_3$, $f^2 = 0.114$). This holds even for the indirect path ($H_2 \rightarrow H_1$ versus $H_3$) through *Passive use* as a mediator and underlines that *Passive use* is a much more important prerequisite for *Active use* than any other factor.

Interestingly, the negative aspects do not seem to influence the active usage behaviour of OSN members. Neither the path coefficients nor the effect sizes of the hypotheses $H_5$ and $H_7$, i.e. the relationship between *Negative consequences* and *Active use* as well as between *Perceived risk* and Active *use*, exceed any threshold. There is only an indirect relationship between *Perceived risk* and *Active use* via *Passive use*. We investigated this further and also tested the relationships between the constructs that influence the *Perceived risk*, namely *Perceived control* and *Trust in networks & providers*, on the one side and *Active use* on the other side. In addition, also the relationship between *Negative consequences* and *Passive use* was tested. Again, no significant relationship could be found. Thus, it seems that negative aspects like identity theft or job consequences do not play a role for the decision on actively using OSN. This result is quite surprising and contradicts the findings of [17] who could confirm a relation between perceived risks and the disclosure of private information. Several reasons for this result are conceivable. First of all, time has passed with many data leak scandals over the past years. As a result, users may be blunted by this and commonly accepted the danger of privacy violation. Furthermore, it could be caused by our investigated user group, namely Gen Y people who have a more relaxed attitude towards such risks. Secondly, [17] used reflective indicators for the perceived risk that measure the construct more generally while we used formative constructs so that we can distinguish the influence of the different factors. Doing so, we found that all negative aspects (risks and consequences) are perceived as high or very high by more than 40% of all interviewees for the consequences and more than 57% for the risks. In particular, this is interesting because at the same time users' trust towards OSNs and their providers is very low and they do not feel in control of their data. Only 4–16% report high or very high trust and between 8% and 25% assesses the control mechanisms as suitable. As a result, the relation between *Perceived control* and *Perceived risk* ($H_8$) is confirmed without a great effect ($f^2 = 0.012$). Instead, the indirect effect of *Perceived control* ($H_9 \rightarrow H_{10}$ versus $H_8$) through *Trust in networks & providers* as a mediator on *Perceived risk* is greater.

## 5.2    Managerial Implications for the OSN Provider

Several implications can be derived from these results. OSN are usually ad sponsored and therefore benefit from a large number of users who visit the network as often as possible. While 82% of the interviewees visit Facebook multiple times each day, only 2.3% publish own posts, 7.8% comment posts, and 1.06% share photos but more than 93% read posts of other users. Therefore, it is crucial for the providers of OSN to attract active users who regularly provide new content that then can be consumed. The most influential factor to turn a user into an active user who provides content is the passive use itself. If the OSN could manage to attract a user, s/he will most probably turn into an active user by time. This holds in particular, as the most influencing indicator of motivational aspects to use Facebook is – according to our survey – to "let others participate in one's life". Once this wish is strong enough, a user will turn into an active user. As classic network externalities seem to hold for OSN, providers just need to hype these network effects. Therefore, OSN providers should concentrate on two issues: First to get as many passive users as possible by providing low entrance barriers and interesting services that can be consumed. Secondly to make it as easy as possible for users to generate content, i.e. publishing posts and pictures, commenting other posts etc. so that others can react to these actions.

However, this is not a sure-fire success. If prerequisites are missing, people may resign to use OSN. For example, if users do not feel good when using an OSN they may resign to visit it. Serious concerns about the security and privacy or severely bad experiences might be reasons for this. As our results indicate, users mistrust OSNs and their providers. They fear several risks and consequences and do not assess the provided control mechanisms as sufficient. This is an alarming situation for providers. Although all this does not seem to have any direct effect on the active usage behaviour, OSN providers should not neglect this problem. While there are no direct effects of risks and consequences on the active use, there is a slight but significant effect of perceived risks on the passive use that in turn has a strong effect on active use. That means that if risks are perceived as too high, first the passive use may decline and then with it also the active use. Therefore, the quite comfortable situation may change quickly. For example the permanent user complaints about how Facebook has treated private data and privacy during the past years and the broad discussions about that increased the danger to lose passive users and in the consequence active users. A dangerous downward spiral could arise.

As a consequence, OSN should work on improving their privacy functions to protect the users' data. This would reduce the perceived risk and enhance the reputation of providers. Users want to be private in OSN; they do not want their data to be forwarded to third parties [22]. Still, when registering at Facebook for example, many privacy functions are disabled and have to be actively enabled by new users. Although OSN are interested in much user generated content, it would be a better signal to activate privacy functions in advance. Then, users would probably perceive OSN and its providers as more caring and more reliable than they currently do.

### 5.3  Limitations and Future Research

As always, some limitations accrue. First of all, our survey was limited to German Gen Y users and can therefore not be transferred to other countries without restriction. Secondly, as we focused on characteristics of OSNs and their providers and motivational aspects, positive and negative experiences and gratifications attained through OSN were not considered. These may better explain the perceived risk as well as the usage behaviour. The explanatory power of these constructs can still be improved. Lastly, interviewees were not asked about their knowledge on safety functions and possible misuse of their data resulting from the use of social networks. This knowledge may moderate the effects of trust and perceived risks on the model.

This points us directly to possible following research. Future research should focus on the relation between positive and negative experiences, trust, perceived risk and usage behaviour. Most probably, there is a time gap between experiences and self-disclosure. This time gap should be considered when examining if users make negative experiences due to self-disclosure or vice versa. Another toehold is the relation between passive and active use. In the current form, we measure passive and active use of the same interviewee. But it seems likely that users become active because of the great number of their peers being in the OSN. The motivational aspect of using OSN as a platform to promote oneself in front of as many peers as possible would be interesting for OSN providers: Then, lurking users would contribute as much as active users to the success of OSN. Due to cultural differences between Germany and other countries, a cross-cultural study should be undertaken. Another interesting research question would be to investigate the factors that influence the active usage negatively and prevent users from visiting OSN like increasing professional content, increasing number of advertising, the usage of personalized advertising etc.

## References

1. Amichai-Hamburger, Y., Vinitzky, G.: Social networks use and personality. Comput. Hum. Behav. **26**, 1289–1295 (2010). doi:10.1016/j.chb.2010.03.018
2. Cheung, C., Chiu, P.Y., Lee, M.K.O.: Online social networks: Why do students use facebook? Comput. Hum. Behav. **27**, 1337–1343 (2011). doi:10.1016/j.chb.2010.07.028
3. Chin, W.W.: Issues and opinion on structural equation modelling. Manag. Inform. Syst. Quart. **22**, 7–16 (1998)
4. Chin, W.W.: The partial least squares approach for structural equation modelling. In: Marcoulides, G.A. (ed.) Modern methods for business research, pp. 295–336. Lawrence Erlbaum Associates, Mahwah (1998)
5. Correa, T., Hinsley, A.W., de Zuniga, H.G.: Who interacts on the Web? The intersection of users' personality and social media use. Comput. Hum. Behav. **26**, 247–253 (2010). doi:10.1016/j.chb.2009.09.003
6. Culnan, M.J., Armstrong, P.K.: Information privacy concerns, procedural fairness, and impersonal trust: an empirical investigation. Organ. Sci. **10**, 104–115 (1999). doi:10.1287/orsc.10.1.104

7. Davis, F.D.: Perceived usefulness, perceived ease of use, and user acceptance of information technology. Manag. Inform. Syst. Quart. **13**, 319–340 (1989). doi:10.2307/249008

8. Dinev, T., Hart, P.: Privacy concerns and internet use – a model of trade-off factors. In: Academy of Management Proceedings 2003, pp. D1–D6 (2003). doi:10.5465/AMBPP.2003. 13792464

9. Dunne, A., Lawlor, M.A., Rowley, J.: Young people's use of online social networking sites: a uses and gratifications perspective. J. Interact. Mark **4**, 46–58 (2010). doi:10.1108/ 17505931011033551

10. Ellison, N.B., Steinfield, C., Lampe, C.: The benefits of Facebook 'friends': social capital and college students use of online social network sites. J. Comput. Mediat. Commun. **12**, 1143–1168 (2007). doi:10.1111/j.1083-6101.2007.00367.x

11. Facebook: Annual Report 2014 (2015). http://investor.fb.com/common/download/download. cfm?companyid=AMDA-NJ5DZ&fileid=852173&filekey=F61276C5-0AE9-49DE-BFD9- 087398F85EC8&filename=FB2014AR.pdf

12. Fornell, C., Larcker, D.F.: Evaluating structural equation models with unobservable variables and measurement error. J. Market. Res. **18**, 39–50 (1981)

13. Fung, R.K.K., Lee, M.K.O.: EC-trust (trust in electronic commerce): exploring the antecedent factors. In: Proceedings of 5th Americas Conference on Information Systems, pp. 517–519 (1999)

14. Hair, J.F., Ringle, C.M., Sarstedt, M.: PLS-SEM: indeed a silver bullet. J. Mark Theor. Pract. **19**, 139–151 (2011). doi:10.2753/MTP1069-6679190202

15. Hair Jr., J.F., Hult, G.T.M., Ringle, S.M.: A Primer on Partial Least Squares Structural Equation Modeling (PLS-SEM). Sage Publications, Los Angeles (2014)

16. Kim, D.J., Ferrin, D.L., Rao, H.R.: A trust-based consumer decision-making model in electronic commerce: The role of trust, perceived risk, and their antecedents. Decis. Support Syst. **44**, 544–564 (2008). doi:10.1016/j.dss.2007.07.001

17. Krasnova, H., Spiekermann, S., Koroleva, K., Hildebrand, T.: Online social networks: why we disclose. J. Inf. Technol. **25**, 109–125 (2010). doi:10.1057/jit.2010.6

18. Kwon, O., Wen, Y.: An empirical study of the factors affecting social network service use. Comput. Hum. Behav. **26**, 254–263 (2010)

19. Lin, H.F., Lee, G.G.: Determinants of success for online communities: an empirical study. Behav. Inform. Technol. **25**, 479–488 (2006). doi:10.1080/01449290500330422

20. Lin, K.Y., Lu, H.P.: Why people use social network sites: an empirical study integrating network externalities and motivation theory. Comput. Hum. Behav. **27**, 1152–1161 (2011). doi:10.1016/j.chb.2010.12.009

21. Lohmöller, J.B.: Latent variable path modelling with partial least squares. Physica (1989). doi:10.1007/978-3-642-52512-4. Heidelberg

22. Madden, M.: Privacy management on social media sites (2012). http://pewintternet.org/ Reports/2012/Privacy-management-on-social-media.asp

23. Mayer, R.C., Davis, J.H., Schoorman, F.D.: An integrative model of organizational trust. Acad. Manag. Rev. **20**, 709–734 (1995). doi:10.5465/AMR.1995.9508080335

24. McCrae, R.R.: The five factor model: issues and applications. J. Pers. **60**, 175–215 (1992). doi:10.1111/j.1467-6494.1992.tb00970.x

25. McKnight, D.H., Choudhury, V., Kacmar, C.: The impact of initial consumer trust on intentions to transact with a web site: a trust building model. J. Strateg. Inf. Syst. **11**, 297– 323 (2002). doi:10.1016/S0963-8687(02)00020-3

26. Menon, N.M., Konana, P., Browne, G.J., Balasubramanian, S.: Understanding trustworthiness beliefs in electronic brokerage usage. In: Proceedings of the 20th International Conference on Information Systems, pp. 552–555 (1999)

27. Moore, K., Mc Elroy, J.C.: The influence of personality on Facebook usage, wall postings, and regret. Comput. Hum. Behav. **28**, 267–274 (2012). doi:10.1016/j.chb.2011.09.009
28. Nonnecke, B., Preece, J., Andrews, D., Voutour, R.: Online lurkers tell why. In: Proceedings of the 10th Americas Conference on Information Systems, New York, pp. 1–7 (2004)
29. Preece, J., Nonnecke, B., Andrews, D.: The top five reasons for lurking: improving community experiences for everyone. Comput. Hum. Behav. **20**, 201–223 (2004). doi:10.1016/j.chb.2003.10.015
30. Quan-Haase, A., Young, A.L.: Uses and gratifications of social media: a comparison of Facebook and instant messaging. Bull. Sci. Technol. Soc. **30**, 350–361 (2010). doi:10.1177/0270467610380009
31. Rau, P.L.P., Gao, Q., Ding, Y.: Relationship between the level of intimacy and lurking in online social network services. Comput. Hum. Behav. **24**, 2757–2770 (2008). doi:10.1016/j.chb.2008.04.001
32. Rauniar, R., Rawski, G., Yang, J., Johnson, B.: Technology acceptance model (TAM) and social media usage: an empirical study on Facebook. J. Enterp. Inf. Manage. **27**, 6–30 (2014). doi:10.1108/JEIM-04-2012-0011
33. Ringle, C.M., Wende, S., Will. A.: SmartPLS 2.0.M3 (2005). http://www.smartpls.de
34. Ross, C., Orr, E.S., Sisic, M., Arseneault, J.M., Simmering, M.G., Orr, R.R.: Personality and motivations associated with Facebook use. Comput. Hum. Behav. **25**, 578–586 (2009). doi:10.1016/j.chb.2008.12.024
35. Sarstedt, M., Ringle, C.M., Smith, D., Reams, R., Hair Jr., J.F.: Partial least squares structural equation modeling (PLS-SEM): a useful tool for family business researchers. J. Fam. Bus. Strateg. **5**, 105–115 (2014)
36. Seidman, G.: Self-presentation and belonging on Facebook: how personality influences social media use and motivations. Pers. Individ. Differ. **54**, 402–407 (2013). doi:10.1016/j.paid.2012.10.009
37. Tan, Y.H., Thoen, W.: Toward a generic model of trust for electronic commerce. Int. J. Electron. Commun. **5**, 61–74 (2000)
38. Vodanovich, S., Sundaram, D., Myers, M.: Research commentary: digital natives and ubiquitous information systems. Inform. Syst. Res. **21**, 711–723 (2010). doi:10.1287/isre.1100.0324
39. Wang, Z., Tchernev, J.M., Solloway, T.: A dynamic longitudinal examination of social media use, needs, and gratifications among college students. Comput. Hum. Behav. **28**, 1829–1839 (2012). doi:10.1016/j.chb.2012.05.001
40. Weiber, R., Mühlhaus, D.: Strukturgleichungsmodellierung. Eine anwendungsorientierte Einführung in die Kausalanalyse mit Hilfe von AMOS, SmartPLS und SPSS Springer-Lehrbuch. Springer, Heidelberg (2014). doi:10.1007/978-3-642-35012-2
41. Zhao, S., Grasmuck, S., Martin, J.: Identity construction on Facebook: Digital empowerment in anchored relationships. Comput. Hum. Behav. **24**, 1816–1836 (2008). doi:10.1016/j.chb.2008.02.012

# Pooling Supply and Demand: Collaboration for Community Broadcasts

Jean-Charles Grégoire[1]([⊠]), Angèle M. Hamel[2], and D. Marc Kilgour[2]

[1] INRS–EMT, Montreal, QC, Canada
gregoire@emt.inrs.ca
[2] Department of Mathematics, Wilfrid Laurier University,
Waterloo, ON, Canada
{ahamel,mkilgour}@wlu.ca

**Abstract.** Geographical communities are now poised to take advantage of newly-available technology that enables them to broadcast events of specialized local interest using streaming video. The relatively low cost is key, but nevertheless activating a server gives rise to a fixed cost, a capacity and a duration, and these may not properly match the community's needs, which themselves can fluctuate widely. We investigate a "pooling" approach which handles excess demand by utilizing the resources of a neighbouring community, in return for payment or reciprocal service. We show how to use data to characterize needs and introduce a formal model. Using the price structure of currently available commercial solutions, we explore practical ways in which basic demand can be met, the sharing of supply and demand could be organized, and how participating communities could allocate their costs.

**Keywords:** Community cooperation · Community event broadcasting · Video streaming · Hosting costs · Resource pool · Trading · Community networking

## 1 Introduction and Context

Today's geographical communities have a singular opportunity: live streaming video is widely available and relatively cheap, and getting cheaper. The convergence of several "more" factors–more computing cycles, more bandwidth, more affordable hosting–is making live streaming of local community events feasible, even on a small scale to allow members who cannot physically attend to participate in, say, a relative's game, a concert or simply a town hall meeting. Nevertheless, resources on the right scale are unlikely to be available; it is hard to determine the right amount when cyclical patterns are not known, and even harder to take account of extreme (in terms of participation) events. The first problem we address is the identification of cost-effective approaches to the problem of just-enough resources for live-streaming by smaller communities.

Now suppose there is an event of great interest, both for physical and remote access, such that additional demand comes from keen outsiders. As the host

C. Pham et al. (Eds.): GECON 2017, LNCS 10537, pp. 106–116, 2017.
DOI: 10.1007/978-3-319-68066-8_9

community, you want to serve this demand. It may be practical to broadcast community events to an audience in the 10 s to 100 s, and special events may increase this by an order of magnitude. But still it is so small that the cost of large scale broadcast infrastructure, such as a Content Delivery Network (CDN), would be prohibitive. The second challenge is to cater for such situations.

We target a small- to mid-size community that manages some form of Web infrastructure to deliver live or recorded content to members and typically has a community centre, equipped with A/V broadcasting equipment, where it would host events of interest. Access to content would be protected with a control mechanism incorporating credentials and authorization. This kind of broadcast is just now technologically feasible and affordable; our predicted system may be conjectural, but it is based on currently available technology, which we now describe.

A community service platform would be composed of a Web server; an authentication/authorization module, supporting federation; a streaming server for live/stored content; a large storage capacity (for media) and possibly a Content Management System (CMS) platform. These components can run on one or more (virtual) machines.

We make the following assumptions about a community's infrastructure:

1. The software platform implements an Infrastructure as a Service model (IaaS) [1], probably using open-source components. For Linux platforms [2], most of the building blocks (Web server, database, authentication, ...) are readily available off-the-shelf;
2. Local and remote connection requests can be distinguished under a federated authorization and access control system (e.g. [3]);
3. If a stream is rebroadcast (through a partner server), it is possible to know it is a rebroadcast and to know and control the total number of people viewing.

Streaming resources are primarily acquired for a community's own use but commercial offerings are inflexible and result in a mismatch with needs. This leads us to explore pooling as an option to manage resources in excess in a form of community network. In essence, once the baseline of resources for the community proper is known, the community may decide to invest in greater capacity, with a view to sharing to meet occasional excess demand while mitigating costs. If several neighbouring communities have servers, capacity may be loaned by one community to another in several forms: (a) directly from the "home" community server; (b) indirectly through a remote community server; or (c) indirectly through a broadcast server. We illustrate the configurations of live-stream delivery in Fig. 1. The components are labelled L (local), R (Remote), E (Everyone) and B (Broadcast Server), permitting us to describe the alternatives as L2L, R2L, and B2L (for services to a client), L2R, R2R, and B2R, for services to a remote client, and or the global alternative B2E, as could be accomplished with a CDN. In the later sections we will explore issues arising out of this configuration.

Finally, we note that costs are based on a combination of fixed and dynamic elements—rental, administrative, and running time are all fixed, while bandwidth consumption is not. In the next section, we explore more specifically the

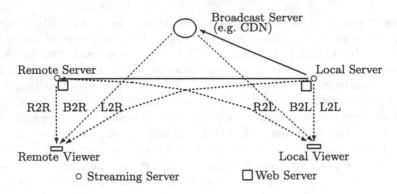

**Fig. 1.** Live stream delivery alternatives.

cost dimension of broadcasting. We then proceed to study of acquisition for a single community before exploring the forms of pooling, and then conclude.

## 2    Broadcasting Costs

Broadcasting costs are an important issue as they strongly depend on, or limit, the degree of participation in an event. Requirements for video delivery and storage and hosting formulæ vary, as do costs. Here we give a few sample costs from Canadian providers and in Canadian dollars. We believe them to be roughly similar worldwide, as these infrastructures have now become commodities.

*Basic Web Hosting.* Hosted Web servers can be cheap, starting at less than $100 annually [12], but such services are not suitable for our purposes as they do not support large transfers of data. Web services are usually offered in heavily mutualized environments, which operate on the assumption that traffic remains low on average. Performance can therefore vary wildly—which is not acceptable for a reliable live streaming service.

*Virtual Private Server Hosting.* The next choice on the same model of shared resources is a Virtual Private Server (VPS), essentially a virtual machine running Linux (or another operating system). Although several VPSs shares the same physical processor, a VPS runs as if it were a real server. Vendors describe this model as offering "unlimited" bandwidth based on "reasonable" use, or fixed quotas. As an example, 100 GB of storage and 2 TB of bandwidth costs $69.99 month/year, or $79.99 per month without a yearly subscription [13].

While market prices can vary, the bottom is fairly well-defined with the only elements of differentiation being the amount of memory and the amount of storage. In the case of streaming, the first factor is always important; the second one is a concern only for stored content.

*Dedicated Server.* A dedicated server is a machine entirely dedicated to the customer, without virtualization. As an example, 2 GB of memory with 150 GB of storage and 10 TB of bandwidth is $225 month/year [14]. In general, dedicated servers tend to offer more storage and more bandwidth, but prices are about four times greater than VPS for lower capacities, falling to about two times for higher capacities.

Other offers are more flexible in terms of parameters: CPU, memory, storage, and bandwidth are available on an "a la carte" basis. Nevertheless, prices for similar configurations are comparable. The objective would be to select the right size to satisfy demand while avoiding systematic over-provisioning.

*Streaming Service.* For streaming content, the services of a CDN provider seem appealing. Resellers offer CDN platforms with software environments tuned for media streaming, live or not. Such services ensure that features are well-tuned for media delivery, which may not be the case with some alternatives. Although these systems provide good live-streaming performance, storage can be a limiting factor.

An offer [15] for a streaming service based on a CDN provides 100 GB of bandwidth a month and 20 GB of storage at $19 per month (based on annual subscription). We note that there is a huge gap between this level and the next one (2000 GB of bandwidth), but an incremental price over quota (overage) is also offered. As usual, it is important to read the fine print: some services offer bandwidth rollover for a fixed time period, while the prices of others depend on a minimal duration subscription. Also noteworthy is storage pricing, which is usually biased towards a large-scale broadcast of a narrow variety of content, as is to be expected because a CDN essentially behaves like a hierarchical cache [6].

In order to exploit this information about costs and capacities, we require an assessment of the community's needs in terms of bandwidth, which requires consideration of both the number of unique viewing events and the audience for each event. We address these in the next section.

# 3  Community Needs and Associated Costs

Table 1 shows estimates of bandwidth (throughput) requirements for different levels of video quality, based on information given by Netflix. Note that 3 Mbps for a one hour video translates into a volume of 1.35 GB. These levels of compression of a raw video stream may not be achievable for a live video, but they are a reasonable first approximation.

The total bandwidth (in TB/mo) is related to the attendance and duration of events by the following formula:

$$\sum_{e \in \mathcal{E}} \text{attendance}(e) \times \text{duration}(e) \times \text{average coding rate}$$

where $\mathcal{E}$ is the set of events, attendance $(e)$ is the number of viewers for event $e$, duration $(e)$ is in seconds, and coding rate is in bps.

We use one month as the fundamental time period for this computation, as hosting is almost always charged on a monthly basis. A problem, however,

**Table 1.** Required throughputs for different quality levels.

| Throughput (Mbps) | Video quality |
|---|---|
| 0.5 | Lowest required speed for streaming |
| 1.5 | Recommended speed for quality viewing |
| 3 | Standard Definition video |
| 5–8 | 720p and 1080p High Definition |
| 25 | 4K Ultra High Definition |

is that there will typically be large month to month variations. Moreover, if there are several linked communities, large audiences will often be correlated, as many viewers are attracted to events that are exceptional. We first discuss the audience distribution for a single community, and then go on to the case of events involving multiple communities.

### 3.1 Monthly Requirements: Single Community

Assessing requirements presents a challenge: a community will start with a history of hosting events without broadcasting them, thus without any data. We propose two approaches, one historical and the other formal.

**Historical Perspective.** We begin by assuming that a historical log of events held over the years is available, and that the subset of events suitable for broadcasting can be identified. We also require the attendance per event in the subset.

Events will be considered to be recurring if they happen at least once per year, and non-recurring otherwise. With the history of recurring events, we can establish how demand evolves from month to month during the year. Clearly, some months with lower event frequency can be expected. Consider the top three months in terms of bandwidth required for broadcast events. If they are relatively similar, take the highest one to define peak demand. If demand in one month conspicuously stands out, exclude it as an outlier and take the next highest month to define peak demand.

We will use the peak demand as a baseline for selecting a hosting option. Note that our process ignores non-recurring events, which include extreme events where participation could be massive. We will discuss later how to make provisions for outliers or extreme events.

**Formal Model.** The other approach to assessing demand is to work with a formal model, i.e., a probability distribution. Clearly any formal model must be consistent with empirical data, but the benefit of moving to abstraction is to allow fine tuning and to support prediction. Note that probability models do not account for non-recurring events; the heavy-tail character of real-world distributions is an issue [10].

Let us consider the following example. We start from a fixed uniform distribution of events, such as three events per week. We then assume an underlying

Poisson process for participation in any event and accordingly obtain an exponentially distributed audience size.

Recall that commercial offerings are organized in fixed sizes: you rent a whole server, not a fraction of a server. This lack of flexibility creates an inherent partitioning—to reach more than a certain number of viewers, the community must incur the cost of another server. To take this into account we set thresholds matching different degrees of participation and define the following categories, assuming a three level bandwidth service offering with options 1 TB, 2 TB and 4 TB, reflecting an operator's offer [14]:

$Z_a$  Below 1 TB
$Z_b$  Between 1 TB and 2 TB
$Z_c$  Between 2 TB and 4 TB
$Z_d$  Above 4 TB

Note that $\frac{Z_d}{Z_c+Z_d}$ is the (conditional) probability that an observation above 2 TB is also above 4 TB.

For a distribution with CDF $1-e^{-\mu x}$, suppose that $\mu = 0.75$. The breakpoints above produce the probabilities $Z_a = 73.64\%$ and $Z_b = 19.41\%$. Thus, with probability 6.95%, the audience is type $Z_c$ or $Z_d$, and it exceeds 2 TB. The (conditional) probability is 6.95% that one of those exceptionally high audiences actually exceeds 4 TB. (The unconditional probability of an audience exceeding 4 TB is 0.48%.) Setting another threshold at 8 TB, we see that the probability that it is reached is close to 0 (barring extreme events).

From the event distribution, assuming independence, and the degree of participation computed above, we can derive monthly requirements by simple superposition. Similarly, we can evaluate the probability of demand exceeding a chosen subscription quota.

Note that, so far, this model assumes uniform distribution of events not only for a particular month, but across the full year. It is also possible to modulate $\mu$ from month to month, e.g. with a Markov process to reflect seasonal factors [5].

**Extreme Events.** Events that are extreme in a statistical sense [4] are of course an issue. We must make special provisions for events for which participation rates fall outside the usual distribution, those that might be called the "event of the decade" or similar. In most cases, the value of $Z_d$ should be understood to underestimate the proportion of extreme events. The community cannot be expected to support such extreme events on its own and may have to pool resources.

## 3.2  Costs: Single Community

Let us illustrate this discussion with a conjectural but realistic example. Assuming a video coding at 1.5 Mbps and an average of three event-hours for 100 viewers per week, we end up with a total of approximately 0.9 TB for a month. Storage for this data would take about 9 GB. It follows that 50 GB storage with

1 TB bandwidth (a real service offering from [13]) would be sufficient to support this service, provided most content could be available online for a limited period of time, say a week. The next level from this service provider (100 GB storage with 2 TB bandwidth) might be required if the community wishes to make more content available for longer.

We have concluded that a dedicated Web server is necessary to support online services, so this option seems appropriate. But are the cost and capacity reasonable, and do they scale up? Let us examine more deeply the 100 viewers per week assumption above. One hundred is 1% of a community of 10 000. The different boroughs of Montreal, for example, range in size from 20 000 to 180 000 inhabitants, which already puts us at the low end of population estimates. Moreover, one event per week means approximately 4 or 5 per month and about 50 events per year, which may not be many; it is likely that attendance is far greater than average a few times over the year. Thus, this model does not scale: the cost of doubling the monthly volume is reasonable, but prices explode beyond that, and the only alternative is a dedicated server.

Table 2. Best option per monthly transfer volume.

| Global volume (TB) | Option | Cost ($/month/yr) |
|---|---|---|
| 1 | VPS | 40 |
| 2 | VPS | 70 |
| 5 | Dedicated | 175 |
| 10 | Dedicated | 225 |
| 20 | Dedicated | N.A |

Table 2 summarizes the options and their costs for increasing monthly transmitted volume. A detailed consideration of service options, such as those provided by [15] shows that streaming services are not really an option for a base service. Before we discuss how they could be complemented, we extend our study beyond the single community case and look for opportunities for sharing.

## 3.3   Monthly Requirements: Multiple Communities

Events such as sports tournaments may involve many communities, beyond what a regular tournament would involve, although not as much as playoffs. In addition to classifying events according to attendance and recurrence, as previously, we now keep track of the number of communities involved. We assume that each community involved in the event will be willing to share the burden of broadcasting it to their own members, no matter where the event occurs. The greatest problem arises for events that generate interest beyond the communities that participate directly. As the number of participating communities increases, the cost of forwarding traffic among them may become significant, as it amounts to an increase in local community participation. These cost increases could be alleviated by a tree structure to relay the feeds [7]. In any case, it is clear that the extra needs associated with such events must be taken into account when planning for capacity.

As we have seen in this section, commercial offerings set thresholds against which a community must compare its needs and under- or over-provisioning is always a danger. This reality motivates communities to pool resources. In the next section we explore fair practices and pricing for pooling supply and demand.

# 4  Pooling Supply and Demand

Our model for the estimation of consumption can be generalized to all communities, on a per-month basis, for all months of the year. We assume that all communities share information openly with each other. This model applies for any non-overlapping subset of communities: trading can be done in groups, or globally. Note that a community cannot benefit by belonging to more than one group.

On this basis, we propose a three-step process to access extra capacity: (1) freely share extra capacity, either first come–first served or systematically, in either case as in a purely altruistic fashion, (2) enter into a year-long trade agreement with specific communities, with a compensation formula and a specific trading platform, or (3) manage a global pool of resources for all communities, on top of the individual infrastructures located within each community. Still, it must be accepted that, when capacity runs out for whatever reason, viewers will be denied service.

Once capacity for sharing is identified, the issue is how to guarantee a fair return, given that it is uncertain a priori exactly how much will be required, and that risk should be shared. Our approach is based on three steps: foundational, static and dynamic.

1. First, identify what capacity, if any, is offered, and how much is required (and when) on top of what is already owned. This gives the foundation of the pool.
2. Second, carry out a static rebalancing of supply and demand, establishing prices for the capacity offered, as discussed below.
3. Third, if necessary, implement dynamic readjustment of offers and demands through the month. It is possible that demand will be below or above expectations, so releases into the pool, and captures from the pool, can both occur. This process is comparable to a "spot" market. To avoid pricing distortions, dynamic readjustment would require the same compensation basis as the static step.

To guarantee fairness, consumption must be tracked for each member community, which is feasible thanks to the federated authentication and authorization process described above. Quota limits must be enforced. We have assumed honesty in both pooling supply and demand. Without it, communities could not appropriately decide to switch to higher capacity and share more, for example. Agreements should run through a full year, not only because of expected month to month variability, but also to reward communities that commit to purchasing, and sharing, additional resources. Alternatively, rather than hoping that "infrastructure leaders" will commit to increase broadcast resources for the common good, it is possible that several communities will decide to collectively purchase a larger resource. This can be decided in part by the level of need that forced the transition to a hosting model.

The level of pricing establishes the compensation a community received for upgrading capacity and providing more resources. A well-regulated system will encourage contributors while avoiding gouging or oversupply. Pooling supply and demand is key to this process, as it rewards transparency while increasing the probability that excess demands are met at reasonable cost. The primary reason why a community acquires extra resources should be its own needs. All communities should participate, which is an option now that technology has ensured that costs not be prohibitive. Capacity should be offered at a price that closely reflects costs, augmented by a small overhead of a few percent. Consumers should pay at a rate that reflects the amount of content they subscribe to. A rebate—effectively, lower overhead—should be offered for small users only, to encourage consumers to avoid waste. It is also preferable that offers be rounded in multiples of flow aggregates, to facilitate management. Based on our example above in Sect. 3.2 and the size of the commercial offers, 10 GB could be considered a reasonable unit.

The pooling supply and demand process would ideally be supported by a automated platform that includes request for bandwidth, offer for bandwidth, global advertisement of supply and demand, pricing establishment, pairing request and offer, pairing agreements, and monitoring and reporting. None of these elements are particularly challenging. These functions could be carried out on an asset exchange platform, some of which are available in open source. Another idea is that these interactions could be coordinated by a local operator (i.e. a reseller), who would also find an interest in "right-sizing" infrastructures.

Finally, beyond our proposal of pooling supply and demand, another option might be the use of local relays, which we studied earlier [9]. A community member could recursively rebroadcast to another member the live flow it receives, in a restricted form of peer-to-peer exchange [8]. However, we note several caveats: (1) the performance asymmetry of residential Internet access, and the typical limits on uplink throughput, imply that many members will be unable to upload a quality live stream; (2) those who upload may face quotas and risk significant financial penalties for excessive consumption of bandwidth; (3) client programs would have to be reconfigured to retransmit received flow; and (4) because of restrictions on home routers, direct communication between two members may not be possible. All these considered, local relays may help to exploit extra capacity, but their contribution is unlikely to be significant.

## 5  Conclusion

We have proposed ways in which geographical communities with common interests in broadcasting but distinct interests in content could cooperate to overcome pricing difficulties. While Internet-based streaming technology is now readily available on a commodity basis, bandwidth and storage can be expensive, especially for users forced to over-provision in order to cover expected peak demands. The problem is rooted in inflexible pricing structures used by service providers, which make it impossible to match the exact needs of a community. Across the telecommunications industry, operators encourage an over-subscription model.

The pooling supply and demand model lays a foundation upon which communities can advertise, trade, acquire and be compensated for resources required collectively. Underlying this model is the transparent sharing of information on resources available and required, on prices charged, and on monitored usage.

Altruistic communities may jump to higher capacities for the greater good. But there are risks associated with uncertain demand as well as issues of coordination among communities. In future work we plan to explore these risk aspects, along with their relation to fair pricing. There is relevant work in the area of community networking (e.g. [11]) that we plan to exploit.

One fundamental issue for our study has been the lack of appropriate data. With better data, a more precise and detailed formal study could be carried out. This lack of data is also a challenge for a community considering broadcasting, as the first step must be a set of community trials to gauge popularity. But communities will benefit, even in the earliest stages, from the knowledge that investment risks can be shared.

## References

1. Bhardwaj, S., Jain, L., Jain, S.: Cloud computing: A study of infrastructure as a service (IAAS). Int. J. Eng. Inf. Technol. **2**(1), 60–63 (2010)
2. Dougherty, D.: LAMP: The open source web platform. ONLamp (2001)
3. Hardt, E.D.: The OAuth 2.0 Authorization Framework. Internet Requests for Comments RFC 6749. http://tools.ietf.org/html/rfc6749
4. Castillo, E.: Extreme Value Theory in Engineering. Academic Press, Boston (1988)
5. Fischer, W., Meier-Hellstern, K.: The markov-modulated poisson process (MMPP) cookbook. Perform. Eval. **18**(2), 149–171 (1993)
6. Vakali, A., Pallis, G.: Content delivery networks: Status and trends. IEEE Internet Comput. **7**(6), 68–74 (2003)
7. Chu, Y., Rao, S.G., Zhang, H.: A case for end system multicast. In: ACM SIGMETRICS (2000)
8. Schollmeier, R.: A definition of peer-to-peer networking for the classification of peer-to-peer architectures and applications. In: First International Conference on Peer-to-Peer Computing. IEEE (2001)
9. Gregoire, J.-C., Hamel, A.M., Kilgour, D.M.: Pricing for a hybrid delivery model of video streaming. SIGMETRICS Perform. Eval. Rev. **44**(3), 33–36 (2016)
10. Resnick, S.I.: Heavy tail modeling and teletraffic data: special invited paper. Ann. Stat. **25**(5), 1805–1869 (1997)

11. Khan, A.M., et al.: Towards incentive-compatible pricing for bandwidth reservation in community network clouds. In: International Conference on Grid Economics and Business Model, pp. 251–264 (2015)
12. Based on Web Hosting Canada offers. www.whc.ca. Last Accessed May 2017
13. Based on HostPapa offers. https://www.hostpapa.ca. Last Accessed May 2017
14. Based on HostUpon offers. https://www.hostupon.ca. Last Accessed May 2017
15. Based on DAcast offers. www.dacast.com. Last Accessed May 2017

# Work in Progress on Energy Efficiency and Resource Management

# Towards Virtual Machine Energy-Aware Cost Prediction in Clouds

Mohammad Aldossary[1,2(✉)], Ibrahim Alzamil[3],
and Karim Djemame[1]

[1] School of Computing, University of Leeds, Leeds, UK
{scmmald, K.Djemame}@leeds.ac.uk
[2] Prince Sattam Bin Abdulaziz University, Al Kharj, Kingdom of Saudi Arabia
MM.Aldossary@psau.edu.sa
[3] Majmaah University, Al Majmaah, Kingdom of Saudi Arabia
I.Alzamil@mu.edu.sa

**Abstract.** Pricing mechanisms employed by different service providers significantly influence the role of cloud computing within the IT industry. With the increasing cost of electricity, Cloud providers consider power consumption as one of the major cost factors to be maintained within their infrastructures. Consequently, modelling a new pricing mechanism that allow Cloud providers to determine the potential cost of resource usage and power consumption has attracted the attention of many researchers. Furthermore, predicting the future cost of Cloud services can help the service providers to offer the suitable services to the customers that meet their requirements. This paper introduces an Energy-Aware Cost Prediction Framework to estimate the total cost of Virtual Machines (VMs) by considering the resource usage and power consumption. The VMs' workload is firstly predicted based on an Autoregressive Integrated Moving Average (ARIMA) model. The power consumption is then predicted using regression models. The comparison between the predicted and actual results obtained in a real Cloud testbed shows that this framework is capable of predicting the workload, power consumption and total cost for different VMs with good prediction accuracy, e.g. with 0.06 absolute percentage error for the predicted total cost of the VM.

**Keywords:** Cloud computing · Cost Prediction · Workload prediction · ARIMA model · Power consumption · Energy efficiency

## 1 Introduction

Cloud computing is an important and growing business model that has attracted the attention of many researchers. Pricing mechanisms that are employed by different service providers significantly influence the role of cloud computing within the IT industry. Billing mechanisms have become even more sophisticated, as customers are charged per month, hour or minute. Nevertheless, there are still limited as customers are charged based on a pre-defined tariff for the resource usage which include CPU, Memory, Storage and Network. This pre-defined tariff does not consider the variable cost of electricity [1]. Consequently, modelling a new pricing mechanism for services

© Springer International Publishing AG 2017
C. Pham et al. (Eds.): GECON 2017, LNCS 10537, pp. 119–131, 2017.
DOI: 10.1007/978-3-319-68066-8_10

offered that can be adjusted to the actual energy costs has become an interesting research topic.

There are limited works on cost models that measure the actual resource usage of a cloud service while taking consideration of variation in costs, power consumption, and performance together. Most cloud computing service providers charge their customers on a timely basis for the virtualised systems usage (with no performance guarantee) instead of the actual resource usage [3]. In other words, cloud service providers charge customers for the services offered on a timely basis, regardless of the actual resource usage and consideration of power consumption, which is considered one of the biggest operational cost factors by cloud infrastructure providers.

Another limitation of the cost mechanism is not only dependent on the actual resource usage and power consumption, but also on other factors that may affect the VMs total cost such as performance variation. Most of the existing studies have focused on minimising the power consumption and maximising the total resource usage, instead of improving VM performance. Further, Cloud providers (e.g. Amazon EC2) [4], have established their Service Level Agreements (SLAs) based on service availability without such an assurance of the performance. For instance, during the service operation, when the number of VMs increases on the same Physical Machine (PM)(overbooking), the resource competition may occur (e.g. once the workload exceeds the acceptable level of CPU utilisation) leading to VMs performance degradation. Thus, cloud service providers do not consider the VMs performance variation, while the VMs performance is a very important factor to satisfy cloud customers' requirements. Therefore, it is essential to consider VM performance variations in the composition of VM costs.

The first step towards this is an Energy-Aware Cost Prediction Framework that may influence the decision making of other problems. This paper focuses on the problem of estimating the resource usage, power consumption, and the total cost of the VMs at service operation. Therefore, a framework is proposed to predict VMs workload using an Autoregressive Integrated Moving Average (ARIMA) model. The relationship between the VMs and PMs workload (CPU utilisation) is investigated using regression models in order to estimate the VMs power consumption and predict the total cost of the VMs. This paper's main contributions are summarized as follow:

- A proposed Energy-Aware Cost Modeller for Cloud system architecture to assess the actual consumption of Cloud infrastructure resources.
- Energy-Aware Cost Prediction Framework that predicts the total cost for heterogeneous VMs by considering their resource usage and power consumption.
- Evaluation of the proposed framework in an existing Cloud testbed in order to verify the capability of the prediction models.

The remainder of this paper is organised as follows: a discussion of the related work is summarised in Sect. 2. Section 3 presents the system architecture followed by a discussion of the Energy-Aware Cost Prediction Framework. Section 4 presents the experimental set up followed by results and discussion in Sect. 5. Finally, Sect. 6 concludes this paper and discusses the future work.

## 2  Related Work

This paper discusses the cost that is associated with the resource usage and power consumption of the VMs. Previous work has looked into the area of calculating the cost of running services on Cloud infrastructure. Altmann and Kashef [13] presented the service placement optimisation based on the cost model in federated clouds to guarantee the cost minimisation for Cloud customers. This approach depends on a brute-force algorithm to evaluate the cost of each possible service placement. The cost model defined in their work as the sum of the fixed costs and the variable costs. The fixed costs include the costs for hardware and the variable costs include (e.g. the electricity cost). However, the cost model proposed in their work does not consider predicting the cost in the future. Also, more factors need to be considered (e.g. performance variation) to guarantee the SLAs. Horri and Dastghaibyfard [8] emphasised the difficulty of dealing with minimising Cloud infrastructure energy consumption while conducting the Quality of Service (QoS), especially since there is a trade-off between energy consumption and SLA. Therefore, they have proposed and implemented a cost model in CloudSim. Their approach considers the total cost including the cost of energy consumption based on (e.g. number of VMs and data size). Nonetheless, their objectives do not consider predicting the total cost or power consumption.

In terms of prediction based on historical data, estimating the resources usage and power consumption of the VMs would require understanding the characteristics of the underlying physical resources, like idle power consumption and variable power under different workload, and the projected virtual resources usage, as stated in [20]. Thus, it is essential to get the predicted VMs' workload first in order to get their predicted power. Some work has predicted future workload in a Cloud environment based on Autoregressive Integrated Moving Average (ARIMA) model; nonetheless, their objectives do not consider predicting the power consumption. For example, Calhciros et al. [24] introduced a Cloud workload prediction module based on the ARIMA model to proactively and dynamically provision resources. They define their workload as the expected number of requests received by the users, which are then mapped to predict the number of VMs needed to execute customers' requests and meet the QoS. Caron et al. [11] presented a resource usage prediction algorithm based on identifying similar usage patterns of the short-term workload history. The algorithm has shown a good result within 4.8% prediction error. Khan et al. [16] proposed a method of characterising and predicting workload based on Hidden Markov Modeling to discover the correlations between VMs workload that can be used to predict the changes of workload patterns. Further, Wood et al. [12] focused on estimating the resource requirements when deploying an application into a virtualised environment using a regression-based model to predict future CPU utilisation. While the evaluation has shown that the prediction error is less than 5%, however these approaches do not consider the prediction of costs or power consumption of the VMs.

Other work focuses on predicting power consumption based on historical data while others use performance counters, which are queried directly from the hardware or the operating system. But, relying on performance counters would not work appropriately in heterogeneous environments with different server characteristics, as argued by Zhang et al. [17]. Therefore, they presented a best fit energy prediction model (BFEPM) that flexibly selects the best model for a given server based on a series of equations that consider only CPU utilisation [17]. Dargie [18] proposed a stochastic model to estimate the power consumption for a multi-core processor based on the CPU utilisation workload and found out that the relationship between the workload and power is best estimated using a linear function in a dual-core processor and using a quadratic function in a single-core processor. Further, Fan et al. [19] have introduced a framework to estimate the power consumption of servers based on CPU utilisation only and argued in their results that the power consumption correlates well with the CPU usage. As their framework produced accurate results, they argued that it is not necessary to use more complex signals, like hardware performance counters, to model power usage.

Compared with the work presented in this paper, the ARIMA model is used to predict the VMs workload, which is then mapped within the prediction framework to get the predicted VMs power consumption. Then, having predicted the VMs' workload and power consumption, the total cost of the VMs is predicted accordingly.

## 3   Resource Usage and Power Consumption for VMs

This section presents the proposed Energy-Aware Cost Prediction Framework to predict the resource usage, power consumption and total cost for VMs. The overall system architecture of this work will be discussed in the next subsection.

### 3.1   System Architecture

Cloud computing architecture consists of three standard layers, which are software as a service (SaaS), platform as a service (PaaS), and infrastructure as a service (IaaS). This paper focuses on the IaaS layer, where service operations take place (Fig. 1).

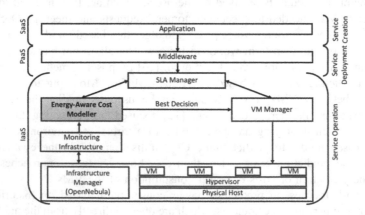

**Fig. 1.** System architecture.

In the IaaS layer, the admission, allocation and management of VMs are performed through the interaction between the components. The highlighted component Energy-Aware Cost Modeller is the main focus of our work.

- **SLA Manager**: this component monitors and measures the SLA's agreed terms.
- **VM Manager**: considers the best decision in order to improve resource usage and reduce the power consumption cost and consequently the total cost of the VMs. For instance, if performance degrades, this component will have actuators to attempt to get the performance to the agreed level. This component interacts with the **Energy-Aware Cost Modeller** to request predictions related to the resource usage, power consumption and cost that VMs would have for a particular host.
- **Monitoring Infrastructure**: this will monitor resource usage, power consumption and performance related metrics.
- **Energy-Aware Cost Modeller**: this component supports:

  (1) Energy-Aware Pricing Model that considers the actual resource usage and power consumption, as introduced in our previous work [5], and
  (2) Energy-Aware Cost Prediction Framework that estimates the resource usage, power consumption and total cost for the VMs.

### 3.2 Energy-Aware Cost Prediction Framework

In our previous work [5], we introduced an **Energy-Aware Pricing Model** that considers power consumption as a key parameter with respect to performance and cost. The proposed model charges the customer based on the actual resource usage and considers the cost of power consumption of the VMs.

In this paper, we extend our work and introduce a new **Energy-Aware Cost Prediction Framework** that would predict VMs workload (CPU, RAM, Disk and Network), power consumption and total cost using the ARIMA model and regression models. This is the main focus of this paper as shown in Fig. 2.

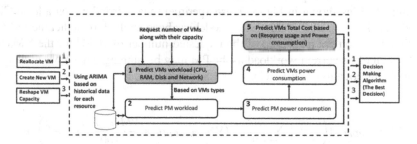

**Fig. 2.** Energy-aware cost prediction framework.

The ARIMA model is a time series prediction model that has been used widely in different domains, including finance, owing to its sophistication and accuracy; further details about the ARIMA model can be found in [14]. Unlike other prediction methods, like sample average, ARIMA takes multiple inputs as historical observations and outputs multiple future observations depicting the seasonal trend. It can be used for seasonal or non-seasonal time-series data. The type of seasonal ARIMA model is used in this work as the targeted workload patterns are reoccurring and showing seasonality in time intervals. In order to use the ARIMA model for predicting the VMs workload in this work, the historical time series workload data has to be stationary, otherwise Box and Cox transformation [15] and data differencing methods are used to make these data stationary. The model selection is based on the best fit model of ARIMA based on Akaike Information Criterion (AIC) or Bayesian Information Criterion (BIC) value.

This framework is aimed towards predicting the total cost of the VMs. In order to achieve that, the VMs workload is first predicted for the next time interval using the ARIMA model based on historical workload patterns. Then, the predicted VMs CPU utilisation is correlated with the PM CPU utilisation in order to predict the power consumption of PM, from which the VMs power consumption is estimated. Finally, the total cost for the VMs is predicted based on the predicted workload and power consumption of the VMs.

As depicted in Fig. 2, the framework includes five main steps in order to predict the VMs workload and power consumption, then predict the total cost of VMs. To reach this goal, the following steps are required.

**Step 1:** to predict (CPU, RAM, Disk and Network) utilisations for the next time interval, ARIMA model is used to identify the best fit model. After predicting the VM workload using the ARIMA model based on historical data, the next steps take place to predict the PM workload and the PM/VM power consumption using regression models.

Before predicting the power consumption for PM/VM, understanding how the resource usage affects the power consumption is required. Therefore, we did an experimental study to investigate the effect of the resource usage (CPU, RAM, Disk and Network) on the power consumption. The findings show that the CPU utilisation correlates well with the power consumption, as this finding is supported in other work [17–19].

**Step 2:** to predict the PM workload which is (PM CPU utilisation), would require measuring the relationship between the number of vCPU and the PM CPU utilisation for a single PM, as shown in Fig. 3. This experiment was carried out on a local Cloud Testbed (see Sect. 4). Linear regression model has been applied to predict the PM CPU utilisation based on the used ratio of the requested number of vCPU for the VMs with consideration of its current workload as the PM may be running other VMs already [6]. The following equation is used (1):

$$
\mathrm{PM}x_{PredUtil} = \left( \alpha \times \left( \sum_{y=1}^{VMCount} \left( \mathrm{VM}y_{ReqvCPUs} \times \frac{\mathrm{VM}y_{PredUtil}}{100} \right) \right) + \beta \right) + \tag{1}
$$
$$
(PM_{xCurrUtil} - PM_{xIdleUtil})
$$

$\mathrm{PM}x_{PredUtil}$ is the predicted PM CPU utilisation; $\alpha$ is the slope and $\beta$ is the intercept of the CPU utilisation. The $\mathrm{VM}y_{ReqvCPUs}$ is the number of requested vCPU for each VM and $\mathrm{VM}y_{PredUtil}$ is the predicted utilisation for each VMs. The $PM_{xCurrUtil}$ is the current PM utilisation and $PM_{xIdleUtil}$ is the idle PM utilisation.

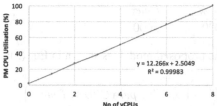
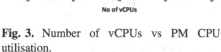
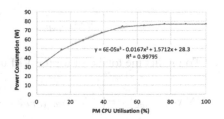

**Fig. 3.** Number of vCPUs vs PM CPU utilisation.

**Fig. 4.** PM CPU utilisation vs power consumption.

**Step 3:** the PM power consumption is predicted based on the relationship between the predicted PM workload (PM CPU utilisation) with PM power consumption on the same PM. Using a regression analysis, the relation is best described using polynomial model with order three for this particular PM, as shown in Fig. 4. Thus, the predicted PM power consumption $PMx_{PredPwr}$ measured by Watt, can be identified using the following formula (2).

$$PMx_{PredPwr} = \left( \alpha(PMx_{PredUtil})^3 + \gamma(PMx_{PredUtil})^2 + \delta(PMx_{PredUtil}) + \beta \right) \qquad (2)$$

Where $\alpha$, $\gamma$ and $\delta$ are all slopes, $\beta$ is the intercept and $PMx_{PredUtil}$ is predicted PM CPU utilization.

**Step 4:** based on the requested number of vCPU and the predicted vCPU utilisation, the VM power consumption is predicted using the proposed formula in [6], as shown in Eq. (3).

$$VMx_{Predpwr} = PMx_{IdlePwr} \times \left( \frac{VMx_{ReqvCPUs}}{\sum_{y=1}^{VMcount} VMy_{ReqvCPUs}} \right) + (PMx_{PredPwr} - PMx_{IdlePwr})$$

$$\times \left( \frac{VMx_{(PredUtil*ReqvCPUs)}}{\sum_{y=1}^{VMcount} VMy_{(PredUtil*ReqvCPUs)}} \right)$$

$$(3)$$

Where $VMx_{Predpwr}$ is the predicted power consumption for one VM measured by Watt. $VMx_{ReqvCPUs}$ is the requested number of vCPU and $VMx_{predUtil}$ the predicted VM CPU utilisation. $\sum_{y=1}^{VMcount} VMy_{ReqvCPUs}$ is the total of vCPU for all VMs in the same PM. The $PMx_{IdlePwr}$ is idle power consumption and $PMx_{PredPwr}$ is the predicted power consumption for a single PM.

**Step 5:** finally, this step predicts the total cost for the VM based on the predicted VM resource usage from step 1 and the predicted VM power consumption from step 4. The energy providers usually charge by the Kilowatt per hour (kWh). Therefore, convert the power consumption to energy is required using the following Eq. (4):

$$VMx_{PredEnergy} = \frac{VMx_{AvgPredpwr}}{1000} \times \frac{Time_s}{3600} \tag{4}$$

To predict the total cost for the VM using the proposed model, as shown in Eq. (5):

$$VMx_{PredTotalCost} = \left( \left( VMx_{ReqvCPUs} \times \frac{VMx_{PredUtil}}{100} \right) \times (Cost\,per\,vCPU \times Time_s) \right)$$
$$+ \left( VMx_{PredRAMUsage} \times (Cost\,per\,GB \times Time_s) \right)$$
$$+ \left( VMx_{PredDiskUsage} \times (Cost\,per\,GB \times Time_s) \right)$$
$$+ \left( VMx_{PredNetUsage} \times (Cost\,per\,GB \times Time_s) \right)$$
$$+ \left( VMx_{PredEnergy} \times Cost\,per\,kWh \right)$$

$$\tag{5}$$

where $VMx_{PredTotalCost}$ is the predicted total cost of the VM. $VMx_{PredRAMUsage}$ is the predicted resource usage of RAM times the cost for that resource for a period of time and so on for each resource such as CPU, Disk and Network. $VMx_{PredEnergy}$ is the predicted energy consumption of the VM times the electricity price as announced by the energy providers.

## 4   Experimental Set up

This section describes the environment and the details of the experiments conducted in order to evaluate the work presented in this paper.

In terms of the experimental design, the aim is to evaluate the new Energy-Aware Cost Prediction Framework presented in terms of predicting the workload, power consumption and total cost for heterogeneous VMs based on historical periodic workload. The prediction process starts by firstly predicting the VM workload using the (auto.arima) function in R package [25] and then completing the cycle of the framework and considering the correlation between the physical and virtual resources to predict power consumption of the VMs on a single PM. After that, the total cost is predicted for the VMs based on their predicted workload and power consumption.

A number of experiments have been designed and implemented on a local Cloud Testbed with the support of the Virtual Infrastructure Manager (VIM), OpenNebula [7] version 4.10, and KVM hypervisor for the Virtual Machine Manager (VMM). This Cloud Testbed includes a cluster of commodity Dell servers, and one of these servers with eight core E31230 V2 Intel Xeon CPU was used. The server includes 16 GB RAM and 1000 GB hard drives. Also, the server has a WattsUp meter [9] attached to directly measure the power consumption. Heterogeneous VMs are created and their monitoring is performed through Zabbix [10], which is also used for resources usage monitoring purposes. Rackspace [26] is used as a reference for the VMs configurations. Three types of VMs, small, medium and large are provided with different capacities. The VMs are allocated with 1, 2 and 4 vCPUs, 1, 2 and 4 GB RAM, 10 GB Disk and 1 GB Network, respectively. In terms of the cost of the virtual resources, ElasticHosts

[27] and VMware [28] prices are followed: where 1 vCPU = £0.008/hr, 1 GB Memory = £0.016/hr, 1 GB Storage = £0.0001/hr, 1 GB Network = £0.0001/hr; and the cost of Energy = £0.14/kWh [21].

In terms of the workload patterns, Cloud applications can experience different workload patterns based on the customers' usage behaviours, and these workload patterns consume power differently based on the resources they utilise. There are several workload patterns, such as *static, periodic, continuously changing, unpredicted*, and *once-in-a-life-time*, as stated in [23]. This paper considers the periodic workload pattern as this work is driven towards solving the issue of the performance variation.

Thus, a number of direct experiments have been conducted to synthetically generate periodic workload by using Stress-ng [2] tool in order to stress all resources (CPU, RAM, Disk and Network) on different types of VMs. The generated workload of each VM type has four time intervals of 30 min each. The first three intervals will be used as the historical data set for prediction, and the last interval will be used as the testing data set to evaluate the predicted results.

# 5 Results and Discussion

This section presents the evaluation of the Energy-Aware Cost Prediction Framework. The figures below show the predicted results for three types of VMs, small, medium and large, running on a single PM based on historical periodic workload pattern. Because of space limitation, only large VMs results are shown. As mentioned earlier, the generated VMs workload along with their power consumption and cost for the last interval are used as the testing data set.

Figure 5 (a, b, c and d) depict the results of the predicted versus the actual VMs workload, including CPU, RAM, Disk, and Network usage for the VMs. Despite the periodic utilisation peaks, the predicted VMs' CPU and RAM workload results closely match the actual results, which reflects the capability of the ARIMA model to capture the historical seasonal trend and give a very accurate prediction accordingly. The predicted VMs' Disk and Network workload is also matching the actual workload, but with less accuracy as compared to the CPU and RAM prediction results. This can be justified because of the high variations in the generated historical periodic workload pattern of the Disk and Network not closely matching in each interval, whereas the generated historical periodic workload pattern for the RAM and CPU usage are closely matched in each interval. Beside the predicted mean values, the figures also show the high and low 95% and 80% confidence intervals.

The proposed framework can predict the power consumption for a number of VMs with only a small variation as compared to the actual one as shown in Fig. 5 (e). The predicted power consumption attribution for each VM is affected by the variation in the predicted CPU utilisation of all the VMs, hence the predicted power consumption of the medium VM matches its predicted CPU utilisation as it has the highest variation than the other predicted VMs' CPU utilisation.

In terms of prediction accuracy, a number of metrics have been used to evaluate the results. These metrics include, *Absolute Percentage Error (APE)* which measures the absolute value of the ratio of the error to the actual observed value; *Mean Error (ME)* which measures the average error of the predicted values; *Root Mean Squared Error (RMSE)* which depicts the square root of the variance measured by the mean absolute error; *Mean Absolute Error (MAE)* is the average of the absolute value of the difference between predicted value and the actual value; *Mean Percentage Error (MPE)* is the computed average of percentage errors by which the predicted values vary from the actual values; and *Mean Absolute Percent Error (MAPE)* is the average of the absolute value of the difference between the predicted value and the actual value explained as a percentage of the actual value [22].

This framework is also capable of predicting the total cost for a number of VMs as shown in Fig. 5(f), with 0.06 of APE for predicted total cost of the large VM, 17.23 of APE for the medium VM and 14.7 of APE for the small VM as shown in Fig. (6).

The accuracy of the predicted VMs workload (CPU, RAM, Disk, Network) and their power consumption based on periodic workload is evaluated using these accuracy metrics, as summarised in Table 1. In addition, Fig. (6) shows the results of the predicted versus the actual total cost for all VMs with the absolute percent error for the predicted total cost. Despite the high variation of the workload utilisation in the

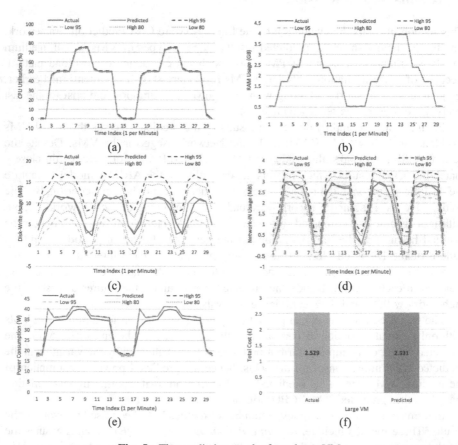

**Fig. 5.** The prediction results for a large VM.

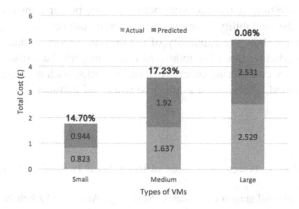

**Fig. 6.** The predicted versus the actual VMs total cost.

**Table 1.** Prediction accuracy for a large VM.

| Parameters | ME | RMSE | MAE | MPE | MAPE |
|---|---|---|---|---|---|
| CPU Utilisation | 0.03765 | 0.299769 | 0.137823 | 0.309809 | 6.615192 |
| RAM Usage | 0.000004 | 0.008671 | 0.002587 | −0.00675 | 0.107601 |
| Disk-Write Usage | 0.1838898 | 1.116114 | 0.733408 | 0.924781 | 12.64005 |
| Network-IN Usage | 0.0657477 | 0.225631 | 0.132185 | −6.13982 | 17.56377 |
| Power Consumption | 1.648176 | 2.617798 | 1.648176 | 4.358135 | 4.358135 |

periodic pattern, the accuracy metrics indicate that the predicted VMs workload and power consumption achieve good prediction accuracy along with the predicted total cost.

# 6   Conclusion and Future Work

This paper has presented and evaluated a new Energy-Aware Cost Prediction Framework that predicts the total cost of VMs by considering the resource usage and power consumption of heterogeneous VMs based on their usage and size, which reflect the physical resource usage by each VM. A number of direct experiments were conducted on a local Cloud Testbed to evaluate the capability of the prediction models. Overall, the results show that the proposed Energy-Aware Cost Prediction Framework can predict the resource usage, power consumption and the total cost for the VMs with a good prediction accuracy based on periodic Cloud workload patterns.

Unlike other existing works, this approach considers the heterogeneity of VMs with respect to predicting the resource usage, power consumption and the total cost.

In future work, we intend to extend our approach and integrate it with performance prediction models to determine the costs of different scenarios. Besides, further investigation will focus on VM performance prediction models, dynamic placement of

VMs, and demonstration of the trade-off between cost, power consumption and performance. Also, the scalability aspects with different prediction algorithms will be considered to further show the capability of the proposed work. Finally, as this paper has focused on predicting the VMs total cost based on periodic workload pattern, we aim to extend this by considering other workload patterns, such as static, continuously changing, unpredicted, and once-in-a-life time workload patterns.

# References

1. Narayan, A., Rao, S.: Power-aware cloud metering. IEEE Trans. Serv. Comput. **7**(3), 440–451 (2014)
2. Stress-ng. http://kernel.ubuntu.com/∼cking/stress-ng/. Accessed 19 Feb 2017
3. Berndt, P., Maier, A.: Towards sustainable IaaS pricing. In: Altmann, J., Vanmechelen, K., Rana, Omer F. (eds.) GECON 2013. LNCS, vol. 8193, pp. 173–184. Springer, Cham (2013). doi:10.1007/978-3-319-02414-1_13
4. Amazon EC2 Service Level Agreement. https://aws.amazon.com/ec2/sla/. Accessed 26 Feb 2017
5. Aldossary, M., Djemame, K.: Energy consumption-based pricing model for cloud computing. In: 32nd UK Performance Engineering Workshop, UKPEW 2016, Bradford, UK, 8–9 September, pp. 16–27 (2016)
6. Alzamil, I., Djemame, K.: Energy prediction for cloud workload patterns. In: Bañares, J., Tserpes, K., Altmann, J. (eds.) GECON 2016. LNCS, vol. 10382, pp. 160–174. Springer, Cham (2013). doi:10.1007/978-3-319-02414-1_13
7. Sunstone Cloud Testbed: OpenNebula.org. http://opennebula.org/. Accessed 20 Feb 2017
8. Horri, A., Dastghaibyfard, G.: A novel cost based model for energy consumption in cloud computing. Sci. World J. **2015**, 724524 (2015)
9. Watt's Up Power Meter: watts up? https://www.wattsupmeters.com/secure/products.php?pn=0. Accessed 20 Feb 2017
10. "Zabbix Monitoring," Zabbix. http://www.zabbix.com/. Accessed 20 Feb 2017
11. Caron, E., Desprez, F., Muresan, A.: Forecasting for grid and cloud computing on-demand resources based on pattern matching. In: Proceedings of 2nd IEEE International Conference on Cloud Computing Technology and Science CloudCom 2010, pp. 456–463 (2010)
12. Wood, T., Cherkasova, L., Ozonat, K., Shenoy, P.: Profiling and modeling resource usage of virtualized applications. In: Issarny, V., Schantz, R. (eds.) Middleware 2008. LNCS, vol. 5346, pp. 366–387. Springer, Heidelberg (2008). doi:10.1007/978-3-540-89856-6_19
13. Altmann, J., Kashef, M.M.: Cost model based service placement in federated hybrid clouds. Futur. Gener. Comput. Syst. **41**(1), 79–90 (2014)
14. Box, G.E.P., Jenkins, G.M., Reinsel, G.C.: Time Series Analysis: Forecasting and Control, 4th edn. Wiley, Hoboken (2008)
15. Box, G.E.P., Cox, D.R.: An analysis of transformations. J. R. Stat. Soc. Ser. B. **26**, 211–252 (1964)
16. Khan, A., Yan, X., Tao, S., Anerousis, N.: Workload characterization and prediction in the cloud: a multiple time series approach. In: Proceedings of the IEEE Network Operations and Management Symposium (NOMS), Maui, HI, April 16–20 (2012)
17. Zhang, X., Lu, J., Qin, X.: BFEPM: "Best Fit Energy Prediction Modeling Based on CPU Utilization". In: 2013 IEEE Eighth International Conference on Networking, Architecture Storage, pp. 41–49 (2013)

18. Dargie, W.: A stochastic model for estimating the power consumption of a processor. IEEE Trans. Comput. **63**, 1311–1322 (2015)
19. Fan, X., Weber, W.-D., Barroso, L.A.: Power provisioning for a warehouse-sized computer. In: Proceedings of the 34th Annual International Symposium on Computer Architecture, pp. 13–23. ACM, New York (2007)
20. Kavanagh, R., Armstrong, D., Djemame, K., Sommacampagna, D., Blasi, L.: Towards an energy-aware cloud architecture for smart grids. In: Altmann, J., Silaghi, G.C., Rana, Omer F. (eds.) GECON 2015. LNCS, vol. 9512, pp. 190–204. Springer, Cham (2016). doi:10.1007/978-3-319-43177-2_13
21. Electricity Price Electricity Price per kWh Comparison of Big Six Energy Companies - CompareMySolar.co.uk Blog. http://blog.comparemysolar.co.uk/electricity-price-per-kwh-comparison-of-big-six-energy-companies/. Accessed 16 Feb 2017
22. Hyndman, R.J., Athanasopoulos, G.: Forecasting: Principles and Practice, OTexts (2017). https://www.otexts.org/fpp/2/5/. Accessed 16 Feb 2017
23. Fehling, C., Leymann, F., Retter, R., Schupeck, W., Arbitter, P.: Cloud Computing Patterns. Springer, New York (2014)
24. Calheiros, R.N., Masoumi, E., Ranjan, R., Buyya, R.: Workload prediction using ARIMA model and its impact on cloud applications' QoS. IEEE Trans. Cloud Comput. **3**, 449–458 (2015)
25. R Core Team: R: A Language and Environment for Statistical Computing. https://www.r-project.org/. Accessed 19 Feb 2017
26. Rackspace, Cloud Servers Pricing and Cloud Server Costs. http://www.rackspace.co.uk/cloud/servers/pricing. Accessed 20 Feb 2017
27. Elastichosts, Pricing - ElasticHosts Linux, Windows VPS Hosting. https://www.elastichosts.co.uk/pricing/. Accessed 16 Feb 2017
28. VMware - OnDemand Pricing Calculator. http://vcloud.vmware.com/uk/service-offering/pricing-calculator/on-demand/. Accessed 16 Feb 2017

# Economic Implications of Energy-Aware Pricing in Clouds

Antonis Dimakis, Alexandros Kostopoulos[✉], and Eleni Agiatzidou

Network Economics and Services Research Group, Department of Informatics,
Athens University of Economics and Business, Athens, Greece
{dimakis, alexkosto, agiatzidou}@aueb.gr

**Abstract.** Cloud computing is a promising approach for delivering ICT services by improving the utilization of data centre resources. One candidate solution for accomplishing energy efficiency within clouds is the adoption of energy-aware pricing by the cloud service providers. In this paper, we compare the economic implications of the choice of pricing schemes under different scenarios.

**Keywords:** Energy-Awareness · Cloud computing · Pricing · Economics

## 1 Introduction

Cloud computing has received considerable attention as a promising approach for delivering ICT services. One candidate solution for accomplishing energy-efficiency is the adoption of energy-aware pricing by the cloud service providers. Charging cloud services based on energy could potentially provide the necessary incentives to the customers for achieving a more efficient resource usage.

Pricing in cloud computing has been studied extensively in the past (see [2] and references therein) and most approaches consist of a combination of a fixed or variable price per VM instance and an additional usage charge based on the actual use of computing resources such as CPU cycles, network bandwidth, memory and storage space. Recently, [3, 4] proposed pricing schemes which incorporate direct energy consumption charges. In [3] the authors do not focus on the economic implications of the proposed scheme, while [4] proposes a demand-response mechanism which the cloud employs to cope with the variability in electricity prices.

In our recent paper [1], we proposed a novel pricing scheme based on energy consumption of cloud resources. In this *two-part tariff energy-based pricing* scheme, the actual form of the price is comprised by two parts: a *fixed* one depending only on static information of a VM, and a *dynamic* one, which depends on its average power usage. For comparison, we have also considered *static pricing*, whereby the price is selected based on VM characteristics and does not vary in time.

To evaluate the effect of pricing, one needs to consider the actions taken by all the economic agents involved. For example, a price increase by an IaaS provider does not necessarily lead to an increase in its profits, as the demand of applications for VMs might drop considerably. For this reason, we consider a microeconomic model, which

C. Pham et al. (Eds.): GECON 2017, LNCS 10537, pp. 132–144, 2017.
DOI: 10.1007/978-3-319-68066-8_11

incorporates the actions of IaaS/PaaS providers, applications and their users. Since an action of any of these agents triggers a chain of subsequent responses by the others, we are interested in determining the equilibrium of such interactions.

The goal of our analysis is to compare the economic implications of the choice of pricing schemes by a service provider. In particular, our aim is to compare the static and energy-based pricing schemes proposed in [1]. To do this we consider models of cloud service providers sharing the same capabilities and the same cost structure, their only difference being the pricing scheme adopted by each. The economic quantities we consider are the level of (i) *profits for each type of provider*, (ii) *payments made by the customers of each provider type*, (iii) *overall satisfaction of the customers of each provider type*. Since the comparison depends on the market structure, we consider the actions of service providers under *monopoly* and *perfect competition*. We prove that charging VM energy in addition to a flat fee per VM, as done by the two-part tariff, is optimal for IaaS/PaaS providers in a monopoly market, as well as under competition. Similarly, we show that the profits of SaaS providers are higher when their applications are energy-aware too.

## 2  Model

**IaaS providers:** each has an infinite number of physical servers at his disposal. Each server is populated by VMs belonging to possibly different applications and the CPU speed is split equally among the VMs. Let $v_i$ be the number of VMs used by application $i$. The provider is able to freely scale, i.e., the server consolidation policy is such that the number of *active* physical servers $m$ scales in proportion to the number of VMs in the infrastructure, i.e., $\sum_i v_i/m = \rho$, where the constant $\rho$ is the *consolidation degree*. If the CPU speed of a physical server is $\mu$ then $\mu/\rho$ is the CPU speed dedicated to each VM running in the infrastructure.

We consider a two-part tariff specified by the parameters $\pi_0, \pi_1$ where $\pi_0$ is the static price (in €/hour) and $\pi_1$ is the energy price (in €/watthour). Notice that a static pricing scheme has $\pi_1 = 0$. The profit per unit of time (in €/hour) for the provider is

$$\pi_0 \sum_i v_i + \pi_1 \sum_i P_i(v_i) - \pi_e \sum_i P_i(v_i) - c(m) \tag{1}$$

where $P_i(v_i)$ is the average power (in watts) consumed by the $i$-th application when it uses $v_i$ VMs. $\pi_e$ is the price per watthour charged by the energy provider. $c(m)$ is the per hour maintenance cost involved in operating $m$ servers; we assume it is linear, i.e., $c(m) = cm$ for some constant $c > 0$. More specifically,

$$P_i(v_i) = p_0 m \frac{v_i}{\sum_j v_j} + p_1 \lambda_i(v_i) = \frac{p_0 v_i}{\rho} + p_1 \lambda_i(v_i)$$

where $p_0$ is the host's base power consumption (while no application workload is executed), $p_1$ is the energy in watt hours consumed in the execution of each application request (or per CPU instruction) excluding base consumption, and $\lambda_i(v_i)$ is the throughput of application $i$ expressed e.g., in requests (or CPU instructions) per second.

**PaaS providers:** we assume they are not economic agents on their own; rather they follow the strategies of IaaS providers. This is the case for example, when the PaaS layer is offered by the same economic entity, which offers the IaaS. Thus, whenever we refer to IaaS we mean the combination of IaaS/PaaS. In a more complete model, we would have considered the case where the PaaS providers are separate economic agents, which follow their own strategies.

**User demand for application requests:** each application $i$ has a different throughput demand (rate of instructions or requests to be executed at the VMs of this application) $\lambda_i^{max}$ which decreases to 0 if the average processing delay of each instruction/request becomes too high. In particular, we assume each request derives a benefit $R_i - \beta_i d_i(\lambda_i)$ from its execution, where $R_i, \beta_i$ are constants and $d_i(\lambda_i) = 1/\left(\frac{\mu}{\rho} - \frac{\lambda_i}{v_i}\right)$ is the average processing delay based on an M/M/1 queueing model. According to this model, the benefit decreases as response delay increases. If the delay becomes too great, the benefit will become negative and requests will start balking at this point. Thus, either $R_i > \beta_i d_i(\lambda_i^{max})$ and $\lambda_i(v_i) = \lambda_i^{max}$, or $R_i = \beta_i d_i(\lambda_i(v_i))$, i.e., $\lambda_i(v_i) = \left(\frac{\mu}{\rho} - \frac{\beta_i}{R_i}\right)v_i$. More compactly: $\lambda_i(v_i) = \min\left\{\left(\frac{\mu}{\rho} - \frac{\beta_i}{R_i}\right)v_i, \lambda_i^{max}\right\}$.

**Applications:** Consider application $i$ employing $v_i$ VMs. The profit per unit of time for the SaaS provider of this application is assumed to be given by $r_i\lambda_i(v_i) - \pi_0 v_i - \pi_1 P_i(v_i)$, where $\pi_0, \pi_1$ are the parameters of the two-part tariff employed by the IaaS provider, $\lambda_i(v_i)$ is the throughput of requests served by application $i$, and $r_i$ is the revenue per completed request (e.g., in €/request).

The application decides how many VMs to buy from a particular IaaS provider such that its profit is maximized. Observe that it will never use more than $\lambda_i^{max}/\left(\frac{\mu}{\rho} - \frac{\beta_i}{R_i}\right)$ VMs needed to attain the maximum demand, since additional VMs only increase payments to the IaaS provider without a corresponding increase in application revenues. Thus the profit maximization problem for the SaaS provider of the $i$-th application is:

$$\max r_i\lambda_i(v) - \pi_0 v - \pi_1 P_i(v)$$
$$\text{over } \quad 0 \le v \le \lambda_i^{max}/\left(\frac{\mu}{\rho} - \frac{\beta_i}{R_i}\right) \tag{2}$$

Since $\lambda_i(v), P_i(v)$ are linear functions of $v$ in $0 \le v \le \lambda_i^{max}/\left(\frac{\mu}{\rho} - \frac{\beta_i}{R_i}\right)$, the optimal number $v_i(\pi_0, \pi_1)$ of VMs is either 0 or $\lambda_i^{max}/\left(\frac{\mu}{\rho} - \frac{\beta_i}{R_i}\right)$. It is nonzero whenever the slope of the objective function in (3) is nonnegative, i.e.,

$$r_i\left(\frac{\mu}{\rho} - \frac{\beta_i}{R_i}\right) \ge \pi_0 + \pi_1\left[\frac{p_0}{\rho} - p_1\left(\frac{\mu}{\rho} - \frac{\beta_i}{R_i}\right)\right] \tag{3}$$

In this idealized model, the number of VMs $v$ can take any real positive value. Although this is done for simplicity, we note that a discrete model would not add anything important to our understanding, as we are mainly interested in fundamental properties of these systems. Apart from that, a continuous model is accurate for applications using a large number of VMs.

In Sect. 3, we first analyse whether energy-awareness of IaaS/PaaS providers is profitable for IaaS/PaaS and SaaS providers in the case where the latter are not energy-aware in the sense that they do not take decisions (e.g., which tasks to schedule on which VMs) on the basis of energy consumption. (Note however that they do get to decide which IaaS/PaaS provider to use on the basis of total price charged; this depends on whether the pricing scheme is energy-based or not). Section 4 considers whether energy-awareness of SaaS providers is profitable for both themselves and IaaS/PaaS providers.

## 3    Energy-Awareness of IaaS/PaaS Providers

### 3.1    Monopoly

Since the two-part tariff has two degrees of freedom while the static pricing scheme is one-dimensional (since $\pi_1 = 0$), the maximum profit achieved by an IaaS/PaaS provider acting as a monopolist is never below its profits if a static pricing scheme is used instead.

Actually, *a two part tariff yields strictly higher profits* as the following simple example shows. Consider the case of two applications with the parameters $\pi_e, p_0, p_1, \rho, \mu, \beta_i, R_i, r_i$ satisfying

$$\pi_e\left(\frac{p_0}{\rho} - p_1\left(\frac{\mu}{\rho} - \frac{\beta_2}{R_2}\right)\right) > r_2\left(\frac{\mu}{\rho} - \frac{\beta_2}{R_2}\right) > r_1\left(\frac{\mu}{\rho} - \frac{\beta_1}{R_1}\right) > \pi_e\left(\frac{p_0}{\rho} - p_1\left(\frac{\mu}{\rho} - \frac{\beta_1}{R_1}\right)\right)$$

Let us compute the profits of a monopolist using the static pricing scheme (where $\pi_1 = 0$) due to application 2:

$$\pi_0 v_2 - c\frac{v_2}{\rho} - \pi_e\left[p_0\frac{v_2}{\rho} + p_1 v_2\left(\frac{\mu}{\rho} - \frac{\beta_2}{R_2}\right)\right] \leq r_2 v_2\left(\frac{\mu}{\rho} - \frac{\beta_2}{R_2}\right) - \pi_e\left[p_0\frac{v_2}{\rho} + p_1 v_2\left(\frac{\mu}{\rho} - \frac{\beta_2}{R_2}\right)\right]$$

$$\leq r_2 v_2\left(\frac{\mu}{\rho} - \frac{\beta_2}{R_2}\right) - \pi_e\left[p_0\frac{v_2}{\rho} - p_1 v_2\left(\frac{\mu}{\rho} - \frac{\beta_2}{R_2}\right)\right]$$

where the first inequality follows from (3) if $v_2 > 0$. (If $v_2 = 0$ then the profits due to application 2 are obviously zero). By our selection of parameter values, the profits due to 2 are strictly negative if $v_2 > 0$. Thus, a monopolist who uses static pricing clearly would not want to serve application 2 since he will suffer losses.

Now if application 1 demands a positive number of VMs under static pricing, condition (3) (with $\pi_1 = 0$) implies $r_1\left(\frac{\mu}{\rho} - \frac{\beta_1}{R_1}\right) \geq \pi_0$ holds. But then $r_2\left(\frac{\mu}{\rho} - \frac{\beta_2}{R_2}\right) > \pi_0$ must also hold, i.e., application 2 also demands a strictly positive number of VMs.

Thus under the static pricing scheme, (3) implies that it is not possible to avoid including application 2.

This does not happen under a two-part tariff with $\pi_0 = 0, \pi_1 > \pi_e$, since then $\pi_1(p_0/\rho - p_1(\mu/\rho - \beta_2/R_2)) > r_2(\mu/\rho - \beta_2/R_2)$ (i.e., application 2 is excluded) but $r_1(\mu/\rho - \beta_1/R_1) > \pi_e(p_0/\rho - p_1(\mu/\rho - \beta_1/R_1))$ (i.e., application 1 is included) and so strictly higher profits result.

As a numerical exposition, we evaluate the profits of a monopolistic provider given by (1), under two scenarios: in the first the provider employs a two-part tariff, while in the second it uses a static price. The parameter values are $R_1 = R_2 = 20, r_1 = r_2 = 1.5, \rho = 10, \pi_e = 0.285, p_0 = 10, p_1 = 5, \lambda_1^{max} = \lambda_2^{max} = 50, \mu = 50, c = 0$.

Figure 1(a) depicts the profits as a function of the maximum average request response delay tolerated by the users of application 1 (normalized by the max tolerated delay for application 2). The profits brought by the two-part tariff are always greater than those brought by the static pricing scheme. They coincide only if the quality-of-service characteristics of the two applications are the same. The greater the diversity between the applications is, the greater the difference in their profits.

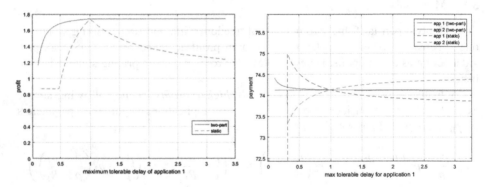

**Fig. 1.** (a) IaaS provider profits in a monopoly – Using a two-part tariff incorporating energy charges (solid curve), and a static pricing (dashed); (b) Comparison of payments by two applications to IaaS providers as a function of application QoS diversity.

## 3.2    Competition

In this section we show that for an IaaS/PaaS provider, *charging VM energy in addition to a flat fee per VM, as done by the two-part tariff, is optimal under competition*: at equilibrium prices only this type of IaaS/PaaS providers offers the maximum possible profits to SaaS providers without suffering losses (i.e., negative profits) himself.

Under ideal competition without entry costs, no IaaS provider is able to make strictly positive profits because in that case he is left without demand. This is because the demand is attracted by other providers, which choose to operate at a smaller albeit nonzero profit margin by slightly reducing their prices. Thus at market equilibrium, competitive IaaS/PaaS providers obtain zero profits and barely cover their costs. Since we are interested in comparing the effect of the pricing scheme on competition, we will compare IaaS providers under the same characterizing parameters (i.e. $\rho, \mu, p_0, p_1$)

except those concerning their pricing scheme. Further, we assume that all IaaS providers face the same maintenance and energy costs, i.e., the $c, \pi_e$ parameters are common.

We say that the IaaS provider is *competitive for applications of type i* if he makes zero profits from applications of this type, i.e., $\pi_0 v_i + \pi_1 P_i(v_i) = \frac{c}{\rho} v_i + \pi_e P_i(v_i)$ for any $v_i > 0$ with $v_i \le \lambda_i^{max}/(\mu/\rho - \beta_i/R_i)$. (Since the profits from application $i$ are linear in $v_i$, it suffices that the previous equality holds for a single $v_i$ for it to hold over the entire range.) Observe that from application types for which an IaaS provider is competitive, the latter is able to attract a nonzero demand. This is because any application of this type pays exactly the minimum possible costs, as all IaaS providers have the same characteristics (apart of their pricing scheme). Thus, if an IaaS/PaaS provider charges prices $\pi_0 = c/\rho, \pi_1 = \pi_e$, i.e., charging by the true factor cost he is facing his own, he is competitive for any application irrespective of its type. This is obvious as the equation defining competitiveness is trivially satisfied for any application. In this tariff, the true energy price is passed onto the application, while the flat fee part covers the per server maintenance costs.

In contrast, IaaS providers, which use static pricing, can only be competitive for a single application type in general. This follows since $\pi_0 v_i = v_i c/\rho + \pi_e P_i(v_i)$ is possible only for $\pi_0 = c/\rho + \pi_e(p_0/\rho + p_1(\mu/\rho - \beta_i/R_i))$, using the definitions of $P_i(v_i), \lambda_i(v_i)$. Thus, the only static price which makes the IaaS provider competitive to application $i$ depends on the application type through $\beta_i/R_i$. This means that the static price used by IaaS providers not charging energy, targets competition for a narrow set of applications. In order for these providers to attract more application types they need to offer multiple statically priced plans so that applications can select the one who find more profitable. This is essentially a pricing strategy which tries to emulate energy-based pricing using application-level information (i.e., $\beta_i/R_i$) which the IaaS provider is difficult to obtain or guess. In contrast, true energy-based pricing which uses application-independent prices is a more robust strategy by relying on industry-wide factor costs.

As an exposition of the competition between IaaS providers and the effect of the pricing scheme, we consider an example, which examines the profits of two applications as a function of their diversity. We assume the users of the applications do not tolerate average request response delays above some value, which is specific to each application. Figure 1 (b) depicts the payments per time unit incurred by each application under two different pricing schemes: i) the static price scheme, which does not take energy consumption into account, and ii) the two-part, which incorporates energy consumption. The parameter values used are $R_1 = R_2 = 20, r_1 = r_2 = 1.5, \rho = 10, \pi_e = 0.285, p_0 = 10, p_1 = 5, \lambda_1^{max} = \lambda_2^{max} = 50, \mu = 50, c = 0$. The price parameters of each scheme are chosen under the assumption of ideal competition, i.e., they are chosen as described in the previous section. The horizontal axis represents the maximum tolerable delay by users of application 1 (normalized to that of application 2).

For stringent delay requirements, when max tolerable delay is less than 0.3, application 1 does not at all use the provider with static pricing since the high costs outweigh benefits. The latter hosts application 2 only, at a competitive price. When the delay requirements of application 1 are not so stringent, the demand rises and application 1 starts using the static provider, but at a cost which is not competitive: application 1 payments exceed the ones offered by the provider employing a two-part tariff. As applications become less diverse (i.e., max tolerable delay close to 1) the two providers are equally attractive, although the provider offering the two-part tariff is slightly more. For values of the max tolerable delay above 1, the less tolerable users belong to application 2 now, and they bare most of the costs in both providers. Nevertheless, the static provider continues not to be competitive as the payments resulting for application 2 exceed those by the provider employing the two-part tariff.

In Fig. 2 the aggregate profits over all applications is depicted for the two-part tariff and the static pricing scheme. The profits under static pricing may decrease if some applications have stringent delay requirements.

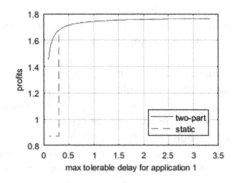

**Fig. 2.** Comparison of SaaS provider profits under IaaS providers competition.

## 4    Energy-Awareness of SaaS Providers

In this section, we analyse whether energy-awareness of SaaS providers is economically sensible. In order to make the effects of energy-awareness clearly visible, we refine the model in Sect. 2 to allow for (i) *physical hosts with different power efficiency*, (ii) *requests with different energy consumption*.

Such situations are quite common; in the sequel we consider the simplest possible case with two different host types (with the one being more power efficient) and two request types (with the one being more energy consuming).

### 4.1    Assumptions

**Host power efficiency:** The efficiency parameters of the two host types are given by (Table 1):

For simplicity, both host types consume the same power while their CPU idles. While active, type $i$ consumes $p_1^i$ extra power where we assume type 1 is more efficient, i.e., $p_1^1 < p_1^2$.

Table 1. Efficiency parameters of the two host types.

| Host type | Idle power consumption | Active power consumption | # of hosts |
|-----------|------------------------|--------------------------|------------|
| 1 | $p_0$ | $p_1^1$ | $H_1$ |
| 2 | $p_0$ | $p_1^2$ | $H_2 = \infty$ |

**VM scheduling:** The fact that type 1 hosts are more power efficient has an implication for the VM scheduling policy of the IaaS provider. Since the latter strives to have minimal energy costs, more power efficient hosts are preferred to less efficient ones. Thus, the VM scheduling will try to allocate type 1 hosts first to meet demand; type 2 hosts will be used only if it is not possible to meet demand only by utilizing type 1 hosts. Since the VM scheduler maintains a fixed number $\rho$ of VMs per host, the maximum number of VMs that can be carried by type 1 hosts is $\rho H_1$. Thus if an application employs $v$ VMs, the number of these hosted in type 1 hosts is $\min(v, \rho H_1)$ while $\max(v - \rho H_1, 0)$ are hosted in type 2 hosts. (This is under the assumption that the VM scheduling algorithm is allowed to freely reallocate all VMs on the available hosts.) Note that if there were an infinite number of hosts for both types, the VM scheduling would never use type 2 hosts. Thus, we assume the number $H_1$ of type 1 hosts is finite. As in Sect. 2, to simplify the analysis the number $H_2$ of type 2 hosts is assumed to be infinite.

**Application request types:** All requests are categorized in two types described by the following parameters (Table 2):

Table 2. Request categorization.

| Request type | Relative power consumption due to a unit rate of requests (normalized to type 2) | Proportion of total requests | Power consumption due to a unit rate of requests |
|--------------|-----------------------------------------------------------------------------------|------------------------------|--------------------------------------------------|
| 1 | $w_1 > 1$ | $\theta_1$ | $p_1^i w_1$ |
| 2 | $w_2 = 1$ | $\theta_2 = 1 - \theta_1$ | $p_1^i w_2$ |

We assume a unit rate of type 1 requests consumes $w_1 > 1$ times the one of type 2. The precise power consumption depends on the host type the request is executed, so the average power consumption is $p_1^i w_1$ if executed on a type $i$ host. Let the total request rate be $\lambda(v)$ when the application employs $v$ VMs, where we have dropped the subscript since we consider a single application. Then the power consumption (excluding idle power) due to type 1 requests is $\theta_1 \lambda(v) p_1^i w_1$ if all were executed on type $i$ hosts. If both host types are used, the average power consumption is given by a corresponding linear combination.

**Request scheduling by the application:** Here we consider the implications in power consumption due to the application being energy-aware or not. First we consider the "legacy" case, where an application has no information about the power consumption of its components. In this case, the application cannot differentiate between the more and less energy consuming request types. Moreover, it cannot have information about the energy efficiency of its VMs. Thus, the requests are scheduled on VMs independently of their type.

Now each VM receives requests of any type at rate $\lambda(v)/v$, where $v$ is the total number of VMs. A proportion $\theta_j$ of those are type $j$, and so their power consumption is $p_1^i w_j$. Thus the power consumed by a VM (excluding the idle state) running on host type $i$ is $p_1^i \frac{\lambda(v)}{v}(\theta_1 w_1 + \theta_2 w_2)$. Considering the VM scheduling algorithm outlined above, the power consumption $P(v)$ of the entire "legacy" application, including power consumption in the idle state, is:

$$P(v) = \frac{p_0 v}{\rho} + [p_1^1 \min(v, \rho H_1) + p_1^2 \max(v - \rho H_1, 0)] \frac{\lambda(v)}{v} \sum_j \theta_j w_j \qquad (4)$$

Let us now consider how an energy-aware application allocates requests on its VMs. Since type 1 hosts are more power efficient and type 1 requests are more energy consuming (as $w_1 > w_2$), an energy-minimizing scheduling policy ought to place type 1 requests on type 1 hosts and use type 2 hosts only if necessary or for serving (the less consuming) type 2 requests. Under such a policy, the power consumption of the energy-aware application is given by

$$P(v) = p_0 \frac{v}{\rho} + \frac{\lambda(v)}{v} \{\min(\theta_1 v, \rho H_1) p_1^1 w_1 + \max(\theta_1 v - \rho H_1, 0) p_1^2 w_1$$
$$+ [\min(v, \rho H_1) - \min(\theta_1 v, \rho H_1)] p_1^1 w_2 + \max(v - \max(\theta_1 v, \rho H_1), 0) p_2^2 w_2\} \qquad (5)$$

### 4.2  Monopoly

Let $v(\pi_0, \pi_1)$ be the optimal number of VMs requested by the application which is obtained by solving the optimization problem (3), where we have dropped the subscript since we have only one application. The IaaS/PaaS provider chooses prices $\pi_0, \pi_1$ which maximize his profits, i.e., he solves:

$$\max \pi_0 v(\pi_0, \pi_1) + \pi_1 P(v(\pi_0, \pi_1)) - c \frac{v(\pi_0, \pi_1)}{\rho} - \pi_e P(v(\pi_0, \pi_1))$$

$$\text{over } \pi_0, \pi_1 \geq 0$$

In Fig. 3 (a), we numerically solve the above problem and depict the maximum profits for the monopolist as a function of the number of power efficient hosts $H_1$. All curves in Fig. 3 (a) were produced under the parameters: $p_0 = 1$, $p_1^1 = 1$, $p_1^2 = 3$, $w_1 = 3$, $w_2 = 1$, $\theta_1 = 0.5$, $\rho = 0.5$, $\mu = 1$, $\lambda^{max} = 50$, $\beta = 1$, $R = 2$, $r = 1$, $c = 0.1$.

The solid curve corresponds to the case where the application is energy aware, and the dashed curve is for a "legacy" application. Energy awareness at the application level increases profits for any choice of parameters. The relative increase is at most 10%, when the energy price of the energy provider is $\pi_e = 0.05$. For cheaper energy, energy-awareness brings a smaller profit increase to the IaaS/PaaS provider.

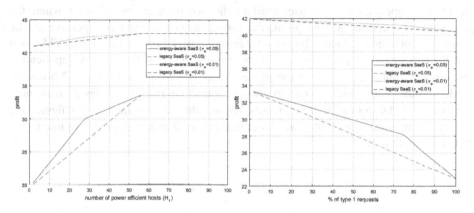

**Fig. 3.** (a) IaaS/PaaS provider profits in the case of monopoly as a function of the number of power efficient hosts; (b) IaaS/PaaS provider profits in a monopoly as a function of the workload mix.

For low numbers of type 1 hosts, the profits are almost identical as the majority of VMs are hosted in type 2 hosts. As the number of type 1 hosts increases, the energy-saving effect of the scheduling of requests performed by the application becomes more significant. Beyond $H_1 = 55$ there is no profit difference as all requests are served by type 1 hosts and request scheduling does not have any effect, since VM scheduling makes sure only the power efficient hosts are utilized.

It is interesting to see where the profit increase is coming from: is it because applications need to pay more or it is mostly due to a decrease in energy costs? For all parameters in Fig. 3 (a) the applications' payments are constant (and equal to 50), so the difference in profits is due to energy savings. The magnitude of the savings seems to be greater for higher energy costs ($\pi_e = 0.05$ case).

In Fig. 3 (b), we again compare profits but now as a function of the percentage of energy consuming requests, i.e., the parameter $\theta_1$ as it ranges from 0 to 1, for $H_1 = 50$. Type 1 requests can be thought as being more CPU intensive (since they consume more energy), while type 2 as more RAM intensive. Therefore, Fig. 3 (b) shows the effect of the workload mix in profits.

All profits are decreasing in $\theta_1$ as type 1 requests are more energy consuming. Again, *the profits with energy-aware applications are higher*. The relative profit increase due to energy-awareness is observed at approximately $\theta_1 \approx 73\%$, which involves a mix of both request types.

Figure 4 (a) depicts IaaS/PaaS provider profits in a monopoly for energy-aware (solid curves) and "legacy" (dashed) SaaS providers, as a function of how much more energy consuming type 1 requests are relative to type 2, i.e., the $w_1$ parameter. The profit difference increases as the energy difference between the request types increases. At $w_1 = 10$ the profit gain due to energy awareness is 20%.

In Fig. 4 (b), we show the profits as the function of the power consumption of type-2 hosts, i.e., the parameter $p_1^2$. As $p_1^2$ increases, so type-2 hosts become less efficient, the profit gain (for IaaS providers when hosting energy-aware with respect to legacy SaaS applications) increases until a deflection point around $p_1^2 = 5.6$ where the gain start to decrease. At this point, the type-2 hosts become too expensive so the "legacy" application (which is hit most by energy costs) drops its demanded VMs such that it ceases to use type-2 hosts. (This is why the profit of the "legacy" application remains constant after $p_1^2 = 5.6$: the $p_1^1$ parameter is constant and no type-2 hosts are used.) On the other hand, the energy-aware application always satisfies its maximum demand $\lambda^{max}$. Of course, if $p_1^2$ increases beyond the range shown in the figure, the energy-aware application will lower its demand as well and meet the profit line of the "legacy" application.

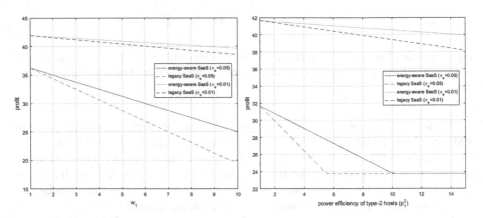

**Fig. 4.** (a). IaaS/PaaS provider profits in a monopoly as a function of $w_1$; (b) IaaS/PaaS provider profits as a function of the power efficiency of type 2 hosts.

Given the attractive properties for the IaaS/PaaS provider that application level energy awareness has, we conclude that he has the incentive of sharing some of the cost involved for the applications to adopt energy-aware technologies. In particular, the introduction of energy awareness at the application level can have important (up to 20%) gains in IaaS/PaaS provider profitability, and does not increase the payments made by applications to IaaS compared to the "legacy" case. Additionally, the profit gains are due to energy savings resulting from scheduling diverse requests to diverse hosts, executed by the application. The more diverse the requests and hosts are the more significant the effect of application-level scheduling becomes. Finally, when either the requests consume similar energies, or the hosts have similar power efficiencies, the additional optimization performed by application does not have a significant effect.

### 4.3 Competition

When IaaS/PaaS providers compete with each other with no entry costs, they have zero profit margins as explained in Sect. 3. Applications however have strictly positive profits and we will see that their profits increase by being energy-aware. As the analysis of the competitive case in Sect. 3 does not depend on the precise form of power consumption function $P(v)$, the same results regarding equilibrium prices carry over to the present case, i.e., the market prices are $\pi_0 = c/\rho$, $\pi_1 = \pi_e$.

Given the market prices, an application solves problem (3) for $\pi_0 = c/\rho$, $\pi_1 = \pi_e$ to obtain the maximum profits. We show that (4) is greater than (5) for any $v$, and so energy-awareness increases application profits. Notice that one can move from the legacy allocation of type 1 requests, where these are distributed equally among all VMs (irrespective of the host they are running on), to the allocation produced by energy-awareness, by shifting small loads of type 1 requests that reside on any VMs on type 2 hosts to VMs on type 1 hosts. If we move a small load $\epsilon$ then the change in the total power is $-p_1^2 \epsilon w_1 + p_1^1 \epsilon w_1$. To keep the load of each VM balanced, the previous shift is complemented by another shift of size $\epsilon$ in the reverse direction, of type 2 requests from the VM running on the type 1 host to the VM on the type 2 host. The change in the power due to the reverse move is $-p_1^1 \epsilon w_2 + p_1^2 \epsilon w_2$. The total power difference is $-p_1^2 \epsilon w_1 + p_1^1 \epsilon w_1 - p_1^1 \epsilon w_2 + p_1^2 \epsilon w_2 = \epsilon(w_2 - w_1)(p_1^2 - p_1^1) < 0$, since $w_2 \langle w_1, p_1^2 \rangle p_1^1$. Thus, the total move yields a decreased power and so (4) is greater than (5). We conclude that *application level energy-awareness increases applications' profits*. To get a sense of the magnitude of the profit increase we numerically evaluate profits.

In Fig. 5 (a), we show the application profits for energy-aware and "legacy" applications. As expected by the previous argument, the profits of energy-aware applications surpass those of "legacy". (The parameters values were the same as those in the previous section). The maximum gain (of about 11%) is obtained for high energy costs, $\pi_e = 0.05$. The gain is marginal for low costs such as $\pi_e = 0.01$.

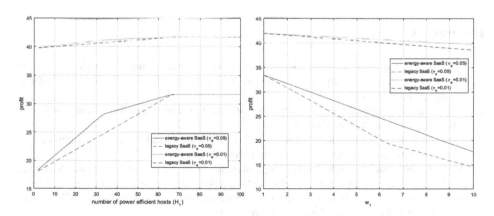

**Fig. 5.** (a) Profits of energy-aware (solid curve) and "legacy" applications (dashed) in competitive markets for IaaS/PaaS; (b) Application profits as a function of energy consumption of type-1 requests.

In Fig. 5 (b), we show application's profits as a function of energy consumption of type 1 requests. The profit gain becomes marginal for homogenous requests. Notice though that there is a saturation effect for $\pi_e = 0.05$ around $w_1 = 6.3$: for too large values of $w_1$ the energy savings due to utilization of type 1 hosts are dominated by the high energy consumption of type 1 requests on type 2 hosts. In this case, the number of type 1 hosts is too small to completely avoid the high energy consumed by type 1 requests.

We observe that in competitive markets for IaaS/PaaS, energy aware applications extract higher profits from energy-based scheduling of requests, and the profit gain is higher if the request energy characteristics are more diverse. Thus, applications themselves would want to adopt energy-based technologies because they become more profitable if IaaS/PaaS charge according to energy consumption.

## 5    Conclusions

In this paper, we considered a mathematical model of applications and IaaS/PaaS providers and showed that applications which adapt to energy-based information and the proposed energy-based pricing schemes by appropriately scheduling requests to VMs, extract higher profits compared to being non-adaptive. Although the model is a gross simplification of reality, it is valuable in that it clearly shows the potential economic benefits for applications to respond to appropriate pricing signals. Thus, it is not only that applications become more power efficient once they utilize an energy-aware framework (e.g., ASCETiC [5]), but they have an economic incentive to utilize it. We saw that IaaS/PaaS providers are the likely first adopters of energy-aware layers as it increases their profits even when the application providers are not energy-aware. Even if the aforementioned analysis shows that if SaaS providers adopt the energy-aware SaaS layer they will also see their profits increase, this does not mean that they will adopt an energy-aware framework as they have no means of evaluating the benefit of doing so. Our future work focuses on defining a more complete model, considering the case where the PaaS providers are separate economic agents.

## References

1. Kostopoulos, A., Agiatzidou, E., Dimakis, A.: Energy-aware pricing within cloud environments. In: Bañares, J., Tserpes, K., Altmann, J. (eds.) GECON 2016. LNCS, vol. 10382. Springer, Cham (2016)
2. Al-Roomi, M., Al-Ebrahim, S., Buqrais, S., Ahman, I.: Cloud computing pricing models: a survey. Int. J. Grid Distrib. Comput. 6(5) (2013)
3. Aldossary, M., Djemame, K.: Consumption-based pricing model for cloud computing. In: 32nd Performance Engineering Workshop, Bradford, UK (2016)
4. Wang, C., Nasiriani, N., Kesidis, G., Urgaonkar, B., Wang, Q., Chen, L., Gupta, A., Birke, R.: Recouping energy costs from cloud tenants: tenant demand response aware pricing design. In: Proceedings ACM 6th International Conference on Future Energy Systems. ACM (2015)
5. ASCETiC, EU FP-7 project. http://ascetic-project.eu/

# Resource Management

# Cost Minimization of Virtual Machine Allocation in Public Clouds Considering Multiple Applications

Joaquín Entrialgo[(✉)], José Luis Díaz, Javier García, Manuel García,
and Daniel F. García

University of Oviedo, 33204 Gijón, Asturias, Spain
{joaquin,jldiaz,javier,mgarcia,dfgarcia}@uniovi.es

**Abstract.** This paper presents a virtual machine (VM) allocation strategy to optimize the cost of VM deployments in public clouds. It can simultaneously deal with multiple applications and it is formulated as an optimization problem that takes the level of performance to be reached by a set of applications as inputs. It considers real characteristics of infrastructure providers such as VM types, limits on the number VMs that can be deployed, and pricing schemes. As output, it generates a VM allocation to support the performance requirements of all the applications. The strategy combines short-term and long-term allocation phases in order to take advantage of VMs belonging to two different pricing categories: on-demand and reserved. A quantization technique is introduced to reduce the size of the allocation problem and, thus, significantly decrease the computational complexity. The experiments show that the strategy can optimize costs for problems that could not be solved with previous approaches.

**Keywords:** Cloud computing · Cost optimization · Virtual Machine Allocation · Multi-application

## 1 Introduction

Cloud computing has evolved quickly in recent years, becoming a useful and attractive alternative for deploying new applications. Cloud computing offers almost unlimited computing capacity (scalability), which can be immediately increased or decreased following the users' demand (elasticity). All of these characteristics are available through a "pay-as-you-go" model.

However, users who want to deploy their applications on the cloud have to answer an important question: how much cloud computing power should they hire? Hiring too much means a waste of money; on the other hand, hiring too little may reduce profits or, even worse, incur economic penalties if SLAs are not met. Therefore, there is a broad research in order to answer this question and to find the most cost-effective allocation, such as [1,4–6,9,10,14,15] or [18].

Among the services provided by cloud computing, here we consider Infrastructure as a Service (IaaS), one of the fastest growing fields. Cloud providers

© Springer International Publishing AG 2017
C. Pham et al. (Eds.): GECON 2017, LNCS 10537, pp. 147–161, 2017.
DOI: 10.1007/978-3-319-68066-8_12

offer different Virtual Machine (VM) types (for example, a VM type provided by Amazon EC2 is m4.large, which offers 2 virtual CPUs and 8 GiB of RAM [3]). Moreover, with regard to pricing, VMs can belong to two different categories: on-demand and reserved [2]. Thus, the cost optimization problem is complex. Firstly users have to choose the cloud provider and the datacenters, each of them with different costs, where to carry out their deployments. Then, users should choose the most appropriate VM types to execute their applications. Finally, if the applications will run for a long time, users should consider to take advantage of the lower price of reserved instances.

Therefore, minimizing deployment costs, while guaranteeing the fulfillment of a determined level of performance, is a usual objective of cloud computing users. To achieve this goal, a significant number of VM allocation strategies have been developed.

An allocation strategy produces a VM allocation that represents the number, types and pricing categories of the VMs to be deployed in a given time period. In order to determine the instants in which an allocation strategy is applied, the time is usually divided in regular time slots. A typical length for these slots is one hour, coinciding with the billing period of some important providers, such as Amazon EC2.

VM allocation strategies can be focused in the short or in the long term. A short-term strategy generates an allocation for the next time slot. In contrast, a long-term strategy usually operates with a yearly period, and it generates a VM allocation for each time slot of a year. Short-term strategies rely on on-demand VMs, because these are oriented to be started or stopped as required, following the instant variations of the workload. In contrast, long-term strategies can take advantage of reserved VMs in addition to on-demand VMs. Reserved VMs support the base workload of the applications, and on-demand VMs supplement the computing capacity provided by reserved VMs as required by the application demands.

Long-term strategies have to deal with severe difficulties. The allocation problems to be solved are huge (for example, considering a reservation period of one year and a time slot of one hour, 8760 allocations must be calculated and they can not be solved independently). Moreover, a significant number of VM types may have to be taken into account, so the solution space to be explored for each allocation may be vast, and the limits imposed by providers (that is, the maximum number of VMs that can be deployed in a region or in an availability zone) also hinder the computation of a solution.

A previous VM allocation approach, referred to as LLOOVIA (Load Level based OptimizatiOn for VIrtual machine Allocation) [6], combined a long-term and a short-term strategy, organized in two phases, to take advantage of both reserved and on demand VMs. LLOOVIA is designed to minimize allocation costs, while guaranteeing the fulfillment of a determined level of performance. However, LLOOVIA lacks the ability to deal with multiple applications: it is designed for managing only one application. To overcome this shortcoming, an improved version of LLOOVIA, named MALLOOVIA (Multi-Application Load

Level based OpimizatiOn for Virtual Machine Allocation), has been designed and is presented in this paper.

MALLOOVIA can deal with multiple applications, each one of them considered perfectly scalable by horizontal replication. MALLOOVIA is formulated as an optimization problem that takes the levels of performance to be reached by a set of applications as input, and generates a VM allocation to support the performance requirements of all the applications as output. The generated allocation minimizes the deployment cost of the applications, guaranteeing the required performance for each one of them. The applications managed by MALLOOVIA can be totally independent or can be part of a service. An example of the latter case is a multi-tier service, which can be considered as composed of different applications, corresponding each one of them to a different tier.

The management of multiple applications increases the size of the problems to be solved extraordinarily, and usually problems become intractable. To overcome this shortcoming, MALLOOVIA employs a quantization method that has the ability of reducing the number of performance levels to be dealt with for each application very significantly. This method has proven to be very effective in the experimental cases analyzed with MALLOOVIA.

## 2  Related Work

In this research, we focus on allocation cost minimization, while guaranteeing the fulfilment of performance requirements. We consider the problem of the deployment of several applications, in a multi-cloud environment. In this multi-cloud environment several types of VM, each of them with different prices and performance, can be chosen. Furthermore, cloud providers impose limits to the number of VMs that can be hired by the user. Finally two pricing models are considered, on-demand and reserved instances.

In the literature, there are several papers that approach the cost optimization problem of VM allocation. However, none of them cover all the previously mentioned aspects simultaneously. There are two main approaches to study this problem. They differ on the way they represent the system workload.

There is a first group of papers [5,8,11,12,16,18] where the workload is represented as the number of VMs required in each period, instead of as the arrival rate of requests to the system, which is more frequently used in transactional applications. The approach presented in these works solves only part of the problem, namely, to find the optimal allocation of VMs to providers, but it does not address the issue of determining the appropriate type and number of VMs to support a given arrival rate. This issue is not solved in those papers, because it is assumed to be known in advance.

In [12] the authors develop a heuristic approach to minimize the cost using a single cloud provider. They also consider reserved and on-demand VMs, but they do not consider any VM type distinction or limit. Their model is based on a prediction over historical data, and in a first stage, using this prediction, the number of reserved VMs to hire are estimated. In a second stage, using the real demand, the number of on-demand VMs needed to fulfill the requirements are obtained.

In [5] the authors propose an optimal cloud resource provisioning algorithm whose aim is to minimize the total cost for provisioning resources in a certain time period. The authors consider the cost resulting from both reserved and on-demand resources from multiple clouds. This model is able to manage different types of applications, but each application must be supported by the same VM type, that is, different types of VM cannot be mixed in the same application. In this model, the VMs are specified as a set of resources: computational power, storage, network bandwidth and electricity power, and in the same way, each cloud provider is represented as a pool of these resources. However, nowadays cloud providers offer VMs as a discrete set of configurations called VM types. The algorithm proceeds in two steps: in the first step a prediction of the VM demand is calculated, in the second step the number of reserved VMs to hire is obtained. In this paper, it is not clear how the on-demand VMs needed to cover the real demand are chosen.

The authors of [18] follow the same approach that [5], but with the difference that they rely on a combination of heuristic methods to find the optimal allocation in a reasonable time.

A more limited study can be found in [8], where the authors develop a heuristic to calculate only the number of reserved VM required for a given prediction. The heuristic provides a sub-optimal solution when it supports different reserved VM contracts. This heuristic is limited to only one application, not considering VM types or VM limits.

In [11] the authors apply a stochastic model based on Inventory Theory to find the optimal combination of reserved and on-demand VMs which minimizes the cost. Applying this model, the authors find an equation to calculate the number of reserved VMs to be leased. From this expression, they apply a heuristic process to find a purchase plan. The main drawback of this model is that it is limited to only one application, one VM type and one cloud provider, and the model does not consider any limit in the number of VMs that can be hired.

The last paper in which workload is given as number of required VMs is [16]. The authors propose a global broker which receives the users' demands and allocates them among a set of cloud providers working cooperatively. The proposed method works in two phases. In the first phase the number of reserved VMs needed is obtained, in a similar way to [8]. In the second phase, a heuristic algorithm is executed to minimize the users' usage cost of provisioning on-demand VMs. The main limitations of this work are that it is limited to only one application and it does not support VM types or any kind of limit.

There is a second group of papers [4, 7, 10, 17] where the optimization problem is analyzed considering the workload as an arrival rate of requests that must be served using the allocated VMs. This represents a more common problem of cloud resource optimization.

In [10] the authors study the VM allocation problem for multimedia application providers. The providers aim to minimize the resource cost while meeting the round trip time requirements. They propose two optimal schemes for VM allocation for both single-site and multi-site clouds. In this work, both reserved and on-demand pricing schemes are considered, but the number of reserved VMs is known and fixed at the beginning of the algorithm. The algorithm only decides how many of them are used. This is not a valid approach because reserved VMs imply an initial cost, whether the VMs are used or not.

In [7] the authors investigate the time-cost optimization problem of tasks with deadline taking advantage of reserved VMs. They present two solutions: the cost optimization problem, where they look for the cheapest allocation, and the time optimization problem, where for a given budget, they find the allocation with the best processing time. This work considers only an application and it is guided by the VM leasing time, more than VM types or limits.

In [4] the authors present a model that optimizes the cost of a deployment of a multi-site application in a multi-cloud environment. The model considers both reserved and on-demand VMs and their pricing schemes. However, it only uses one application and one VM type in the analysis.

In [17] the authors propose a cloud brokerage service that aggregates the cloud user demands to take advantage of cheaper prices of reserved VMs. The service handles the cloud user demands with a pool of VMs that are either reserved or launched on-demand. The aim is to minimize the cost using as few on-demand VMs as possible. This work is limited to one VM type and only one cloud provider.

Finally, the most related work is [6]. This work covers all the characteristics considered here, except that it only deals with a single application. The objective of our paper is to extend [6] to solve the cost optimization problem when several applications have to be allocated on the same cloud resources.

In the literature there are only two similar works [9,15] that consider cost optimization of several applications on a cloud computing environment. However, they are limited by the type of resources they support and they only perform an static (off-line) analysis. Thus, in [9] the authors propose an algorithm that finds the most cost-effective allocation which meets the QoS requirements with the lowest cost. Its main drawbacks are that it is limited to on-demand VMs and it does not take advantage of reserved VMs. Finally, in [15] the authors solve the problem of cost optimization of concurrent services when they are executed on a multi-cloud environment considering different VM types, but as in the previous work it does not take advantage of reserved VMs.

Our paper approaches the cost optimization problem in a more complete way than previous works: it considers several application simultaneously; it can be used in multi-cloud environments; it takes into account how cloud providers support different VM types and their restrictions; and it considers both reserved and on-demand price schemes.

# 3   System Model and Resolution

## 3.1   Overview

The model presented in this paper is very similar to the one in [6], but extended to allow multiple applications to be deployed in the same (shared) cloud infrastructure. Most of the concepts and notation in [6] are still relevant, being the main differences: (a) the workload is not longer a single number per timeslot, but a set of numbers, one per application, and (b) the performance of any given instance class (defined later) is not a single number, but also a set of numbers.

The problem to solve is to find, for each timeslot, the number and types of VMs which should be acquired (both reserved and on-demand VMs), to run each of the applications. The number and types of reserved VMs will be fixed after the purchase, and will be the same for all timeslots, while the number and types of on-demand instances will vary. The problem is solved in two phases. Phase I tries to find the optimal number of reserved VMs of each type. This phase requires a long-term prediction of the workload, for the whole reservation period and for each application. This phase is carried out off-line, before the deployment. The result of this phase is used to buy reserved VMs for a whole reservation period. Phase II starts assuming that those reserved VMs are available, and uses a short-term workload prediction for each application, which consists of the expected workload per application, for the next timeslot. During phase II, at each timeslot, the expected workload is supported by a mix of the available reserved VMs, plus some extra on-demand VMs whose number and type is to be found in this second phase.

The problem is complicated by the fact that cloud providers can impose a limit on the maximum number of allocated VMs of each type, or a maximum total number of VMs allocated per region, or a maximum total number of CPU cores allocated per region, or a mix of several of these limits. Since these limits are on the infrastructure, and are not set per application, they make impossible to decompose the problem in several independent problems, one per application.

## 3.2   Infrastructure Model

To unify the different kinds of limits imposed by different cloud providers, we use the concept of **Limiting Set**, denoted by $LS_j$, which are sets in which VMs are deployed and which impose some kind of global limit on the VMs in that set. Each $LS_j$ defines two limits: $LS_j^{vms}$, which is the maximum number of virtual machines which can run simultaneously in $LS_j$, and $LS_j^{cores}$, which is the maximum number of CPU cores which can run simultaneously in $LS_j$.

To unify the different VM types offered by different cloud providers in their different availability zones, and under different pricing schemas, we use the concept of **Instance Class**, denoted by IC. For example, an on-demand c4.large on Amazon EC2 on region us-east-2, is a different instance class than a reserved c4.large on Amazon EC2 on availability zone us-east-1b. For each $IC_i$ the following attributes are defined:

- $p_i$ is the price per time slot of the class. For reserved VMs this price should include the upfront payment prorated over the duration of the reservation period, and the per-hour cost.
- $perf_{ai}$ is the performance of that class when it is used to run the application $A_a$, under the considered kind of load for that application, and expressed in the same units as the load. These values can be obtained via benchmarking or monitoring.
- $rsv_i$ is a boolean denoting whether this instance class is reserved or not.
- $c_i$ is the number of CPU cores provided by this class.
- $ls_i$ is an integer, $j$, which is the index of the $LS_j$ to which this instance class belongs.
- $max_i$ is the maximum number of VMs of this class which can be instantiated in its limiting set. Some cloud providers also impose this kind of restriction, especially for high performance VM types.

Without loss of generality we can divide the set of all $IC_i$ into two disjoint subsets, depending on the value of $rsv_i$. We will use the superindex $^{res}$ to refer to attributes of reserved instance classes and $^{dem}$ for on-demand ones. For example, $p_i^{res}$, $perf_{ia}^{dem}$, etc.

## 3.3 Applications and Workload Model

An application is the software that will be run in the instance classes. It can be thought as the disk image used to boot the VM. For example, one application can be a database and a second application can be a web server. The set of possible applications $A = \{A_1, A_2, ..., A_{N_A}\}$ is fixed. Each application has a different performance for each possible instance class, and this is captured by the attribute $perf_{ia}$ previously seen, which is assumed to be known for all instance classes and applications.

We assume time divided into *slots* of length $t$ (e.g., 1 h), and denote each of these time slots by $t_k$. At any timeslot $t_k$, the workload is a vector $l_k = \{l_{k,1}, l_{k,2}, \ldots, l_{k,N_A}\}$. The component $l_{k,a}$ is the expected workload for application $A_a$ during timeslot $t_k$.

Note that for Phase I the sequence of $l_k$ for all timeslots $t_k$ is required in advance. This is a prediction that we will denote by LTWP (Long Term Workload Prediction). For Phase II, however, only the workload for the next timeslot is required, and we will denote it by STWP (Short Term Workload Prediction).

To reduce the problem size for Phase I we choose to represent the LTWP as a histogram. Given an arbitrary workload vector $L = \{L_1, \ldots, L_{N_A}\}$, the histogram $H(L)$ is the number repetitions of that workload in the LTWP. More formally $H(L) = \sum_{k=1}^{T/t} eq(L, l_k)$, being $eq(x, y) = 1$ if $x = y$, and 0 otherwise.

We define the effective workload, and denote it by $\mathbb{L}$, as the set of all vector loads which appear at least once in the LTWP, or, more formally $\mathbb{L} = \{L : H(L) > 0\}$. Note that, if some $L$ appears twice or more times in the LTWP, then the size of $\mathbb{L}$ will be smaller than the size of LTWP, so this representation saves space, being equal in the worst case (when no workload vector ever repeats).

## 3.4   Optimization Problem for Phase I

The optimization problem can be formulated as an integer linear programming problem, with the unknown integer variables $Y_{ai}$, which is the number of reserved VMs of class $\mathrm{IC}_i^{\mathrm{res}}$ to be purchased at the beginning of the reservation period $T$ to run application $A_a$, and $X_{aiL}$ which is the number of on-demand VMs of class $\mathrm{IC}_i^{\mathrm{dem}}$ to run application $A_a$ to be purchased at any time slot for which the predicted vector load is $\boldsymbol{L}$. Since reserved instances are paid even if not used, the analysis assumes those machines to be always available.

The function to optimize is the cost for the whole reservation period, which can be calculated as:

$$C = \sum_{a=1}^{N_A} \sum_{i=1}^{N^{\mathrm{res}}} Y_{ai} p_i^{\mathrm{res}} T/t + \sum_{a=1}^{N_A} \sum_{i=1}^{N^{\mathrm{dem}}} \sum_{L\in\mathbb{L}} X_{aiL} p_i^{\mathrm{dem}} H(\boldsymbol{L}) \tag{1}$$

This cost is minimized subject to restrictions:

$$\sum_{i=1}^{N^{\mathrm{res}}} \mathrm{perf}_{ai}^{\mathrm{res}} Y_{ai} + \sum_{i=1}^{N^{\mathrm{dem}}} \mathrm{perf}_{ai}^{\mathrm{dem}} X_{aiL} \geq L_a \qquad \forall \boldsymbol{L} \in \mathbb{L}, \forall a = 1, \dots, N_A \tag{2}$$

$$\sum_{a=1}^{N_A} Y_{ai} \leq \max_i^{\mathrm{res}} \qquad \forall i = 1, \dots, N^{\mathrm{res}} \tag{3}$$

$$\sum_{a=1}^{N_A} X_{aiL} \leq \max_i^{\mathrm{dem}} \qquad \forall \boldsymbol{L} \in \mathbb{L}, i = 1, \dots, N^{\mathrm{dem}} \tag{4}$$

$$\sum_{a=1}^{N_A} \sum_{i\in S_j^{\mathrm{res}}} Y_{ai} + \sum_{a=1}^{N_A} \sum_{i\in S_j^{\mathrm{dem}}} X_{aiL} \leq \mathrm{LS}_j^{\mathrm{vms}} \qquad \forall \boldsymbol{L} \in \mathbb{L}, j = 1, \dots, N^{\mathrm{LS}} \tag{5}$$

$$\sum_{a=1}^{N_A} \sum_{i\in S_j^{\mathrm{res}}} c_i Y_{ai} + \sum_{a=1}^{N_A} \sum_{i\in S_j^{\mathrm{dem}}} c_i X_{aiL} \leq \mathrm{LS}_j^{\mathrm{cores}} \qquad \forall \boldsymbol{L} \in \mathbb{L}, j = 1, \dots, N^{\mathrm{LS}} \tag{6}$$

Restriction (2) states that, for each application, the performance given by the solution should be at least equal to the workload for that application, for all predicted workload vectors. Restrictions (3) to (6) represent the limits imposed by cloud providers on the total number of VMs of ech type, the total number of VMs per region and the total number of CPU cores per region, respectively. In the last two restrictions, the symbol $S_j$ represents the set of instance classes which share the same limiting set $\mathrm{LS}_j$, i.e.: $S_j = \{i : \mathrm{ls}_i = j\}$.

## 3.5   Optimization Problem for Phase II

Phase II is very similar to Phase I, but much simpler. The set of equations to solve are the same already seen in Phase I, but now $L$ is a set with a single element: the vector load for the next time slot (STWP).

During Phase II only on-demand instances can be hired, so it is necessary to include new restrictions which fix the number of reserved instances to the values found by Phase I. However, we can allow Phase II to reuse reserved instances for a different application than the one given by the allocation generated in Phase I. This way we can accommodate discrepancies between the long term prediction and the short term prediction (which will be in general more accurate).

To formalize this idea, lets call $Y'_{ia}$ the solution found by Phase I. Then, in Phase II the following restriction is added:

$$\sum_{a=1}^{N_A} Y_{ia} = \sum_{a=1}^{N_A} Y'_{ia} \quad \forall i = 1, \ldots, N^{\text{res}} \tag{7}$$

## 3.6   Solving Strategies and Approximations

The size of the problem in Phase I is usually huge, especially when no workload vector repeats in the LTWP, and thus the size of $\mathbb{L}$ is large. This can be alleviated if the LTWP is approximated by a quantized version.

Formally, given a set of quantization steps $\{Q_a\}$, one per application, the quantized long-term workload prediction, QLTWP, is defined as the sequence of vector loads $\bar{l}_k$, for $k = 1, \ldots, T/t$, being:

$$\bar{l}_k = \{\bar{l}_{ka}\} = \left\{ \left\lceil \frac{l_{ka}}{Q_a} \right\rceil Q_a \right\} \quad a = 1, \ldots, N_A \tag{8}$$

Note that, by taking the ceiling operator, QLTWP is a pessimistic approximation of LTWP, assuming workloads greater than or equal to the ones predicted. This is to ensure that the performance restriction in (2) is still fulfilled.

Since the quantization reduces the number of possible values that the workload can take, it increases the chance of observing repetitions of the same vector load $L$, and thus the histogram of QLTWP, $\bar{H}(L)$, will have a smaller number of non-zero points than $H(L)$, i.e.: the size of the effective quantized workload $\bar{\mathbb{L}}$ will be smaller (or equal in the worst case) than the size of the original effective workload $\mathbb{L}$.

Using QLTWP instead of LTWP the size of the problem can be thus reduced. The quantization steps $\{Q_a\}$ gives us control over the size of the problem, at the cost of possibly introducing suboptimality in the solution.

There is one choice of $\{Q_a\}$ which is particularly intesting because it does not introduce suboptimality in the solution. This is the case in which each $Q_a$ is the greatest common divisor of the performances for that application among all instance classes, i.e.:

$$Q_a = \gcd_i \text{perf}_{ia} \tag{9}$$

Using $Q_a$ chosen as in Eq. (9) the solution of Phase I gives the same values for $Y_{ia}$ than in the case without quantization, but the quantized version is a smaller problem, easier to solve, as shown in the experimental results section.

## 4   Experimental Results

In order to show how the technique proposed in this paper can solve problems that previous state-of-the-art techniques are not able to address, a synthetic case study is presented in this section. In this case study, a hypothetical analytics company uses three applications: a data extraction application that every six hours fetches the data from different external sources, an analysis application that the customers use and a database that is used by the extraction application to save the data and by the analysis application to carry out the analysis.

These three applications are executed in Amazon's EC2 cloud. The analytics company has statistics about the number of expected requests for the next year and wants to obtain the allocation with the minimum cost that fulfills the performance requirements. Figure 1 shows the synthetic workload that has been generated to simulate the statistics from the company. As can be seen the three applications have different request patterns. In particular, the extraction application only executes every six hours; the analysis application exhibits periodic behaviour with daily, weekly and yearly cycles; finally, the database application workload is compounded from the other two application workloads, using different visit ratios to the database.

In order to have real prices and limits, we are going to assume that the applications have to be deployed in region US West (N. California) of Amazon's EC2 cloud, where there are three availability zones. There is a limit of 20 reserved VMs in each zone. In addition, there is a limit of 20 VMs for each type of on-demand instance. In order to provide a variety of options, VM types m3.medium, m3.large, c3.large and c3.xlarge have been selected as possible types to execute the application. Table 1 shows the performances and price for each VM type. The values of the performances have been generated synthetically, but the relation between them follows the relation between ECU (the performance metric used

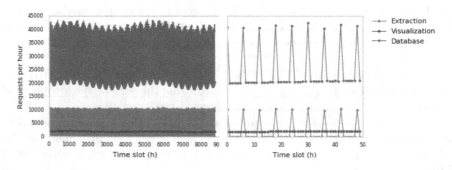

**Fig. 1.** Workload of the case study, for a year (left) and for the first 50 hours (right).

**Table 1.** Performance and price of different VM types.

| VM type | Application performance (rph) | | | Price ($/h) | |
|---|---|---|---|---|---|
| | Extraction | Analysis | Database | On-demand | Reserved |
| c3.large | 5750 | 30 | 18900 | 0.12 | 0.0766 |
| c3.xlarge | 10350 | 50 | 34020 | 0.239 | 0.154 |
| m3.large | 4600 | 20 | 15120 | 0.154 | 0.105 |
| m3.medium | 2300 | 10 | 7560 | 0.077 | 0.0532 |

**Table 2.** Quantization amounts used in phase I.

| Quantization amount | GCD multiplier | Number of variables | Quantization step $Q_a$ (rph) | | |
|---|---|---|---|---|---|
| | | | Extraction | Analysis | Database |
| 0 | N/A | 91632 | None | None | None |
| 1 | 1 | 8544 | 1150 | 10 | 3780 |
| 2 | 3 | 2256 | 3450 | 30 | 11340 |
| 3 | 5 | 1200 | 5750 | 50 | 18900 |
| 4 | 7 | 672 | 8050 | 70 | 26460 |
| 5 | 10 | 720 | 11500 | 100 | 37800 |
| 6 | 15 | 384 | 17250 | 150 | 56700 |

by Amazon) for each type. In addition, compute optimized VM types (c3.large and c3.xlarge) have been given more performance for the analysis application to provide a more interesting case study where different applications behave differently in different VM types.

As the goal of the experimentation is showing how this new technique compares to previous works, the case study has been analyzed with MALLOOVIA and LLOOVIA. However, since LLOOVIA can only handle one application, the three applications have been analyzed independently, generating three solutions, one per application, and the total cost has been computed as the sum of the cost of the three solutions. Notice that, since LLOOVIA considers the limits independently in each application, there is a risk that total number of VMs for the combined solution exceeds the limits, so the solution obtained with LLOOVIA would be unfeasible.

To study how quantization affects the results, the problem has been solved without quantization and with several amounts of quantization using different quantization steps, and to isolate the error introduced by quantization from the error in the workload predictions the same workload has been used as LTWP and STWP. In the first case, the quantization step for each application is the greatest common divisor (GCD) of the performance of each VM type. This quantization step does not introduce error. In the rest of the cases, the quantization step is multiplied by 3, 5, 7, 10 and 15, giving the values shown in Table 2. As can

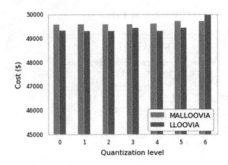
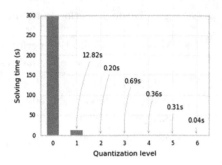

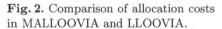

**Fig. 2.** Comparison of allocation costs in MALLOOVIA and LLOOVIA.

**Fig. 3.** Time required for solving phase I of MALLOOVIA.

be seen, increasing the quantization steps reduces the number of variables in the optimization problem for phase I. Using the GCD, the number of variables decreases from 91632 to 8544.

Figure 2 shows that in MALLOOVIA, the cost increases very little when the quantization step is increased (notice that the y axis starts in 45 000). As expected, when the quantization step is the greatest common divisor, the cost is the same as with no quantization. In the worst case, the cost is incremented in less than 0.3%. On the other hand, Fig. 3 shows that the solving time for phase I of MALLOOVIA is greatly reduced using quantization. Using the GCD, the solving time is one order of magnitude smaller than without quantization, but the solution obtained is also optimal.

Figure 2 shows a result that may be unexpected at first: except when the quantization amount is maximum, costs are higher in MALLOOVIA than in LLOOVIA. As it was mentioned before, there is a reason that explains why, in fact, MALLOVIA is better: as LLOOVIA is not prepared for working with several applications, the allocation obtained by combining the three independently generated allocations does not respect the limits imposed by the providers and, thus, is not feasible.

This can be seen in Fig. 4, which shows the number and types of VMs allocated for each application in MALLOVIA and LLOOVIA for the 50 first hours. Reserved VMs are represented with different colors (depending on the type and zone), while on-demand VMs are depicted with levels of grey. It can be seen that LLOOVIA allocates 60 reserved VMs for the analysis application. That is the maximum number of reserved VMs that can be allocated with the 20 limit per region and the three regions available, and it is a valid solution when only that application is taken into account. However, when solving for the database application, LLOOVIA also allocates two reserved VMs, making the combined allocation not compliant with the limits imposed by the provider; thus, the combined solution is unfeasible. On the other hand, MALLOOVIA allocates 60 VMs between the three applications, obtaining a feasible solution.

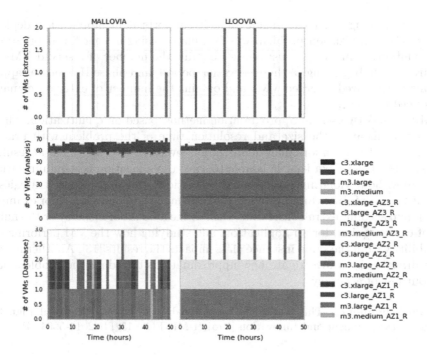

**Fig. 4.** Comparison of number of VMs allocated in MALLOOVIA and LLOOVIA. In the legend, the suffix "_R" indicates that the VM is reserved and "_AZn" indicates that it is deployed in availability zone $n$.

In addition, MALLOVIA has another advantage: if for any time-slots the STWP for an application were smaller than the LTWP, some reserved instances for that application would not be needed and could be reused for another application, avoiding to hire new on-demand VMs and, thus, reducing the cost.

This case study has demonstrated that MALLOOVIA can solve problems that strategies not prepared for multi-applications solve incorrectly. In addition, it has shown that using quantization the solving time can be significantly reduced without increasing the cost significantly.

## 5    Conclusions and Future Work

In this paper we have presented the MALLOOVIA allocation strategy. It enables the cloud user to find the most economical allocation that meets performance when the user wants to deploy several applications running simultaneously and for a long time period.

MALLOOVIA succeeds in representing the real characteristics found in the cloud market: different cloud providers, several types of VMs, constraints imposed by the providers to the number of VMs that can be simultaneously hired and pricing schemes. In addition, it supports multi-application deployments. The optimization problem was formulated using integer linear programming and solved in two phases: phase I obtains the number of reserved VMs to be hired at the beginning of the reservation period, and phase II allocates applications to the hired reserved VMs and obtains the number of extra on-demand VMs needed at each time slot.

MALLOOVIA uses an approximation method based on quantization, which reduces significantly the size and resolution time of the problem with practically no cost deviation for small quantization levels. In the experimental results, this strategy has shown that it is able to solve the allocation cost-minimization problem without violating the imposed restrictions, unlike previous strategies.

Future work focuses on improving the realism of the cloud model, for example taking into account extra constraints, such as the amount of memory or the number of cores required for an application, and studying how the VM performance variability within the same instance class impacts the results [13]. Another future work direction is to investigate new approximations to reduce the problem size without lost of accuracy.

**Acknowledgements.** This work was supported by the Spanish National Plan for Research, Development and Innovation [Project MINECO-15-TIN2014-56047-P].

# References

1. Álvarez, P., Hernández, S., Fabra, J., Ezpeleta, J.: Cost estimation for the provisioning of computing resources to execute bag-of-tasks applications in the amazon cloud. In: Altmann, J., Silaghi, G.C., Rana, O.F. (eds.) GECON 2015. LNCS, vol. 9512, pp. 65–77. Springer, Cham (2016). doi:10.1007/978-3-319-43177-2_5
2. Amazon: Amazon EC2 pricing (2016). https://aws.amazon.com/ec2/pricing/
3. Amazon: Amazon EC2 - instance types (2017). https://aws.amazon.com/ec2/instance-types/
4. Bellur, U., Malani, A., Narendra, N.C.: Cost optimization in multi-site multi-cloud environments with multiple pricing schemes. In: 2014 IEEE 7th International Conference on Cloud Computing, pp. 689–696. IEEE, June 2014
5. Chaisiri, S., Lee, B.S., Niyato, D.: Optimization of resource provisioning cost in cloud computing. IEEE Trans. Serv. Comput. **5**(2), 164–177 (2012)
6. Díaz, J.L., Entrialgo, J., García, M., García, J., García, D.F.: Optimal allocation of virtual machines in multi-cloud environments with reserved and on-demand pricing. Future Gener. Comput. Syst. **71**, 129–144 (2017)
7. Hu, M., Luo, J., Veeravalli, B.: Optimal provisioning for scheduling divisible loads with reserved cloud resources, pp. 204–209. IEEE, December 2012
8. Khatua, S., Sur, P.K., Das, R.K., Mukherjee, N.: Heuristic-based optimal resource provisioning in application-centric cloud. CoRR abs/1403.2508 (2014)
9. Mireslami, S., Rakai, L., Wang, M., Far, B.H.: Minimizing deployment cost of cloud-based web application with guaranteed QoS, pp. 1–6. IEEE, December 2015
10. Nan, X., He, Y., Guan, L.: Optimal allocation of virtual machines for cloud-based multimedia applications. In: 2012 IEEE 14th International Workshop on Multimedia Signal Processing (MMSP), pp. 175–180. IEEE, September 2012

11. Nodari, A., Nurminen, J.K., Frühwirth, C.: Inventory theory applied to cost optimization in cloud computing. In: Proceedings of the 31st Annual ACM Symposium on Applied Computing, pp. 470–473. ACM Press (2016)
12. Orbegozo, I.S.A., Moreno-Vozmediano, R., Montero, R.S., Llorente, I.M.: Cloud capacity reservation for optimal service deployment. In: CLOUD COMPUTING 2011, The Second International Conference on Cloud Computing, GRIDs, and Virtualization, pp. 52–59. IARIA, September 2011
13. O'Loughlin, J., Gillam, L.: Performance evaluation for cost-efficient public infrastructure cloud use. In: Altmann, J., Vanmechelen, K., Rana, O.F. (eds.) GECON 2014. LNCS, vol. 8914, pp. 133–145. Springer, Cham (2014). doi:10.1007/978-3-319-14609-6_9
14. Pietri, I., Sakellariou, R.: Cost-efficient CPU provisioning for scientific workflows on clouds. In: Altmann, J., Silaghi, G.C., Rana, O.F. (eds.) GECON 2015. LNCS, vol. 9512, pp. 49–64. Springer, Cham (2016). doi:10.1007/978-3-319-43177-2_4
15. Ran, Y., Yang, B., Cai, W., Xi, H., Yang, J.: Cost-efficient provisioning strategy for multiple services in distributed clouds, pp. 1–8. IEEE, May 2016
16. Reddy, K.H.K., Mudali, G., Sinha Roy, D.: A novel coordinated resource provisioning approach for cooperative cloud market. J. Cloud Comput. 6(1), 8 (2017)
17. Wang, W., Niu, D., Liang, B., Li, B.: Dynamic cloud instance acquisition via IaaS cloud brokerage. IEEE Trans. Parallel Distrib. Syst. 26(6), 1580–1593 (2015)
18. Yousefyan, S., Dastjerdi, A.V., Salehnamadi, M.R.: Cost effective cloud resource provisioning with imperialist competitive algorithm optimization. In: 2013 5th Conference on Information and Knowledge Technology (IKT), pp. 55–60. IEEE, May 2013

# Client-Side Scheduling Based on Application Characterization on Kubernetes

Víctor Medel[1(✉)], Carlos Tolón[1], Unai Arronategui[1],
Rafael Tolosana-Calasanz[1], José Ángel Bañares[1], and Omer F. Rana[2]

[1] Computer Science and Systems Engineering Department, Aragón Institute
of Engineering Research (I3A), University of Zaragoza, Zaragoza, Spain
{vmedel,unai,rafaelt,banares}@unizar.es, ctolon@hotmail.com
[2] School of Computer Science and Informatics, Cardiff University, Cardiff, UK
ranaof@cardiff.ac.uk

**Abstract.** In container management systems, such as Kubernetes, the scheduler has to place containers in physical machines and it should be aware of the degradation in performance caused by placing together containers that are barely isolated. We propose that clients provide a characterization of their applications to allow a scheduler to evaluate what is the best configuration to deal with the workload at a given moment. The default Kubernetes Scheduler only takes into account the sum of requested resources in each machine, which is insufficient to deal with the performance degradation. In this paper, we show how specifying resource limits is not enough to avoid resource contention, and we propose the architecture of a scheduler, based on the client application characterization, to avoid the resource contention.

**Keywords:** Containers · Scheduling · Resource contention · Resource management

## 1 Introduction

With the advent of the cloud computing paradigm and the emergence of its technologies, computational power can be adjusted on demand to the processing needs of applications. Developers can currently choose among a number of cloud computational resources such as virtual machines (VMs), containers, or bare-metal resources, having each their own characteristics. A VM can be seen as a piece of software that emulates a hardware computing system and typically multiple VMs share the same hardware to be executed. Nevertheless, VM utilization can sometimes be difficult to achieve, e.g. when the applications to run do not consume all the resources of a VM.

Containers are rapidly replacing Virtual Machines (VM) as virtual encapsulation technology to share physical machines [8,16,19,20]. The advantages over VMs are a much faster launching and termination time overheads, and an improved utilization of computing resources. Indeed, the process management origin of

© Springer International Publishing AG 2017
C. Pham et al. (Eds.): GECON 2017, LNCS 10537, pp. 162–176, 2017.
DOI: 10.1007/978-3-319-68066-8_13

container-based systems allows users to adjust resources in a fine-grained fashion more closely with the granularity of many applications enabling single or groups of containers to be deployed on-demand [4]. Finally, container-based platforms, such as Kubernetes, also provide automating deployment and scaling of containerized applications, simplifying the scaling of elastic applications.

Nevertheless, as happened with VMs, containers also exhibit resource contention, which leads to unexpected performance degradation. In general terms, resource contention arises when the computing demand from the applications being executed exceeds the overall computing power of the shared host machine. In particular, resource contention appears in containers, when the demand of multiple containers in the same host machine exceeds the supply, understood in terms of CPU, memory, disk or network. This phenomenon can happen in spite of the isolation mechanisms integrated with container technologies, namely Linux namespaces and Linux Control Groups, which isolate the view of the system and limit the amount of computational resources, respectively. Therefore, the development of applications on these platforms requires new research on scheduling and resource management algorithms that reduces resource contention while maximizes resource utilization. Existing platforms like Kubernetes already incorporate a reservation mechanism in order to reduce resource contention. However, such mechanism is only for CPU and for the maximum amount of memory, and can decrease resource utilization.

In this paper, we propose a client-side scheduling approach in Kubernetes that aims at reducing the resource contention phenomenon in container technologies. Our approach makes use of application characterization in terms of the usage of resources, and extends the Kubernetes scheduler so that it can take better allocation decisions on containers based on such characterization. Our application characterization consists of dividing applications in two categories, namely high and low usage of resources and then, in this early stage work, we delegate the classification process of applications to the client or developer: He or she needs to provide the category which fits better into his/her application. Then, we extend the Kubernetes scheduler behaviour, in essence, we try to avoid that containers wrapping applications with high usage of a resource (i.e. CPU or disk) coincide in the same host machine. Finally, we conducted experiments with real-world applications, such as WordCount and PageRank, in operational stream processing frameworks, such as Thrill [6] and Flink [3], and compared the results with the standard Kubernetes scheduler.

The rest of this paper is structured as follows. In Sect. 2 a brief overview of related work is presented. Section 3 describes basic technological aspects of Docker and Kubernetes, and Sect. 4 shows the effects of resource contention. Section 5 presents our proposed architecture to deal with interference, and shows how an application characterization can help the scheduler to improve overall performance. Finally, our paper ends with conclusions and future work in Sect. 6.

## 2  Related Work

Container scheduling in cloud environments is an emergent research topic. Google has developed and used several schedulers for large scale infrastructures over past years based on a centralized architecture [5,21]. They are oriented for internal global use or as a global service provider. Some works have been proposed to improve the algorithms available as a standard in practical cloud infrastructures, such as Kubernetes[1], Mesos[2] [10] and Docker Swarm[3]. However, in [7], the authors point out the lack of works about resource management with containers, and they propose a scheduling framework that provides useful management functions that can be used to apply customized scheduling policies, mainly, in local environments. We can find few more works that complements to our approach: In [9], the authors propose a generational scheduler to map containers to different generations of servers, based on the requirements and properties learned from running containers. It shows an improved energy efficiency over Docker Swarm built-in scheduling policies. The work in [11] uses an ant colony meta-heuristic to improve application performance, also over Docker Swarm base scheduling policies. In contrast, in our paper, we consider both, resource utilization and application performance. The authors in [2] address the problem of scheduling micro-services across multiple VM clouds to reduce overall turnaround time and total traffic generated. Finally, in [1], the authors introduce a container management service which offers an intelligent resource scheduling that increase deployment density, scalability and resource efficiency. It considers an holistic view of all registered applications and available resources in the cloud. The main difference from our approach is that we focus on the client side requirements to optimize a subset of applications and resources.

Outside the container technologies, similar approaches exist. For instance, CASH [12] is a Context Aware Scheduler for Hadoop. It takes into account the heterogeneity of the computational resources of a Hadoop cluster as well as the job characteristics, whether they are cpu or I/O intensive. In [17], the authors use k-means as a classification mechanism for Hadoop workloads (jobs), so that jobs can be automatically classified based on their requirements. They plan to improve the performance of their scheduler by separating data intensive and computation intensive jobs in performing the classification. On the other hand, job interference was also studied in Hadoop, and acknowledged as one of the key performance aspects. In [23], the authors analyse the high level of interference between interactive and batch processing jobs and they propose a scheduler for the virtualization layer, designed to minimize interference, and a scheduler for the Hadoop framework. Similarly, the authors in [22] analyse the interference occurring among Apache Spark jobs in virtualized environments. They develop an analytical model to estimate the interference effect, which could be exploited for improving the Apache Spark Scheduler in the future.

---

[1] https://kubernetes.io/.

[2] http://mesos.apache.org/.

[3] https://docs.docker.com/swarm/, https://github.com/docker/swarmkit.

## 3   Kubernetes Architecture

Kubernetes is a platform to facilitate the deployment and management of containerized applications abstracting away from the underlaying infrastructure (see footnote 1). The system is composed of the Kubernetes *Control plane*, i.e. the master node and any number of *worker nodes* that execute the deployed applications. Applications are submitted to the control plane, which deploys them automatically across the worker nodes. Components of the control plane can reside on a single master node, or can be split across multiple nodes. The components of the control plane are: (1) The API server, implemented with a RESTful interface, which gives an entry point to the cluster. The API service is used as a proxy to expose the services which are executed inside the cluster to external clients. (2) The Scheduler that assigns a worker node to each component of your application. (3) *etcd*, a key-value distributed storage system, used to coordinate resources and to share configuration data of the cluster. And (4) The *Controller manager*, a process that combines and coordinates several controllers such as the replication controller, the node controller, the namespace or the deployment controller.

Each worker, which runs containerized applications, has the following components: (1) Docker, or any other container runtime. (2) The *kubelet* service that communicates with the master and the containers on the node. (3) *Kube-proxy* that balances client request across all containers that configure a service. The basic components considered on this paper are shown in Fig. 1. For a more detailed description of the chain of events triggered when a pod is created see [13].

The deployment unit in Kubernetes is a pod, an abstraction of a set of containers tightly coupled with some shared resources (the network interface and

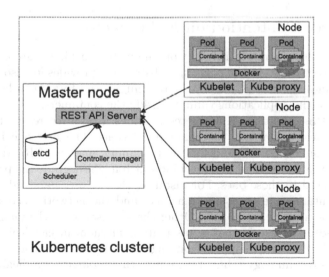

**Fig. 1.** Kubernetes architecture.

the storage system). Each pod, and all its containers, are executed on one allocated machine, and has a IP address that is shared by all containers. Therefore, two services listening on the same port cannot be deployed in a pod.

Developers can specify pod resource requests and limits. A pod *resource request* is the minimum amount of resources needed by all containers in the pod, and the pod *resource limits* is the maximum resources allocated to the containers in a pod. Once the pod is running on a node, it consumes as much CPU time as it can. CPU time is distributed between pods running on the pod in the same ratio than the pod request specifications. CPU is considered a compressible resource, which means that is acceptable a performance degradation due to a CPU resource contention. However, memory is incompressible, and it is not admissible for a pod to be running if it has not enough memory as requested. Consequently, developers should limit the amount of memory a container can consume.

The Kubernetes scheduler allocates pods into nodes taking into account factors that have a significant impact on the availability, performance and capacity – e.g. the cluster topology, individual and collective resources, service quality requirements, hardware and software restrictions, policies, etc. The scheduler uses request and limits to filter the nodes that have enough resources to execute a pod, and from them, it chooses the best one. Pods can be categories in three Quality of Service (QoS) classes: *Best effort* (lowest priority), *Burstable*, and *Guaranteed* (highest priority). The QoS classes is inferred from the request and limits manifests. A *Guaranteed* pod has all containers with limits equal to requests; a *Best effort* pod has not request or limit manifest for any container; and the rest of pods are *Burstable*. Once a pod is deployed in a node, if *pod request manifest < pod request limits* resource requested are guaranteed by the scheduler, but it is possible to use resources beyond the request manifest if they are idle resources.

## 4    Resource Contention on Kubernetes

When several containers are running on the same machine, they compete for the available resources. As the container abstraction provides less isolation than virtual machines, sharing physical resources might lead to a degradation in the performance of the applications running inside the containers.

To avoid this situation, Kubernetes provides a resource reservation mechanism. That mechanism has two main restrictions. The first one is that the reservation is only for CPU and for the maximum amount of RAM. However, the resources that are shared in a machine which might degrade the performance are not restricted to those ones. For instance, the network bandwidth is shared among all containers in the same machine, and the network access is shared for all containers inside a pod [15]. Other shared resource is the memory bandwidth. The second issue is that a reservation mechanism can lead to unused resources in the cluster. An application might reserve an entire core – CPU limit in Kubernetes terminology – but it only uses the resource sporadically.

**Table 1.** Reference applications used as a background workload with the resource which they use intensively and with the chosen execution parameters.

| Application | Resource | Notes |
|---|---|---|
| Pov-ray | CPU | Version 3.7 with default parallelism |
| STREAM [14] | Memory bandwidth | - DSTREAM_ARRAY_SIZE=100000000 <br> - DNTIMES=100 |
| dd | Disk I/O bandwidth | dd if=/dev/zero of=/root/testfile <br> bs=1G count=1 oflag=direct > dev/null |

We executed several applications on the same machine to characterise how the performance degrades. The machine has two E6750 cores and 8 GB of RAM. The chosen applications are a map-reduce application, *WordCount*, and a webgraph application, *PageRank* [18], expecting that PageRank makes a higher usage of CPU than WordCount. Additionally, we ran both applications inside two different frameworks for data stream processing: Flink [6] and Thrill [3]. We chose both of them because they are implemented in different programming languages – Flink is implemented in Java, whereas Thrill is implemented in C++. We ran each experiment ten times, and we plotted their mean values.

The first set of experiments consists in running one application per experiment – WordCount inside Flink, WordCount inside Thrill, PageRank inside Flink and PageRank inside Thrill – along with a background execution caused by another application which makes an intensive usage of a certain resource: a ray tracing program, Pov-ray[4], the STREAM benchmark [14], and a file transfer and conversion Unix command, dd[5], are used as workload background applications. These three applications were executed in a continuous loop. A summary of the parameters used, their version, as well as the resource they use intensively is depicted in Table 1.

For the experiments, we ran WordCound and PageRank and varied the input size in order to observe how their performance degrades for long executions. For PageRank applications, we selected the Barabasi-Albert graph which was generated using the NetworkX package[6]. As a reference time, we take the execution time of each application in isolation, without the background application, $App_0$. Given the execution time of that application with a certain background workload, for instance $App_{pv}$, we calculate the performance degradation as $\frac{App_{pv}}{App_0}$. Results are shown in Fig. 2. We can see that: (i) the implementation of Thrill is much more efficient than Flink in all cases; (ii) there is a significant performance degradation when we execute WordCount in all cases for big input sizes – 1 thousand million –, which is caused when dd is very high (about four times). The explanation is that the size of the input is 6.76 GB, so there are a lot of

---

[4] Persistence of vision raytracer (version 3.7) [computer software], http://www.povray.org/download/.
[5] dd(1) linux user's manual (2010).
[6] https://networkx.github.io/.

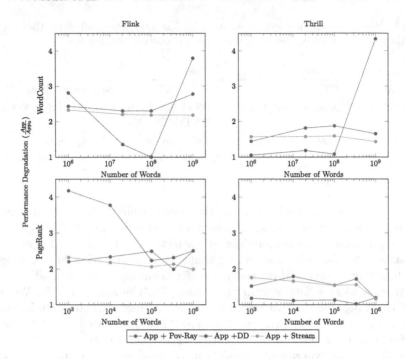

**Fig. 2.** Performance degradation for several Apps – WordCount inside Flink, Word-Count inside Thrill, PageRank inside Flink and PageRank inside Thrill – with a background workload.

page faults in the execution and the application is continuously accessing to the storage system. (iii) Finally, there is also a significant performance anomaly when executing WordCount and Flink and dd for small input sizes. This is due to internal implementation of Flink regarding I/O access, as for such small input sizes the computational times are reduced in comparison with the overheads for accessing disk.

In the second set of experiments, we have measured the degradation caused in real scenarios. We execute on the same physical machine the following scenarios for each application – WordCount and PageRank–: (i) one instance of Flink – Thrill–; two instances of Flink –Thrill– and four instances of Flink –Thrill–. (ii) one instance of Flink + one instance of Thrill; two instances of Flink + two instances of Thrill. Results are shown in Fig. 3. We can observe that in Flink, the degradation is similar when there is another Flink or Thrill application. When there are four applications, the performance is degraded in a high degree with Flink applications in WordCount example. The results are very similar in Thrill experiments.

In general, we can see that the degradation is higher when two or more instances of the same container are scheduled in the same machine. The reason for this behaviour is that both applications make use of the same resources at the same time, so the contention is higher.

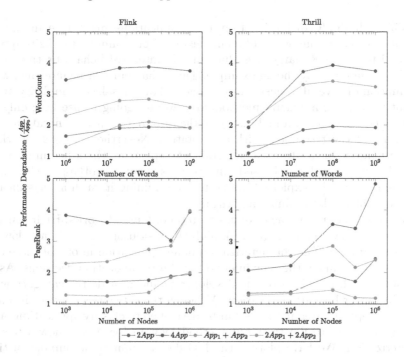

**Fig. 3.** Performance degradation for several Apps – WordCount inside Flink, Word-Count inside Thrill, PageRank inside Flink and PageRank inside Thrill – when executed in different configurations.

## 5  Client-Side Scheduling

As we presented in Sect. 3, pods are allocated into machines by Kubernetes Scheduler. Kubernetes provides a label mechanism, which allows it to place the pods in machines which satisfy certain conditions. For example, the application can request a machine with a solid disk. However, the client should know which kind of labels the cluster provides. This mechanism is insufficient to deal with the problem presented in Sect. 4. In this section, we introduce a methodology to characterize applications in an informal way. The implemented client-side scheduler uses the characterization as a guideline to allocate pods inside machines.

### 5.1  Application Characterization

In certain cases, applications can be classified depending on which resource they use more intensively – CPU, I/O disk, network bandwidth, or memory bandwidth. An application which is writing in disk continuously has a different behaviour from another one which makes an intensive use of CPU. For the lack of space, in this paper, we only consider applications that make an intensive use of CPU or an intensive use of I/O disk. In our previous experiments, `pov-ray` was the application which exemplifies a high CPU application and the `dd` command exemplifies a high I/O disk utilisation. Real applications might have an intensive usage of a resource, but with different degrees. For example, the bzip application, used to compress large files, has an I/O intensive behaviour that is less than the usage made by the **dd** example. This behaviour can be modelled which the definition of several intensity usage grades. For the sake of simplicity and as we want to propose a general methodology, we are going to use here only two grades of resource usage, a high usage of the resource – with a ↑ notation – and a low usage of the resource – with a ↓ notation. Nevertheless, we acknowledge that the number of grades is a determinant aspect for the scheduling performance that needs to be addressed, and there is a number of approaches in the literature that can be exploited for better determining it, such as classification and clusterization data mining algorithms.

Therefore, in our approach, we have a total of four categories: High cpu utilisation ($cpu\ \uparrow$), low cpu usage ($cpu\ \downarrow$), high I/O disk usage ($disk\ \uparrow$), and low I/O disk usage ($disk\ \downarrow$). The characterization of an application in one of these categories is going to allow the scheduler to take better allocation decisions. As the simplest method, the client or the developer should provide the category which better fits better his/her application. Although the categories are very intuitive, alternative sophisticated methods can be developed to classify applications automatically. In order to illustrate our methodology, in Fig. 4, we show a possible characterization. We have plotted the I/O degradation – the number of times the application is slower when it is scheduled in the same machine along with **dd**– vs the CPU degradation – the same procedure using **pov-ray**. We used **dd** and **pov-ray** as benchmarking applications, however, other applications which make a high usage of a single resource can be used. The values were taken from the experiments shown in Fig. 2. The red lines split the four categories, and they were obtained with qualitative criteria. Then, we classified each application

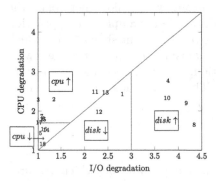

| App | Input Size | Id | Categoría |
|---|---|---|---|
| FlinkWC | $1 \cdot 10^6$ | 1 | $cpu \uparrow$ |
| FlinkWC | $20 \cdot 10^6$ | 2 | $cpu \uparrow$ |
| FlinkWC | $100 \cdot 10^6$ | 3 | $cpu \uparrow$ |
| FlinkWC | $1000 \cdot 10^6$ | 4 | $disk \uparrow$ |
| ThrillWC | $1 \cdot 10^6$ | 5 | $cpu \downarrow$ |
| ThrillWC | $20 \cdot 10^6$ | 6 | $cpu \uparrow$ |
| ThrillWC | $100 \cdot 10^6$ | 7 | $cpu \uparrow$ |
| ThrillWC | $1000 \cdot 10^6$ | 8 | $disk \uparrow$ |
| FlinkPR | 1000 | 9 | $disk \uparrow$ |
| FlinkPR | 10000 | 10 | $disk \uparrow$ |
| FlinkPR | 100000 | 11 | $cpu \uparrow$ |
| FlinkPR | 334863 | 12 | $disk \downarrow$ |
| FlinkPR | $1 \cdot 10^6$ | 13 | $cpu \uparrow$ |
| ThrillPR | 1000 | 14 | $cpu \downarrow$ |
| ThrillPR | 10000 | 15 | $cpu \uparrow$ |
| ThrillPR | 100000 | 16 | $cpu \downarrow$ |
| ThrillPR | 334863 | 17 | $cpu \uparrow$ |
| ThrillPR | $1 \cdot 10^6$ | 18 | $cpu \downarrow$ |

**(a)** CPU degradation vs. I/O Degradation.

**(b)** Application Identification and Characterization.

**Fig. 4.** Application characterization based on the CPU degradation and the I/O degradation. Numbers in subfigure a are application identifiers in table b. (Color figure online)

---

**Algorithm 1.** Client-Side Scheduler

1: **procedure** *Client-Side Scheduler*$(l_{app}, W)$
2:    $S = GetClusterState()$
3:    $minValue := \infty$
4:    $bestNode := 0$
5:    **for** $N$ in $S$ **do**
6:       **if** $|N| \le min\{|M|, \forall M \in S\})$ **then**
7:          **if** $minValue > \sum_{j}^{|N|} w_{j,app}$ **then**
8:             $minValue := \sum_{j}^{|N|} w_{j,app}$
9:             $bestNode := N$
10:          **end if**
11:       **end if**
12:    **end for**
13:    $Allocate(l_{app}, bestNode)$
14: **end procedure**

---

Table 2. Example weight matrix $W$ for two resources and two usage grades.

| $App_1 \backslash App_2$ | cpu ↑ | cpu ↓ | disk ↑ | disk ↓ |
|---|---|---|---|---|
| cpu ↑ | 5 | 4 | 2 | 1 |
| cpu ↓ | 4 | 3 | 1 | 0 |
| disk ↑ | 2 | 1 | 5 | 4 |
| disk ↓ | 1 | 0 | 4 | 3 |

taking as criteria the resource which caused more contention. The plotted numbers are the identifier of the corresponding application, which are shown in Fig. 4b.

## 5.2   Client-Side Scheduling

We propose a scheduler design which has two criteria: (i) Balancing the number of applications in each node; (ii) minimising the degradation in a machine caused by the resource competition. Formally, let us define a node $N$ as a multi-set of labels. Each label represents an application that is running inside that node. In our example, we have four kind of labels – $l_0$ equivalents to cpu ↑; $l_1$ equivalents to cpu ↓, and so on. In a certain moment, the state of the cluster $S$ can be modelled as a set of nodes. Given a new application whose label is $l_{app}$, the best node to allocate $l_{app}$ is given by:

$$\operatorname*{argmin}_{i \in 0}^{|E|} \sum_{j} w_{E_{i,j}, app}$$

where $w_{k,l}$ is the weight of the $k$-$th$ row and $l$-$th$ column of a weight matrix $W$. Each $w_{k,l}$ models the penalty to schedule a new application labelled as $l$, if in that node is running an application labelled as $k$. $E_{i,j}$ is the $j$-th application label of $i$-th node in $E$ set. $E$ is defined as $E = \{N \in \boldsymbol{S} \land \forall M \in \boldsymbol{S}, |N| \leq |M|\}$. The $E$ set contains the nodes with less applications. Algorithm 1 implements the previous formalisation.

In order to obtain the weight matrix $W$, we provide the following rules: For each element $w_{k,l}$, we observe if the labels are associated with the same resource. If that is the case, then we set high values of penalty: 3, 4, or 5. Then, we observe the grade of usage. From the previous values, if both grades are high we set the highest penalty value (5); if only one is high, then we associate the medium value (4), and if both are low, then the lowest penalty value is set (3). In case the labels are not associated with the same resource, we repeat the same process to associate the low values (0, 1, or 2) if $i$ and $j$ correspond to different resources. From the experiments made in Sect. 4, we can build a weight matrix $W$, as depicted in Table 2.

## 5.3  Experiments

We made some experiments to compare our client-side scheduler with the default Kubernetes scheduler. The proposed scheduler was implemented in Python. The experiments were run in a Kubernetes cluster with 8 machines (each machine has four i5-4690 cores and 8 GB of RAM). One of the machines acts as a dedicated Master Node. In the proposed scenario, we ran six applications three times – dd and pov-ray with parameters from Table 1; PageRank in Thrill and Flink with 1 million nodes and WordCount in Thrill and Flink with 1,000 million words– with the default Kubernetes scheduler. The scenario was executed ten times. As the Kubernetes scheduler has a non-deterministic behaviour, we show three reference cases in Fig. 5. Each bar represents the execution time of the application, and its colour indicates the machine where the scheduler placed the application. The vertical line shows the total time measured for the experiment (time to create the pods plus execution time plus time to delete the pods). Case number 1 represents the worst case. Kubernetes allocated WCFlink1 and WCFlink2 in the same machine, with an execution of dd and PRFlink1. As a result, the execution time of WCFlink1 is more than 10 min, due to the degradation caused by sharing the machine with WCFlink2. Case number 2 represents a balanced case, with an execution time about 10 min. The Scheduler placed again WCFlink3 and WCFlink2 in the same, so there is certain degradation in the performance. The best case corresponds to Case 3. In this situation, Kubernetes allocated WCFlink1, WCFlink2, WCFlink3 in different machines and the result is better (about eight minutes). From these experiments, we can conclude that, as Kubernetes has a non-deterministic behaviour, the execution time of the applications has a high variance. If the scheduler splits the applications with an intensive CPU usage along different machines, the results are better; however the decision is taken randomly. Additionally, we can see in Case 2 that the default Scheduler does not try to balance the number of applications along the number of machines – the scheduler places four applications in node3 and only one application in node5.

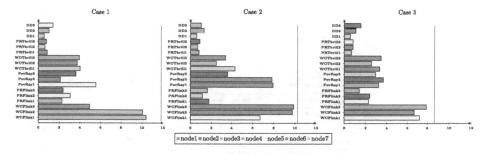

**Fig. 5.** Execution time and machine allocation with the default Kubernetes scheduler. The blue line shows the total measured time (Execution time + time to create pods + time to delete pods). (Color figure online)

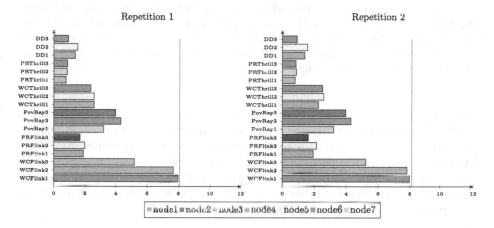

**Fig. 6.** Execution time and machine allocation with the proposed scheduler. The blue line shows the total measured time (Execution time + time to create pods + time to delete pods) (Color figure online)

The results of the same experiment with our scheduler are shown in Fig. 6. Its behaviour is deterministic, so under the same conditions, the scheduler allocates the applications in the same machine – in the figure we only show two of the ten executions, due to the low variance. The overall execution time of the experiment is about eight minutes. This value is 20% better than the mean time of the Kubernetes scheduler –about 10 min–, and it is significantly better –33%– than the worst case – about 12 min –. The total time is similar to the best case of the default scheduler. Additionally, the variance in the execution time is lower. The improvement is achieved splitting the application with a high CPU utilisation –WCFlink1, WCFLink2, and WCFlink3– in different machines.

In our last set of experiments, we executed the same batch of applications using the reservation mechanism available in Kubernetes. As WCFlink1, WCFlink2, WCFlink3 have the highest execution time, we reserved two cores for them. For the rest applications, we reserved only one core. The results are dis-

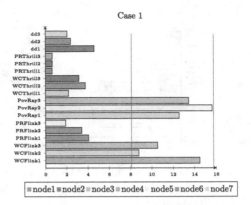

**Fig. 7.** Execution time and machine allocation with CPU limit mechanism. `WCFlink1`, `WCFlink2`, `WCFlink3` are executed with two cores and the rest application with one core. The blue line shows the total time obtained with the proposed scheduler and the red line shows the total measured time (Execution time + time to create pods + time to delete pods) (Color figure online)

played in Fig. 7. The red line compares the total time with our scheduler with the blue line. We can see that the total time is almost twice. The reason for this behaviour is that there are a lot of unused resources in the machines. Additionally, the variance of the execution time is very high – for instance, `pov-ray1` has an execution time about 12 min and `pov-ray2` has an execution time about 16 min–. It can be explained due to the fact that there are other resources that cause performance degradation which are not reserved.

## 6   Conclusions and Future Work

Container virtualization provides a quick and flexible mechanism to share computational resources in machines, while improving resource utilization as compared to other Cloud resource such as Virtual Machines. However, the low isolation between container based applications can lead to performance degradation in those applications. In our paper, we have shown that the default mechanism to isolate resources between containers in Kubernetes are not sufficient to lead with the performance degradation. Although CPU is the main source of degradation, the competition for other resources – I/O disk, memory bandwidth and network – should be included in the model. Moreover, our experiments show that the CPU reservation mechanism can lead to unused resources in the cluster, and the execution time of applications might have a high variance caused by degradation caused by other sources distinct than the CPU.

As a solution to deal with the competition of resources between containers, we propose a scheduling technique based on the characterization of applications. Clients or developers provide informal information about their applications – for instance, which resource the application uses more intensively – and in turn, the scheduler uses that information to allocate the applications using the same resource in different machines. In our experiments, we achieved about a 20 percent improvement in the execution time of a simple scenario compared with the default Kubernetes non-deterministic scheduler. The total execution time is about the half compared to a scenario were resources are reserved in Kubernetes. Additionally, the behaviour of our scheduler is deterministic, so it can be used for further analysis. As future work, for the classification stage of applications, machine learning algorithms can be exploited, which can even automate the classification process and can achieve more sophisticated classification results, while targeting more complex applications in order to improve our scheduling approach.

**Acknowledgements.** This work was co-financed by the Industry and Innovation department of the Aragonese Government and European Social Funds (COSMOS research group, ref. T93); and by the Spanish Ministry of Economy under the program "Programa de I+D+i Estatal de Investigación, Desarrollo e innovación Orientada a los Retos de la Sociedad", project id TIN2013-40809-R. V. Medel was the recipient of a fellowship from the Spanish Ministry of Economy.

# References

1. Awada, U., Barker, A.D.: Improving resource efficiency of container-instance clusters on clouds. In: 17th IEEE/ACM International Symposium on Cluster, Cloud and Grid Computing (CCGrid 2017). IEEE (2017)
2. Bhamare, D., Samaka, M., Erbad, A., Jain, R., Gupta, L., Chan, H.A.: Multiobjective scheduling of micro-services for optimal service function chains. In: IEEE International Conference on Communications (ICC 2017). IEEE (2017)
3. Bingmann, T., Axtmann, M., Jöbstl, E., Lamm, S., Nguyen, H.C., Noe, A., Schlag, S., Stumpp, M., Sturm, T., Sanders, P.: Thrill: high-performance algorithmic distributed batch data processing with c++. arXiv preprint arXiv:1608.05634 (2016)
4. Brunner, S., Blochlinger, M., Toffetti, G., Spillner, J., Bohnert, T.M.: Experimental evaluation of the cloud-native application design. In: IEEE/ACM 8th International Conference on Utility and Cloud Computing (UCC), pp. 488–493 (2015)
5. Burns, B., Grant, B., Oppenheimer, D., Brewer, E., Wilkes, J.: Borg, omega, and Kubernetes. ACM Queue **14**, 70–93 (2016)
6. Carbone, P., Katsifodimos, A., Ewen, S., Markl, V., Haridi, S., Tzoumas, K.: Apache Flink: stream and batch processing in a single engine. Bull. IEEE Comput. Soc. Techn. Comm. Data Eng. **38**(4), 28–38 (2015)
7. Choi, S., Myung, R., Choi, H., Chung, K., Gil, J., Yu, H.: Gpsf: general-purpose scheduling framework for container based on cloud environment. In: International Conference on Internet of Things (iThings) and IEEE Green Computing and Communications (GreenCom) and IEEE Cyber, Physical and Social Computing (CPSCom) and IEEE Smart Data (SmartData), pp. 769–772. IEEE (2016)
8. Felter, W., Ferreira, A., Rajamony, R., Rubio, J.: An updated performance comparison of virtual machines and linux containers. In: International Symposium on Performance Analysis of Systems and Software (ISPASS), pp. 171–172 (2015)
9. Havet, A., Schiavoni, V., Felber, P., Colmant, M., Rouvoy, R., Fetzer, C.: Genpack: a generational scheduler for cloud data centers. In: 2017 IEEE International Conference on Cloud Engineering (IC2E), pp. 95–104. IEEE (2017)

10. Hindman, B., Konwinski, A., Zaharia, M., Ghodsi, A., Joseph, A.D., Katz, R.H., Shenker, S., Stoica, I.: Mesos: a platform for fine-grained resource sharing in the data center. In: NSDI, vol. 11, p. 22 (2011)

11. Kaewkasi, C., Chuenmuneewong, K.: Improvement of container scheduling for Docker using ant colony optimization. In: 2017 9th International Conference on Knowledge and Smart Technology (KST), pp. 254–259. IEEE (2017)

12. Kumar, K.A., Konishetty, V.K., Voruganti, K., Rao, G.V.P.: CASH: context aware scheduler for hadoop. In: 2012 International Conference on Advances in Computing, Communications and Informatics, ICACCI 2012, 3–5 August 2012, Chennai, India, pp. 52–61 (2012)

13. Lukša, M.: Kubernetes in Action (MEAP). Manning Publications, Greenwich (2017)

14. McCalpin, J.D.: Memory bandwidth and machine balance in current high performance computers. In: IEEE Computer Society Technical Committee on Computer Architecture (TCCA) Newsletter, pp. 19–25, December 1995

15. Medel, V., Rana, O., Arronategui, U., et al.: Modelling performance & resource management in Kubernetes. In: Proceedings of the 9th International Conference on Utility and Cloud Computing, pp. 257–262. ACM (2016)

16. Morabito, R., Kjällman, J., Komu, M.: Hypervisors vs. lightweight virtualization: a performance comparison. In: 2015 IEEE International Conference on Cloud Engineering (IC2E), pp. 386–393. IEEE (2015)

17. Oskooei, A.R., Down, D.G.: COSHH: a classification and optimization based scheduler for heterogeneous hadoop systems. Future Generation Comp. Syst. **36**, 1–15 (2014)

18. Page, L., Brin, S., Motwani, R., Winograd, T.: The pagerank citation ranking: bringing order to the web. Technical report, Stanford InfoLab (1999)

19. Raho, M., Spyridakis, A., Paolino, M., Raho, D.: Kvm, Xen and Docker: a performance analysis for ARM based NFV and cloud computing. In: 3rd Workshop on Advances in Information, Electronic and Electrical Engineering (AIEEE), pp. 1–8. IEEE (2015)

20. Seo, K.T., Hwang, H.S., Moon, I.Y., Kwon, O.Y., Kim, B.J.: Performance comparison analysis of linux container and virtual machine for building cloud. Adv. Sci. Technol. Lett. **66**(105–111), 2 (2014)

21. Verma, A., Pedrosa, L., Korupolu, M.R., Oppenheimer, D., Tune, E., Wilkes, J.: Large-scale cluster management at Google with Borg. In: Proceedings of the European Conference on Computer Systems (EuroSys), Bordeaux, France (2015)

22. Wang, K., Khan, M.M.H., Nguyen, N., Gokhale, S.S.: Modeling interference for apache spark jobs. In: 9th IEEE International Conference on Cloud Computing, CLOUD 2016, USA, pp. 423–431 (2016)

23. Zhang, W., Rajasekaran, S., Duan, S., Wood, T., Zhu, M.: Minimizing interference and maximizing progress for hadoop virtual machines. SIGMETRICS Perform. Eval. Rev. **42**(4), 62–71 (2015)

# Performance and Economic Evaluations in Adopting Low Power Architectures: A Real Case Analysis

Daniele D'Agostino[1]([⊠]), Daniele Cesini[2], Elena Corni[2], Andrea Ferraro[2],
Lucia Morganti[2], Alfonso Quarati[1], and Ivan Merelli[3]

[1] Institute for Applied Mathematics and Information Technologies "E. Magenes",
National Research Council of Italy, Genoa, Italy
`dagostino@ge.imati.cnr.it`
[2] CNAF Section, Italian Institute for Nuclear Physics, Bologna, Italy
[3] Institute for Biomedical Technologies, National Research Council of Italy,
Segrate, MI, Italy

**Abstract.** The continuous technological advances made energy efficiency a major topic for greener Information Technology systems. Low power Systems-on-Chip (SoC), originally developed in the context of mobile and embedded technologies, are becoming attractive also for scientific and industrial applications given their increasing computing performances, coupled with relatively low cost and power demands. In this work, we investigate the potential of the most representative SoCs for a real life application taken from the field of molecular biology. In particular, we investigate the opportunity of using SoCs for Next-Generation Sequencing (NGS) analysis, considering different applicative scenarios, with different timing and costs requirements. We evaluate the achievable performance together with economical aspects related to the total cost of ownership for a small medium enterprise offering services of NGS sequence alignment, supporting analysis performed in hospitals, research institutes, farms and industries.

**Keywords:** Low power Systems-on-Chip · Next-generation sequencing · Performance and economic evaluations

## 1  Introduction

Information Technology is increasingly a place where companies can save money and energy [1]. This is of particular importance for current HPC systems [2], which are more and more bound by their power consumption, but also for all the ICT companies, where this aspect is only expected to worsen in the foreseeable future [3]. In response to this problem, high-end processors are quickly introducing more advanced power-saving and power-monitoring technologies [4]. On the other hand, low power processors are gaining interest in many applicative fields. Designed for the mobile market, they are progressively reducing the

© Springer International Publishing AG 2017
C. Pham et al. (Eds.): GECON 2017, LNCS 10537, pp. 177–189, 2017.
DOI: 10.1007/978-3-319-68066-8_14

performance gap with high-end processors, with the added values of keeping a competitive edge on costs, reducing their carbon footprint and preserving the environment.

In particular, low power Systems-on-Chip (SoCs) are designed to meet the best computing performance with the lowest power consumption. The SoCs superior performance/consumption ratio is driven by the growing demands for hand-held devices and energy-savvy boards in mobile and embedded industries. Indeed, the primary design goal for embedded processors has been low power consumption because of their use in battery-powered devices. On the contrary, the current power-hungry traditional servers were designed for high floating-point performance. Moving away from their primordial mobile and embedded worlds, SoCs are conceivably becoming an interesting alternative architecture for running scientific but also commercial-oriented applications without sacrificing too much the performances and functionalities of traditional servers.

Investigating the potential and performances of low power SoC architectures for scientific and non-scientific workloads is the aim of the COSA project (COmputing on SoC Architectures, http://cosa-project.it), an ongoing initiative funded by the Italian Institute for Nuclear Physics (INFN) started in January 2015. The COSA project [5] exploring limits and benefits of low power SoCs compared to the current mainstream high-end x86 server architectures, e.g. [6].

The COSA lab is equipped with an unconventional cluster of ARMv7, ARMv8 and x86 low-power SoCs nodes (connected through 1 Gb/s and 10 Gb/s ethernet switches) currently used as a test-bed for scientific benchmarks and real-life scientific applications in both single-node and multi-node fashion.

The aim of this work is to explore the feasibility, performances and cost requirements for a small-medium enterprise (SME) offering a service based on a real-life application taken from the field of molecular biology, namely the Next-Generation Sequencing (NGS) analysis.

Intriguingly, low-power and low-costs architectures can be used to develop a number of bioinformatic applications. An example is represented by portable sequencing machines, such as the Oxford Nanopore Minion [7], where power consumption represents a major issue. This will lead to the direct analysis of genomes of humans, animals or plants in remote regions of the world, or to analyse the composition of the microbioma in air-filters, water or soil samples in a simple and portable way.

The focus of the paper is on adopting state-of-the-art SoC architectures in a commercial environment: this mean that the trade-off among acquisition costs, energy costs and achievable performance comparing standards enterprise-oriented hosts in relation to the most representative SoCs of the COSA cluster are discussed.

The paper is organized as follows. Section 2 discusses the related works and the test-bed, i.e. the hardware, energy and economic specifications of the architectures employed in our tests. Section 3 provides details on the Next-Generation Sequencing application. The experimental results are shown and discussed in Sect. 4, considering different applicative scenarios. Finally, the paper closes in Sect. 5.

# 2  Materials and Methods

In the following we provide a brief overview of related works in the area, followed by the description of the test-bed used in our tests.

## 2.1  Related Works

The first HPC system able to provide a computational power of 1 Petaflop appeared in 2008. One year later the scientific community, considering that its power consumption was of about 2.4 MW, started the discussion on how to scale up to 1 Exaflop while staying in a power envelope of 20–30 MW [8]. So far, several research project were funded to tackle the key issue of designing new hardware components, together with suitable programming environments.

The Mont-Blanc project [9,10], coordinated by the Barcelona Supercomputing Center and by Bull, has deployed several generations of HPC clusters based on ARM processors, developing also the corresponding eco-system of HPC tools targeted to this architecture. Another project along this direction is the EU-FP7 EUROSERVER [11,12] coordinated by CEA, which aims to design and prototype technology, architecture, and systems software for the next generation of data center "Micro-Servers", exploiting 64-bit ARM cores. Many research groups that are on the same research line, exploring different hardware low power platforms or software techniques: some are exploring Dynamic Voltage and Frequency Scaling (DVFS) techniques as a way to modulate power consumption of processor and memory, scaling the clock frequency of one or both sub-systems according to the execution of memory- or compute-bound application kernels [13]. More recently, other projects are focusing also on Near Threshold Voltage (NTV) computing [14] making the processor to work at even lower voltages. Other initiatives dealing with the creation of low power based machines are the SpiNNaker (Spiking Neural Network Architecture) project [15,16], proposed by the Advanced Processor Technologies Research group at the University of Manchester and the EU FET-HPC project ExaNeSt [17].

## 2.2  Experimental Setup

To validate our approach we experimented on the 7 machines heterogeneous test-bed reported in Table 1. We tested two classes of machines: HPC-201, HPC-08 and Xeon Phi are server-grade machines hosted in the server room of a production data center, while Xeon-D, avoton, J4205 and N3710 are mini-ITX boards hosted in a laboratory of the data center. The latter are shown in Fig. 1.

In this work we have considered only X86-based hardware because the porting to these platforms was straightforward with respect to other platforms, i.e. ARM based, having all the dependencies already compiled and available. However, a comparison that includes also ARM platforms using several applications as benchmarks can be found in [6,18,19]. On the basis of our experience ARM based low power platforms can be fruitfully exploited for CUDA applications thanks to the availability of developments boards such as the Jetson TK1/TX1.

**Table 1.** Technical, energy and BOM (Bill Of Material) comparative view of the test-bed. Max power for HPC-201, HPC-08 and Xeon Phi is estimated or gathered from previous stress tests. BOM for HPC-201, HPC-08 and Xeon Phi is calculated from real tenders of a production data center.

|  | HPC-201 | HPC-08 | Xeon Phi | Xeon D | avoton | J4205 | N3710 |
|---|---|---|---|---|---|---|---|
| CPU Brand | Xeon | Xeon | Xeon | Xeon | Atom | Pentium | Pentium |
| Model | E5-2683v4 | E5-2640v2 | Phi 7230 | D-1540 | C2750 | J4205 | N3710 |
| Architecture | Broadwell | Ivy Bridge | Airmont | Broadwell | Silvermont (Avoton) | Goldmont (Apollo Lake) | Airmont (Braswell) |
| Year | Q1 2016 | Q3 2013 | Q2 2016 | Q1 2015 | Q3 2013 | Q3 2016 | Q1 2016 |
| HyperTH | Yes | Yes | Yes | Yes | No | No | No |
| Freq (GHz) | 2.10 | 2.00/2.50 | 1.30/1.50 | 2.0/2.60 | 2.40/2.60 | 1.50 | 1.60 |
| Cache (MB) | 40 | 20 | 32 | 12 | 4 | 2 | 2 |
| N CPUs | 2 | 2 | 1 | 1 | 1 | 1 | 1 |
| N Cores | 32 | 16 | 64 | 8 | 8 | 4 | 4 |
| Memory (GB) | 256 | 128 | 64 | 16 | 8 | 8 | 8 |
| TDP (W) | 250 | 250 | 215 | 55 | 20 | 7 | 8 |
| BOM (€) | 6,000 | 5,000 | 6,000 | 1,100 | 800 | 300 | 300 |

4xINTEL AVOTON C-2750        4xINTEL XEOND-1540                 2xINTEL J4205                         2xINTEL N3700
                                                                                                      4xINTEL N3710

**Fig. 1.** The SOC clusters at INFN Bologna.

In the other case they are equivalent to N3700. However, the applications under study in this work were developed for CPU only.

A master server was used as a monitoring station and a power meter was attached to the monitoring station to measure the energy consumption for every test or real-life application.

An external network file system hosting all software and datasets is mounted on every cluster node. The differences between the two classes is evident looking at the last two rows at the bottom of the table showing the thermal design power (TDP) and median Bill Of Material (BOM) of each platform.

In particular the laboratory power measurement equipment consists of a high precision DC power supply, a high precision digital multimeter connected to a National Instruments data logging software, and a high precision AC power meter. To monitor the consumption of the SoCs, the DC current absorbed is measured by a Voltech PM300 Power Analyzer downstream of the power supply. The measured Thermal Design Power (TDP) of all the considered machines ranges from 7 W of J4205 to 250 W of the Intel Xeon E5 Processors. As regards the BOM, the considered prices are mainly related to the motherboard, the processor, the memory and a SATA hard disk.

The operative system of all platforms is Ubuntu 16.04.2 LTS except for HPC-201 (CentOS release 6.5), HPC-08 (Ubuntu 14.04.5 LTS) and Xeon Phi (CentOS release 7). Moreover for our testbed we used the GCC compiler, version 6.2.0, and MPI library, version 1.10.2 on each machine except on HPC-201 (GCC: 4.9.0, MPI: 1.8.1) and on HPC-08 (GCC: 4.8.4, MPI: 1.6.5).

## 3   The NGS Application

The increasing availability of molecular biology data resulting from improvements in experimental techniques represents an unprecedented opportunity for Bioinformatics and Computational Biology, but also a major challenge [20]. Due to the increasing number of experiments involving genomic research, in particular due to the spreading of these techniques from research centres to hospitals and from farms to food industries, the amount and complexity of biological data is increasing very fast.

In particular, the high demand for low-cost sequencing has driven the development of high-throughput technologies that parallelize the sequencing process, producing thousands or millions of sequences concurrently [21]. High-throughput, or next-generation, sequencing (NGS) applies to genome sequencing, genome resequencing, variant identification (Genotyping), transcriptome profiling (RNA-Seq), DNA-protein interactions (ChIP-sequencing), and epigenome characterization [22].

Such huge and heterogeneous amount of digital information is an incredible resource for uncovering disease associated hidden patterns in data [23,24], allowing the creation of predictive models for real-life biomedical applications [25,26]. But suitable analysis tools should be available to life scientists, biologists and physicians to properly treat this information in a fast and reliable way.

The first step to accomplish for each analysis is the alignment of the reads achieved through sequencing to the reference genome. This is usually done on a single server using parallel applications, such as Bowtie [27], BWA [28] or STAR [29]. All these tools rely on the Burrows Wheeler transform (also called block-sorting compression), which is useful to compress the reference database in order to make the search very fast. A pipeline of operations to perform this analysis is shown in Fig. 2. Moreover, the transformation is reversible, without needing to store any additional data.

These programs are very fast, basically CPU-bound and they scale linearly with the dimension of the input. Although each input sequence takes a different computational effort to align against the reference dataset, relying on the number of hits found and the general similarity with the reference genome (considering gaps and mismatches) these algorithms are usually implemented using

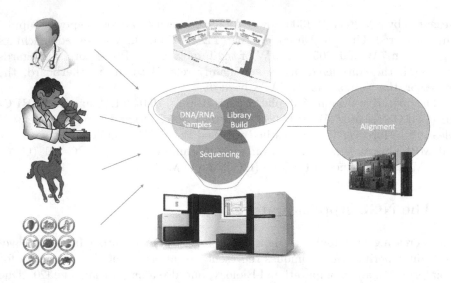

**Fig. 2.** Examples of applications of the next-generation sequencing pipeline that can be commercially addressed using SoCs.

smart multi-thread approaches that are able to balance the load between threads. On the other hand, network-based implementations of these aligners, generally relying on splitting the database, despite being tested by different groups, had little success, since its usually better to split the input sequences in chunks and compute them separately.

Therefore, considering that the amount of NGS data to analyse is huge and is growing faster than the computing power available to data scientists [30], some important infrastructural challenges are near to come. Different scenarios can be drawn for NGS application, presenting different data dimensions (depending on the depth of sequencing), number of experiments and urgency of getting the results back.

Indeed, while for research purpose the number of datasets to analyse are a few in a specific amount of time, but experiments are usually huge to allow new discoveries, hospitals have a daily incoming of patients, although in this case the single experiments has a lower throughput of data.

Sequencing and genotyping are becoming very popular also in farms, to verify the pedigree of animals or to prevent diseases, such as mastitis, and in food industry, to check product for contaminating from other species or animals. Typically, these experiments are in large number, but with a lower through of reads, since they aim at the identification of peculiar and well-known patterns.

Another growing application field for NGS is the food industry, in order to certify food safety [31]. From one hand, sequencing technology provides rapid identification and characterization of micro-organisms with a level of precision not previously possible. On the other hand, NGS is used to certify that food is contamination free, both to be compliant with allergenic-free nutritions and for religious related diet constrains.

# 4    Experimental Results and Discussion

The experimental evaluations have been conducted considering an NGS application for performing clinical, zoo-technical, research and industrial analysis. In detail, we considered that the input dataset for a clinical and zoo-technical analysis has a size of about 10 GB, while an in depth analysis - as those performed for research purposes - requires to process about 50 GB. Food industry analysis' datasets are assumed to be of 1 GB size. As regards the software, the porting on all the platforms is straightforward.

Table 2 summarizes the four applicative scenarios considered.

**Table 2.** Applicative scenarios considered for the execution of the NGS application for performing clinical and research analysis.

|  | Potential customers | Experiments per day | Amount of data for experiment | Note |
|---|---|---|---|---|
| Research Labs | 7 | 1 | From 10 GB to 50 GB | Usually an experiment corresponds to many samples to analyze. There are also breaks periods |
| Hospitals | 15 | 3 | From 1 GB to 10 GB | The rate is constant |
| Farms | 10 | 5 | From 1 GB to 10 GB | The rate is constant |
| Food industry | 5 | 10 | From 500 MB to 1 GB | The rate is constant and quite urgent |

## 4.1    Performance Evaluation

Although each sequence takes a different computational effort to align against the reference genome, the running times are normally distributed [32], resulting in an application that has almost linear scalability. In other words, this means that doubling the dimension of the dataset results in doubling the time required for the computation and so on and so forth.

Table 3 shows the execution times, in minutes, required for performing the analysis of a 10 GB dataset using the seven platforms, while the related scalability trends are presented in Fig. 3. Analogously, an analysis for a dataset of 1 GB, tenfold smaller than the original one, has been performed for the seven platforms, achieving the same scalability figures, as expected. For sake of completeness, we repeated the analysis considering a dataset of 50 GB, five time bigger than the original one, achieving the same speed-up trends.

Clearly, the best result has been achieved using HPC-201, which is equipped with the most powerful, traditional CPU. Using a single core we get the result after 7 h, whereas using all the cores in hyper-threading we reduce this time down

**Table 3.** Execution times, in minutes, for performing a clinical analysis on the considered platforms.

| Threads | HPC-201 | HPC-08 | Xeon Phi | Xeon D | avoton | J4205 | N3710 |
|---------|---------|--------|----------|--------|--------|-------|-------|
| 1 | 438.4 | 531.5 | 830.1 | 406.0 | 877.0 | 752.2 | 897.6 |
| 4 | 121.9 | 148.1 | 434.5 | 112.0 | 223.3 | 204.4 | 247.1 |
| 8 | 65.7 | 79.4 | 218.0 | 59.2 | 119.1 | | |
| 16 | 35.5 | 46.1 | 117.2 | 47.8 | | | |
| 32 | 20.6 | 39.2 | 68.4 | | | | |
| 64 | 17.2 | | 49.8 | | | | |
| 128 | | | 45.7 | | | | |

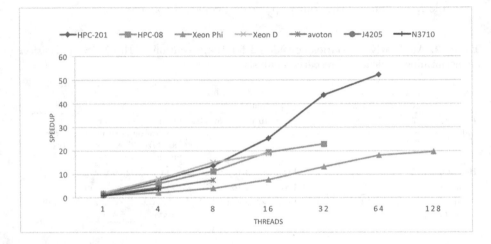

**Fig. 3.** Performance figures of the considered platforms. Speed-up values are computed considering the slowest sequential time, i.e. the 897.6 min necessary to N3710 to produce the result for the clinical analysis.

to 17 min. It is worth noticing that the scalability is nearly good, considering the data parallel nature of the application. Using the physical 32 cores we get a speed-up of 21 with respect to using a single core, and 43.5 with respect to the reference represented by the slowest processor N3710, as shown in Fig. 3, while the gain using the hyper-threading technology is limited.

The other two high performance computing (HPC) platforms, i.e. HPC-08 and Xeon Phi, shows performance which are comparable to the low power Xeon D platform, requiring between 39 and 47 min, respectively. In particular, this application is not able to exploit the full potential of the Xeon Phi processor, whose architectural features make its 64 physical cores providing the same performance of the 8 cores of the Xeon D with hyper-threading.

The other three platforms require between 2 and 4 h to compute the results. Such time is absolutely acceptable also in clinical examination, where normally results are required to be ready in 12 h for humans and in 1–2 days for animals. In particular, while the performance using 4 cores are comparable for all the three platforms, the Intel avoton is able to exploit 8 physical cores and to reduce by half the time needed to process the data, with a speed-up figure of 7.3.

## 4.2    Economic Evaluation

We collected all the data used for an economic evaluation of the 7 platforms in Table 4. In particular, we considered the scenario where a SME provides such analysis service on a regional basis. In Lombardia, where ITB has its own head-quarter, it is possible to forecast requests from fifteen hospitals and ten farms, for a total amount of 95 clinical/zoo-technical analysis per day, while the demand of research analysis can be evaluated as an average of seven per day and of fifty daily arrivals for Industry (see Table 2).

At first we evaluated the number of hosts the SME have to acquire to assure all the analysis are performed on the due time. On the basis of the best performance achieved, a single HPC-201 platform can accomplish up to 85 clinical/zoo-technical or 17 research analysis every 24 h, therefore there is the need to buy two hosts. The worst case is represented by the Intel N3710, where a single host can process only 6 clinical/zoo-technical or 1 research analyses per day. The time required for the analysis of food industries is very limited except for J4205 and again N3710, that can accomplish respectively only 72 and 48 of these tasks. It is worth to note that, in every case, each host behaves independently for each analysis and it is not considered as part of a cluster.

On the contrary, if we consider the cost to buy all the necessary hosts, the N3710 is the third cheapest choice, because each host costs about €300, as the Intel J4205. The best choice is represented by the acquisition of 5 hosts equipped with Xeon D processors, because such infrastructure is the cheapest one and however provides clinical results in less than one hour. The worst choice is represented the acquisition of 4 hosts equipped with Xeon Phi processors, as we saw they do not perform very well for the considered application, behaving like the Xeon D platform but at a cost four time bigger.

From the power consumption point of view, we measured the Watt needed to perform the analyses in the fastest cases. We can see HPC-201 requires half the power needed by the other two HPC systems but about twice those of Xeon D. The lowest value are achieved with the Intel J4025, having a factor 7 with respect to the most demanding HPC-08 platform.

In Table 4 we also report the daily energy consumption (in Kw/h) of the platforms along with the yearly cost, computed by assuming an hourly energy price per Kw of €0.119, determined by the average price supplied by Eustat (http://ec.europa.eu/eurostat/statistics-explained/index.php/Energy). As known, the energy market has strong spatial/temporal scale variations. Just to mention spatial fluctuations, we remind the 2015 price per kilowatt-hours in three US states[1]: ¢ 7.4 (Washington), ¢ 15.42 (California) and ¢ 26.17 (Hawaii), with

---

[1] https://www.eia.gov/electricity/state/.

**Table 4.** Summary of performance and economic figures of the considered platforms.

|  | HPC-201 | HPC-08 | Xeon Phi | Xeon D | avoton | J4205 | N3710 |
|---|---|---|---|---|---|---|---|
| Clinical (min) | 17.2 | 39.2 | 45.7 | 47.8 | 119.1 | 204.4 | 247.1 |
| Research (min) | 86.0 | 196.0 | 237.7 | 239.1 | 595.3 | 1021.9 | 1235.5 |
| Industry (min) | 1.8 | 3.9 | 4.7 | 4.8 | 11.5 | 20.2 | 24.9 |
| N. Hosts | 2 | 4 | 4 | 5 | 12 | 22 | 24 |
| Acquisition (€) | 12,000 | 20,000 | 24,000 | 5,500 | 9,600 | 6,600 | 7,200 |
| Clinical (W) | 71.7 | 163.3 | 142.3 | 43.8 | 39.7 | 23.8 | 28.8 |
| Research (W) | 358.0 | 816.6 | 792.5 | 219.2 | 198.4 | 119.2 | 144.1 |
| Industry (W) | 7.2 | 16.3 | 14.2 | 4.4 | 4 | 2.4 | 2.9 |
| Kw per day | 9.7 | 22 | 19.8 | 5.9 | 5.4 | 3.2 | 3.9 |
| Annual Energy (€) | 301 | 683 | 615 | 183 | 168 | 99 | 121 |

a US average price of ¢ 10.41. In Europe for the same period, the price per kilowatt-hours ranges from ¢ 7.8 (Bulgaria) to ¢ 16 (Italy), with EU-28 average of ¢ 11.9.

We observe that notwithstanding consumption noticeably varies amongst the architectures, due to the different computation times, the energy cost is rather negligible if compared to the fixed cost due to the acquisition of each system. Given these costs figures, one can be inclined to assume that no energy-saving policy, like those adopting *flexibility mechanisms* for the Computing Resources of Data Centres [33], is worthwhile to be implemented with such a reduced capacity system.

Indeed power-reducing techniques are more adequate for medium/large distributed infrastructures like Grids [34], Clouds [35] or Data Centres [36] where thousand up to million servers are deployed. In those cases the costs reduction associated to such energy-saving measures are effectively significant, considered the scale of the infrastructure.

Nevertheless, starting from these energetic considerations, it is possible to conclude that low power architectures still represent a suitable solution for SME providing services because of the trade-off between performance and costs. As said before, in the considered scenario the acquisition of 5 Xeon D hosts is the cheapest solution that allows to support the considered workload, and it is able to satisfy the expectation of customers in terms of delivering results on time.

We would stress the fact that the analysis presented here has the purpose to answer the question if low-power SoC architectures are feasible also in a commercial environments where SMEs offer their services, as stated in the introduction. In general, the two HPC-201 systems represents in facts resources suitable for other types of workloads that need HPC-oriented capabilities. Moreover, higher cost servers are typically equipped with enterprise-level components as opposed to low-end system, which require service in the long run. However, for the purpose of our analysis, we demonstrated that low-power architectures can represent an equivalent or even better choice with respect to traditional enterprise system.

# 5   Conclusions and Future Works

This paper presented an analysis of performance and economic aspects for a SME willing to offer a service based on a real life application taken from the field of molecular biology using low power system-on-chips.

It is to note that comparing high-end HPC servers with motherboards based on low power SoC taken from the mobile and embedded world is "unfair", but nevertheless the results presented shows that also for time-consuming applications, like NGS data analysis, the use of low power architectures represents a feasible choice in terms of trade-off between execution times and power consumption.

Future developments of this work are represented by the evaluation of other application domains, with different requirements and also able to exploit multiple hosts at a time, in particular MPI-based ones. In particular, we are considering problems of real-time video surveillance and the possibility of using low power devices in pharmaceutical industries for the development of new drugs through in-silico simulations of proteins-chemicals interactions. In these scenarios also the costs and power consumption of switches will be considered, together with a more emphasis on the scalability figures.

**Acknowledgements.** This work has been supported by the Italian Ministry of Education and Research (MIUR) through the Flagship (PB05) InterOmics, the EC-FP7 innovation project MIMOMICS (no. 305280), and the EC- FP7 strep project REPARA (no. 609666), and it was partly funded by the Scientific Commission 5 of the Italian Institute for Nuclear Physics (INFN) through the COSA project.

# References

1. Winston, A., Favaloro, G., Healy, T.: Energy strategy for the c-suite. Harvard Bus. Rev. 138–146 (2017)
2. Rajovic, N., Carpenter, P., Gelado, I., Puzovic, N., Ramirez, A., Valero, M.: Supercomputing with commodity CPUs: are mobile SoCs ready for HPC? In: Proceedings of SC13: International Conference for High Performance Computing, Networking, Storage and Analysis (2013)
3. Calore, E., Schifano, S.F., Tripiccione, R.: Energy-performance tradeoffs for HPC applications on low power processors. In: Hunold, S., et al. (eds.) Euro-Par 2015. LNCS, vol. 9523, pp. 737–748. Springer, Cham (2015). doi:10.1007/978-3-319-27308-2_59
4. Hackenberg, D., Ilsche, T., Schone, R., Molka, D., Schmidt, M., Nagel, W.: Power measurement techniques on standard compute nodes: a quantitative comparison. In: 2013 IEEE International Symposium on Performance Analysis of Systems and Software (ISPASS), pp. 194–204 (2013)
5. Cesini, D., Corni, E., Falabella, A., Ferraro, A., Morganti, L., Calore, E., Schifano, S.F., Michelotto, M., Alfieri, R., De Pietri, R., Boccali, T., Biagioni, A., Lo Cicero, F., Lonardo, A., Martinelli, M., Paolucci, P.S., Pastorelli, E., Vicini, P.: Power efficient computing: the experience of the COSA project

6. Morganti, L., Cesini, D., Ferraro, A.: Evaluating systems on chip through HPC bioinformatics and astrophysics applications. In: Proceedings of the 24th Euromicro International Conference on Parallel, Distributed, and Network-Based Processing (PDP) 2016, pp. 541–544 (2016)
7. Jain, M., Olsen, H.E., Paten, B., et al.: The Oxford Nanopore MinION: delivery of nanopore sequencing to the genomics community. Genome Biol. **17**(1), 239 (2016)
8. Geist, A., Lucas, R.: Major computer science challenges at exascale. Int. J. High Perform. Comput. Appl. **23**(4), 427–436 (2009)
9. The Mont-Blanc prototype: an alternative approach for HPC systems. In SC16: International Conference for High Performance Computing, Networking, Storage and Analysis, pp. 444–455, November 2016. doi:10.1109/SC.2016.37
10. http://www.montblanc-project.eu/
11. Marazakis, M., et al.: EUROSERVER: share-anything scale-out microserver design. In: 2016 Design, Automation & Test in Europe Conference & Exhibition, DATE 2016, Dresden, Germany, 14–18 March 2016, pp. 678–683 (2016)
12. http://www.euroserver-project.eu/
13. Horak, D., et al.: Energy consumption optimization of the Total-FETI solver and BLAS routines by changing the CPU frequency. In: 2016 International Conference on High Performance Computing Simulation (HPCS), pp. 1031–1032, July 2016. doi:10.1109/HPCSim.2016.7568453
14. Catalan, S., et al.: Energy balance between voltage-frequency scaling and resilience for linear algebra routines on low-power multicore architectures. Parallel Comput. (2017). doi:10.1016/j.parco.2017.05.004
15. Furber, S., Temple, S.: Neural systems engineering. J. R. Soc. Interface **4**(13), 193–206 (2007). doi:10.1098/rsif.2006.0177
16. http://apt.cs.manchester.ac.uk/projects/SpiNNaker/
17. Katevenis, M., et al.: The ExaNeSt project: interconnects, storage and packaging for exascale systems. In: 2016 Euromicro Conference on Digital System Design (DSD), pp. 60–67 (2016). doi:10.1109/DSD.2016.106
18. Corni, E., Morganti, L., Morigi, M.P., Brancaccio, R., Bettuzzi, M., Levi, G., Peccenini, E., Cesini, D., Ferraro, A.: X-Ray computed tomography applied to objects of cultural heritage: porting and testing the filtered back-projection reconstruction algorithm on low power systems-on-chip. In: 24th Euromicro International Conference on Parallel, Distributed, and Network-Based Processing (PDP) 2016, pp. 369–372 (2016)
19. Morganti, L., Corni, E., Ferraro, A., Cesini, D., D'Agostino, D., Marelli, I.: Implementing a space-aware stochastic simulator on low-power architectures: a systems biology case study. In: 25th Euromicro International Conference on Parallel, Distributed, and Network-Based Processing (PDP) 2017 (2017)
20. Fuller, J.C., Khoueiry, P., Dinkel, H., et al.: Biggest challenges in bioinformatics. EMBO Rep. **14**(4), 302–304 (2013)
21. Church, G.M.: Genomes for all. Sci. Am. **294**(1), 46–54 (2006)
22. de Magalhes, J.P., Finch, C.E., Janssens, G.: Next-generation sequencing in aging research: emerging applications, problems, pitfalls and possible solutions. Ageing Res. Rev. **9**(3), 315–323 (2010)
23. Merelli, I., Calabria, A., Cozzi, P., et al.: SNPranker 2.0: a gene-centric data mining tool for diseases associated SNP prioritization in GWAS. BMC Bioinform. **14**(1), S9 (2013)
24. Merelli, I., Cozzi, P., D'Agostino, D., Clematis, A., Milanesi, L.: Image-based surface matching algorithm oriented to structural biology. IEEE/ACM Trans. Comput. Biol. Bioinform. (TCBB) **8**(4), 1004–1016 (2011)

25. Chiappori, F., Merelli, I., Milanesi, L., Marabotti, A.: Static and dynamic interactions between GALK enzyme and known inhibitors: guidelines to design new drugs for galactosemic patients. Eur. J. Med. Chem. **63**, 423–434 (2013)
26. Chiappori, F., D'Ursi, P., Merelli, I., Milanesi, L., Rovida, E.: In silico saturation mutagenesis and docking screening for the analysis of protein-ligand interaction: the Endothelial Protein C Receptor case study. BMC Bioinform. **10**(12), S3 (2009)
27. Langmead, B., Trapnell, C., Pop, M., Salzberg, S.L.: Ultrafast and memory-efficient alignment of short DNA sequences to the human genome. Genome Biol. **10**(3), R25 (2009)
28. Li, H., Durbin, R.: Fast and accurate short read alignment with Burrows Wheeler transform. Bioinformatics **25**(14), 1754–1760 (2009)
29. Dobin, A., Davis, C.A., Schlesinger, F., Drenkow, J., Zaleski, C., Jha, S., Batut, P., Chaisson, M., Gingeras, T.R.: STAR: ultrafast universal RNA-seq aligner. Bioinformatics **29**(1), 15–21 (2013)
30. DNA Sequencing Is Now Improving Faster Than Moore's Law! https://www.forbes.com/sites/techonomy/2012/01/12/dna-sequencing-is-now-improving-faster-than-moores-law
31. Applications of Whole Genome Sequencing in food safety management. www.fao.org/3/a-i5619e.pdf
32. Misale, C., Ferrero, G., Torquati, M., Aldinucci, M.: Sequence alignment tools: one parallel pattern to rule them all? BioMed Res. Int. (2014)
33. Antal, M., Pop, C., Valea, D., Cioara, T., Anghel, I., Salomie, I.: Optimizing data centres operation to provide ancillary services on-demand. In: Altmann, J., Silaghi, G.C., Rana, O.F. (eds.) GECON 2015. LNCS, vol. 9512, pp. 133–146. Springer, Cham (2016). doi:10.1007/978-3-319-43177-2_9
34. Galizia, A., Quarati, A.: Job allocation strategies for energy-aware and efficient Grid infrastructures. J. Syst. Softw. **85**(7), 1588–1606 (2012)
35. Quarati, A., Clematis, A., D'Agostino, D.: Delivering cloud services with QoS requirements: business opportunities, architectural solutions and energy-saving aspects. Future Gener. Comput. Syst. **55**, 403–427 (2016)
36. Goiri, I., Katsak, W., Le, K., Nguyen, T.D., Bianchini, R.: Parasol and GreenSwitch: managing datacenters powered by renewable energy. In Proceedings of the Eighteenth International Conference on Architectural Support for Programming Languages and Operating Systems (ASPLOS 2013), pp. 51–64. ACM, New York (2013)

# Edge Computing

# User Behavior and Application Modeling in Decentralized Edge Cloud Infrastructures

John Violos[1]([✉]), Vinicius Monteiro de Lira[2], Patrizio Dazzi[2], Jörn Altmann[3],
Baseem Al-Athwari[3], Antonia Schwichtenberg[4], Young-Woo Jung[5],
Theodora Varvarigou[1], and Konstantinos Tserpes[1,6]

[1] School of Electrical and Computer Engineering,
National Technical University of Athens, 15771 Zografou, Greece
violos@mail.ntua.gr,dora@telecom.ntua.gr
[2] Institute of Information Science and Technologies,
National Research Council of Italy (CNR), Pisa, Italy
{vinicius.monteirodelira,patrizio.dazzi}@isti.cnr.it
[3] Technology Management, Economics, and Policy Program, College of Engineering,
Seoul National University, Seoul, Republic of Korea
{altmann,baseem}@snu.ac.kr
[4] CAS Software AG, Karlsruhe, Germany
Antonia.Schwichtenberg@cas.de
[5] Cloud Computing Research Department,
Electronics and Telecommunications Research Institute (ETRI),
Daejeon, Republic of Korea
jungyw@etri.re.kr
[6] Department of Informatics and Telematcs,
Harokopio University of Athens, Tavros, Greece
tserpes@hua.gr

**Abstract.** Edge computing has emerged as a solution that can accommodate complex application requirements by shifting data and computation to infrastructure elements that are more suitable to manage them given the current circumstances. The BASMATI Knowledge Extractor is a component that facilitates the modeling of the resource utilization by providing tools to analyze application usage together with user behavior. This is particularly relevant in the case of mobile applications where user context and activity are tightly coupled to the application performance.

**Keywords:** Performance modeling · Resource utilization · User behavior modeling · Application usage modeling · BASMATI project

## 1 Introduction

The rate at which mobile applications expand to take over a large share in the software market is unprecedented. The supporting infrastructures are undergoing a continuous development in order to cope with the demanding setting. The advent of decentralized edge clouds has managed to stick out among the viable

© Springer International Publishing AG 2017
C. Pham et al. (Eds.): GECON 2017, LNCS 10537, pp. 193–203, 2017.
DOI: 10.1007/978-3-319-68066-8_15

solutions and has been quickly adopted by application developers. This type of infrastructure assumes a dynamic orchestration of multiple computing and storage elements from which it may be comprised.

The BASMATI Knowledge Extractor (BKE) contributes towards this direction by providing decision support services to federated cloud brokers and job offloading managers. It does so by investigating the contribution of the user behavior (and in particular mobility since we are referring to mobile applications), of the application model, as well as their combination, to the resource utilization patterns.

This investigation is relying on data analysis for building predictive models for user behavior and application usage. The work suggests a number of possible approaches that yield different results under various conditions. The BKE can be seen as a toolkit that can contribute in the preservation of QoS through a more efficient resource utilization.

This work describes the design of such a component in the context of a federated, decentralized edge cloud platform supporting mobile applications. It continues with details about the data management and concludes with the tools that are to enable the knowledge acquisition.

## 2   Functionality and Architecture of the Knowledge Extractor

The general architecture of the BKE component is presented in Fig. 1. It is comprised of three knowledge acquisition subcomponents and an auxiliary data preprocessing subcomponent. The three knowledge acquisition components are the User Mobility Behavior, Application Usage Modeling and the Situation Knowledge Acquisition. These subcomponents rely on prediction techniques that are described in Sect. 4 regarding the knowledge acquisition. The preprocessing of data takes place in the Unified Representation subcomponent and uses data fusion and feature engineering techniques described in Sect. 3.

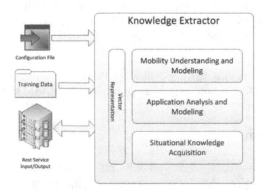

**Fig. 1.** Knowledge extractor component.

Figure 2 depicts the formalization of the problem that resolves the BKE. Given the available data from various data resources, the BKE refines and fuses them in a unified representation upon which it then applies a prediction technique in combination with the Knowledge base to produce the outcome predictions. The outcome predictions can be defined in terms of user mobility or applications and sessions demands on resources. With the term "session" we refer to an application session running at a specific time for a specific user.

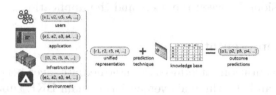

**Fig. 2.** Flow of logic of the knowledge extractor process.

## 2.1 User Mobility Behavior Modeling

The Mobility understanding and modeling is the subcomponent of the BKE that analyzes and predicts the behavior of the mobile app users. It is application-dependent and operates on the assumption that the user behavior affects the provision of application services and the utilization of the federated resources. For instance, for location-based mobile applications supported by decentralized edge cloud infrastructures, the resource utilization may vary based on the mobility patterns of the end users. As such, analysis of semantic trajectories (that is, trajectories enhanced with e.g. event metadata) may assist in dynamically balancing the load among the various infrastructure elements and thus preserving the QoS guarantees. The extraction of these trajectories requires the fusion and analysis of multiple data sources including textual, geo-spatial and other types of data.

The actions for a Basmati end user to adapt the mobility modeling to a new specific given application are the following two: firstly, a compatible dataset based on previous observations should be passed to the BKE in order to construct the representation knowledge base that will be used from the supervised machine learning techniques. Afterwards, in the configuration file should be declared which prediction technique will be used and the type of the input data.

## 2.2 Application Usage Modeling

Based on the application usage modeling, predictions related to resource demands came be made, this time from the application's perspective. Different applications pose different resource demands under the same load. These predictions in combination with the QoS should be examined by the resource broker for the optimal resource management and the avoidance of bottlenecks. Some of the resource demand parameters that are modeled are CPU, memory, bandwidth, average file size, application duration usage and time interval between two application requests.

## 2.3  Situational Knowledge Acquisition

The Situational Knowledge Acquisition is the third main subcomponent of the BKE. This subcomponent makes predictions of the resource demands that are generated for sessions between the users and the applications.

## 2.4  Unified Representation

The unified representation introduces an intermediate layer between the sources of incoming data and the three abovementioned main BKE subcomponents. Its purpose is to unify and transform the input data in a form compatible and readable by the predictive algorithms.

Heterogeneous data sources will constantly feed the BKE with observations. They include human trajectories, web-based data, user contextual data, resource utilization per application, etc. Feature engineering techniques are applied to gauge the best feature representation of the observations. Then, the users behavior, application model and combinations of user-application can be represented with a composite data structure as illustrated in Fig. 3.

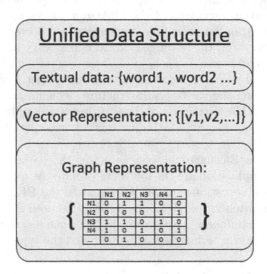

**Fig. 3.** Unified data structure.

Respectively each prediction model can process different kind of data such as textual data, vectors or graphs and retrieve them from the compatible field of the unified data structure.

## 2.5  Configuration

The BKE components can be used on demand, based on the particular application scenario requirements. Each case can have its own specific data as input and expect its own specific data as outcome predictions. The form of the input data, the expected outcomes, and the selection of the predictor techniques can be passed to the BKE through a configuration service. This configuration service orchestrates how the BKE works. Technically, it comprises a REST endpoint that receives the configurations in the form of an XML or JSON document, allowing for the implementation of a usable web interface for its creation.

## 2.6  Training Data

According to the supervised machine learning techniques, the three main subcomponents use training data to build their internal knowledge representations. Initially these training data can be provided by files in the hosted servers of the components.

## 2.7  Input/Output

The input and the output of the BKE are provided and stored in a local relational database, accessed through a RESTful API. Similarly, user context and application data can be persisted to the database through the API so they can then be transformed to the form expected by the unified data structure.

# 3  Data Preprocessing

The data preprocessing is carried out in order to fit the data to the unified representation structure's schema involving three consequent steps. The data fusion that gathers the data from the data sources performing operations to join them, the feature engineering that produce the most representative features and the normalization of the value features. The aim of the data preprocessing stage is to combine relevant information from various sources into a single structure that provides a more accurate and flexible description in contrast with the individual data sources.

The varying input instances are mapped in the unified representation structures. The knowledge base files are loaded and used by the prediction techniques in combination with the representation of the input instances so as to produce the requested predictions. There is no need to store and retrieve the input data in any kind of database. The unified representation subcomponent is responsible to handle the varying input data and the extra effort of a database should be avoided. Furthermore, the knowledge base files are stored in files such as JSON and arff. The prediction techniques do not need specific parts of the stored data and specific queries on them, but they need entire length of the knowledge base to carry out their processes (Fig. 4).

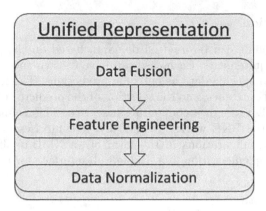

**Fig. 4.** Unified representation.

## 3.1 Data Fusion

The fusion of data is a very powerful tool and enriches the prediction methods. For the BKE component the data is comprised of user profile data and application, service and resource usage data. These data are integrated, using any of the two following models according to the frequency and the size of the data load from the data sources.

– The Multi-sensor integration fusion model [11] follows a hierarchical fashion to combine data in fusion centers. The first fusion center retrieves data from two peer sensors. The following fusion centers combine the data from a new data sensor with the output of the previous Fusion center. The last fusion center outputs the integrated data in a unified structure. This method is used in case of a heavy data workload.
– The second option for the data fusion from multiple sensors is the Behaviour knowledge-based model [12]. This model consists of a series of stages. The first stage retrieves the data from all the data sensors. In the next stage a feature vector is extracted from the retrieved data. The third stage associates a data structure to the predefined needs. In the last stage, a set of rules is applied according to formalism of the representation. This method will be used in case of a frequent data update.

## 3.2 Feature Engineering

The intrinsic structure of the available data and the needs of the end users may constitute a supervised learning problem that involves features that do not have a positive contribution to the method accuracy. The concept the more data the better results is not applied in the prediction methods and large amounts of data may produce low accuracy and performance in data analytic applications.

Two different set of techniques are used to mitigate the issue of the redundant features of the datasets: the feature extraction and the feature selection. Both of them reduce the data representation using fewer features. Features, attributes, variables, terms, dimensions are interchangeable notions for the needs of BKE. Feature extraction methods represent features in a new dimensional space making a fusion or a transformation of the features. On the contrary, feature selection methods do not transform the dimensions. They select the dimensions that contain more bits of information based on a certain objective function.

**Feature Extraction.** The Feature extraction methods introduce a new lower feature-dimensional space that combines the initial data features. The derived features should satisfy the following three properties. They should be informative and non-redundant, facilitate the machine learning and predictions methods in which they will be used, and in some case to provide a better human understanding of the problem. Two feature extraction techniques are presented below the technique that satisfy the aforementioned criteria in a better way will be implemented in the unified representation subcomponent.

A common dimensionality reduction method is the Principal Component Analysis (PCA) [8]. PCA is a statistical method that orthogonally transforms the original dimensions into a new component set of dimensions. The new set of dimensions is called principal components, it is smaller and it retains most of the information. The basic idea is to convert the correlated features into a new set of features that are linearly uncorrelated. The PCA is an iterative process. The first principal component should have the largest variance and the following components should have the highest variance under the restriction to be orthogonal to the previous components.

The Independent Component Analysis (ICA) [6] is a statistical and computation feature extraction method that detects the latent features that underline sets of random observations. ICA is based on a generative model for multivariate data. The instances can be linear or nonlinear mixtures of the unknown latent variables while how they are mixed is unknown. The latent variables that will be found by ICA are assumed to be non-Gaussian, linear and mutually independent and they are called the independent components of the observed data. The feature extraction process is not reversible because some information is lost in the process of transformation.

**Feature Selection.** Feature selection is the process of choosing a subset of features from a set of candidate features based on a statistical score such as variation of variable correlation. The features that will be selected are the most important and representative of the available features. These methods require a good understanding of the aspects of the prediction problem that have to be resolved.

The three main feature selection approaches are wrapper method, filter method and the embedded method. The wrapper and the embedded Feature selection techniques cannot be applied to the KE because of the computation demands and their inability to discriminate the feature selection stage with the prediction stage. On the other hand, the filter methods produce good results with low computation demands. Other filter techniques are Information gain, Chi-square, Mutual Information, Fisher score, Low variance criterion.

### 3.3 Data Normalization

The data sources may provide values in a different scale than the internal representation of the predefined knowledge of the BKE. A standardization and normalization process bridges this gap reproducing the feature values to lie between a specified minimum and a maximum value.

## 4 Knowledge Acquisition

The BKE predictions can be carried out by classification, clustering or regression methods. The decision of what prediction approach is used depends on the type and the amount of provided data and the parameters to be predicted which vary in each use case. The following proposed method can be enhanced to take into consideration the time evolution of the observations and the predicted parameters.

### 4.1 Natural Language Processing

Predictions based on the textual data can be carried out using a Graph representation model in combination with Graph similarity metrics. The Graph model has been used for classification [2] and clustering purposes [16] and it can be also applied for regression analysis. The graph model has been used with N-Grams being represented as nodes yet there is the option to use words instead. In the following description of the Graph model we use the term implying a word or N-gram.

### 4.2 Vector Processing

The classification, clustering and regression of vectors have been extensively researched and applied in many fields. We use two of the main vector prediction methods as the baseline models of the BKE: the Support Vector Machine (SVM) and Bayes Classification. The SVM [14] model represents the instances as points in an N-dimensional space. Then a planar is gauged to divide the instances that belong to different categories. The gap between instances that belong to different categories should be as wide as possible. The Gaussian Bayes classifier [7] uses a conditional probability model in which the values of the vector are the independent variables and the category is the dependent variable y.

## 4.3    Graph Partitioning

To identify categories of users or the correlation between users and applications a graph partition method can be applied. Typically the graph partitioning problems are NP-hard. Heuristic and approximation algorithms have been proposed that produce sufficient results. The KernighanLin algorithm [3] is a graph partition algorithm that performs well in a dense graph with less than 10000 nodes. It uses a technique that exchanges nodes between the partitions using the betweenness metric of internal and external cost. Girvan and Newman [5] inctroduced the K-Means partition algorithm. K-Means produce good results with the limitation that the observations should be linear. In this method each observation is assigned in the cluster with the nearest mean value.

## 4.4    Artificial Neural Network Method

Literacy research [10, 15] suggests that another option that achieves the same goal is to employ artificial neural networks (ANN). ANN may provide an accurate model of the application deployment allowing to estimate the computational requirements of a given user.

# 5    Implementation of Knowledge Extractor

The implementation of the BKE took place using the Java programming language and it complies with the specifications of Open Cloud Computing Inter face (OCCI) [4]. The BKE uses a variety of prediction techniques, some of them are implemented based on available java libraries such as Weka [17], deeplearning4java [1] and some others such as NgramsGraphs NLP classification and Markov chains developed from the researchers and developers of the Basmati project. In order to provide more prediction techniques that are based on the scikit-learn library [13] of the python programming language we have examined the use of wrappers such as Jython [9].

The BKE interfaces with the other components of Basmati through a restful API using JSON for data representation. The Decision Maker (DM) is the component of the Basmati platform that requests the predictions of the users mobility and the application resources. The Application Monitoring is the component that is responsible to store and retrieve the data that can be used to update the knowledge base.

# 6    Conclusions

Predicting the resource requirements in an edge cloud platform supporting mobile applications calls for the development of a complex model. This model maps user behavior and application usage to resource utilization. The BKE provides an architecture that facilitates a number of machine learning techniques that can be adapted to the given data and provide estimations of the resource utilization.

**Acknowledgements.** BASMATI (http://basmati.cloud) has received funding from the European Unions Horizon 2020 research and innovation programme under grant agreement no. 723131 and from ICT R&D program of Korean Ministry of Science, ICT and Future Planning no. R0115-16-0001.

# References

1. Deeplearning4j: Open-source distributed deep learning for the jvm. https://deeplearning4j.org. Accessed 17 July 17
2. Aisopos, F., Tzannetos, D., Violos, J., Varvarigou, T.A.: Using n-gram graphs for sentiment analysis: an extended study on twitter. In: Second IEEE International Conference on Big Data Computing Service and Applications, BigDataService 2016, Oxford, United Kingdom, March 29 - April 1, 2016, pp. 44–51 (2016). http://dx.doi.org/10.1109/BigDataService.2016.13
3. Dutt, S.: New faster kernighan-lin-type graph-partitioning algorithms. In: Proceedings of 1993 International Conference on Computer Aided Design (ICCAD), pp. 370–377, November 1993
4. Edmonds, A., Metsch, T., Papaspyrou, A.: Open cloud computing interface in data management-related setups. In: Fiore, S., Aloisio, G. (eds.) Grid and Cloud Database Management, pp. 23–48. Springer, Heidelberg (2011). doi:10.1007/978-3-642-20045-8_2
5. Girvan, M., Newman, M.E.: Community structure in social and biological networks. Proc. Natl. Acad. Sci. **99**(12), 7821–7826 (2002)
6. Hyvärinen, A., Oja, E.: Independent component analysis: algorithms and applications. Neural Netw. **13**(4–5), 411–430 (2000)
7. John, G.H., Langley, P.: Estimating continuous distributions in bayesian classifiers. In: Proceedings of the Eleventh Conference on Uncertainty in Artificial Intelligence, UAI 1995, pp. 338–345. Morgan Kaufmann Publishers Inc., San Francisco (1995)
8. Jolliffe, I.: Principal Component Analysis. Wiley, New York (2014)
9. Juneau, J., Baker, J., Wierzbicki, F., Muoz, L.S., Ng, V., Ng, A., Baker, D.L.: The Definitive Guide to Jython: Python for the Java Platform. Apress, Berkeley (2010)
10. Kousiouris, G., Menychtas, A., Kyriazis, D., Gogouvitis, S., Varvarigou, T.: Dynamic, behavioral-based estimation of resource provisioning based on high-level application terms in cloud platforms. Future Gener. Comput. Syst. **32**, 27–40 (2014)
11. Luo, R.C., Kay, M.G.: Multisensor integration and fusion in intelligent systems. IEEE Trans. Syst. Man Cybern. **19**(5), 901–931 (1989)
12. Pau, L.F.: Sensor data fusion. J. Intell. Robot. Syst. **1**(2), 103–116 (1988)
13. Pedregosa, F., Varoquaux, G., Gramfort, A., Michel, V., Thirion, B., Grisel, O., Blondel, M., Prettenhofer, P., Weiss, R., Dubourg, V., et al.: Scikit-learn: machine learning in python. J. Mach. Learn. Res. **12**, 2825–2830 (2011)
14. Singla, A., Patra, S., Bruzzone, L.: A novel classification technique based on progressive transductive SVM learning. Pattern Recogn. Lett. **42**, 101–106 (2014)
15. Tserpes, K., Kyriazis, D., Menychtas, A., Varvarigou, T.: A novel mechanism for provisioning of high-level quality of service information in grid environments. Eur. J. Oper. Res. **191**(3), 1113–1131 (2008)

16. Violos, J., Tserpes, K., Papaoikonomou, A., Kardara, M., Varvarigou, T.A.: Clustering documents using the 3-gram graph representation model. In: 18th Panhellenic Conference on Informatics, PCI 2014, Athens, Greece, October 2–4, 2014, pp. 29:1–29:5 (2014). http://doi.acm.org/10.1145/2645791.2645812
17. Witten, I.H., Frank, E., Hall, M.A., Pal, C.J.: Data Mining: Practical Machine Learning Tools and Techniques. Morgan Kaufmann, San Francisco (2016)

# Incentivising Resource Sharing in Edge Computing Applications

Ioan Petri[1][✉], Omer F. Rana[2], Joseph Bignell[2], Surya Nepal[3], and Nitin Auluck[4]

[1] School of Engineering, Cardiff University, Cardiff, UK
petrii@cardiff.ac.uk
[2] School of Computer Science and Informatics, Cardiff University, Cardiff, UK
[3] CSIRO, Canberra, Australia
[4] Indian Institute of Technology Ropar, Rupnagar, India

**Abstract.** There is increasing realisation that edge devices, which are closer to a user, can play an important part in supporting latency and privacy sensitive applications. Such devices have also continued to increase in capability over recent years, ranging in complexity from embedded resources (e.g. Raspberry Pi, Arduino boards) placed alongside data capture devices to more complex "micro data centres". Using such resources, a user is able to carry out task execution and data storage in proximity to their location, often making use of computing resources that can have varying ownership and access rights. Increasing performance requirements for stream processing applications (for instance), which incur delays between the client and the cloud have led to newer models of computation, which requires an application workflow to be split across data centre and edge resource capabilities. With recent emergence of edge/fog computing it has become possible to migrate services to micro-data centres and to address the performance limitations of traditional (centralised data centre) cloud based applications. Such migration can be represented as a cost function that involves incentives for micro-data centres to host services with associated quality of services and experience. Business models need to be developed for creating an open edge cloud environment where micro-data centres have the right incentives to support service hosting, and for large scale data centre operators to outsource service execution to such micro data centres. We describe potential revenue models for micro-data centers to support service migration and serve incoming requests for edge based applications. We present several cost models which involve combined use of edge devices and centralised data centres.

**Keywords:** Edge computing · Micro-data centres · Resource sharing · Cost · Business models

## 1 Introduction and Motivation

With the increasing number of devices that are now generating data, it is necessary to understand how this data should be stored, processed and archived.

© Springer International Publishing AG 2017
C. Pham et al. (Eds.): GECON 2017, LNCS 10537, pp. 204–215, 2017.
DOI: 10.1007/978-3-319-68066-8_16

Various projections have been made about the number of Internet of Things (IoT) devices we are likely to see over the next few years (often around 2020) – from Cisco, Gartner, etc. The numbers vary, but there is general agreement that this is likely to be in the order of billions, and 40% of generated data will come from sensors [5] by this projected time period. Currently, most data generated in this way is transmitted to a cloud-based data centre, processed and returned back to the user. Although this has become the dominant mode of operation, this introduces significant limitations for applications that have latency constraints, or which require response times to be within a particular threshold. Supporting application requirements through a cloud-based data centre is constrained by the last-mile network connecting the user to the network. Whereas the network around the data centre is often high speed and of high capacity, the network from the user to the first hop network component can have varying properties (especially true for mobile users).

To overcome these constraints, the fog and edge computing paradigm has been proposed, to enable processing and data storage between the user and the data centre. Fog and edge computing (FEC) resources can have significant heterogeneity (performance, data formats, energy use, type, security capability, etc.), and may be offered by a variety of different vendors, e.g. coffee shops, University campuses, Point of Presence from mobile network providers, etc [11]. There is also differing terminology associated with such FEC resources, for instance, some also refer to these as "cloudlets" [9] "micro data centres" (MDC) [1] that exist at the network edge, and peer with cloud-based data centres, etc. Many also consider a Peer-2-Peer approach for aggregating edge capacity, by enabling such cloudlets to interact with each other directly. A variety of applications have been suggested to benefit from FEC infrastructure, such as supporting storage and caching, partial processing of video feeds, monitoring physical assets (e.g. in retail or supply chain applications), on-line and interactive gaming etc. There is also emerging literature on how potential *interference* caused by co-located workloads in a cloud environment can be migrated to FEC devices, focusing on just-in-time migration of services, e.g. INDICIES [10], Caglar et al. [3].

There is now increasing literature on how such FEC infrastructure can be realised in practice [6–8]. Approaches range from the use of Raspberry Pi/Arduino-based resources that can host a Web Server (such as Flask), to more specialist micro data centres that can implemented using a computing cluster. There is however limited coverage on business and revenue models that would incentivise resource providers to offer FEC resources for third party use. We investigate this aspect in here using two application scenarios. An architecture is proposed for supporting these business models, which can be generalised to a variety of applications. We use simulations using iFogSim [4] to demonstrate the benefit of using FEC resources using our prototype applications. Section 2 provides an architecture to give context to the discussion in this paper. The reminder of the paper is as follows: In Sect. 2 we present our micro-data centre architecture and description. In Sect. 3 we describe the application scenario and overall methodology followed by the performance evaluation in Subsect. 3.3). In Sect. 4 we present business models for fog computing and conclude our work in Sect. 5.

## 2   FEC Architecture

Figure 1 illustrates a conceptual architecture for FEC application orchestration. A mobile device (D) has the ability to generate/ingest data and submit tasks for processing. The tasks are submitted to a micro data centre (MDC), that is "closer" to the user device (geographically or based on access latency). MDCs are capable of holding data and executing tasks with a very low latency (compared to a cloud data centre). For simplicity, we assume that each device is connected to one MDC (their "home MDC"). However, it is possible for user devices to connect to multiple MDCs. Similarly, each MDC is connected to its Cloud Data Center (CDC), i.e., home CDC; it is possible for one MDC to be connected to multiple CDCs. Existence of an MDC therefore data transfer from a user to this MDC in the first instance. The MDC can also act as a data cache to to subsequently transfer this data to a CDC if needed. To ensure support for data privacy and security (a major constraint in use of MDC at present), we assume that a device D can trust its home MDC. The home CDC is classified as semi-trusted, i.e., it can do the task as requested, but cannot guarantee the privacy of data and tasks. Here, the data and tasks are exposed to potential attacks such as an insider attack. Other MDCs and CDCs are untrusted.

We consider a decentralised distributed orchestration model, in which each computing device in the network has an orchestration agent. Agents work collaboratively towards achieving the goal, i.e. complete a user task within a budget and a given deadline, subject to security constraints.

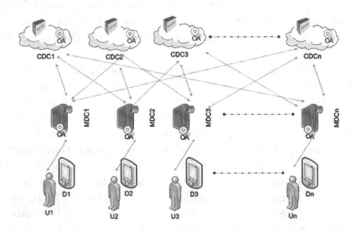

**Fig. 1.** Conceptual architecture for FEC application orchestration.

## 2.1    Best Effort Orchestration Protocol

Orchestration Agents (OAs) at both MDC and CDC work together to schedule user submitted tasks. Consider three task execution scenarios, at: (a) home MDC, (b) home CDC, and (c) remote MDC, as illustrated in Fig. 2. The diagram demonstrates a best effort orchestration protocol as an example to illustrate the concept.

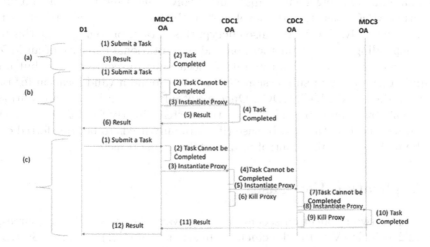

**Fig. 2.** Orchestration Protocol between MDC and CDC.

In scenario 1, device (D) submits a task to its home MDC (MDC1), which can meet the cost, deadline and security requirements. The task is then executed at the local MDC and result returned to D. As local MDCs are trusted, this case uses the highest level of security. In scenario 2, the task submitted by D cannot be executed at the local MDC, being unable to meet task deadline due to existing workload. The local OA forwards to CDC (CDC1) OA to create a proxy agent. The proxy agent then takes over the responsibility for task completion. The task is then completed by CDC1 and the result is returned to D via MDC1. As CDC1 is considered to be semi-trusted, this scenario represents a semi-trusted task execution at CDC (meeting the other two constraints of cost and deadline). In scenario 3, the task cannot be completed by the home CDC (CDC1), requiring other CDCs or MDCs that can complete the task. In our example, the CDC1 first contacts CDC2, but it cannot meet the latency requirement as the result of the task is much bigger in size than the original task. This means the task has to be computed closer to the device to meet the latency requirement. The CDC2 finds another MDC closer to D that can meet the latency requirement. It instantiates a new proxy agent at the remote MDC (MDC3) and passes the task to it – and the local agent is terminated. MDC3 completes the task and returns the results directly to MDC1, which then passes this to D. All proxy agent instances for a specific task are killed once the task is completed. Note that we have described normal execution scenarios using a best effort orchestration protocol. Our multi-agent based distributed orchestration can handle variations in the execution of the protocol due to failures, including failures to meet the specified requirements (cost, security and deadline).

Data transfer between OAs remains an important challenge in these scenarios, which may involve two aspects: (i) a user device submits data to the "local" MDC, and from this point onwards requires the OA at the MDC to manage and coordinate data management. This could involve migrating the data to a CDC or another MDC, based on the level of "trust" that has been identified by the user. Alternatively, the OA can also encrypt this data prior to migrating this to a CDC, depending on the sophistication and computational capacity of an MDC; (ii) a user device aims to find a suitable location to execute a task, but does not undertake any data submission before it has found a valid location for task execution (i.e. local MDC, CDC). Once a suitable location has been confirmed, and an OA has been deployed, data is transferred directly from the user device to the device hosting the OA. In case (ii), data only needs to be transferred once and the user device takes control of undertaking this transfer.

## 3    Application Use Cases

We consider two application scenarios to motivate the use of FEC resources, a Vehicle-2-Vehicle (V2V) and Vehicle-to-Infastructure (V2I) scenario (Sect. 3.1) and a healthcare data processing scenario (Sect. 3.2).

### 3.1    Vehicle-2-Infrastructure Interaction

This scenario involves determining congestion within a particular area by using: (i) localised information and alerting; (ii) global processing of the information at a CDC. The scenario is realised using three agents, represented as *controllers* in Fig. 3. A camera monitors a given traffic area, and based on observed motion, alerts an "Area Traffic Controller" (acting as MDC) – which takes into account location of vehicles (and co-position to each other), and sends updates to a "Car Controller" (alongside the road, another MDC) and a "Global Traffic Controller" (running in a CDC) – the last of these can aggregate forecast received from other Area Traffic Controllers across multiple regions. Each of these controllers have different resource capacities and latencies from the Car Controller. The Car Controller measures speed of each passing vehicle in its vicinity, and sends this data for aggregation to the other controllers. We simulate this scenario using iFogSim, giving different capacities to each of these controllers (including an energy consumption profile), as illustrated in Table 1.

In this scenario both the MDC and CDC are considered to be "trusted", i.e. data can be exchanged between any MDC and the CDC. Trust in this case can also be related to potential availability of an MDC, i.e. if the network connecting the MDC to the CDC is likely to fail, then multiple MDCs may co-exist at the same location to provide greater resilience. Trust in this instance measures the

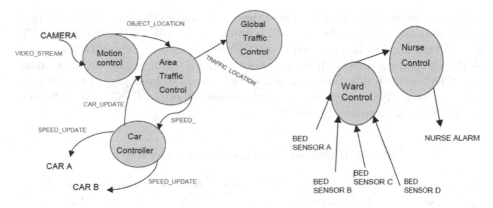

**Fig. 3.** Controllers for V2V/V2I scenario.

**Fig. 4.** Controllers for healthcare scenario.

**Table 1.** V2V configuration for iFogSim.

| Src | Dest. | CPU (MIPS) | Network (pckts) | Data type | Direc. |
| --- | --- | --- | --- | --- | --- |
| Camera | Motion Detec. | 1000 | 20000 | Stream | Up |
| Motion Detec. | Area Traffic Contr. | 3000 | 2000 | Obj. Loc. | Up |
| Area Traffic Contr. | Glob. Traf. Contr. | 5000 | 2000 | Traf. Loc. | Up |
| Car Contr. | Area Traffic Contr. | 500 | 2000 | Car Update | Up |
| Car Contr. | Speed | 100 | 100 | Speed Upd | Down |

likelihood that an MDC will return a suitable reading to a CDC within a given time interval.

## 3.2 Healthcare Data Processing

In this scenario, all beds within a hospital ward have sensors that monitor vital signs of a patient (such as heart rate, movement pattern, ECG data, etc.). The "Ward Controller" takes this raw data and performs analysis of the data locally, and acts as an MDC in this case. Data from each patient can be analysed to identify any particular triggers or anomalies that should be identified to a clinician – referred to as the "allNurse" alarm tuple in Fig. 4. In this instance, the data remains within the ward (i.e. the context of the local MDC), and does not need to be exported to any external system. The "Nurse Control" involves interaction with local nurses, and if an alarm is received a "nurseAlarm" actuator is triggered.

Where an anomaly has been found and further analysis needs to be carried out, the data is exported to an extended data centre (CDC). This analysis could involve: (i) integrating this data with other sources available about the same individual; (ii) carrying out a multi-patient population study to investigate patients with a similar profile. In both case, the data can be presented to a clinician for further analysis. The objective in this application scenario is that in the majority of cases the data will remain within a Ward Controller (MDC), and will not need to be exported to a CDC. In this instance, the MDC is trusted as it collects data directly from a patient within a ward. Migration of the data to a CDC would imply that confidential data needs to be exported to a remote location for analysis, requiring security credentials of the CDC to be validated before this is undertaken (Table 2).

**Table 2.** Healthcare scenario configuration for iFogSim.

| Src | Dest. | CPU (MIPS) | Network (pckts) | Data type | Direc. |
|---|---|---|---|---|---|
| Bed sensor | Heart Rate Detec. | 1000 | 200 | Raw data | Up |
| Heart Rate Detec. | Nurse Contrl. | 2000 | 1000 | Call Nurse | Up |
| Nurse Contrl. | Alarm | 100 | 100 | Alarm | Down |

### 3.3    Evaluation: Performance

Both scenarios have been simulated via iFogSim changing a number of parameters associated with each. For the V2V scenario, the number of areas and cars/area were modified, to investigate the impact of executing car updates at local MDC (Area Controller) vs. at the CDC (Global Controller). As illustrated in Fig. 5, the benefit of using an MDC alongside a CDC is illustrated, where the processing time on a CDC which takes 11000 simulation cycles is reduced to 4000 cycles using a combination of CDC+MDC for 100 cars per area. In his simulation a total of 10 areas were considered, with this graph representing the average obtained from the simulation.

Figure 6 illustrates how data exchanged between the MDC and CDC varies, due to network congestion. The aim is to demonstrate that due to network congestion between the MDC and CDC, it does not make sense to transmit local data to the CDC for processing, necessitating se of local MDC. This could

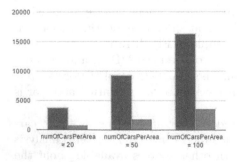

**Fig. 5.** MDC+CDC – Sim. Time on y-axis.

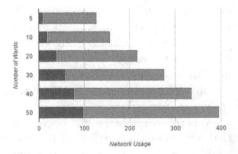

**Fig. 6.** MDC vs. CDC – Net. Traffic.

occur, for instance, if more wards or more beds per ward are introduced into the simulation. For this particular simulation, we maintain the number of beds/ward at 10 and increase the number of wards to 50. The y-axis shows total network usage when the simulation was run at CDC (the red bars) being significantly larger than the total network usage with MDC (blue bars). Utilizing local MDC reduces network traffic, as smaller amounts of data need to be shipped outside the local region/area of the MDC, thereby leading to lower network congestion. Within a decentralised hospital we would expect to have thousands of sensors constantly sending data so network congestion would be a real problem, looking at the results from this scenario we can see that a decentralised hospital would not be possible without use of FEC devices.

### 3.4 Evaluation: Cost Analysis

Based on the V2V scenario in Sect. 3.1, we consider that we have a set of MDCs – $N = \{n_1, ..., n_m\}$, responsible for managing data from Car Controllers $C = \{c_1, ..., c_n\}$. Each $c_i$ broadcasts data to an MDC based on an analysis of congestion within a given area. Therefore, we have a number of computational jobs that need to be processed to calculate this congestion profile, with a preference for execution at a particular $n_j$. We consider that a job has an associated cost $c$, calculated as:

$$c = exec._{time} \times cost_{excution} + net._{tranfer} \times cost_{transfer} + storage_{time} \times cost_{storage}$$

where $cost_{execution}$ is the cost per CPU, $cost_{transfer}$ represents data size transferred and $cost_{storage}$ represents cost for storage of data. The costs reported in the experiments are calculated based on Amazon EC2 small instances in dollars(\$). We present only the MCDs cost perspective and we are not taking into consideration aspects related to delays in execution and time-to-execute constraints.

Increasing number of cars: In this scenario we investigate the impact on cost when increasing the number of vehicles for a fixed number of areas. As illustrated in Fig. 7, on the x-axis the parameters [5, 10] refer to 5 areas and 10 cars per area.

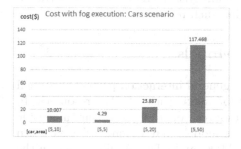

**Fig. 7.** Transaction costs – Cars.

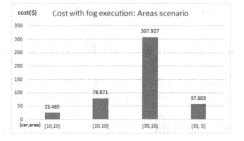

**Fig. 8.** Transaction costs – Areas.

We observe that the cost fluctuates with the number of cars. When increasing the number of cars per area, due to an increase in the number of devices submitting jobs, the network communication increases requiring greater congestion on FEC devices. We observe that when using 5 areas and 50 cars [5, 50] the cost reaches the highest level.

Increasing number of areas: We measure the impact of changing the number of areas with associated FEC devices monitoring a number of vehicles in their proximity. An area can host an MDC that can be used to carry out analysis on data from the vehicles. In this experiment the number of vehicles is fixed while the number of areas is modified.

In Fig. 8 we observe that changing the number of areas has a more significant impact than number of vehicles. Areas have a specific number of Car Controllers that can execute jobs by estimating car speeds and locations. The maximum cost is recorded when using 30 areas with 10 cars per area, expressed as [30, 10]. We also consider how the system reacts to different loading scenarios (i.e. changes in number of jobs that need to be processed) when both cars and areas change. Figure 9 shows how execution time changes with increasing number of cars and areas, and subsequent impact on execution time due to increase in network traffic and number of tasks.

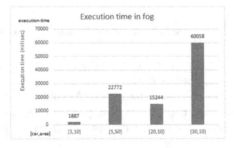

**Fig. 9.** Execution time: increasing cars & areas.

These simulations demonstrate how FEC devices (represented as Car and Area Controllers) can be used alongside a cloud system (represented as a Global Controller), and the associated cost of using such resources.

## 4   Business and Coordination Models

Given the two scenarios in Sect. 3 and the general interaction protocol outlined in Sect. 2, we generalise business models for making use of FEC resources. In this discussion we are not using FEC resources on their own, but alongside the availability of CDC(s). Several business models may become relevant when considering migration of services between MDC and CDC. As illustrated in the V2I scenario, multiple MDCs may exist between the user device (D) and the

CDC, and the potential revenue generation for each of these MDC layers should be taken on board. Similar to current broad availability of WiFi access points, we envisage three general ways of funding MDCs: (i) by cloud providers; (ii) by local businesses; (iii) by public funding. We expand on each of these aspects below. In a previous analysis [2] we investigate similar approaches for Virtual Machine migration in Fog systems.

Our business models are centered on the use of an Orchestration Agent (OA), as described in Sect. 2. An OA is responsible for executing one or more tasks on the behalf of a user application, and can launch proxy OAs on remote resources (e.g. other MDC or CDC) to achieve this. An OA also interrogates remote resources to determine potential costs of execution, and ensure that security credentials of the remote resource are valid. Our business models are centered on the use of the OA-based abstraction:

- **Dynamic MDC discovery:** In this model, an OA would be able to choose an MDC provider on-the-go, according to the MDC availability profile, security credentials, or type. The use of a service-based approach enables loose coupling, enabling an eco-system of providers to co-exist. However, there is no guarantee that integrating externally provisioned services will lead to the fulfilment of the OA objectives. An OA can therefore record "preferred" MDCs and cache this information locally. We envision cloud providers maintaining and operating MDCs in order to extend their revenue beyond resource provisioning in CDCs. Dynamic MDC discovery equates to finding an MDC in the vicinity of a user device.
- **Pre-agreed MDC contracts:** In this model, the OA would rely on informative/detailed contracts that adequately capture the circumstances and criteria that influence the performance of the externally provisioned services that are subject of the contract. An OA would therefore have pre-agreed contracts with specific MDC operators, and would interact with them preferentially. This also reduces the potential risks incurred by the OA. In performance-based contracts, an MDC would need to provide a minimum level of performance (e.g. availability) to the OA which is reflected in the associated price. This could be achieved by interaction between MDCs being managed by the same operator, or by MDC outsourcing some of their tasks to a CDC.

  Consider the following scenario to illustrate the pre-agreed MDC contracts business model: a coffee chain offers contracts for use of MDCs operated by this coffee chain across a city or country. A user wishing to make use of MDCs owned and operated by this coffee chain would need to agree to a: (i) security certificate provided by this coffee chain; (ii) have a pre-agreed subscription for use of resources provided at MDCs operated by this coffee chain. With an increasing number of branches/locations of this coffee chain, a user would have a greater choice of locations available for use of an MDC. This is equivalent to accessing wireless networks (Wifi) at locations offered by a particular provider which can have presence at multiple locations. Such a coffee shop chain may also decide to enter into preferential agreements with cloud data centre operators (e.g. public cloud providers) to integrate their regional

MDCs with CDCs operated by the data centre provider. This aligns closely with expansion of Amazon Web Services (AWS) from an infrastructure owned and operated by an ecommerce provider, to a more globally accessible public cloud infrastructure. In the same way, a coffee shop chain which operates local infrastructure to offer Wifi services to customers, could also operated micro data centres that can offer additional services to customers.

- **MDC federation:** In this model multiple MDC operators can collaborate to share workload within a particular area, and have preferred costs for exchange of such workload. This is equivalent to alliances established between airline operators to serve particular routes. To support such federation, security credentials between MDCs must be pre-agreed. This is equivalent to an extension of the *pre-agreed MDC contracts* business model, where MDCs across multiple coffee shop chains can be federated, offering greater potential choice for a user.

- **MDC – CDC exchange:** In this model an OA would contact a CDC in the first instance, which could then outsource computation to an MDC if it unable to meet the required Quality of Service targets (e.g. latency). A CDC could use any of the three approaches outlined above – i.e. dynamic MDC discovery, preferred MDCs, or choice of an MDC within a particular group. A CDC operator needs to consider whether outsourcing could still be profitable given the type of workload a user device is generating.

## 5    Conclusion

In this paper we present how micro-data centres can be used to support service migration and serve incoming requests from applications. We consider that micro-data centres have a cost function that involves incentives for micro-data centres for hosting various services and an associated quality of services.

We describe, using two scenarios, how FEC resources can enhance the capability of a cloud-based data centre. Revenue models for supporting the combined use of such resources are outlined, demonstrating how latency sensitive applications can be supported across such infrastructure. We use a V2V application to demonstrate how FEC resources, closer to the data generation source, can reduce processing times as the data sources are scaled.

We demonstrate that in our applications cost is directly related to the number of fog devices, network architecture and application specificities. Such factors should be considered when developing corresponding business models.

## References

1. Bahl, V.: Micro datacenter middleware for mobile computing (keynote). In: ACM Middleware, Vancouver, Canada, 7–11 December 2015. http://2015.middleware-conference.org/keynote-talk-victor-bahl/. Accessed June 2017
2. Bittencourt, L., Lopes, M.M., Petri, I., Rana, O.F.: Towards virtual machine migration in fog computing. In: 10th International 3PGCIC Conference 2015, Poland, pp. 1–8, November 2015

3. Caglar, F., Shekhar, S., Gokhale, A., Koutsoukos, X.: An intelligent, performance interference-aware resource management scheme for IoT cloud backends. In: Proceedings of the 1st IEEE International Conference on Internet-of-Things: Design and Implementation, Berlin, Germany, pp. 95–105, April 2016

4. Gupta, H., Dastjerdi, A.V., Ghosh, S.K., Buyya, R.: iFogSim: a toolkit for modeling and simulation of resource management techniques in Internet of Things, edge and fog computing environments. https://arxiv.org/abs/1606.02007. Accessed June 2017

5. Noronha, A., Moriarty, R., OConnell, K., Villa, N.: Attaining IoT value: how to move from connecting things to capturing insights: gain an edge by taking analytics to the edge. Cisco White Paper (2014). http://www.cisco.com/c/dam/en_us/solutions/trends/iot/docs/iot-data-analytics-white-paper.PDF. Accessed June 2017

6. Aazam, M., Huh, E.-N.: Fog computing and smart gateway based communication for cloud of things. In: International Conference on Future Internet of Things and Cloud (FiCloud), pp. 464–470. IEEE (2014)

7. Yannuzzi, M., Milito, R., Serral-Gracia, R., Montero, D., Nemirovsky, M.: Key ingredients in an IoT recipe: fog computing, cloud computing, and more fog computing. In: IEEE 19th International Workshop on Computer Aided Modeling and Design of Communication Links and Networks (CAMAD), pp. 325–329. IEEE (2014)

8. Vaquero, L.M., Rodero-Merino, L.: Finding your way in the fog: towards a comprehensive definition of fog computing. ACM SIGCOMM Comput. Commun. Rev. 44(5), 27–32 (2014)

9. Satyanarayanan, M., Bahl, P., Caceres, R., Davies, N.: The case for VM-based cloudlets in mobile computing. IEEE Pervasive Comput. Mag. 8(4), 14–23 (2009)

10. Shekhar, S., Chhokra, A., Bhattacharjee, A., Aupy, G., Gokhale, A.: INDICES: exploiting edge resources for performance-aware cloud-hosted services. In: 1st IEEE International Conference on Fog and Edge Computing (ICFEC), Madrid, Spain (2017)

11. Yi, S., Li, C., Li, Q.: A survey of fog computing: concepts, applications and issues. In: Proceedings of Workshop on Mobile Big Data, Mobidata 2015, Hangzhou, China, pp. 37–42. ACM Press (2015)

# Cloud Federation

# Fairness in Revenue Sharing for Stable Cloud Federations

Ram Govinda Aryal[✉] and Jörn Altmann

Technology Management, Economics and Policy Program,
College of Engineering, Seoul National University,
Gwanak-Ro 1, Gwanak-Gu, Seoul 08826, South Korea
aryal.rg@gmail.com, jorn.altmann@acm.org

**Abstract.** A cloud federation is a platform, on which a number of cloud service providers (CSPs) builds an alliance and cooperates to share cloud resources. It is an appropriate way to address cloud elasticity needs. It expands resources beyond the limited capacity of a single CSP. It also helps maximizing profit for any CSP by improving the utilization of their resources. An alliance can be formed, only if potential members (CSPs) see marginal benefits in joining a federation. Once the alliance is formed, a fair distribution of revenue among the members of the alliance becomes important for the alliance to sustain. The distribution can be proportional to the contribution to the alliance. This paper analyzes the Shapley value method as a revenue sharing model for cloud federations. Our simulation results of the model show that the model increases the revenue for the federation due to the aggregation of spare capacity. The model provides a fair distribution of the revenue to the members of the federation, improving the stability of cloud federations.

**Keywords:** Cloud computing · Cloud federation · Resource sharing · Revenue sharing model

## 1 Introduction

### 1.1 Background

The development of computing has been driven by the constant increase in computational demand [1]. During this development, computing has evolved through cluster computing, grid computing, and cloud computing [2], with cloud computing being the most popular paradigm.

Basically, cloud computing is a form of computing, in which resources are outsourced through the Internet to data centers that pool large computing resources [3]. The capability of resource pooling and service metering enables cloud computing to offer services on demand and as pay-per-use [4, 29], allowing users to fulfill their computing needs rapidly, minimal technical skills, and no upfront cost. Cloud services can be provisioned as one of three service models (infrastructure as a service (IaaS), platform as a service (PaaS), and software as a service (SaaS)) and one of three deployment models (private cloud, community cloud, and public cloud) [4, 7].

© Springer International Publishing AG 2017
C. Pham et al. (Eds.): GECON 2017, LNCS 10537, pp. 219–232, 2017.
DOI: 10.1007/978-3-319-68066-8_17

The ability to offer on-demand computing services has created a big demand for cloud computing and, hence, a significant market growth in the cloud computing field.

However, the demand for cloud computing services is not steady and changes with the change in customer needs. The fluctuating computational demand for cloud services brings in significant challenges to the CSPs. For example, if CSPs make sure to fulfill any extreme demand by over provisioning of resources, it leads to resource underutilization for most of the time and, hence, the approach becomes economically inefficient.

One of the effective approaches to deal with fluctuating computational demand is to outsource the computing jobs beyond any CSPs resource limitation to other CSPs that have their resources underutilized. Cloud federation is a platform that is named for such an approach [26]. CSPs, by being the member of the cloud federation [36], cooperate with each other by providing resources to fulfill user demand and increase their profits [30, 31, 33].

Besides, according to a recent study, more than 68% of the global cloud market is being captured by six big providers [6]. In such an oligopolistic market, network externalities and economies of scale can provide potential limitation for small CSPs to compete with these big players [7, 36]. Cloud federation can provide a way for small CSPs to increase their competitive strength and increase their market share [36].

## 1.2 Study Objectives and Contributions

Cloud federation is an appropriate way to address the need of cloud elasticity by expanding resources beyond the limited capacity of a single CSP. It is also a way to get profit out of, otherwise, unused resources for any CSP. However, an alliance can be formed, only if potential members (CSPs) see marginal benefits in joining the federation. For this, a proper economic model is necessary for achieving a fair distribution of revenue. The revenue distribution can depend on the contributions made by each member CSPs in the federation. Such a fair revenue sharing model is also essential for sustaining an alliance.

With the realization for the need of cloud federation, studies on economic models applicable for cloud federations emerged. In particular, previous works focus on revenue sharing models that maximize total social benefits of federations [8, 9]. Other works attempt maximizing the profit of an individual CSP in an federation that operates in a non-cooperative environment [10, 11]. So far, however, no work provides a revenue sharing model for cloud federation within a cooperative environment that is proportionate to the contributions of each member of the federation, which is addressed in this article. Therefore, our objective is to determine whether the Shapley value method could be applied to cloud federations.

For the analysis, we developed a Java program for simulating an environment with five CSPs making available a certain number of virtual machines (VMs). Each simulation run included 100 job requests demanding a random number of VM instances. The simulation runs were carried out for four different scenarios, to capture the effectiveness of the model with respect to the size of job requests and resources made available by CSPs to the federation.

The contributions of this paper are twofold: First, we state that the Shapley value method is an appropriate method for sharing revenue among the members of a cloud federation. The Shapley value method calculates the revenue share for each member CSP according to their marginal contributions to the federation [12, 24]. Second, we verify through simulation that: (i) the total revenue is maximized for large job requests, if the CSPs work in a federation; (ii) the Shapley value method provides a fair way of dividing the revenue; and (iii) the Shapley value method achieves a higher revenue than the basic method that calculates revenue share on the basis a CSP's resources made available as a fraction of total available resources of the federation.

The remainder of the paper is organized as follows: Sect. 2 describes related works. The system model is presented in Sect. 3. Section 3.2 discusses the proposed approach of revenue sharing based on Shapley values in cloud federations. Details on the simulation experiments and result analyses are presented in Sect. 4. Finally, the paper concludes with a discussion and conclusion in Sect. 5.

## 2   Related Works

Several works have addressed cloud federations. A vision, challenges, and architectural elements of federated cloud computing environments are presented by Buyya et al. and Jeffery et al. [13, 38]. These works support application scaling across multiple CSPs and consider policy impact as also outline by Hofäcker et al. [37]. Frameworks for cloud federations that employs the role of broker have also been proposed [14, 35]. Multi-agent protocol is proposed by Messina et al. and is applicable for negotiations of service level agreements in cloud federations [17]. Suzic et al. propose an architecture for security governance that aims to provide a transparent and secure sharing of infrastructure and data within the heterogeneous environment of cloud federation [22].

Economic benefits of cloud federation are also discussed [16, 28, 32]. With a survey of conceptual background about federation of small CSPs, Kim et al. provide a guidance for defining economic problems of cloud federation [7]. Drivers and barriers have been discussed as well [36]. A cost model for federated hybrid clouds is presented by Kashef and Altmann [15, 26].

An economic model for the federation of cloud service providers is presented by Goiri, Guitart, and Torres as well as Kashef and Altmann [19, 26]. The proposed model helps CSPs to make decisions with regards to outsourcing, in-sourcing and turning off unused nodes based on different environmental factors. As a solution to the problem of limited resources, Bouabdallah et al. propose a distributed approach relying on contract net protocol [20]. It considers various parameters relating to a service provider, client and quality of service for virtual machine placement. Interoperability and openness aspects have also been discussed [27, 28]. Hadji et al. propose an algorithm for allocation of critical resources in a cloud federation (i.e., for selecting hosting resources and placing applications and services) that aims at optimizing cost efficiency [18]. Li et al. studied on auction methods (non-cooperative method) as a way of maximizing profits in cloud federation where buying and selling of the resources between customer and provider of cloud services [10, 34]. In their work [8], Hassan et al. present a mechanism to share resources and revenue among cooperative members in an alliance of CSPs that aim at maximizing social welfare.

In their work [21], Barril et al. analyze the organizational as well as technology integration challenges and identify incentives that make CSPs willing to aggregate the resources and form a federation. It is argued that the Internet of Things (IoT) will be the main business driver and motivation for cloud federation. Another mechanism for the formation of cloud federation is proposed by Mashayekhy et al. The mechanism aims at maximizing the profit of the federation [5].

A game-theoretic policy-based decision-making process is presented by Lu et al., which helps cloud providers to form an alliance that helps improving resource utilization and maximizing profit [9]. Samaan presents an economic model for sharing resources by modeling the interactions of CSPs as a repeated game among selfish players [11], where the CSPs maximize their profit by selling their unused resources to the spot market.

## 3   System Model

### 3.1   Stakeholders and Parameter Definitions

For developing the system model of a cloud federation, we consider the broker-based architecture as proposed by the National Institute of Science and Technology [23] and further researchers [27, 31, 40]. It considers five types of stakeholders (Fig. 1).

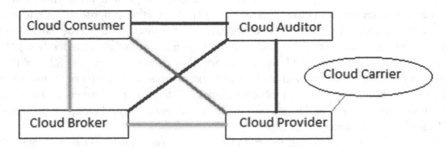

**Fig. 1.** Interaction between stakeholders in a cloud federation.

The cloud brokers maintain information about cloud providers, such as the cost for each type of VM instance. In detail, for each cloud provider (CSP) in the federation, the availability and the cost of resources is periodically updated by cloud brokers. The cloud consumers specify the resource requirements for various time slots. They place service requests to brokers for such resource requirements. Cloud providers maintain resources and update their price list. These cloud providers provide resources to cloud service users in the form of virtual machines. They communicate with the cloud brokers about their offers for cloud resources. The cloud auditors make sure that the transactions between consumers, providers, and brokers follow regulations. The cloud carriers provide the communication service for the other stakeholders. Formally, the stakeholders are represented as follows in the system model. Cloud providers $P_i$ are represented as a set of size n, as shown in Eq. 1.

$$P = \{P_1,\ldots,P_n\} \tag{1}$$

Each virtual machine is defined by a certain capacity of the processing core, memory, and storage. For our system model, we limit the types of virtual machines to m. Therefore, VMs can only be provisioned as one of m VM types (Eq. 2).

$$V = \{V_1,\ldots,V_m\} \tag{2}$$

Cloud consumers send requests R for a number of instances of different VM types. It is defined as a set of requested numbers of VM instances $R_j$ of type $V_j$ (Eq. 3).

$$R = \{R_1,\ldots,R_m\} \tag{3}$$

Although there are different costs for running different VM types of different CSPs, the broker sets a fixed retail price for each of the VM types. The retail prices are represented as a set S (Eq. 4), where $S_j$ refers to the retail price of one instance of VM type $V_j$ per unit of time.

$$S = \{S_1,\ldots,S_m\} \tag{4}$$

The charge A to be paid by the user depends on the number of instances of VM requested and the retail price of the VM instance of VM types $V_j$ (Eq. 5).

$$A = \sum_{j=1}^{m} R_j * S_j \tag{5}$$

A federation is made up of a set of cloud service providers that build an alliance to provide a cloud service package. Mathematically it is represented as a subset of the set of cloud service providers $F \subseteq P$.

### 3.2 Revenue Sharing in Cloud Federations

Revenue sharing in cloud federations requires four steps: (i) calculation of the cost of operation (service provisioning), which depends on the CSPs that the jobs are assigned to; (ii) calculation of the total revenue and the total profit; (iii) maximizing the revenue and profit; and (iv) a method for calculating the revenue share.

**Cost of VMs.** There is some cost associated with running the virtual machines at a CSP's data center. The cost includes power consumption, operation cost, and maintenance cost. The cost for running same type of virtual machine may be different for different service providers depending on the geographical location as well as security and other provisions implemented by individual CSP [15, 26]. The cost of running a VM of type $V_j$ at the data center of service provider $P_i$ is represented as $C_{ij}$.

The cost may also be affected by dynamic factors, like the current work load at the CSP's data center. A CSP, who is not willing to accept many requests from the federation due to an internal high workload, assigns a price higher than the actual cost for the resource.

However, the retail price $S_j$ is fixed, independent of which CSP within the federation is provisioning the resources.

This distinction between retail price and cost is important as it is used as a basis for calculating the profit for job requests within the federation. For each job request, the cloud broker receives the status of resource availability and cost from the CSPs.

**Revenue and Profit Calculation.** The total revenue is calculated as the sum of the retail price of all the VM instances running at all the CSPs of a federation F. The total profit from a cloud service provisioning R is calculated similarly as the sum of the differences between the retail price and cost of all the VM instances running at all the CSPs of a federation F (Eq. 6).

$$\text{Revenue}(F, R) = \sum_{i=1}^{n} \sum_{j=1}^{m} R_j * S_j; \quad \text{Profit}(F, R) = \sum_{i=1}^{n} \sum_{j=1}^{m} R_j * \left(S_j - C_{ij}\right)$$

$$(6)$$

where $S_j$ is the retail price set by the broker for a virtual machine of type $V_j$, and $C_{ij}$ is the cost of running a virtual machine of type $V_j$ at the data center of provider $P_i$.

**Revenue and Profit Maximization Through Federation Selection.** A job assignment is performed with the objective of maximizing the total revenue or the total profit of the federation $P_F$. Mathematically, the maximization problem can expressed as:

$$\max_{F \subseteq P} \text{Revenue}(F, R); \quad \max_{F \subseteq P} \text{Profit}(F, R) \tag{7}$$

Due to the differences in the cost of service provisioning through different service providers, the profit for the federation varies for different combinations of CSPs provisioning the cloud service request. In order to maximize the total profit of the federation, it is desirable to bundle the cloud services from the top of a list, which lists service providers with available resources in ascending order of price imposed by them. Job requests, for which no services can be bundled due to lack of adequate available resources, need to be rejected.

**Profit Sharing.** In order to continue working in cooperation within a federation, CSPs should be able to receive a fair share of the total benefits of the alliance. Thus, the question is: what is a fair way to divide the payoffs among the members of the alliance. Therefore, it is necessary to define fairness. One approach of defining fairness is to identify axioms that exhibit the properties of a fair payoff division. Lloyd Shapley [24] presents such axioms for a coalitional game in general and states that, the fairness is achieved, if each member of the alliance receives a payoff in proportion to its marginal contribution to the alliance. We apply these axioms to cloud federations:

*Axiom 1 (Symmetry):* Two cloud service providers, who offer exactly the same (quality and quantity of) resources to the federation (i.e., alliance), are considered to be inter-changeable and should receive the equal revenue share. Therefore, if two CSPs i and j are interchangeable in a federation of $|F|$ CSPs and a job request R, then the revenue of both CSPs is equal:

$$\text{Revenue}_i(F, R) = \text{Revenue}_j(F, R) \tag{8}$$

where Revenue$_i$(F,R) and Revenue$_j$(F,R) represent revenues of CSPs i and j, respectively. Both CSPs are part of a federation F of $|F|$ CSPs, handling a job request R.

*Axiom 2 (Dummy Players):* A member CSP of a federation that has no resources available for the alliance is considered to be a dummy player and should receive zero benefits from the alliance. Therefore, if a CSP i contributes no resources to a federation of $|F|$ CSPs and a job request R, then the revenue of CSP i is zero:

$$\text{Revenue}_i(F, R) = 0 \tag{9}$$

where Revenue$_i$(F,R) is the profit share of CSP i with respect to service provisioning of job request R in a federation F.

*Axiom 3 (Additivity):* If it is possible to decompose a job request R, then it should be possible to decompose the revenues. Therefore, if a job request R can be decomposed into $R^1$ and $R^2$ in a federation F of $|F|$ CSPs, then:

$$\text{Revenue}_i\left(F, R^1 + R^2\right) = \text{Revenue}_i\left(F, R^1\right) + \text{Revenue}_i\left(F, R^2\right) \tag{10}$$

where Revenue$_i\left(F, R^1 \mid R^2\right)$ is the revenue share of CSP i gained by the service provisioning of job request R (i.e., $R^1 + R^2$), while Revenue$_i\left(F, R^1\right)$ and Revenue$_i\left(N, R^2\right)$ are the revenue share of CSP i gained by the service provisioning of job request $R^1$ and $R^2$, respectively.

*Shapley Value Method:* It is a method that satisfies the three axioms [12, 39]. It divides the revenue among the members of an alliance. In detail, it is calculated as:

$$\phi_i(P, v) = \frac{1}{|P|!} \sum_{F \subseteq P} |F|!(|P| - |F| - 1)![v(F \cup \{i\}) - v(F)] \tag{11}$$

where $\phi_i$(P,v) is the Shapley value of CSP i, and v is a function (v: $2^N \rightarrow \Re$) that represents the worth of an alliance. The term $[v(F \cup \{i\}) - v(F)]$ represents the marginal value that CSP i adds to the alliance F, where $v(F \cup \{i\})$ is the value of the alliance includes F and i, and $v(F)$ is the value of the alliance F that does not include i. The term $|F|!(|P| - |F| - 1)!/|P|!$ is used for normalized weighting for the different possible alliances of size $|F|$ and the total number of possible alliance members $|P|$. $|F|!$

represents all possible number of alliances that could be made before CSP i is added to the alliance and $(|P| - |F| - 1)!$ represents the number of other possible alliance.

## 4 Simulation

### 4.1 Simulation Setup

For our simulations, five CSPs having homogeneous cloud resources (i.e., VMs) are considered. The specification of the VM type is based on the Amazon Web Service EC2 t2.xlarge. The retail price for the virtual machine is fixed as per AWS EC2 on-demand pricing for Seoul, South Korea as of May 30th, 2017. The details on the VM type specification and the retail price are shown in Table 1. For the simulation, we also consider a uniform cost for all VMs of all CSPs. As CSPs operate with profit margins at a level of 23% [25], we fixed the cost at a level of 80% of the retail price for all CSPs (Table 1). However, it has to be noted that the approach presented is applicable for scenarios with different cost of VM instances for different providers.

**Table 1.** Specification and cost of the VM instance for simulation.

| VM instance | vCPU | Memory | Price / hour | Per-unit cost |
|-------------|------|--------|--------------|---------------|
| AWS EC2 t2.xlarge | 4 | 16 GB | $0.256 | $0.2048 |

Per scenario, multiple simulation runs were carried out with 100 job requests in each run. Each job request included different numbers of VM instances, but for simplicity reasons, we considered only one type of VM instances. The entire simulation experiment comprised simulation runs for four different demand scenarios that were created by varying the average size of job requests and the number of VM instances made available by the five CSPs. These scenarios are listed and briefly described in Table 2.

**Table 2.** Simulation scenarios.

| Scenario name | Scenario description |
|---------------|----------------------|
| 1 | Each of the job requests can be fulfilled, only if all member CSPs contribute resources |
| 2 | Each of the job requests can be fulfilled by a limited number of different sub-alliances, but no job request can be fulfilled by an individual CSP |
| 3 | Each of the job requests is of small size, such that every job request can be fulfilled by any of the member CSPs individually |
| 4 | Each of the job requests can be fulfilled by a large number of different sub-alliances, but no job request can be fulfilled by an individual CSP |

## 4.2   Result and Analysis

As shown in Fig. 2, among the four scenarios considered in the simulation, only in one of the scenarios (Scenario 3), in which job sizes are small enough to be fulfilled by individual CSPs, profit could also be generated in absence of a federation. In every other scenario, the absence of a federation yields no profit. It is not unexpected, as no job request was small enough to be provisioned by a CSP without extending their resource capability beyond their limit. Thus, in absence of a federation, all job requests were dropped, thereby providing zero profit for all CSPs. The result of the simulation demonstrates that a group of CSPs can maximize their total profit by working within a federation.

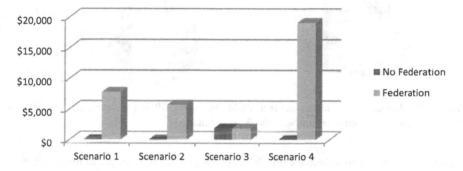

**Fig. 2.** Comparison of the total profit for no federation and federations for four scenarios.

Table 3 depicts the Shapley values for each of the CSPs for all four scenarios (number of VM instances made available by each CSP) and the average job size. It indicates the value of the contributions given by each CSP in the federation. The Shapley values were calculated following Eq. 9 and averaging over all repeated simulation runs with 100 job requests per run.

**Table 3.** Individual CSP contribution (Shapley values) for all four scenarios.

| Scenario name | Job size (Mean number of VMs) | Number of VM instances available | | | | | Weighted mean of contributions (Shapley value) | | | | |
|---|---|---|---|---|---|---|---|---|---|---|---|
| | | CSP 1 | CSP 2 | CSP 3 | CSP 4 | CSP 5 | CSP 1 | CSP 2 | CSP 3 | CSP 4 | CSP 5 |
| 1 | 152.11 | 32 | 30 | 32 | 33 | 33 | 0.2000 | 0.1869 | 0.2000 | 0.2066 | 0.2066 |
| 2 | 111.80 | 35 | 33 | 38 | 37 | 35 | 0.1963 | 0.1844 | 0.2146 | 0.2084 | 0.1963 |
| 3 | 36.45 | 192 | 153 | 107 | 104 | 166 | 0.2000 | 0.2000 | 0.2000 | 0.2000 | 0.2000 |
| 4 | 373.09 | 107 | 148 | 151 | 187 | 127 | 0.1482 | 0.2054 | 0.2096 | 0.2609 | 0.1759 |

As depicted from the result (Scenario 3 and Scenario 4 in Fig. 3 and Table 3), it is observed that the marginal contributions (Shapley values) for each CSP is not only dependent on the resources on offer but also on the size of the job requests. The Shapley values for Scenario 4 correspond to the resources made available, while

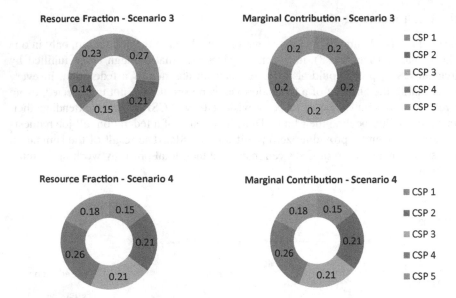

**Fig. 3.** Number of VM instances made available by each CSP and the marginal contributions (Shapley values) of each CSP for Scenario 3 and Scenario 4.

Scenario 3 show equal values for all CSPs despite similar differences in resources made available. These equal values are not unexpected. Job requests for Scenario 3 were small enough, such that they could be fulfilled with available resources by any of the CSPs individually. For such job requests, the contributions by each CSP are equal, despite the differences in the number of available resources that the CSPs have on offer. No additional value could be created with surplus resources in that scenario. This result is acceptable and demonstrates the fairness property of the Shapley value method.

Furthermore, if the job requests are large, CSPs with a similar number of resources on offer are evaluated with similar Shapley values and, hence, similar revenue and, as the cost is fixed, similar profits. This is shown for Scenario 1 and Scenario 2 (Fig. 4 and Table 3). With regards to a large job request, these CSPs are interchangeable with each other. Therefore, they provide a similar marginal contribution to the federation. Hence,

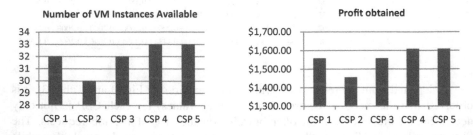

**Fig. 4.** Number of VM instances made available and the profit shares of CSPs for Scenario 1.

a similar evaluation of their contributions in the federation is justifiable and demonstrates fairness of the method.

## 5 Discussion and Conclusion

As seen from the simulation results, if CSPs work independently, any job request, which comes to a CSP and requires resources beyond the CSP's current free resources, has to be rejected, leading to a loss of revenue (Fig. 2). In the case of CSPs working in a federation, the same job request can be accepted due to resource aggregation from multiple CSPs, thereby leading to additional revenue. This demonstrates that a federation can play an important role in maximizing the total revenue of CSPs. Furthermore, if resources from all CSPs needed to be aggregated to fulfill a job request (Table 3 and Fig. 4), the simulation result showed that the profit share calculated with the Shapley value method is close to the profit share calculated with a basic method (i.e., the fraction of resources made available), which also demonstrate fairness of the Shapley method.

In addition to this, if job requests can be fulfilled by any of the CSP individually, unlike to the basic method, in which the revenue varies based on the resource made available by the CSP, the Shapley model yields an equal revenue share for each of the CSPs independent to the number of resources made available. The marginal contributions of all CSPs are equal. This essentially demonstrates the feature of the Shapley model. It provides the desired property of fairness by considering the contribution of the CSP to a job request.

The simulation results also demonstrate that two CSPs making an equal number of VM instances available to the federation receive an equal revenue share, if the revenue is calculated following the Shapley value method. This also exhibits fairness.

Considering these results, we can conclude that a revenue sharing model based on the Shapley value method can provide an increased total revenue for CSPs in cloud federations compared to CSPs working independently. The revenue sharing model based on Shapley values provides a fair distribution of revenues to member CSPs in cloud federations.

We believe that both CSPs and a cloud federation can benefit from a fair revenue sharing model. For individual CSPs, the assurance of receiving a fair share of the revenue according to their contribution to fulfilling a job request encourages them to join and continue cooperation within the federation. For the federation, the Shapley value method provides a way of distributing revenue to federation members, which have been generated from an increase in the overall resource utilization. These benefits improve the stability of a federation.

Our Future work will address technical aspects of implementing the Shapley value method as well as making our current investigation more realistic. This includes refined scenarios, a system architecture, the consideration of selfish-behavior of CSPs.

**Acknowledgements.** The research was conducted within the project BASMATI (Cloud Brokerage Across Borders for Mobile Users and Applications), which was supported from the ICT R&D program of the Korean MSIT/IITP [R0115-16-0001].

# References

1. Rimal, B.P., Choi, E., Lumb, I.: A taxonomy and survey of cloud computing systems. In: INC, IMS and IDC, pp. 44–51 (2009)
2. Mustafa, S., Nazir, B., Hayat, A., Khan, A.U.R., Madani, S.A.: Resource management in cloud computing: taxonomy, prospects, and challenges. Comput. Electr. Eng. **47**, 186–203 (2015)
3. Venters, W., Whitley, E.A.: A critical review of cloud computing: researching desires and realities. J. Inf. Technol. **27**(3), 179–197 (2012)
4. Mell, P., Grance, T.: The NIST definition of cloud computing (2011)
5. Mashayekhy, L., Nejad, M.M., Grosu, D.: Cloud federations in the sky: formation game and mechanism. IEEE Trans. Cloud Comput. **3**(1), 14–27 (2015)
6. Ranger, S.: AWS dominates cloud computing infrastructure market, bigger than IBM/Google/Microsoft combined (2017). http://www.zdnet.com/article/aws-dominates-cloud-computing-infrastructure-market-bigger-than-ibmgooglemicrosoft-combined. Accessed July 2017
7. Kim, K., Kang, S., Altmann, J.: Cloud goliath versus a federation of cloud davids. In: Altmann, J., Vanmechelen, K., Rana, O.F. (eds.) GECON 2014. LNCS, vol. 8914, pp. 55–66. Springer, Cham (2014). doi:10.1007/978-3-319-14609-6_4
8. Hassan, M.M., Al-Wadud, M.A., Fortino, G.: A socially optimal resource and revenue sharing mechanism in cloud federations. In: CSCWD, 19th International Conference on Computer Supported Cooperative Work in Design. IEEE (2015)
9. Lu, Z., Wen, X., Sun, Y.: A game theory based resource sharing scheme in cloud computing environment. In: WICT, World Congress on Information and Communication Technology (2012)
10. Li, H., Wu, C., Li, Z., Lau, F.C.M.: Profit-maximizing virtual machine trading in a federation of selfish clouds. In: INFOCOM. IEEE (2013)
11. Samaan, N.: A novel economic sharing model in a federation of selfish cloud providers. IEEE Trans. Parallel Distrib. Syst. **25**(1), 12–21 (2014)
12. Jackson, M.O., Leyton-Brown, K., Shoham, Y.: Game Theory Online (2016). http://www.game-theory-class.org. Accessed July 2017
13. Buyya, R., Ranjan, R., Calheiros, R.N.: InterCloud: utility-oriented federation of cloud computing environments for scaling of application services. In: Hsu, C.-H., Yang, L.T., Park, J.H., Yeo, S.-S. (eds.) ICA3PP 2010. LNCS, vol. 6081, pp. 13–31. Springer, Heidelberg (2010). doi:10.1007/978-3-642-13119-6_2
14. Chauhan, S.S., Pilli, E.S., Joshi, R.: A broker based framework for federated cloud environment. In: ETCT, International Conference on Emerging Trends in Communic Technology. IEEE (2016)
15. Kashef, M.M., Altmann, J.: A cost model for hybrid clouds. In: Vanmechelen, K., Altmann, J., Rana, O.F. (eds.) GECON 2011. LNCS, vol. 7150, pp. 46–60. Springer, Heidelberg (2012). doi:10.1007/978-3-642-28675-9_4
16. Darzanos, G., Koutsopoulos, I., Stamoulis, G.D.: Economics models and policies for cloud federations. In: IFIP Networking Conference and Workshops. IEEE (2016)
17. Messina, F., Pappalardo, G., Santoro, C., Rosaci, D., Sarné, G.M.L.: A multi-agent protocol for service level agreement negotiation in cloud federations. Int. J. Grid Util. Comput. **7**(2), 101–112 (2016)
18. Hadji, M., Aupetit, B., Zeghlache, D.: Cost-efficient algorithms for critical resource allocation in cloud federations. In: Cloudnet, International Conference on Cloud Networking. IEEE (2016)

19. Goiri, Í., Guitart, J., Torres, J.: Economic model of a cloud provider operating in a federated cloud. Inf. Syst. Front. **14**(4), 827–843 (2012)
20. Bouabdallah, R., Lajmi, S., Ghedira, K.: Resources provisioning within cloud federation. In: SMC, International Conference on Systems, Man, and Cybernetics. IEEE (2016)
21. Barril, J.F.H., Ruyter, J., Tan, Q.: A view on Internet of things driving cloud federation. In: ICCCBDA, International Conference on Cloud Computing and Big Data Analysis. IEEE (2016)
22. Suzic, B., Prünster, B., Ziegler, D., Marsalek, A., Reiter, A.: Balancing utility and security: securing cloud federations of public entities. In: Debruyne, C., et al. (eds.) OTM 2016 Conferences. LNCS, vol. 10033, pp. 943–961. Springer, Heidelberg (2016)
23. Liu, F., Tong, J., Mao, J., Bohn, R.B., Messina, J.V., Badger, M.L., Leaf, D.M.: NIST cloud computing reference architecture. NIST special publication, report, pp. 500–292 (2011)
24. Winter, E.: The shapley value. In: Handbook of Game Theory with Economic Applications, vol. 3, pp. 2025–2054 (2002)
25. Oreskovic, A.: Amazon isn't just growing revenue anymore – it's growing profits (2016). http://www.businessinsider.com/amazons-big-increase-in-aws-operating-margins-2016-4. Accessed May 2017
26. Altmann, J., Kashef, M.M.: Cost model based service placement in federated hybrid clouds. Future Gener. Comput. Syst. (2014). doi:10.1016/j.future.2014.08.014. Elsevier
27. Gebregiorgis, S.A., Altmann, J.: IT service platforms: their value creation model and the impact of their level of openness on their adoption. Procedia Comput. Sci **68**, 173–187 (2015)
28. Haile, N., Altmann, J.: Evaluating investments in portability and interoperability between software service platforms. Future Gener. Comput. Syst. doi:10.1016/j.future.2017.04.040
29. Rohitratana, J., Altmann, J.: Impact of pricing schemes on a market for software-as-a-service and perpetual software. Future Gener. Comput. Syst. **28**(8), 1328–1339 (2012). Elsevier
30. Haile, N., Altmann, J.: Structural analysis of value creation in software service platforms. Electron. Markets (2015). doi:10.1007/s12525-015-0208-8
31. Haile, N., Altmann, J.: Value creation in software service platforms. Future Gener. Comput. Syst. (2015). doi:10.1016/j.future.2015.09.029. Elsevier
32. Kim, K., Altmann, J.: Effect of homophily on network formation. Commun. Nonlinear Sci. Numer. Simul. **44**, 482–494 (2017)
33. Haile, N., Altmann, J.: Estimating the value obtained from using a software service platform. In: Altmann, J., Vanmechelen, K., Rana, O.F. (eds.) GECON 2013. LNCS, vol. 8193, pp. 244–255. Springer, Cham (2013). doi:10.1007/978-3-319-02414-1_18
34. Altmann, J., Courcoubetis, C., Risch, M.: A marketplace and its market mechanism for trading commoditized computing resources. Ann. des Télécommunications **65**, 653–667 (2010)
35. Altmann, J., Carlini, E., Coppola, M., Dazzi, P., Ferrer, A.J., Haile, N., Jung, Y., Kang, D.-J., Marshall, I.-J., Tserpes, K., Varvarigou, T.: BASMATI - a brokerage architecture on federated clouds for mobile applications. In: CGW, International Workshop, Krakow, Poland (2016)
36. Haile, N., Altmann, J.: Risk-benefit-mediated impact of determinants on the adoption of cloud federation. In: PACIS - Pacific Asia Conference on Information Systems. AIS (2015)
37. Hofäcker, D., Schröder, H., Li, Y., Flynn, M.: Trends and determinants of work-retirement transitions under changing institutional conditions: Germany, England and Japan compared. J. Soc. Policy **45**(1), 39–64 (2016)
38. Jeferry, K., Kousiouris, G., Kyriazis, D., Altmann, J., Ciuffoletti, A., Maglogiannis, I., Nesi, P., Suzic, B., Zhao, Z.: Challenges emerging from future cloud application scenarios. Procedia Comput. Sci. **68**, 227–237 (2015)

39. Ernst, F., Klaus, S.M.: A theory of fairness, competition, and cooperation. Quart. J. Econ. **114**(3), 817–868 (1999)
40. Mohammed, A.B., Altmann, J., Hwang, J.: Cloud computing value chains: understanding businesses and value creation in the cloud. In: Neumann, D., Baker, M., Altmann, J., Rana, O. (eds.) Economic Models and Algorithms for Distributed Systems. Autonomic Systems, pp. 187–208. Springer, Heidelberg (2009)

# Model for Incentivizing Cloud Service Federation

Juan Pablo Romero Coronado[✉], and Jörn Altmann[✉]

Technology Management, Economics, and Policy Program,
Department of Industrial Engineering, College of Engineering,
Seoul National University, Seoul, South Korea
jpromero@snu.ac.kr, jorn.altmann@acm.org

**Abstract.** In cloud computing, big service providers rule the market due to the economies of scale. Cloud federation presents a possible solution, allowing small cloud providers to increase their competitiveness by making strategic alliances with one another and, thus, forming a network with shared resources. Previous research suggests several different factors that may incentivize the participation of selfish cloud providers, such as cost disparity, existence of big competitors, and revenue sharing mechanisms. It is also assumed that individual cloud providers aim to maximize their profits and will choose to make alliances as long as there is a benefit in doing so. For deciding on whether to federate, cloud providers take into consideration whether the federation will yield them an increase in profits. Our study models with a repeated game the interactions between selfish heterogeneous agents that aim to maximize individual profits. Each agent starts off as an individual and is allowed to change its strategy and federate with other providers, in order to improve its own performance. By looking at the speed of establishing collaborations and the overall profit of all individuals, we can determine which specific incentives encourage the creation of cloud federations. The results of this study suggest that the factors considered can incentivize the formation of federations. Yet, it also affects the number and size of the resulting federations.

**Keywords:** Cloud federation · Federation formation · Revenue sharing · Business incentive · SMEs · Repeated game · Strategic alliance

## 1 Introduction

### 1.1 Cloud Computing

Cloud computing is commonly defined as "a model for ubiquitous, convenient, on-demand network access to a shared pool of configurable computing resources". It is characterized by providers having a pooled repository of resources, which ensures a measured service with on-demand access for consumers [1]. It is usually divided into three categories depending on the main focus: software as a service (SaaS) [22], platform as a service (PaaS) [23, 24, 27], and infrastructure as a service (IaaS).

This new model gathered the attention of the world quickly and became one of the fastest growing IT markets in the last few years. In fact, 2017 data shows that it is a

© Springer International Publishing AG 2017
C. Pham et al. (Eds.): GECON 2017, LNCS 10537, pp. 233–246, 2017.
DOI: 10.1007/978-3-319-68066-8_18

148-billion-dollar industry that is growing at a 25% rate annually, with a shifting tendency from infrastructure towards services [2].

In recent years, the once emerging cloud computing has become a widely used and deployed technology in the IT market. Each year an increasing number of users are getting on-demand access to services through the cloud. As the market grows, the provisioning of on-demand access to software, platforms, and infrastructure resources benefits from the economies of scale [3].

## 1.2     Problem Description

There are two main issues in the current cloud computing market. The first is related to the volatile change in the number of user requests. In a market, where instant on-demand access is required, providers can find it difficult to keep up with the user requirements of computational resources [4]. Service providers cannot easily scale their capabilities due to the high initial cost of infrastructure and the upkeep cost that may ensue after customer demand drops [19].

The second problem lies in the anti-competitive externalities of the economies of scale in the cloud service sector. Recent data shows that Amazon controls over 30% of the cloud infrastructure market share and 50% is owned by 24 other leading companies, leaving less than 20% of the market share for medium and small providers [5]. Due to the highly efficient and cost effective infrastructure of the big cloud providers (CP), small and medium sized CPs can be hard-pressed to compete against them on the number of resources, service quality, and price [20, 21, 29].

Besides market places [28], cloud federation has been seen as a possible solution for both issues [19]. Horizontally dynamic cloud federation allows small CPs to collaborate and gain access to economies of scale by increasing the amount of infrastructure resources available to them [25]. It also helps ensuring the users' quality of service and minimizing costs [6].

Despite the promises of cloud federation, it is important to state that there is no functional federation in the open market. Extensive research has been done on optimizing the performance of certain federations and on dealing with challenges, such as resource sharing and interoperability [19, 21, 26]. Factors hindering providers to adopt cloud federation have also been investigated [30].

## 1.3     Research Objective

The main objective of this study is to identify the factors that encourage businesses to collaborate with each other and form strategic alliances in the cloud computing industry sector. Based on this research objective, the research questions that are addressed in our study are: Which factors show promising incentives to businesses that collaborate? What are the effects of these factors on the creation speed and the overall performance of cloud federations?

To answer these questions, we propose a game mechanism that simulates the formation of cloud federations. We use agent-based modelling, which allows us to model social interactions between agents, each with their own behaviors and characteristics. This type of modelling allows us to define different CPs, which aids in getting more meaningful results. The resulting model introduces selfish CPs into a cloud market, allowing them to federate for increasing their profits.

This paper makes contributions to the understanding of the formation of cloud federations. The results of the simulations provide some insights regarding how the different factors affect the number, size, and speed of federations.

The implications of our findings are that revenue sharing schemes and other factors (e.g., cost and capacity disparity) can definitely incentivize cloud providers into mutual collaborations, while also affecting the number and the shape of the resulting federations.

The subsequent sections of this paper are organized as follows. Section 2 features a revision of previous research conducted on the subject, focusing primarily on determining the factors that other authors have identified as necessary or desirable for Cloud federations. Section 3 proposes an agent-based model that simulates a cooperative game mechanism between selfish cloud providers, helping examining factors identified in the literature review. In Sect. 4, the results of the simulations are presented. Section 5 concludes with a summary of the main findings and a brief discussion of the implications of the present study.

## 2  Background

After a thorough review of the cloud federation literature, though excluding policy impact on transitions [31], several factors were identified as important for incentivizing federations and coalitions. Amongst them, the concept of capacity-based revenue sharing is perhaps the most prominent one. It is a resource and revenue sharing mechanisms, which determines how CPs in a federation share their computational resources, and more importantly, the profits that result from the collaboration. Having an efficient mechanism is of paramount importance as well, since they encourage CPs to participate in a federation [7].

Samaan created a revenue sharing mechanism for spot markets of cloud resources, featuring self-enforced capacity regulation [14]. Mashayekhy et al. used a game theory model that profit maximizes the resource allocation of a cloud federation [4]. Lu et al. and Hassan et al. developed a revenue sharing mechanism by means of linear stochastic programmed games [10, 15]. Guazzone et al. proposed a framework for the formation of cloud federations in a scenario, in which cost minimization of energy resources is essential [11]. Xu et al. proposed a resource allocation mechanism that uses evolutionary mechanisms and auctioning pricing to obtain optimal allocations [13]. El Zant et al. introduced volatile pricing and changing capacities into a revenue sharing mechanism [7]. Wei et al. suggested that the QoS expectation level of users should be considered in the sharing mechanisms [12].

Besides revenue sharing, some of the articles in literature suggest that any disparity between CPs can affect the potential profits of the federation and should also be considered. In some of these articles, the disparity comes in the form of CPs having different computational power and storage capabilities. Other articles suggest that CPs usually have different cost functions that may influence the difference in their revenues, especially in models that consider different types of service requirements. As these disparities are consistent with reality, they should be studied. A summary of the articles reviewed and the factors mentioned in them is presented in Table 1.

**Table 1.** Factors discussed in related literature.

| Source | Keywords | Revenue sharing | Capacity disparity | Cost disparity |
|---|---|---|---|---|
| Samaan et al. [8] | virtual machine, resource sharing, cooperative game, social welfare | ✓ | ✓ | ✓ |
| El Zant et al. [7] | revenue sharing, spot market | ✓ | ✓ | |
| Niyato et al. [9] | big data, game theory, trust model | ✓ | ✓ | ✓ |
| Lu et al. [10] | resource sharing, game theory | ✓ | ✓ | |
| Guazzone et al. [11] | cooperative game theory, coalition formation | ✓ | ✓ | |
| Wei et al. [12] | resource allocation, cooperative game | ✓ | ✓ | ✓ |
| Xu et al. [13] | game theory, resource allocation | ✓ | | |
| Mashayekhy et al. [4] | virtual machine, game theory | ✓ | | ✓ |
| Hassan et al. [14] | cloud provider, capacity outsourcing, repeated game, perfect equilibrium | ✓ | | |
| Hassan et al. [15] | cooperative game, coalition, game theory, profit | ✓ | | |

In summary, previous studies have suggested different factors that may influence the creation of "guilds" of CPs, in other words, cloud federations between CPs. However, although most of the studies agree that a good revenue sharing mechanism is essential, no study has simulated and measured the impact of such factors.

# 3   Experiment Formulation

In this section, first, we define the model and the coalition game that is used for the simulation. Second, we define the concepts of revenue sharing, capacity disparity, and cost disparity, which were identified in the previous studies as encouragers of cloud federation. Finally, based on these factors, we define four types of scenarios, which are used to test their impact on the formation of federations.

## 3.1   Model

The model consists of a group of independent cloud providers and a user demand generator. Each CP has a certain amount of computational resources in terms of computing units, memory, and storage. The CPs offers these computational resources to the users in the form of virtual machines (VM), as long as they have the capacity to provide them.

The user demand generator plays the role of the customers. This entity generates a variable number of users per day (up to 30 users). In order to represent the flexible demands of users, the model considers that user requests are volatile and, therefore, vary in size, duration, and service type as well. To achieve this, we consider three types of VMs: general purpose, storage specialized, and computing specialized. The specifications of the VMs are detailed in Table 2 and are modelled after the Amazon EC2 Web Services instances for Seoul [16]. The model uses the Mersenne-Twister algorithm to generate random numbers with a normal distribution. Each demand is comprised of a certain number of VMs, type of VM, and duration in days. Then, each generated user with random demand contacts a random CP for service. This allows us to simulate changes in demand and to mimic the cloud services market.

**Table 2.** Specification of three types of virtual machines (VM).

|  | General purpose | Storage specialized | Computing specialized |
|---|---|---|---|
| Computing units | 14 | 14 | 31 |
| GBs of memory | 16 | 30 | 16 |
| TBs of storage | 2 | 6 | 2 |
| Price per day | $ 13.96 | $ 20.26 | $ 18.50 |

For the sake of simplicity, this model comes with some limitations regarding the requirements for cloud federations. In this model, there is the assumption that all CPs trust one another, that there is no administrative cost for collaboration, and that CPs have perfect interoperability. In detail, interoperation between CPs normally incurs a cost that should be covered by the federation [21]. Besides, CPs that do not trust each other would hardly collaborate fully, which would impede alliances. Finally, with regard to collaboration cost, the model assumes that the prices are fixed (i.e., the prices are independent of collaboration cost).

The main feature of this model is that the CPs have the freedom to collaborate with one another. Each CP is considered to be a selfish agent that will strive to increase its revenue. Therefore, CPs will only federate, if there is an incentive to do so (i.e., if there is an increase in utility). In this study, we define a CP's utility to be its total revenue as shown in the following function:

$$U_i = \sum_{j=1}^{n} VM_{ij} \times p_{ij} \tag{1}$$

where $U_i$ represents the total utility of CP $i$, while $VM_{ij}$ represents the number of VMs of type $j$ demanded. The variable $p_{ij}$ represents the VM price, which is the same for all CPs in our simulation model [17].

## 3.2   Experiment Setup

For the simulation, we propose a repeated game that allows CPs to create strategic alliances. The game begins with the CPs having their full capacity available and being part of no federation. Then, the demand generator starts sending requests to the CPs, who in turn will accept the requests, if they have capacity still available to fulfill it.

At any point of the repeated game, a CP may realize that collaborating with another CP would result in an increase in utility. For example, a CP may not have enough resources by itself, to fulfill a user request that would otherwise be lost. Collaboration between CPs allows them to share their resources and other strategic advantages, which in turn leads to increased profit.

During the game, all CPs measure their utility and calculate the expected utility of joining or creating a federation. If a CP concludes that it can increase its utility by collaborating rather than by working alone, then it will decide to federate. Similarly, CPs in a federation measure the expected utility, which they would receive by working alone, and will decide to leave or dissolve the federation, if the expected utility is higher than its current utility.

For the experiments, we define two baseline scenarios (i.e., no-federation scenarios) and three main scenario types that are used to compare the effect of each of the factors to be studied. The three scenario types focus on revenue sharing mechanisms, capacity disparity, or cost disparity. For the no-federation scenario, a group of ten cloud providers is assumed that offer the general purpose VMs only (Table 2). All CPs start with the same capacity limit and cost. As for the revenue sharing mechanism, CPs will get the full revenue from the VMs assigned to the federation. Detailed information about the parameter settings for the two no-federation scenarios is presented in Table 3.

**Table 3.** Parameter values used for the two no-federation scenarios.

| Parameter | Value |
|---|---|
| Revenue sharing mechanism | Assigned VMs |
| Number of cloud providers | 10 |
| Available VM types | General Purpose or All VM Types |
| Computing capacity (CUs) | 500 |
| Storage capacity (TBs) | 100 |
| Cost | Not Considered |

**Revenue Sharing Scenario.** Revenue sharing mechanisms are important to cloud federations due to several factors. First, cloud providers need an effective revenue sharing method, to encourage their participation in a federation. In other words, cloud providers will only cooperate, if they receive a benefit [8].

Second, it determines how the allocation of revenue is performed. A fair system is needed, ensuring that all CPs are properly recompensed for the amount of resources that they invested into the federation [7]. For this study, fairness is defined as self-centered inequity aversion. This term relates to the behavior, at which "people resist inequitable outcomes; i.e., they are willing to give up some material payoff to move in the direction of more equitable outcomes" [18].

There are several well-known mechanisms for resource sharing in coalition and game theory models. However, each one of them provides a different benefit, fairness, and stability values to the collaborations. This may affect how the federations are created, and even how they are dissolved. Therefore, to further test their impact, it is important that those different revenue-sharing mechanisms are compared within scenarios. The revenue sharing parameters that are considered in this scenario type are depicted in Table 4.

*Assigned Resources.* With this mechanism, each CP will obtain a revenue share that is proportional to the amount of resources contributed (proportional revenue sharing mechanism) [7]. This mechanism is particularly strong in its fairness. This is a simple mechanism to implement, as it only considers the resource contributions of collaborating CPs for the calculation of the amount of revenue that each one of them gets. Besides, it allows combining resources that could not be sold separately.

*Outsourcing.* In some instances, cloud federations have been seen as a way for CPs to outsource some of its business to another CP. Following this logic, collaborating CPs can implement a mechanism, in which the outsourcing provider will get a percentage of the revenue or a fixed fee. This revenue sharing would allow a CP to keep some of the revenue of the business it secured, even though it would not be able to fulfill by itself. For this mechanism, the variable alpha is defined as the percentage of revenue that will be forwarded by the outsourcing CP to the service fulfilling CP. For this experiment, alpha is set to 70%, 75%, or 90%.

*Shapley Value.* This mechanism is named after Lloyd Shapley, who proposed a method to calculate the overall gain of all alternatives of a player that participates in a game with a large number of agents. The Shapley Value is calculated through the function:

$$\varphi_i(v) = \sum_{S \subseteq N} \frac{(|S| - 1)!(|N| - |S|)!}{|N|!} [v(S) - v(S - \{i\})] \qquad (2)$$

where $\varphi_i$ represents the Shapley value, which is the gain of player $i$. $S$ represents a possible coalition, which is a subset of all players $N$. The function $v$ ($v: 2^N \rightarrow \mathfrak{R}$) represents the worth of a coalition [17].

In cloud computing, the Shapley value is used to represent the marginal contributions of any CP to the federation it belongs to. In contrast with other revenue sharing schemes, this scheme allows federations to allocate revenue according to the value created. Using this scheme, other types of contributions made by CPs can be considered, not just the resources provided by the CPs.

**Capacity Disparity Scenario.** In this scenario, CPs are given different capacities with respect to storage capacity and computing capacity. In particular, while some CPs have the capacities as used in the base scenario, others derivate from this by being specialized in storage resources or computational resources. Table 4 contains the parameter values for the capacity disparity scenario.

**Table 4.** Parameter values for the three main scenarios.

| Parameter | Revenue-sharing scenario(s) | Capacity disparity scenario | Cost disparity scenario | | |
|---|---|---|---|---|---|
| Revenue sharing mechanism | Assigned resources; outsourcing (70%, 75%, 90%); Shapley value | Assigned resources | Assigned resources | | |
| Number of cloud providers | 10 | 10 | 10 | | |
| Available VM types | 1 (General) | All | All | | |
| Computing capacity [CU] | 500 | CP1&2 [500] CP3&4 [1000] CP5&6 [250] CP7&8 [500] CP9&10 [750] | 500 | | |
| Storage capacity [TB] | 100 | CP1&2 [100] CP3&4 [50] CP5&6 [200] CP7&8 [150] CP9&10 [100] | 100 | | |
| Cost [% of price] | Not considered | Not Considered | | **VM1** | **VM2** | **VM3** |
| | | | CP 1&2 | 80% | 80% | 80% |
| | | | CP 3&4 | **70%** | 80% | 80% |
| | | | CP 5&6 | 80% | **70%** | 80% |
| | | | CP 7&8 | 80% | 80% | **70%** |
| | | | CP 9&10 | **75%** | **75%** | **75%** |

**Cost Disparity Scenario.** All CPs are given the same resource capabilities. However, each CP will have different costs. This scenario accounts for how some CPs can have different costs of resources due to a different efficiency in their infrastructure management. The cost percentages and other parameters are presented in Table 4.

## 4   Results

Each simulation has been executed 100 times, in order to calculate the average result of the three performance indicators. The main indicators of performance considered are the number of federations created, the number of steps needed for the model to reach equilibrium, and the total revenue of the population. The reasons for selecting those three performance indicators are that they enable interpreting the overall result of the simulation from a business perspective. For example, a high number of federations created suggests that the particular scenario fosters collaboration. The number of steps to reach an equilibrium indicates the strength of the incentive mechanism and its performance in a competition with other federations. The total revenue of the agents is an indicator for the benefit of collaboration, where a high value means that a high demand could be covered.

### 4.1   Results for the Revenue Sharing Scenarios

After analyzing the first results obtained in this scenario, we could detect that the revenue sharing mechanism has a significant impact on the way that federations are formed. Furthermore, the comparison of the results of each of the revenue sharing mechanisms, it is easy to observe their traits. Table 5 shows the average outcome of the 100 simulations that were performed for each scenario.

While the total revenue of the population did not vary significantly for all mechanisms, the Shapley value mechanism performs even worse than the no-federation

**Table 5.** Simulation results for revenue sharing scenarios.

| Scenario analyzed | Number of federations | Number of steps to reach equilibrium | Total revenue |
|---|---|---|---|
| No-federation scenario (Only general purposed VMs used) | 0 | 0 | $ 133,021.49 |
| 'Assigned Resource' revenue sharing scenario | 2.53 | 52.15 | $ 137,483.52 |
| 'Outsourcing 70%' revenue sharing scenario | 0 | 0 | $ 133,021.49 |
| 'Outsourcing 75%' revenue sharing scenario | 1.61 | 50.94 | $ 135,582.31 |
| 'Outsourcing 90%' revenue sharing scenario | 3.28 | 54.55 | $ 137,865.75 |
| 'Shapley Value' revenue sharing scenario | 2.4 | 36.68 | $ 131,646.12 |

scenario. Interestingly, analyzing the distribution of revenue reveals that the CPs being part of the federation achieve higher revenues than in the no-federation scenario. The remaining CPs obtain less. The Shapley value mechanism was the fastest in reaching the equilibrium (36.88 steps) compared to the outsourcing revenue sharing scenarios. This means that the Shapely value mechanism substitutes some of the payoff with federation creation speed.

Furthermore, the best mechanism for forming cloud federations, with respect to size and revenue, is the outsourcing mechanism with an outsourcing value of 90%. However, if the outsourcing value is too small (which is the case if alpha is 70% or below in our scenarios), CPs will choose to work always by themselves. Therefore, by comparing the outsourcing scenarios, we can conclude that, if the value of alpha is not set fairly by the collaborating CPs, then federation formation will not happen.

## 4.2    Results for the Capacity Disparity Scenarios

For the capacity scenario, the results show an increase in revenue compared to the no-federation scenario and multiple types of VMs. The results are summarized in Table 6. The results are consistent with results of previous studies. Cloud providers with different capabilities and pools of resources have a hard time managing the volatile demand of customers. This is particularly true, if there are different types of services and requirements. In this case, the presence of different types of VMs causes this effect.

**Table 6.** Simulation results for the capacity disparity scenario and the cost disparity scenario.

| Scenario analyzed | Number of federations | Number of steps to reach equilibrium | Total revenue |
|---|---|---|---|
| No-federation scenario (All VM Types Used) | 0 | 0 | $ 103,223.61 |
| Capacity disparity scenario | 2.9 | 34.62 | $ 114,773.53 |
| Cost disparity scenario | 2.49 | 37.11 | $ 121,276.47[a] |

[a] Note: The performance measure for the cost disparity scenario is cost, which has been measured to be $27,893.59. The corresponding revenue is shown in the table.

Nonetheless, the simulation showed a very particular behavior in this scenario. In most cases, the CPs that formed federations included members with completely different capabilities, resulting in very heterogeneous federations (i.e., federations of CPs that provide very different resources). This behavior shows that CPs could achieve better performances in federations with different capabilities than offering those resources themselves. The CPs allow federations to allocate VMs to the CP that would be able to fulfill it more effectively, which in turn helps the federation saving resources.

### 4.3   Results for the Cost Disparity Scenario

In terms of number and formation speed of the federations, the cost disparity scenario and the capacity disparity scenario yielded similar results, as can be seen in Table 6.

Contrary to expectations, the resulting federations of the cost disparity scenario are quite different to the federations of the capacity disparity scenario. In the capacity disparity scenario, CPs would strive to assign their resources in the most allocation-effective (i.e., cost-effective) way. CPs collaborate with one another, to gain a strategic advantage in terms of cost effectiveness, leading to heterogeneous federations formed by CPs with different capabilities.

In the cost disparity scenario, results show that such an occurrence is rare. From this observation, we can conclude that gaining an advantage in cost effectiveness is less beneficial than selling unused resources. That means, CPs tend to federate with CPs that let them use their resources as much as possible, rather than gaining more profit per VM

## 5   Conclusions

### 5.1   Summary

This paper proposed cloud federation formation scenarios that simulate the interactions of cloud providers. Each one of these scenarios is used to test and study different factors, identified in previous studies as incentives to form cloud federations. The factors that were simulated were revenue-sharing mechanisms, capacity disparity, and cost disparity. The results of the simulations offer some insights regarding the effects of these factors on the creation of cloud federations.

### 5.2   Discussion and Implications

The results obtained from the simulations of the scenarios show the effect of cost disparity, capacity disparity, and revenue sharing mechanisms on cloud federation formations.

The results about the revenue-sharing mechanisms have shown that they are vital to federations. They define the distribution of benefits obtained through collaboration. The Shapley value mechanism showed to be the fastest in reaching an equilibrium but also achieved lower revenue than the other scenarios. In contrast, the outsourcing mechanism was the most efficient in terms of the number and the revenue of federations. However, the results also depicted that it is necessary to have a sufficient revenue percentage to share. Otherwise, the performance of the mechanisms drops significantly, even to the point at which no federation is created. The implications of these findings are that cloud federation must have a fair revenue-sharing mechanism that provides sufficient benefits. Without that, businesses will not have any incentive to collaborate at all.

The results about capacity disparity and cost disparity showed that capacity disparity provides a better incentive than cost disparity. By comparing the resulting performance measures, we can conclude that CPs benefit more by getting all their available resources used, rather than by achieving a cost advantage usable in a fraction of said resources. This coincides with the situation in the IT sector, where technologies can easily be replaced and updated. In other words, although both are inherent characteristics of businesses, the disparity in resources and capabilities is more important than cost competitiveness.

### 5.3 Limitations and Future Work

The limitations of this paper are as follows. First, the model assumes that there are no impediments to federations, as long as CPs decide to collaborate. Potential obstacles such as interoperability, trust between CPs, and QoS are not considered in the model. Second, we assume that the resource prices are fixed and that CPs do not have enough power to affect them. Third, the study has the same limitations as study based on agent-based modeling. The simulations performed were simplified to some extent, in order to easily observe the effect of factors, also limiting its similarity to reality.

With respect to future work, we would recommend testing more factors such as QoS constraints and trust between CPs. Simulations that test several of these incentives simultaneously would also yield considerable insight on cloud federation formations. Additional research is also needed on the effects of demand changes on the formation of federations. Finally, a similar study could be performed, in which prices are variable and the creation of federations may yield monopolies or oligopolies.

**Acknowledgements.** This research was conducted within the project BASMATI (Cloud Brokerage Across Borders for Mobile Users and Applications), which has received funding from the ICT R&D program of the Korean MSIP/IITP (R0115-16-0001) and from the European Union's Horizon 2020 research and innovation programme under grant agreement no. 723131.

## References

1. Mell, P., Grance, T.: The NIST definition of cloud computing. National Institute of Standards and Technology, Gaithersburg (2011)
2. Synergy Research Group, 2016 review shows $148 billion cloud market growing at 25% annually (2017). https://www.srgresearch.com/articles/2016-review-shows-148-billion-cloud-market-growing-25-annually
3. Dikaiakos, M., Katsaros, D., Mehra, P., Pallis, G., Vakali, A.: Cloud computing: distributed internet computing for IT and scientific research. IEEE Internet Comput. 13(5) (2009)
4. Mashayekhy, L., Nejad, M.M., Grosu, D.: Cloud federations in the sky: formation game and mechanism. IEEE Trans. Cloud Comput. 3(1), 14–27 (2015)
5. Synergy Research Group, Big four still dominate in Q1 as cloud market growth exceeds 50% (2016). https://www.srgresearch.com/articles/gang-four-still-racing-away-cloud-market
6. Hassan, M.M., Hossain, M.S., Sarkar, A.J., Huh, E.N.: Cooperative game-based distributed resource allocation in horizontal dynamic cloud federation platform. Inf. Syst. Front. 16(4), 523–542 (2014)
7. El Zant, B., Amigo, I., Gagnaire, M.: Federation and revenue sharing in cloud. In: IEEE International Conference on Cloud Engineering, pp. 446–451 (2014)

8. Samaan, N.: A novel economic sharing model in a federation of selfish cloud providers. Trans. Parallel Distrib. Syst. **25**(1), 12–21 (2014)
9. Niyato, D., Vasilakos, A.V., Kun, Z.: Resource and revenue sharing with coalition formation of cloud providers: game theoretic approach. In: Cluster, Cloud and Grid Computing, pp. 215–224 (2011)
10. Lu, Z., Wen, X., Sun, Y.: A game theory based resource sharing scheme in cloud computing environment. In: Information and Communication Technologies, pp. 1097–1102 (2012)
11. Guazzone, M., Anglano, C., Sereno, M.: A game-theoretic approach to coalition formation in green cloud federations. In: Cluster, Cloud and Grid Computing, pp. 618–625 (2014)
12. Wei, G., Vasilakos, A.V., Zheng, Y., Xiong, N.: A game-theoretic method of fair resource allocation for cloud computing services. J. Supercomputing **54**(2), 252–269 (2010)
13. Xu, X., Yu, H., Cong, X.: A qos-constrained resource allocation game in federated cloud. In: Innovative Mobile and Internet Services in Ubiquitous Computing, pp. 268–275 (2013)
14. Hassan, M.M., Al-Wadud, M.A., Fortino, G.: A socially optimal resource and revenue sharing mechanism in cloud federations. In: IEEE 19th International Conference on Computer Supported Cooperative Work in Design, pp. 620–625 (2015)
15. Hassan, M.M., Abdullah-Al-Wadud, M., Almogren, A., Rahman, S.K., Alamri, A.A.A., Hamid, M.: QoS and trust-aware coalition formation game in data-intensive cloud federations. Concurrency Comput. Pract. Experience **28**(10), 2889–2905 (2015)
16. Amazon: Amazon EC2 pricing (2017). https://aws.amazon.com/ec2/pricing/on-demand
17. Ernst, F., Klaus, S.M.: A theory of fairness, competition, and cooperation. Q. J. Econ. **114** (3), 817–868 (1999)
18. Roth, A.E.: The Shapley Value: Essays in Honor of Lloyd S. Shapley. Cambridge University Press, Cambridge (1988)
19. Altmann, J., Kashef, M.M.: Cost model based service placement in federated hybrid clouds. Future Gener. Comput. Syst. **41**, 79–90 (2014). doi:10.1016/j.future.2014.08.014. Elsevier
20. Gebregiorgis, S.A., Altmann, J.: IT service platforms: their value creation model and the impact of their level of openness on their adoption. Procedia Comput. Sci. **68**, 173–187 (2015)
21. Haile, N., Altmann, J.: Evaluating investments in portability and interoperability between software service platforms. Future Gener. Comput. Syst. (2017). doi:10.1016/j.future.2017.04.040
22. Rohitratana, J., Altmann, J.: Impact of pricing schemes on a market for software-as-a-service and perpetual software. Future Gener. Comput. Syst. **28**(8), 1328–1339 (2012). Elsevier
23. Haile, N., Altmann, J.: Structural analysis of value creation in software service platforms. Electron. Markets (2015). doi:10.1007/s12525-015-0208-8
24. Haile, N., Altmann, J.: Value creation in software service platforms. Future Gener. Comput. Syst. (2015). Elsevier, doi:10.1016/j.future.2015.09.029
25. Kim, K., Kang, S., Altmann, J.: Cloud goliath versus a federation of cloud davids. In: Altmann, J., Vanmechelen, K., Rana, Omer F. (eds.) GECON 2014. LNCS, vol. 8914, pp. 55–66. Springer, Cham (2014). doi:10.1007/978-3-319-14609-6_4
26. Kim, K., Altmann, J.: Effect of homophily on network formation. Commun. Nonlinear Sci. Numer. Simul. **44**, 482–494 (2017)
27. Haile, N., Altmann, J.: Estimating the value obtained from using a software service platform. In: Altmann, J., Vanmechelen, K., Rana, Omer F. (eds.) GECON 2013. LNCS, vol. 8193, pp. 244–255. Springer, Cham (2013). doi:10.1007/978-3-319-02414-1_18
28. Altmann, J., Courcoubetis, C., Risch, M.: A marketplace and its market mechanism for trading commoditized computing resources. Ann. des Télécommunications **65**, 653–667 (2010)

29. Altmann, J., Carlini, E., Coppola, M., Dazzi, P., Juan Ferrer, A., Haile, N., Jung, Y., Kang, D.-J., Marshall, I.-J., Tserpes, K., Varvarigou, T.: BASMATI - a brokerage architecture on federated clouds for mobile applications. In: CGW 2016 International Workshop, Krakow, Poland (2016)
30. Haile, N., Altmann, J.: Risk-benefit-mediated impact of determinants on the adoption of cloud federation. In: PACIS - Pacific Asia Conference on Information Systems, AIS Singapore (2015)
31. Hofäcker, D., Schröder, H., Li, Y., Flynn, M.: Trends and determinants of work-retirement transitions under changing institutional conditions: Germany, England and Japan compared. J. Soc. Policy 45(1), 39–64 (2016)

# Work in Progress on Service Selection and Coordination

# ClouDSS: A Decision Support System for Cloud Service Selection

Umut Şener[✉], Ebru Gökalp, and P. Erhan Eren

Informatics Institute, Middle East Technical University, Ankara, Turkey
{sumut, egokalp, ereren}@metu.edu.tr

**Abstract.** Cloud computing brings in significant technical advantages and enables companies, especially small and medium size enterprises (SMEs), to eliminate up-front capital expenditures. This is due to the various benefits it provides, such as pay-as-you-go service model, flexibility of services, and on-demand accessibility. The proliferation of cloud services leads to their wide spread use and calls for comprehensive evaluation approaches in order to be able to choose the most suitable alternatives. To this end, existing studies in the literature generally provide solutions incorporating a single method for making such decisions. Therefore, this study proposes a more comprehensive solution in the form of a decision support system named as ClouDSS which employs various Multi-Criteria Decision Making (MCDM) methods with the aim of optimizing cloud service selection decisions. ClouDSS has a default decision model, which can be customized according to enterprise-specific requirements, for evaluating the suitability of cloud services with respect to business needs. After presenting the main components of ClouDSS, the employed cloud service selection process is described in order to highlight the associated tasks, including both objective and subjective evaluation approaches. Furthermore, the applicability of the proposed system is demonstrated through a case study.

**Keywords:** Economics of cloud computing · Service selection · Decision support system · SME · Multi-Criteria Decision Making

## 1 Introduction

Enterprises have been adopting Cloud Computing (CC) technologies which provide various opportunities such as scalability, flexibility, and on-demand availability. Indeed, CC provides financial benefits including reduced expenditures for existing applications as well as the availability of innovative IT at an affordable operating cost [1]. Among the main drivers of CC are economics and simplification of software delivery and operation [2]. Due to offered benefits such as competitive advantages, significant cost savings, and enhanced business processes, CC is an attractive proposition for many Small and Medium Size Enterprises (SMEs) [3, 4].

Despite the high rate of IT related advances, the growth of CC adoption by SMEs is relatively slow. Since the CC adoption related concerns are multifaceted, the assessment and selection of a variety of available cloud services with similar functions in the market have become a major challenge [1]. Practitioners in SMEs are faced with

© Springer International Publishing AG 2017
C. Pham et al. (Eds.): GECON 2017, LNCS 10537, pp. 249–261, 2017.
DOI: 10.1007/978-3-319-68066-8_19

complex decisions regarding the selection of most suitable CC services for their business activities. This is because the decision includes a comprehensive analysis of all potential criteria influencing the CC service adoption and utilization. These criteria may vary depending on the business structures of SMEs, and may include improved efficiency, increased availability, fast deployment, and elastic scalability, security concern, privacy issues, and information loss [5–7]. Therefore, the CC service selection for SMEs is a complicated decision-making process, which may benefit from multi criteria decision making (MCDM) methods. Although there has been a growing number of studies regarding CC adoption in SMEs [4, 8, 9], a literature review [10] indicates that only few of them are related to the use of MCDM approaches for CC adoption in SMEs.

The decision support system (DSS) concept is described as *"computer based information systems that provide interactive information support to managers during the decision-making process"* [11]. DSSs are interactive and well-integrated systems which provide managers with data, tools, and models to facilitate semi-structured decisions that are unique, rapidly changing, and not easily specified in advance. The information system architecture is relatively less complex for the case of SMEs, but lacks computer aided decision-making capability. Therefore, the development of computerized decision support for SMEs will contribute to their innovation and prosperity [12].

The aim of this study is to analyze existing work related to cloud service selection decisions in SMEs and to develop a DSS providing a collection of MCDM methods for supporting such decisions. Accordingly, the literature is reviewed systematically to identify studies related to the cloud service selection approaches in SMEs. Then, by analyzing the existing studies, and considering the strengths and weaknesses of them, a DSS named as ClouDSS is proposed. The aim of ClouDSS is to provide a comprehensive approach for assessing cloud service alternatives in order to find the best selection for a given company maximizing the economic benefits of CC technologies.

The remainder of the paper is structured as follows: Sect. 2 provides background information which covers economic benefits of cloud computing for SMEs, a brief description of MCDM methods for cloud service selection, and a systematic literature review of existing proposed DSSs for cloud service selection decision of SMEs. Section 3 presents the components of ClouDSS together with the description of the cloud service selection process. Consequently, a case study that demonstrates the applicability of ClouDSS is presented in Sect. 4, followed by the conclusion of the study.

## 2 Literature Review

### 2.1 Economic Benefits of Cloud Computing for SMEs

CC provides the capability to provision on-demand services at a cheaper cost than on-premises alternatives, with reduced complexity, improved scalability, and broader availability. In CC, various services such as computing, storage, and software are available and accessed over the internet.

SMEs have a significant role in terms of supporting national economies. Because small companies have flexible organizational structures which are easily adaptable to new economic conditions or market trends. Although SMEs are capable of creating innovation, their technical capacities constitute a barrier regarding opportunities and profits resulting from economies of scale obtained by large companies [13]. In addition, SMEs have limited financial capabilities, and new expenditures may cause fatal results in business, therefore they try to carry out cost-effective hardware and software investments. CC addresses these issues and provides on-demand and flexible solutions for SMEs, at lower cost levels, thereby reducing potential risks of investments as well as boosting productivity and creativity in businesses.

The economic benefits of CC for SMEs are identified as follows [14]: strategic flexibility (the ability of quick deployment for entering a new market), reduced cost (no up-front and maintenance costs due to pay-per-use), software availability (reduced or no licensing fees), scalability (practically endless resources and automatic scaling based on changing demand), skills and staffing (reduced need for highly-skilled personnel), energy efficiency (reduced utility cost), and system redundancy (data recovery for better action plan in case of system failure). The quick deployment ability of cloud services and reduced Total Cost of Ownership of cloud solutions such as SaaS seem to be more appropriate for SMEs than large organizations [15]. Accordingly, SMEs are in need of selecting and deploying CC solutions based on their specific business requirements.

## 2.2 Cloud Service Selection by Using MCDM

CC service selection is a complicated decision-making process requiring the use of MCDM approach for identifying the most suitable cloud services among available alternatives [16–18]. As stated in [19], MCDM methods are commonly applied to study complex problems, since they provide a well-structured approach in the operations research domain, and their efficiency is proven in solving complicated and multi-dimensional decision making problems [16]. MCDM includes a set of methods for making comparisons, prioritizing multiple alternatives, and selecting the best-fit choice. Among these methods which include Min-Max, Max-Min, ELECTRE, PROMETHEE, TOPSIS, Compromise Programming, Analytic Hierarchy Process (AHP), Fuzzy AHP, Data Envelopment Analysis (DEA), and Goal Programming, the most widely used one is AHP. It is also quite suitable for cloud service selection decisions [17].

## 2.3 DSSs Developed for Cloud Service Selection Decision

A systematic literature review conducted by following the method given in Kitchenham [20] is presented in this section. DSSs developed for cloud service selection for SMEs is selected as the research topic and the starting point of the search. The search query is defined as {{"decision" OR "decision-making" OR "DSS" OR "decision support system" OR "Service Selection"} AND "cloud"}. Web of Science (www.webofknowledge.com) and Aisel (aisel.aisnet.org) are selected as databases for the search. In Web of Science, 36 papers are collected, while in Aisel only 33 papers are identified. First of all, SSCI, SCI, and AIS index journals, and conference proceedings, series, meetings, and reviews are selected among the resulting papers. Before reading papers fully, keywords, titles, and abstracts of the studies are checked to assess whether they are related to the research topic. Then, the publication date is selected as between 2000 and 2017. A significant portion of the collected studies is related to the decision of cloud services adoption. They mainly investigate the identification of significant decision criteria instead of proposing a DSS. After this elimination, only eight studies remain and they propose a DSS solution which is based on a single model such as AHP, Fuzzy AHP, and DEA:

- The service selection based on user feedback [21] is proposed as a decision model for cloud selection. However, this model covers the subjective assessment of customers and the assessment of third-party organization. Therefore, this model appears to be inconvenient for SMEs.
- Karim et al. [22] propose an AHP-based decision model for cloud service selection.
- Wilson et al. [23], Godse and Mulik [24], Garg et al. [17] propose a DSS based on AHP ranking. But it does not provide additional assessment methods.
- Whaiduzzaman et al. [16] investigate the available MCDM methods. But, they do not present a decision model or DSS.
- Rehman et al. [25] propose a scenario based MCDM for IaaS selection and compare the results of 7 MCDM methods. However, they utilize matlab functions and usage of the model requires domain knowledge, which can be difficult for SMEs to use.
- Eisa et al. [26] investigate the trends in cloud service selection. They present different online assessment tools such as RightCloudz, Intel Cloud Finder, and Cloudorado. They give a comparison of these tools in terms of their capabilities. MCDM methods are not directly incorporated into their proposed solution.

As a result of the systematic literature review, it can be concluded that there is a limited number of studies proposing DSS for cloud service selection. The analysis of existing studies reveals that they provide solutions utilizing a maximum of two decision models and their structures are not customizable according to enterprise specific requirements. Therefore, in order to provide a more comprehensive solution, this study proposes a customizable DSS for selecting the most suitable cloud services. The system is intended to be also accessible for users with limited domain knowledge regarding CC and decision making approaches. The proposed solution is described next.

## 3   Development of ClouDSS

The system architecture of ClouDSS comprises three main components of a typical DSS: Data Management, Model Management, and Knowledge Management, as shown in Fig. 1. The proposed ClouDSS is designed as a DSS for cloud service selection process which contains a set of semi-structured decisions requiring individual judgment. It focuses on determining the best cloud service alternative based on both objective and subjective evaluation by using MCDM methods including AHP, Fuzzy AHP, linear optimization, goal programming, etc. The unique aspect of ClouDSS is that it provides various techniques within a single system, and Decision Makers (DMs) can access the system over the internet for making cloud service selection decisions efficiently and comprehensively.

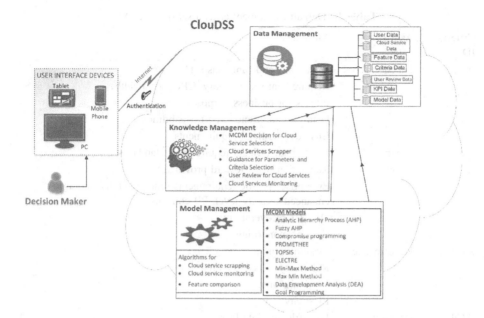

**Fig. 1.** System architecture of ClouDSS.

## 3.1 Identification of the Criteria Set for MCDM

The criteria set for adopting a cloud-based enterprise solution has already been identified in our earlier study [27], based on an extensive literature search. In that study, the factors are ranked by employing the AHP method with 20 experts. Based on these results, the highest ranking factors are chosen as the assessment criteria set to be used in ClouDSS (Table 1). Each criterion consists of several attributes that enable DMs to evaluate cloud service alternatives. While the default assessment criteria set consists of five main items including functionality, security & privacy, performance, usability and economic value, additional criteria can be chosen from an extended collection available in ClouDSS.

## 3.2 Cloud Service Selection Process in ClouDSS

The cloud service selection process and the interrelated set of tasks performed in conjunction with the ClouDSS modules are shown in Fig. 1. The DM accesses ClouDSS after registering and entering the company information such as company size, sector, number of employees, and business structure. After the user is authenticated successfully, the DM selects the type of cloud service, such as Enterprise Information Systems, Enterprise Content Management Systems. The DM can make an objective evaluation by obtaining a feature comparison table for the cloud service alternatives, including objective parameters such as languages provided, hourly pay-as-you-go (yes/no), and SLA level. The DM can also make a subjective evaluation, which means finding the best-fit cloud service alternative by weighing multiple criteria based on his

**Table 1.** Default assessment criteria set of ClouDSS.

| Criteria ID | Assessment criteria | Attributes |
|---|---|---|
| AC1 | Functionality | Operations and functions set |
| | | Requirement set (memory, CPU, bandwidth) |
| | | Fitness for business purposes |
| | | Data migration and export capabilities |
| | | Business partners' requirements |
| AC2 | Security & privacy | Conformance (legal requirements/standards) |
| | | Reputation (trust toward providers) |
| | | Enterprise specific requirements (encrypted data storage, enhanced security level, PII controls) |
| | | Disaster recoverability |
| | | Ease of monitoring |
| AC3 | Performance | System uptime |
| | | Reliability |
| | | Response time |
| | | Elasticity |
| AC4 | Usability | User-friendly interface |
| | | Ease of use |
| AC5 | Economic value | Price of the product |
| | | Additional operating cost of the product |
| | | Cost of the downtime |
| | | Total cost of ownership (i.e. implementation cost, personnel training cost, licensing fees, etc.) |

intuition, judgement, and experience regarding cloud services. If the DM wants to make an objective comparison, he selects the set of features in order to compare the service alternatives to be shown in the comparison table. He also selects a suitable user profile for user reviews matching his own requirements, such as user experience, user review rating, and company size the user works at, and the system displays the reviews. As a result, he obtains the feature comparison table which is in a matrix form showing features versus service alternatives. Reviews of other users are also shown at the end of the table for each cloud service. Once the DM makes the cloud service selection decision based on this table, the option of making additional subjective evaluation before making the final decision is also offered to the DM. If he selects this option, MCDM is performed after the selection of model (the default model is AHP), criteria from the criteria set (the default criteria are functionality, security &privacy, performance, usability, and economic value), and service alternatives from the cloud services set. Then, the system requests the user to perform a pair-wise comparison of the selected criteria followed by a comparison of alternatives for each selected criteria. For example, if the best-fit solution is to be chosen among seven alternatives by using the default criteria set containing the five criteria, six pairwise comparison matrices are requested to be filled by the DM (one for pair-wise comparison of criteria and five for pair-wise comparison of alternatives for each criteria). Upon completion of comparisons, ClouDSS displays the results report including the scores for each alternative and offers to perform additional assessments by using different models. If the DM selects an additional assessment, available models are displayed for selection. After selecting the additional model, the assessment is conducted and the resulting report is obtained. As a result, the process is concluded by making the cloud service selection decision. ClouDSS consists of five modules as described below.

**MCDM for Cloud Service Selection:** This module includes algorithms implementing MCDM Models such as AHP, Fuzzy AHP, DEA and Goal-Programming to provide optimized decision making.

**Cloud Services Information Fetcher:** This module includes APIs developed for extracting up-to-date information about cloud services by constantly checking their provider's websites to find out if there is any new information. The collected data is stored as cloud services data.

**Guidance for Parameters and Criteria Selection:** This module is responsible for providing assistance to DMs with specifying parameters used for objective evaluation and criteria for subjective evaluation. This module also represents parameters and criteria in a uniform way so that users with little knowledge about cloud technologies can easily understand and specify their requirements.

**User Review for Cloud Services:** This module aims to manage user review data related to cloud services. IT experts or other DMs using the services provide reviews for cloud services, which are rated by other DMs based on usefulness and correctness.

**Cloud Services Monitoring:** Some quantitative Key Performance Indicator (KPI) values regarding performance and reliability of cloud services, such as response time and system up-time, are obtained, monitored and managed by this module which regularly checks cloud providers. The real-time values obtained periodically for this kind of KPIs are stored as KPI data. The DM can select the time interval in which the values are collected. ClouDSS gives real-life measures for these KPIs in order to increase the decision quality. However, for some cloud services, it is not possible to monitor them as they may not have interfaces for monitoring purposes.

## 4 Case Study

The applicability of ClouDSS is presented by employing a usage scenario in this section. The SMEs need to assess the different aspects of the alternative cloud solutions before implementing; therefore they need a set of methods in order to evaluate the different aspect of the alternatives and to select the best-fit solution among them.

A small company considers implementing a cloud-based Enterprise Content Management (ECM) solution. This decision is made by following the subjective evaluation path described in Fig. 2. Six Decision Makers (DMs) in a given SME try to determine the best alternative among three cloud service alternatives X, Y, and Z, with respect to the requirement set provided in Table 1. Decision makers employ pairwise

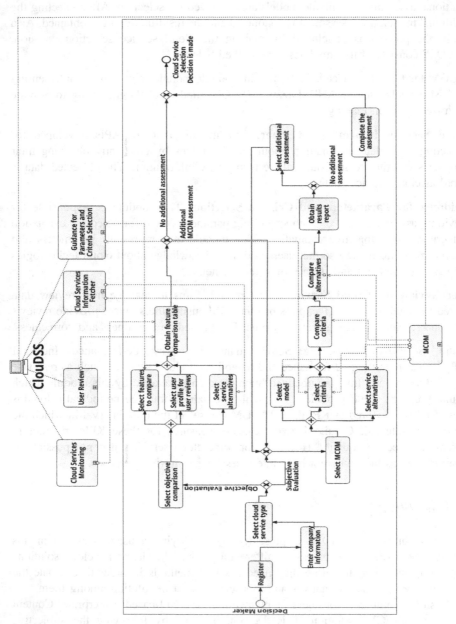

**Fig. 2.** Cloud service selection process in ClouDSS.

Table 2. The weights of the products based on each criterion.

|  | AC1 | AC2 | AC3 | AC4 | AC5 | Overall | Priority |
|---|---|---|---|---|---|---|---|
| Alternative X | 0.36 | 0.53 | 0.47 | 0.37 | 0.37 | 0.42 | 1 |
| Alternative Y | 0.35 | 0.32 | 0.22 | 0.20 | 0.39 | 0.30 | 2 |
| Alternative Z | 0.29 | 0.14 | 0.31 | 0.43 | 0.25 | 0.28 | 3 |

comparisons of the AHP methodology to obtain the following: (i) Prioritize the assessment criteria independently, (ii) Prioritize the feasible products independently, (iii) Merge the results of the prioritization to identify the best solution.

The default decision model in ClouDSS is AHP. The decision criteria together with their descriptions are provided by the ClouDSS user interface. If the company has additional requirements apart from the criteria in the default decision model, the decision model can be enhanced by selecting those items from the criteria pool in ClouDSS. After finalizing the decision criteria, the ClouDSS construct judgment matrix is formed based on the AHP method.

The judgment matrix consists of the pairs that the decision makers compare. In this case, six experts compare each item of the comparison pairs to each other, and express their individual rankings for the comparison by using Saaty's Scale [28]. This scale allows the decision makers to convert their linguistic judgment into a numerical measure which represents the relative importance of items in each pair. The scale is from "1", which represents "equally important", to "9" which represents "extremely important".

ClouDSS checks the consistency of each judgment matrix in order to prevent inconsistent judgments of the experts, and once the consistency ratio is calculated as over 10%, a notification is sent to the corresponding user to revise his judgment. After the consistency check, the weight of each criterion is determined. The resulting weights obtained by combining the comparison results of six DMs are given in Table 2. According to the AHP ranking, the highest weight is assigned to X. But the weights of Y and Z are very close to each other. Therefore, the company may prefer to conduct an additional analysis such as DEA, in order to evaluate them, as described next.

The DM investigates the most cost-effective product among the three different cloud-based enterprise solutions given above, and can employ Input-oriented DEA decision model to select the best alternative. That means, it is investigated whether the selected product can still increase its output (i.e., net income, etc.) or decrease its input when compared to the "ideal" cloud product (Table 3).

- Input 1: Amount of Subscription Payment per Year
- Input 2: Number of IT Personnel Hired

Table 3. The input and output of the DEA model.

| Cloud alternatives | Input 1 (million $) | Input 2 | Output 1 (thousand) | Output 2 (thousand $) | Output 3 |
|---|---|---|---|---|---|
| Alternative X | 2 | 50 | 10 | 100 | 24 |
| Alternative Y | 1.6 | 44 | 8 | 80 | 16 |
| Alternative Z | 1.2 | 30 | 6 | 90 | 12 |

- Output 1: Average Number of Customers of the Enterprise
- Output 2: Expected Net Income from Investment
- Output 3: Expected Number of Business Partnership

According to the given inputs and outputs, for calculation efficiency of the Alternative X, the following linear optimization model is constructed.

**Linear Optimization Model for Alternative X efficiency:**

$$\text{Minimize } \theta; \text{ minimize input resources} \tag{1}$$

Constraints:

$$2\lambda_{A1} + 1.6\lambda_{A2} + 1.2\lambda_{A3} < = 2^*\theta \tag{2}$$

$$50\lambda_{A1} + 44\lambda_{A2} + 30\lambda_{A3} < = 50^*\theta \tag{3}$$

$$10\lambda_{A1} + 8\lambda_{A2} + 6\lambda_{A3} > = 10 \tag{4}$$

$$100\lambda_{A1} + 80\lambda_{A2} + 90\lambda_{A3} > = 100 \tag{5}$$

$$24\lambda_{A1} + 16\lambda_{A2} + 12\lambda_{A3} > = 24 \tag{6}$$

$$\lambda_{A1} + \lambda_{A2} + \lambda_{A3} = 1 \tag{7}$$

$$\lambda_{A1}, \lambda_{A2}, \lambda_{A3} > = 0 \tag{8}$$

Once this model is solved for Alternative X, $\lambda_{A1} = 1$, $\lambda_{A2} = 0$, $\lambda_{A3} = 0$, and; the efficiency coefficient of Alternative X is calculated as "1", which means Alternative X is found as the efficient product. Similarly, each product efficiency can be calculated by the DEA method.

As a result, Alternative X has the highest rank among others in AHP and it is also found as efficient according to DEA. Therefore, the decision to choose Alternative X, as suggested by AHP is further verified by DEA as an efficient selection.

## 5  Conclusion

CC provides significant benefits to SMEs both financially and technically. There are various aspects of CC which are important for its adoption. Accordingly, the selection of suitable cloud services turns into a complex decision problem requiring a comprehensive approach for making an optimal decision. Furthermore, each SME may be operating under a unique set of circumstances which makes this decision even more difficult. Therefore, a DSS that is capable of collecting relevant data as well as providing a set of suitable methods becomes important in helping SMEs with cloud service selection decisions. To this end, this study proposes ClouDSS which is a DSS for cloud service selections.

The conducted systematic literature review reveals that there is a limited number of studies proposing DSS for cloud service selection. Upon analyzing them, the system architecture for ClouDSS is constructed in order to provide a more comprehensive solution. Its system architecture containing data, model and knowledge management components is described. Furthermore, the cloud service selection process by using ClouDSS is presented in order to delineate the set of corresponding tasks. The applicability of the proposed system is demonstrated by providing a case study.

ClouDSS provides a set of assessment methods within a single system without the need of expertise or knowledge in the domain of cloud technologies and decision making approaches. The main contribution of the study is that it proposes a comprehensive DSS while a limited number of existing studies provides solutions utilizing a maximum of two decision models. ClouDSS offers both objective and subjective evaluation approaches for cloud service selection decision. For subjective evaluation, 10 MCDM methods are available to support decisions for identifying the best alternatives according to enterprise-specific requirements. Another significant contribution is that it provides customization of criteria for subjective evaluation and parameters for objective evaluation, as well as the capabilities for searching and filtering of cloud service alternatives and user reviews. Furthermore, it collects real-life measurements for quantitative KPIs and up-to-date service information in order to increase the decision quality. Finally, it also provides guidance to DMs for specifying parameters and criteria through easy to understand representations. While ClouDSS has been designed by considering the needs of SMEs, the solution is suitable for use in large enterprises as well.

As part of future work, additional case studies are planned in order to further assess the applicability of ClouDSS. Furthermore, its usability will be investigated by conducting System Usability Scale (SUS) tests with DMs who are planning to adopt a cloud service.

# References

1. Sultan, N.A.: Reaching for the "cloud": how SMEs can manage. Int. J. Inf. Manage. **31**, 272–278 (2011)
2. Erdogmus, H.: Cloud computing: does Nirvana hide behind the Nebula? IEEE Softw. **26**, 4–6 (2009)
3. Dillon, S., Vossen, G.: SaaS Cloud computing in small and medium enterprises: a comparison between Germany and New Zealand. Int. J. Inf. Technol. Commun. Converge. **3**, 1–16 (2009)
4. Carcary, M., Doherty, E., Conway, G., McLaughlin, S.: Cloud computing adoption readiness and benefit realization in Irish SMEs—an exploratory study. Inf. Syst. Manag. **31**, 313–327 (2014)
5. Dutta, A., Peng, G.C.A., Choudhary, A.: Risks in enterprise cloud computing: the perspective of IT experts. J. Comput. Inf. Syst. **53**, 39–48 (2013)
6. Tse, D.W.K., Chen, D., Liu, Q., Wang, F., Wei, Z.: Emerging issues in cloud storage security: encryption, key management, data redundancy, trust mechanism. In: Wang, L.S.-L., June, J.J., Lee, C.-H., Okuhara, K., Yang, H.-C. (eds.) MISNC 2014. CCIS, vol. 473, pp. 297–310. Springer, Heidelberg (2014). doi:10.1007/978-3-662-45071-0_24
7. Wu, W.-W., Lan, L.W., Lee, Y.-T.: Factors hindering acceptance of using cloud services in university: a case study. Electron. Libr. **31**, 84–98 (2013)

8. El-Gazzar, R.F.: A literature review on cloud computing adoption issues in enterprises. In: Bergvall-Kåreborn, B., Nielsen, P.A. (eds.) TDIT 2014. IAICT, vol. 429, pp. 214–242. Springer, Heidelberg (2014). doi:10.1007/978-3-662-43459-8_14

9. Oliveira, T., Thomas, M., Espadanal, M.: Assessing the determinants of cloud computing adoption: an analysis of the manufacturing and services sectors. Inf. Manag. **51**, 497–510 (2014)

10. Yang, H., Tate, M.: A descriptive literature review and classification of cloud computing research. Commun. Assoc. Inf. Syst. **31**, 35–60 (2012)

11. O'Brien, J.A., Marakas, G.: Introduction to Information Systems. McGraw-Hill, Inc., New York (2005)

12. Szabo, S., Ferencz, V., Pucihar, A.: Trust, Innovation and Prosperity. Qual. Innov. Prosper. **17**, 1–8 (2013)

13. Al-Isma'ili, S., Li, M., Shen, J., He, Q.: Cloud computing adoption decision modelling for SMEs: a conjoint analysis. Int. J. Web Grid Serv. **12**, 296 (2016)

14. Talukder, A.K., Zimmerman, L., Prahalad, H.A.: Cloud economics: principles, costs, and benefits. In: Antonopoulos, N., Gillam, L. (eds.) Cloud Computing. Computer Communications and Networks, pp. 343–360. Springer, London (2010). doi:10.1007/978-1-84996-241-4_20

15. Seethamraju, R.: Adoption of software as a service (SaaS) enterprise resource planning (ERP) systems in small and medium sized enterprises (SMEs). Inf. Syst. Front. **17**, 475–492 (2015)

16. Whaiduzzaman, M., Gani, A., Anuar, N.B., Shiraz, M., Haque, M.N., Haque, I.T.: Cloud service selection using multicriteria decision analysis. Sci. World J. **2014** (2014)

17. Garg, S.K., Versteeg, S., Buyya, R.: SMICloud: a framework for comparing and ranking cloud services. In: 2011 Proceedings of the 4th IEEE International Conference on Utility and Cloud Computing, UCC 2011, pp. 210–218 (2011)

18. Lee, S., Seo, K.-K.: A hybrid multi-criteria decision-making model for a cloud service selection problem using BSC, fuzzy Delphi method and fuzzy AHP. Wirel. Pers. Commun. **86**, 57–75 (2016)

19. Dyer, J.: Multiple criteria decision analysis: state of the art surveys. Int. Ser. Oper. Res. Manag. Sci. **78**, 265–292 (2005)

20. Kitchenham, B.: Procedures for performing systematic reviews. vol. 33, p. 28. Keele University, Keele (2004)

21. Qu, L., Wang, Y., Orgun, M.: A: cloud service selection based on the aggregation of user feedback and quantitative performance assessment. In: 2013 IEEE International Conference on Services Computing, pp. 152–159 (2013)

22. Karim, R., Ding, C., Miri, A.: An end-to-end QoS mapping approach for cloud service selection. In: Proceedings of the 2013 IEEE Ninth World Congress on Services, pp. 341–348 (2013)

23. Wilson, B.M.R., Khazaei, B., Hirsch, L.: Towards a cloud migration decision support system for small and medium enterprises in Tamil Nadu. In: CINTI 2016 - Proceedings of the IEEE 17th International Symposium on Computational Intelligence and Informatics, pp. 341–346 (2017)

24. Godse, M., Mulik, S.: An approach for selecting Software-as-a-Service (SaaS) product. In: CLOUD 2009 - IEEE International Conference on Cloud Computing, pp. 155–158 (2009)

25. Rehman, Z.U., Hussain, O.K., Hussain, F.K.: Iaas cloud selection using MCDM methods. In: Proceedings of the 2012 IEEE Ninth International Conference on e-Business Engineering, ICEBE 2012, pp. 246–251 (2012)

26. Eisa, M., Younas, M., Basu, K., Zhu, H.: Trends and directions in cloud service selection. In: Proceedings - 2016 IEEE Symposium on Service-Oriented System Engineering, SOSE 2016, pp. 423–432 (2016)
27. Şener, U., Gökalp, E., Eren, P.Erhan: Cloud-based enterprise information systems: determinants of adoption in the context of organizations. In: Dregvaite, G., Damasevicius, R. (eds.) ICIST 2016. CCIS, vol. 639, pp. 53–66. Springer, Cham (2016). doi:10.1007/978-3-319-46254-7_5
28. Saaty, T.L.: The analytical hierarchy process, planning, priority. In: Resource Allocation. RWS Publications, USA (1980)

# Coordination Models for 5G Multi-provider Service Orchestration: Specification and Assessment

George Darzanos$^{(\boxtimes)}$, Manos Dramitinos, and George D. Stamoulis

Athens University of Economics and Business (AUEB), Athens, Greece
{ntarzanos,mdramit,gstamoul}@aueb.gr

**Abstract.** The inherently multi-stakeholder value chain of 5G services calls for business and service coordination. In this paper, we introduce and evaluate coordination models for the multi-provider service composition, namely the Fully Centralized, Distributed and per-Provider Centralized models, in the context of the 5GEx multi-provider orchestration framework. We perform a scalability assessment of the models in terms of the message overhead, also investigating the trade-off between service composition efficiency and message overhead. Our sensitivity analysis on the different parameters of our evaluation framework reveal that hybrid models scale better, but also other models may achieve the same level of message overhead under certain conditions.

**Keywords:** 5G · Coordination models · Service orchestration · 5G exchange

## 1 Introduction

5G envisions services with new capabilities over a unified networking and cloud infrastructure impacting verticals such as Infotainment, e-Health, Energy, Automotive, Manufacturing Factories of the Future [1]. These services rely on an all-IP fully *softwarized* network architecture from core to edge that utilizes virtualized resources in order to orchestrate, trade, deploy and manage services jointly over the network, storage and compute domains in a fast, agile and secure way. The 5G customer-facing retail services rely on wholesale infrastructure services, which can be categorized to *Connectivity*, *Virtual Network Function as a Service* (VNFaaS - network and application functions chained to support the service) and *Slice as a Service* (SlaaS - a managed set of Connectivity and VNFaaS services, additionally providing to the customer full control and management access) [2].

The value chain of 5G services inherently involves multiple stakeholders and administrative domains, each contributing to the end-to-end service provisioning. Network Service Providers (NSPs), Network Function Providers, Infrastructure Service Providers (IfSPs), Over-the-top Providers, are only a subset of the stakeholders being part of the 5G ecosystem. This greatly complicates the task of end-to-end service composition and inter-provider coordination, thus the adoption

© Springer International Publishing AG 2017
C. Pham et al. (Eds.): GECON 2017, LNCS 10537, pp. 262–274, 2017.
DOI: 10.1007/978-3-319-68066-8_20

of sophisticated service Orchestrators is vital. The way Orchestrators are organized, how and what information is exchanged amongst them has great impact on the efficiency of the 5G service composition. In this paper we specify concrete coordination models for service composition in the 5G multi-provider setting, which are generic enough to apply to any underlying 5G orchestration framework. We perform qualitative and quantitative, simulations-based assessment of them. We assess their scalability in terms of message overhead and service availability, providing recommendations regarding the information dissemination and management policies over the 5G architecture and service model.

## 2     5G Exchange Framework

5GEx [3] is an open multi-service multi-operator inter-networking approach for orchestrating, trading and composing 5G infrastructure *wholesale services*. Through the 5GEx framework NSPs and Clouds trade, orchestrate and manage services on the fly, so as to meet end user demand for 5G retail services. The fact that there are multiple ways to do this, motivates the work reported in this paper regarding coordination models for service composition in 5G.

The 5GEx architecture, anticipates and specifies standard interfaces, extending the ETSI MANO (Management and Orchestration) architecture [4] to the multi-provider setting of 5G services. A Multi-provider Multi-domain Orchestrator (MdO) orchestrates services over multiple technology and administrative domains using multiple Domain Orchestrators. 5GEx defines three main interfaces: The MdO interacts with Domain Orchestrators via Interface (3) to orchestrate resources and services within the same administrative domain and interacts with other MdOs over Interface (2) to request and orchestrate services across domains. The MdO exposes over Interface (1) service specification APIs that enable the Enterprise Customer, i.e. an Online or Network-Cloud Service Provider to demand a service. 5GEx also considers third party providers, which do not own resource domains but operate MdO to broker resources and services from other providers.

## 3     Related Work

To the best of our knowledge our work is the first study of coordination models for 5G multi-provider service composition. However, there is some related work in other contexts, such as DiffServ, Brokers, Grids, Clouds and Web services. Regarding Brokers, the necessity for coordination models to manage multi-agent systems led to agent-oriented coordination models and collaboration patterns [5]. Similarly, a bandwidth broker architecture for scalable end-to-end network services of guaranteed quality is introduced in [6,7]. These broker architectures relate to 5G Orchestrators, dealing with QoS management and admission control of multi-domain network services. However, contrary to our paper, these works focus only to the network domain, ignoring compute/storage aspects, also lacking an exhaustive investigation of the alternative hierarchies and their properties.

In the context of Cloud, the authors in [8] introduce the Cloud Coordinator, an element that is similar to an MdO of the 5G ecosystem and it is responsible for the inter-cloud interactions of a Cloud Provider. However, the Cloud coordinators focus on the negotiation, trading and exchange of cloud resources among the provider, not on the composition and orchestration of complex multi-provider services.

Closely related to the hybrid approach of our paper is [9], where a virtual and dynamic hierarchical architecture for a scalable e-Science Grid is introduced, based on the notion of virtual groups, consisting of grid nodes that are within the same domain, have similar properties and exchange information frequently. In particular, a three-layers hierarchy of virtual groups is proposed for scalable node discovery and service provisioning. One node with each group act as a coordinator and it is responsible for the information propagation toward all other groups. This is similar to our hybrid hierarchical approach with multiple Orchestrators. However, contrary to the coordinator nodes that only acts as relays, our 5G Orchestrators performs information aggregation, bundling and filtering.

Finally, regarding Web services, an Internet-scale model for servers-to-clients asynchronous event dissemination is specified in [10]. After exploring the design space of a proxy-based architecture, a hierarchy of event forwarding proxies to deliver events from each source to each related receiver is proposed. Again, our 5G Orchestrators are more intelligent and have more functionalities compared to the forwarding proxies that only reduce the extent of the redundant information.

## 4    Coordination Models for 5G Service Composition

### 4.1    Specification Methodology

Prior to presenting the coordination models, we specify the solution space and a baseline scenario and illustrations so as to facilitate the reader. The main design aspects of coordination models for 5G service orchestration are:

*(i) Distributed vs Centralized*: Service exchange and trading may be done in a fully distributed fashion through bilateral (possibly cascading) communications, or by means of a central entity, namely an Orchestrator that serves as the focal point for the aggregation/dissemination of information and service orchestration.

*(ii) Fully Centralized vs per-Provider Centralized*: Centralized models may be Fully or per-Provider Centralized. In the Fully Centralized model, a single Orchestrator does the orchestration for all 5G providers. In the per-Provider Centralized model multiple Orchestrators of multiple providers co-exist, each serving a different cluster of 5G providers. The providers of each cluster communicate with their Orchestrator according to the Fully Centralized model, while the Orchestrators of different clusters communicate in a distributed way. However, contrary to the Distributed model, each Orchestrator can contact all other Orchestrators regardless whether they are directly connected or not.

*(iii) Coordination model phases.* Every coordination model inherently consists of two phases, namely the *publishing phase* and the *service composition phase*. The *publishing phase* specifies the extent and granularity of the information exchanged among the providers regarding the service offerings supported. The publishing phase precedes the *service composition phase* that is triggered when a customer request arrives at a provider who uses the information that has been revealed in the publishing phase to compose the service.

*(iv) Push vs Pull*: The major difference of the pull to push models is the extent and type of information exposed at the publishing phase. In particular, in the push model the providers publish SLA offers, i.e. full service specifications prior to any customer request. On the other hand, in the pull models, each provider's service capabilities are published, a generic aggregate-level set of service types, QoS attributes and price ranges. An actual SLA offer is generated only after a customer's request.

The aforementioned options result in eight generic coordination models, defined below. For the better presentation of the coordination models we consider a specific scenario, depicted in Fig. 1a, with multiple providers operating under an orchestration framework such as 5GEx. The common support of the orchestration framework is depicted by the colored rectangle enclosing the providers. In our scenario, A and C are NSPs, D and E are IfSPs of compute and storage, and B is both NSP and IfSP. SP is an On-line Service Provider who needs a multi-provider service. SP has already an established business relationship with at least one NSP, e.g. in order to purchase connectivity. We henceforth refer to this provider (i.e. A in our scenario) throughout the paper as the primary provider for SP. Note that in the Centralized models, only the providers of the orchestration framework are aware of the Orchestrator's existence and not S, thus SP **always** contacts his primary provider. Fig. 1b introduces some basic notation and illustrations that will be used throughout the paper.

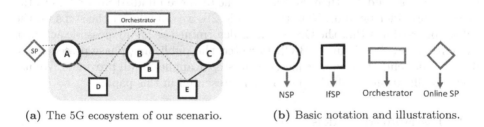

(a) The 5G ecosystem of our scenario.      (b) Basic notation and illustrations.

**Fig. 1.** The 5G ecosystem and actors of our scenario.

## 4.2   Fully Centralized Models

**Push Model.** During the *publishing phase* all providers submit to the Orchestrator their service offers, i.e. their Service Catalogue entries in the form of

SLAs (step 1 of Fig. 2a), which contain on-net destination(s), QoS attributes, price and offer expiration time. The Orchestrator, uses the topology view and the providers' offers gathered during the publishing phase to perform centrally the *service composition phase* for each customer request passed to him (step 3) by some provider that receives it (step 2): The Orchestrator computes a bundle of SLA offers meeting the request and returns a solution to the primary provider (step 4), which in turn returns it to the customer (step 5).

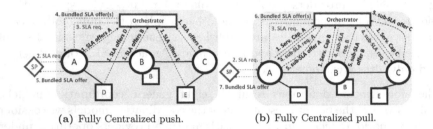

(a) Fully Centralized push.          (b) Fully Centralized pull.

**Fig. 2.** Exchange of messages for the fully centralized models.

**Pull Model.** Figure 2b depicts the sequence of steps for the Fully Centralized pull model. In step 1, the providers publish to the Orchestrator their service capabilities. Again, the service composition phase is initiated upon a customer's request arrival to the primary provider (step 2). The Orchestrator uses the service capabilities collected during the publishing phase to send (sub-)SLA requests to the providers able to satisfy (part of) the request (step 4). For instance, the Orchestrator may push a sub-SLA request only for compute and storage resources to D. Then, these providers reply with offers (step 5) to the Orchestrator, which consolidates them and pushes one or more bundled SLA offers to the primary provider (step 6). Note that, in Fig. 2b, we only depict the steps for the subset of providers that the Orchestrator determined as highly possible actors of the current service chain (A-B-C). However, the publishing phase precedes and does not depend on service requests, thus step 1 applies to all providers. We use this simplification for all the pull models presented in this paper.

### 4.3 Distributed Models

Distributed models rely on bilateral cascading of service capabilities or SLA offers. This means that each provider communicates only with his direct neighbors.

**Push Model.** During the publishing phase each provider exchanges SLA offers with all of his direct neighbors. Each provider can also *bundle* his own SLA offers with those received, and then advertise bundles to his other neighbors. Through the bundling process, a provider can gradually increase the distance (in hops) that his bundled SLA offers can reach, as described in the next paragraph.

Figure 3a depicts the exchange of messages for the Distributed push model. For demonstration purposes, we do not present all the exchanged messages, but we focus in a specific chain (A-B-C-E) in order to show how an offer from A to E is created by means of bundling. In the first iteration (step 1), the providers exchange only their own offers, thus only offers of maximum hop count of two can be created. In each step, the providers use the information gathered in previous steps to create the bundled offers and increase the hops. Thus, after the third iteration (step 3), provider A has received an SLA offer from B that enables him to build a chain to provider E. Whenever SP requests a service from A to E (step 4), service composition is triggered and A can respond immediately because of the bundling done during the publishing phase.

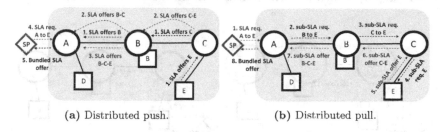

    (a) Distributed push.         (b) Distributed pull.

**Fig. 3.** Exchange of messages for the distributed push models.

Bundling only applies to network services, while compute and storage SLA offers are forwarded as received. Bundling or forwarding all the SLA offers coming from the neighbors may create flood as the length of the service chain becomes large. This motivates smart information dissemination policies taking advantage of the topology hierarchy to avoid flooding, e.g. by defining a maximum length of the bundled SLA offer path. On the other hand, too conservative bundling policies though may lead to low offer availability of multiple hops offers.

**Pull Model.** In the publishing phase of the Distributed pull model, the bundling process we described in the previous paragraph is performed on the announced service capabilities. Contrary to push model, the providers exchange messages also during the service composition phase, as depicted in Fig. 2b. Once the primary provider receives a request (step 1), he extracts the part of the SLA that he cannot satisfy himself. Then, he uses the service capabilities collected at the publishing phase to determine his neighbors that can satisfy the remaining part of the SLA and sends the respective sub-SLA requests (step 2). Each provider receiving a sub-SLA request applies the same process until the request reaches the destination (step 3). All providers receiving a request return a sub-SLA offer in the reverse order of requests until the bundled offer reaches the primary provider (step 7) that delivers the final offer to the customer (step 8).

### 4.4 Per-provider Centralized Models

**Push Model.** The publishing phase is performed in each cluster separately and it is followed the same process as in the Fully Centralized push model (Fig. 2a). Thus, each Orchestrator (A, B, C) acquires full knowledge for the SLA offers within its cluster. As presented in Fig. 4a, these offers are published to a Service Catalogue that is accessible by any other Orchestrator (step 1). Again, the service composition phase is initiated by a customer request (step 2). After receiving the request, the primary provider D forwards the request to the local Orchestrator A (step 3). Then, A calculates the path to the destination and browses the Service Catalogues of the Orchestrators that are part of the service chain. After the evaluation of the available offers, A purchases the desired sub-SLA offers and bundles them himself (step 4). Following the same logic as in the Fully Centralized model, the Orchestrator A returns a bundled offer to the primary provider (step 5), which in turn returns it to the customer (step 6).

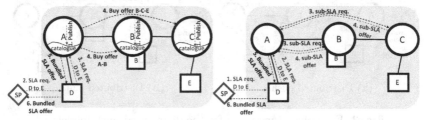

(a) Per-Provider Centralized push.          (b) Per-Provider Centralized pull.

**Fig. 4.** Exchange of messages for the per-provider centralized models.

**Pull Model.** During the publishing phase of the pull, service capabilities are exchanged within each cluster and stored to the Orchestrators' Catalogues. As shown in Fig. 4b, the service composition phase is initiated by a customer request (step 1). The local Orchestrator A, computes the service chain based on the service capabilities and sends sub-SLA requests (step 3) to the other Orchestrators involved in the service chain, bundles the received (step 4) sub-SLA offers and delegates the bundled one to the primary provider (step 5). Finally, the primary provider returns this offer to the customer (step 6).

## 5   Assessment

In this section, we perform a scalability assessment of the proposed models based on total number of messages exchanged among the service orchestration actors. We investigate how the scalability of the proposed models is affected by different parameters of the ecosystem. Also, we examine aspects such as SLA offers availability and redundancy of exchanged messages.

## 5.1   Methodology

**Topology.** We simulate an environment of multiple Transit-NSPs (T-NSPs), Edge-NSPs (E-NSPs) and IfSPs being interconnected in a hierarchical topology of three tiers, resembling the Internet tiered hierarchy: The first tier contains all the T-NSPs connected in a full-mesh fashion, each of them serving a number of E-NSPs from the second tier. With probability 0.5 an E-NSP has a peering link with another randomly selected E-NSP. The IfSPs of the third tier are uniformly distributed connected to the E-NSPs, while with probability 0.5 an IfSP is connected to two E-NSPs. In the Fully Centralized models we assume that the Orchestrator joins the full mesh of the top tier. This means that if an IfSP sends a message to the Orchestrator, it will cross the AS of three different providers in the physical topology resulting in a count of 3. In the per-Provider Centralized models we assume that only the T-NSPs maintain an Orchestrator, therefore the number of clusters created equals the number of T-NSPs.

**SLA Offers and Service Capabilities.** We categorize the services that a provider can offer to network (N), compute (C) and storage (S) domain services. We assume that the T-NSPs offer services only in N domains, E-NSPs in all domains, while IfSP in C and S domains. We assume that each provider offers various service types in each domain. In the push models, a provider may create SLA offers of multiple QoS levels for the same service type; therefore, the total number of SLA offers is also depends on the number of different QoS levels. In the pull models, each provider creates only one service capability for each service type because service capabilities are more generic compared to SLA offers, thus can be more compacted. In the Distributed models we investigate different levels of bundling intensity, i.e. different thresholds on the maximum length of the bundled SLA offer (or service capability) path. Finally, for the forwarding of C/S SLA offers and service capabilities the providers takes advantage of topology hierarchy to reduce the number of duplicates.

**Service Requests.** We assume that the service requests are generated at the edge, hence received at E-NSPs and IfSPs. The requests coming from the customers of an E-NSP demand connectivity from their primary E-NSP to a remote PoP or IfSP, but may also request compute and storage to the source or destination provider. The requests arriving to an IfSP can be of the same type with that of E-NSP customers, or it can be a request for C or S resources in multiple IfSPs with optional connectivity between them.

## 5.2   Scalability Assessment and Sensitivity Analysis

We ran multiple experiments over different topologies generated as described in the previous subsection. We use the results of a single simulation setup as baseline to compare the different model's performance, and then we perform a sensitivity analysis on the ecosystems parameters. Our baseline simulation setup parameters are set to: T-NSP=5, E-NSP=20, IfSP=40, 5 PoPs per E-NSP, 1 PoI per neighbor, 2 levels of QoS per service type, 1 service capability per PoI pair, 30 service request per E-NSP and IfSP. In the Distributed models, we assume that the providers perform *intense bundling*, thus they can reach any destination within the 5G orchestration framework.

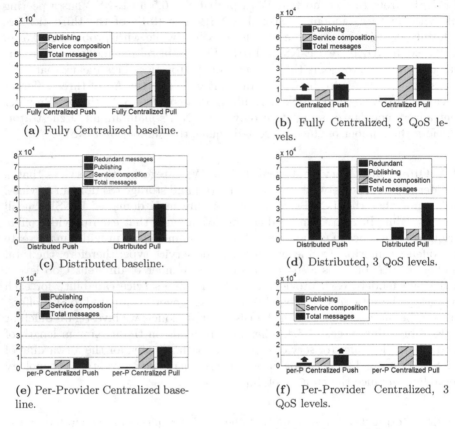

(a) Fully Centralized baseline.

(b) Fully Centralized, 3 QoS levels.

(c) Distributed baseline.

(d) Distributed, 3 QoS levels.

(e) Per-Provider Centralized baseline.

(f) Per-Provider Centralized, 3 QoS levels.

**Fig. 5.** Message overhead for all coordination models under two different setups.

**Single-Setup Observations on Message Overhead.** Figure 5 depicts the message overhead of all models under two different setups. The first one is the baseline setup, while the second one has 3 levels of QoS per service type, i.e. one more compared to the baseline. Focusing on the baseline setup, we can observe that the higher message overhead is observed in the Distributed models, while the per-Provider Centralized models are the ones that generate the fewest messages. As expected, the pull models generate fewer messages than push during the publishing phase, since the service capabilities are more compacted than SLA offers. The push models have an advantage in the composition phase since they require the exchange of fewer messages for the composition of each service. Finally, the duplicates created because of the bundling and forwarding actions are negligible since providers take into account the overall topology for message propagation.

**Impact of the Number of Available QoS Levels.** The number of available levels of QoS per service type does not affect the pull models since 1 service capability message that covers all QoS levels will be pushed. On the other hand, the push models are affected since a different SLA offer will be pushed for each QoS level (Fig. 5b, d, f). We can observe that Distributed push is the most "sensitive" in the number of QoS levels and SLA offers, due to the intense bundling/forwarding. The Fully and per-Provider Centralized push models are also affected, but they are less sensitive.

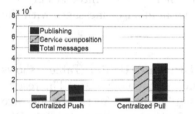

(a) Fully Centralized, 10 PoPs per E-NSP.

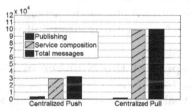

(b) Fully Centralized, 90 requests per E-NSP and IfSP.

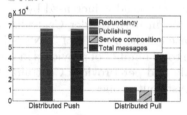

(c) Distributed, 10 PoPs per E-NSP.

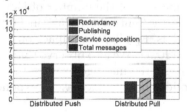

(d) Distributed, 90 requests per E-NSP and IfSP.

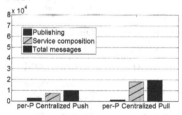

(e) Per-Provider Centralized, 10 PoPs per E-NSP.

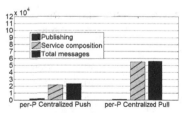

(f) Per-Provider Centralized, 90 requests per per E-NSP and IfSP.

**Fig. 6.** Message overhead for all coordination models under two different setups.

**Impact of the Number of Edge PoPs.** Figure 6a, c and e depict the message overhead for all coordination models for a setup with the double number of edge PoPs per E-NSP compared to the baseline. Again, the Distributed models are affected more than the Centralized ones where the impact is minor. The number of edge PoPs affects the message overhead of push and pull models in the same extent, as depicted in Fig. 5c and Fig. 6c.

**Impact of the Number of Service Requests.** Figure 6b, d and f depict the message overhead of all coordination models for a setup with three times more service requests compared to the baseline setup. The number of requests affects the service composition phase of each model, with the Centralized pull affected the most since the Orchestrator must exchange increased number of messages with E-NSPs and IfSPs being at the edge of the network. The per-Provider Centralized pull is also affected, but not as much since the multiple Orchestrators are closer to the edge providers of their cluster. Interestingly, the Distributed pull model generates almost the same number of messages with the per-Provider Centralized pull.

**Impact of the Number of T-NSPs, E-NSPs and IfSPs.** Table 1 shows the total number of messages exchanged for different topology sizes. The results reveal that increasing the number of IfSPs significantly affects the message exchange of all models, namely 85% increase in Fully Centralized, 180% in Distributed and 83% in per-Provider Centralized models. On the other hand, after an increase of the number of E-NSPs the message overhead is increased by 27% in Fully Centralized, 75% in Distributed and 16% in per-Provider Centralized models. Finally, the impact on a possible increase on the number of T-NSPs is even lower. We also observe that by doubling the total number of providers in the system, the message overhead is doubled in Fully and per-Provider Centralized models, but the increase is exponential in the Distributed ones.

**Table 1.** Message overhead for different topology sizes.

| T-NSPs | E-NSPs | IfSPs | Push | | | Pull | | |
|--------|--------|-------|--------------|--------|----------|--------------|--------|----------|
| | | | Fully centr. | Distr. | per-Prov. | Fully centr. | Distr. | per-Prov. |
| 5 | 20 | 40 | 13022 | 50476 | 9026 | 34813 | 35016 | 19288 |
| 10 | 20 | 40 | 13286 | 54720 | 9226 | 34781 | 37026 | 19354 |
| 5 | 40 | 40 | 16414 | 87421 | 10887 | 43225 | 57301 | 23268 |
| 5 | 20 | 80 | 23952 | 138680 | 16673 | 59914 | 85496 | 33544 |
| 10 | 40 | 80 | 26932 | 207846 | 18651 | 70720 | 123536 | 39120 |

**Bundling Intensity and SLA Offers Availability.** The aforementioned results reveal that the Distributed models do not scale due to the intense bundling and forwarding of the SLA offers and service capabilities. Thus, we investigate how a restriction on the maximum hops a bundled SLA offer can reach may mitigate this issue. We also examine how such restrictions may lead to low availability of SLA offers, hence customer requests for remote PoPs cannot be immediately satisfied. The results show that if the providers adopt a bundling policy of maximum two SLA offers, the message overhead is lower than all the other coordination models but the SLA offers availability drops to 19%. A bundling policy of maximum three SLA offers leads to an availability of 56% but for double the message overhead of the Centralized models. Note that without bundling an SLA offer path has length 2, while after bundling 4 SLA offers all destinations in our topology can be reached.

### 5.3   Discussion

Distributed models do not scale since they are highly affected by multiple parameters of the 5G ecosystem, including service types and QoS levels. Second, as the number of PoPs per E-NSP increases so does the number of possible destinations in the 5G ecosystem, thus the message overhead increases both for pull and push models. Finally, the message overhead increases exponentially with the total number of providers in the ecosystem.

Pull models are advantageous in the publishing phase due to the more compacted nature of service capabilities compared to SLA offers. Push models have an advantage in service composition since they exchange fewer messages per service. Thus, pull models are more suitable for limited demand and early service markets, while the push models are best for mature, liquid markets.

Per-Provider Centralized models scales better than all the others. While the Fully Centralized models appear perform similarly with the per-Provider Centralized for small topology setups, as the number of providers and the service requests increases the performance difference becomes clearer. The advantage of per-Provider Centralized models lies on the fact that during the publishing phase the messages are pushed to closer distance (in hops) cluster-local Orchestrators.

## 6   Conclusions

In this paper we introduced multiple coordination models for 5G multi-provider service orchestration. We simulated an Internet-like environment of multiple 5G providers and evaluated the models under different setups, performing a sensitivity analysis on the different parameters of the ecosystem. Our results reveal that Distributed models scale significantly worse than Fully and per-Provider Centralized models. As the ecosystem becomes larger the hybrid per-Provider Centralized models scale best. Evaluating the coordination models over different topology structures and further assessing smart bundling policies for the Distributed models comprise directions of future work.

**Acknowledgements..** This work has been performed in the framework of the H2020-ICT-2014 project 5GEx, which is partially funded by the European Commission.

This information reflects the consortiums view, but neither the consortium nor the European Commission are liable for any use that may be done of the information contained therein.

# References

1. The 5G Infrastructure PPP whitepapers. https://5g-ppp.eu/white-papers/
2. "NGMN 5G White Paper" by NGMN Alliance (2016). https://www.ngmn.org/uploads/media/NGMN_5G_White_Paper_V1_0.pdf
3. Sgambelluri, A., et al.: Orchestration of network services across multiple operators: The 5G exchange prototype. In: EuCNC (2017). http://www.5gex.eu/
4. Ersue, M.: ETSI NFV management and orchestration-An overview. In: Proceeding of the 88th IETF Meeting (2013)
5. Hayden, S., Carrick, C., Yang, Q.: Architectural design patterns for multiagent coordination. In: Proceeding of the International Conference on Agent Systems, vol. 99 (1999)
6. Zhang, Z., et al.: Decoupling QoS control from core routers: A novel bandwidth broker architecture for scalable support of guaranteed services. In: ACM SIGCOMM Computer Communication Review (2000)
7. Duan, Z., et al.: A core stateless bandwidth broker architecture for scalable support of guaranteed services. IEEE TPDS 15(2), 167–182 (2004)
8. Calheiros, R.N., et al.: A coordinator for scaling elastic applications across multiple clouds. Future Gener. Comput. Syst. 28(8), 1350–1362 (2012)
9. Lican, H., Wu, Z., Pan, Y.: Virtual and dynamic hierarchical architecture for E-science grid. Int. J. HPCA 17(3), 329–347 (2003)
10. Yu, H., Deborah, E., Ramesh, G.: A hierarchical proxy architecture for Internet-scale event services. In: Proceeding of IEEE 8th WET ICE (1999)

# Keynote Topics

# Network Neutrality: Modeling and Challenges and Its Impact on Clouds

Bruno Tuffin[✉]

Inria, Campus Universitaire de Beaulieu, 35042 Rennes Cedex, France
bruno.tuffin@inria.fr
http://www.irisa.fr/dionysos/pages_perso/tuffin/Tuffin_en.htm

**Abstract.** Network neutrality has been a very sensitive topic of discussion all over the world. During this talk, we will first introduce the elements of the debate and introduce how the problem can be modeled and analyzed through game theory. With an Internet ecosystem much more complex now than the simple delivery chain Content-ISP-User, we will in second step highlight how neutrality principles can be bypassed in various ways without violating the rules currently evoked in the debate, for example via CDNs, or via search engines which can affect the visibility and accessibility of content. We describe some other grey zones requiring to be dealt with and spend some time on discussing the (potential) implications for clouds.

**Keywords:** Network economics · Game theory · Network neutrality · Content Delivery Networks · Cloud computing · Search engines

This keynote talk is mostly based on joint works with Patrick Maillé, Pierre L'Ecuyer, Nicolas Stier, and Gwendal Simon.

*Network (non) neutrality* has become a very hot topic in the past few years [6,11], at the same time from political, economic, and daily-life points of view, because it may refashion the Internet business model and in general the telecommunications vision and future. In short, the dispute started in the 2000s between Internet service providers (ISPs) and *major* content providers (CPs). ISPs were, and somewhat still are, complaining about big CPs having their resource-consuming traffic flowing through their networks and not paying any fee for that, while CPs take is an increasing part of the total network-related revenue. As a consequence, ISPs were threatening CPs to cut their access to the network, or at least to downgrade their quality of service, if they were not accepting to pay. This raised a lot of protests, from those CPs but also from user associations, concerned about the change of philosophy of the Internet it would lead to, and the violation of the neutrality principle, stating that all consumers are entitled to reach meaningful content, and that packets should not be differentiated. The underlying question is whether the current telecommunications business model should be sustained, with the transition of the Internet from the initial interconnection of cooperative universities to now revenue-seeking

© Springer International Publishing AG 2017
C. Pham et al. (Eds.): GECON 2017, LNCS 10537, pp. 277–280, 2017.
DOI: 10.1007/978-3-319-68066-8_21

and now often non-cooperative actors. This led to public consultations launched worldwide, and set of recommendations from regulators.

Our goals during this presentation are manyfold:

1. *Introduce the debate*, its history and the pros and cons of neutrality, according to its proponents and opponents (following [7,10]).
2. *Describe how game theory* [12] *can be used* to design and analyze mathematical models illustrating potential outcomes of interactions between Internet actors, and leading sometimes to counter-intuitive results. Some questions we can answer are, among others: (i) Is neutrality or non neutrality beneficial to Internet actors and to society? (ii) Is regulation needed to drive to a "good" outcome, and what level of regulation is required? Two illustrative models we will introduce are the following.
   - In [3], we present a model with ISPs providing direct connectivity to a fixed proportion of the content, and competing for end users. Users choose their ISP based on price. Three connectivity options between ISPs are studied and compared: peering between the ISPs, no transfer of traffic between ISPs (cut transmission with as a consequence exclusivities in terms of content), and volume-based paid transit. From our analysis, the "no transfer" option does not benefit to anybody. Also, compared to peering, paid transit avoids a price war for end users when the price sensitivity of users is high. A suggested rule with minimal regulation is to let the ISPs choose transit prices with the threat to impose peering in case no agreement is reached; then user welfare is close to maximal while still leaving some decision space to ISPs.
   - Another type of model in [1,2] deals with the case of competitive ISPs in front of a (quasi-)monopolistic CP, a situation barely studied while relevant in practice, and a topic of complain from ISPs. Thanks to game theory again, it can be illustrated that, surprisingly, side payments are not always profitable for ISPs, and can even be beneficial to the CP. A computable level of side payments can also maximize social or user welfare, but the neutral case is the most suitable to avoid disparities between ISPs revenues.
3. *Extend the debate.* The network neutrality debate is solely based on the supply chain **CP - ISP - users**. In other words, users want to access the CP and the ISP is the intermediary. But the Internet ecosystem has become much more complex with a lot of other actors serving as intermediaries between content and users [9]: we can mention Content Delivery Networks (CDNs) or cloud providers, service providers such as search engines or web portals sometimes necessary to reach pieces of content, etc. All those providers act as intermediaries who can favor a service in competition with others, sometimes with financial compensation. When side payments are forbidden, ISPs could even differentiate services at a CDN or portal level by vertically integrating those services, without breaching the current neutrality principle according to which all packets are treated equally within the network. Our claim is that net neutrality debate should probably be extended to all actors involved in the Internet delivery chain.

- In [4, 8], we have analyzed the impact of a revenue-maximizing CDN on end-users, network providers and content providers, and compared it with a neutral behavior in order to see if regulation would need to be introduced. When there is competition between CPs, it is illustrated in [4] that an optimal pricing and caching strategy from the CDN can be unfair: a big CP can harm a small one by paying more. In [8], it is also shown that a CDN can also influence competition between ISPs: an ISP can harm the other by "financially welcoming" the CDN.
- In [5], we have determined the optimal ranking policy for a search engine as a trade-off between short-term revenue (based on the potential immediate gain from high-ranked links) and long-term revenue (based on the satisfaction of users due to the relevance of the ranking). A non-neutral search engine can impact innovation non-neutrality impacts innovation. A revenue-oriented search engine may indeed deter innovation at the content level due to lack of visibility. Search biased search engines have been highlighted and have induced the so-called *search neutrality debate*, but our claim is that it could maybe be encompassed in a more general neutrality debate.

4. *Discuss more recent issues such as zero rating.* Zero rating in wireless subscription plans consists in not counting an application in data caps. Should it be allowed to attract customers? Can we authorize *sponsored data*, where a service/content provider can pay for the transfer of data accessed by users so that they are not included in data caps? Is it against the net neutrality principle even if packets are treated the same at network level? Is it bad for customers and does it hurt competition? It is the type of questions regulators are currently investigating.

5. *Discuss the implications of neutrality or non-neutrality for clouds.* A non-neutral network could lead to less accessible cloud services, because requiring payments from users (through access using their data caps), or side payments from cloud providers. Neutrality is therefore central for cloud providers. But could for the other side cloud services unfairly differentiate services, and could this be against innovation at the content level? What about a vertical integration of cloud services by CPs or ISPs? Those questions could ignite an interesting and surely vivid and sensitive discussion within the GECON community.

# References

1. Boussion, F., Maillé, P., Tuffin, B.: Net neutrality debate: impact of competition among ISPs. In: Proceedings of the Fourth International Conference on COMmunication Systems and NETworkS (COMSNETS), Bangalore, India (2012)
2. Coucheney, P., Maillé, P., Tuffin, B.: Impact of reputation-sensitive users and competition between ISPs on the net neutrality debate. IEEE Trans. Netw. Serv. Manage. **10**(4), 425–433 (2013)
3. Coucheney, P., Maillé, P., Tuffin, B.: Network neutrality debate and ISP interrelations: Traffic exchange, revenue sharing, and disconnection threat. Netnomics **1**(3), 155–182 (2014)

4. Gourdin, G., Maillé, P., Simon, G., Tuffin, B.: The economics of CDNs and their impact on service fairness. IEEE Trans. Netw. Serv. Manage. **14**(1), 22–33 (2017)
5. L'Ecuyer, P., Maillé, P., Stier-Moses, N., Tuffin, B.: Revenue-maximizing rankings for online platforms with quality-sensitive consumers. Oper. Res. **65**(2), 408–423 (2017)
6. Lenard, T., May, R.E.: Net Neutrality or Net Neutering: Should Broadband Internet Services be Regulated. Springer, New York (2006)
7. Maillé, P., Reichl, P., Tuffin, B.: Internet governance and economics of network neutrality. In: Hadjiantonis, A.M., Stiller, B. (eds.) Telecommunication Economics. LNCS, vol. 7216, pp. 108–116. Springer, Heidelberg (2012). doi:10.1007/978-3-642-30382-1_15
8. Maillé, P., Simon, G., Tuffin, B.: Impact of revenue-driven CDN on the competition among network operators. In: Proceedings of CNSM (2015)
9. Maillé, P., Simon, G., Tuffin, B.: Toward a net neutrality debate that conforms to the 2010s. IEEE Commun. Mag. **54**(3), 94–99 (2016)
10. Maillé, P., Tuffin, B.: Telecommunication Network Economics: From Theory to Applications. Cambridge University Press, Cambridge (2014)
11. Odlyzko, A.: Network neutrality, search neutrality, and the never-ending conflict between efficiency and fairness in markets. Rev. Netw. Econ. **8**(1), 40–60 (2009)
12. Osborne, M., Rubinstein, A.: A Course in Game theory. MIT Press, Cambridge (1994)

# IoT and Data Analytics for Developing Countries from Research to Business Transformation

Abdur Rahim[✉]

Fondazione Bruno Kessler (FBK)/Create-Net, Trento, Italy
arahim@fbk.eu

**Abstract.** The Internet of Things (IoT) and data analytics is not just the story for the developed economic countries, but it is rather equality importance for developing nations especially in Africa. The IoT has the tremendous opportunity for the human and economical development. Together with IoT and big data are driving improvements to human economic conditions and wellbeing in healthcare, water, agriculture, natural resource management, resiliency to climate change and energy. This talk will outline the experience from H2020 WAZIUP project, an IoT project for African and with African. Hence the talk will provide the IoT and data analytics movement prospective for the developing countries including the opportunity that offers to developing nations with a specific challenge. The talk also outlines the needs to exploit IoT potential and share IoT Technologies best-practices through the involvement of innovation communities and stakeholder (startup, developer, innovation Hub) from local district, regional, national and international-level.

**Keywords:** Africa · Internet of things · Ecosystem · Innovation · WAZIUP · Open source

## 1 Specialized and African Value-Added IoT Solutions

From our experience in WAZIUP project over the past few years, we have seen a lot of interests and early feedback on IoT from African communities and stakeholders. It is clear that the continent is getting ready to adapt IoT in their daily lives and business operations. At the same time, IoT activities are also increasing in different forms through local communities, IoT developer training by Swahili Box in Kenya, e-toll system in South Africa by SANRAL, Smart Africas Transform Africa summit and The Internet of Things Africa Summit and Smart Expo. Different stakeholders are getting involved in active IoT projects on the ground in Africa. These stakeholders include industry members, universities, NGOs, and tech start-ups, each contributing different strengths from capacity building to innovation. Big industries players with experience in IoT like IBM, SAP, Google, have established presence in Africa as well.

© Springer International Publishing AG 2017
C. Pham et al. (Eds.): GECON 2017, LNCS 10537, pp. 281–284, 2017.
DOI: 10.1007/978-3-319-68066-8_22

From technical point of view, the IoT solutions developed by Industrial countries are either too generic or focusing only on industrial market needs. In Africa, there is a need for specialized solutions which addresses fundamental problems like internet and network connectivity, cost of solutions, power requirements, simplicity in terms of deployment and operation, robustness from environment threat, and user-centric design for notification (SMSs, voice, WhatsApp and Facebook) and interaction.

Through our interaction with the average engineers and developers in Africa, they are often good in mobile and web application development but lack the experience, knowledge and capacity on the IoT core technology (e.g. data management, IoT backend, IoT connectivity, data analytics, etc.) to develop a competitive IoT solutions. They often require advanced training so they can develop these kind of solutions.

The internet connection is the major drawback. As a result, developers and engineers have to think of options for IoT without internet. For large-scale systems including hundreds of thousands of sensors, devices and/or readers, high reliability levels are likely to prove important. Cultural context on the ground also matters, and it should be taken into account, along with technical considerations.

African engineer and entrepreneur need specialized IoT big data enterprise solutions including the development kit that are faster (to save the deployment time) and easy to deploy having a very basic IoT knowledge. These solutions have to be affordable in terms of cost, working with and without internet connection, and energy efficient. They need real-life testing environment (close to reality) with large-scale systems including hundreds of sensors.

## 2   IoT Made in Africa

One of the main sources of locally developed applications and innovation is the Techno hubs that are springing up across Africa. With the rise of Fablab, makerspace and tech hubs, young and talented Africans are now coming together to collaborate and to use open source tools to develop and prototype their ideas. Most tech hub members start working on their ideas while in the University. The many of the idea and project start from university (student final year project). It is interesting to note that some of these ideas grow into start-ups once there is the conducive environment to nurture and support them.

From our experience, one of the key features of the African digital innovation renaissance is that, it is increasingly homegrown. They have the vision to redesign the solutions which already exist in developed market, by Africans for the African market, providing homegrown cost-effective alternatives. In addition, entrepreneurs want to create solutions that are appropriate for their challenges and needs like Kenyas seamless payment system, M-PESA and Brick. What is unfolding is a virtuoso system with a started in Africa mindset that could potentially remake what Africans buy. This is especially exciting because it empowers people to use their local expertise, know-how and hands-on skills to solve problems that exist in their daily lives. WOELAB is an example of such a Fablab in Lome, Togo (partner of WAZIUP) that inspires makers to use old and waste electronic part to create working products such as locally made 3D printers.

The African need to create innovative applications and services homegrown Made in Africa like MPesa (from Kenya) that addresses the local problems and requirements. The continent needs more innovation and accelerator programs run by innovation hubs and tech hubs, engagement of young and talent entrepreneurs in the innovation process.

## 3   IoT Local African Ecosystem

While it is very early to assess the impact of African innovation, it is already clear that these makers and innovation hub offer a platform for a new economic system that taps into the brainpower of Africans to seed shared prosperity. The problems to solve in the continent are plentiful- clean water, energy, health, and food processing. In addition, there are significant challenges for the African makers, getting people to take them seriously including the government and even their competitor. Also, these hubs need more innovation business model and revenue generation steam. Hence the sustainable uptake of the results and innovation services within the countries became a major issue. This is valid of all innovation project, hub as well as start-up. Most of the African start-up teams cannot afford to pay someone to develop the competitive solutions for them. For African start-up one main challenges are the go-to-market, often these start-ups need small seed funding to grow and business and technical training.

Most of the innovation projects have difficulties to sustain, since they often vanish after the project completion date. We also need to acknowledge that the sustainability is a long-term process. It often needs continuously (external aid) until reach the critical mass and viability, often additional funding, the need to develop and build on local talent, understanding the behavioral response of users and stakeholder ecosystem, innovation partnership, offer clear benefits to users.

Maximizing the benefits of the IoT is likely to require more coordinated action across all sectors, SMEs and industries, telecom operator, ICT regulators, funding agencies, financial agencies, innovation stakeholders working closely with their counterparts in data protection and competition, but also with government and policy makers. Given the high pervasiveness of the IoTs impact, it is vital that as more countries introduce policy frameworks, they take into account the various factors and implications of the IoT across different sectors. When all stakeholders are included in active dialogue, the IoT represents a promising opportunity for more coherent policy-making and implementation. IoT projects require to setup up innovation partnership and risk sharing business model; they also need a local IoT ecosystem at the same time connected with national and international/European IoT ecosystem.

The African needs to create IoT ecosystem as local as possible with involvement of complement stakeholders and actors including the innovation stakeholders. Members of the ecosystem should complement each other giving opportunity for innovation partnership model (sharing the risks and benefits). The roles of ecosystem should be the sustainability of the technology and business. The project must look for sustainable business and economic model for the hub as well as support on the business model for the start-up. This is one of the key visions of the proposal to sustain the project results and hub.

**Acknowledgements.** This talk has been produced in the context of the H2020 WAZIUP project. The WAZIUP project consortium would like to acknowledge that the research leading to these results has received funding from the European Unions H2020 Research and Innovation Programme under the Grant Agreement H2020-ICT-687607.

# Low-cost IoT, Big Data, and Cloud Platform for Developing Countries

Corentin Dupont[1], Tomas Bures[2], Mehdi Sheikhalishahi[2],
Congduc Pham[3(✉)], and Abdur Rahim[1]

[1] Fondazione Bruno Kessler (FBK)/Create-Net, Trento, Italy
{cdupont,arahim}@fbk.eu
[2] Innotec21 GmbH, Leipzig, Germany
{tomas.bures,mehdi.sheikhalishahi}@innotec21.de
[3] University of Pau, Pau, France
congduc.pham@univ-pau.fr

**Abstract.** Gartner forecasts that 6.4 billion connected things will be in use worldwide in 2016, up 30% from 2015, and will reach 20.8 billion by 2020. In 2016, 5.5 million new things will get connected every day. Furthermore, the current research and marker trends shows the convergence between IoT and Big Data. On the other hand, developing countries are still far from being able to benefit from IoT infrastructures. In this paper we explain how IoT can be made available for everybody and we present WAZIUP, a project aiming at building an open innovation platform able to accelerate innovation in developing countries and rural areas. The WAZIUP IoT platform will allow the development of IoT applications coupled with Big Data capabilities. The platform is tailored to the specific requirements and constraints of developing countries. We will give an overview of the WAZIUP IoT and Big Data platform and then detail its technical aspects.

**Keywords:** IoT · Big Data · Low-cost IoT platform · Cloud computing

## 1 Introduction

ICT developments in developing countries has the potential to cut across traditional sectors: notable examples are the introduction of micro-health insurance and health-savings accounts through mobile devices; index-based crop insurance; crowd-sourcing to monitor and manage the delivery of public services. These innovative applications recognize and leverage commonalities between sectors, blur traditional lines, and open up a new field of opportunities. The opportunity for ICT intervention in developing countries is huge especially for IoT and big data: those technologies are promising a big wave of innovation for our daily life [1, 2].

The era of IoT can connect a large variety of sensors, devices, equipment, systems. In turn, the challenge is about driving business outcomes, consumer benefits, and the creation of new value. The new mantras for the IoT era is

© Springer International Publishing AG 2017
C. Pham et al. (Eds.): GECON 2017, LNCS 10537, pp. 285–299, 2017.
DOI: 10.1007/978-3-319-68066-8_23

the collection, convergence and exploitation of data. The information collection involves data from sensors, devices, gateways, edge equipment and networks. This information allows increasing process efficiency through automation while reducing downtime and improving people productivity. Figure 1 shows some typical applications where remote monitoring facilities could greatly increase quality and productivity in a large variety of rural applications.

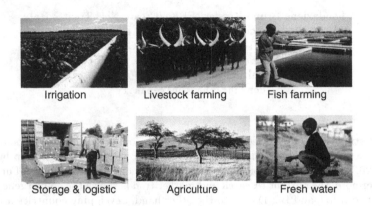

| Irrigation | Livestock farming | Fish farming |
| Storage & logistic | Agriculture | Fresh water |

**Fig. 1.** Some ICT fields of IoT opportunities in rural environments.

However, developing countries are facing many difficulties – lack of infrastructure, high cost of hardware, complexity in deployment, lack of technological ecosystem and background, etc. – when it comes to real deployment of IoT solutions [3], especially in remote and rural areas. In this context, IoT deployment must address four major issues: (a) Longer range for rural access, (b) Cost of hardware and services, (c) Limit dependancy to proprietary infrastructures and (d) Provide local interaction models.

In this article, we present in Sect. 2 the new technologies and trends contributing in making IoT available at a much lower cost for worldwide adoption. Then, we present in Sect. 3 the EU H2020 WAZIUP IoT platform targeting deployment of low-cost IoT and Big Data in developing countries, addressing the aforementioned major issues. Section 4 concludes the article.

## 2 Entering the IoT Era

### 2.1 IoT Connectivity Made Easy

Recent Low-Power Wide Area Networks (LPWAN) technologies for Internet-of-Things (IoT) introduced by Sigfox and Semtech's (LoRa$^{TM}$) [4] are currently gaining incredible interest and are under intense deployment campaigns worldwide. They definitely initiated a new innovation cycle as they obviously provide a much better connectivity answer for IoT (most of IoT devices have small amount to data to send and very limited battery power) compared to traditional cellular-based connectivity (e.g. GSM/GPRS/3G) or short-range technologies such as IEEE 802.15.4. They offer several kilometers range without relay nodes to reach a central gateway, thus greatly simplifying large-scale deployment of IoT devices as opposed to the complex multi-hop approach needed by short-range radio technologies. Figure 2 shows a typical extreme long-range 1-hop connectivity scenario to a long-range gateway, which is the single interface to Internet servers, using low-cost LoRa radio modules available from many vendors. Most of these long-range technologies can achieve 20 km or higher range in line-of-sight (LOS) condition and about 2 km–4 km in non-LOS conditions [5,6] such as in dense urban/city environments.

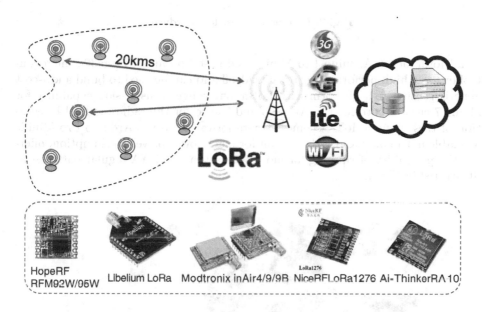

**Fig. 2.** Extreme long-range application with new radio technologies.

## 2.2 Low-Cost DIY IoT Hardware

Commercial IoT devices are getting mature but they are definitely too expensive for very low-income countries. In addition, these highly integrated devices are difficult to repair with their parts being hardly locally replaced. The availability of low-cost, open-source hardware platforms such as Arduino boards and Raspberry-like embedded Linux definitely pushes for a Do-It-Yourself (DIY) and "off-the-shelves" design approach for a large variety of IoT applications [7].

The Arduino ecosystem is large and proposes various board models, from large and powerful prototyping boards to smaller and less energy-consuming boards for final integration purposes as illustrated in Fig. 3. For instance, the

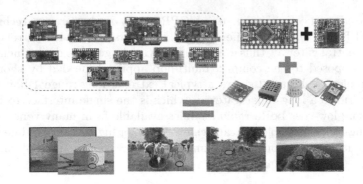

**Fig. 3.** Generic low-cost IoT hardware.

small form factor Arduino Pro Mini board based on an ATmega328 microcontroller has a high performance/price tradeoff and can be used to build a low-cost generic sensing IoT platform with LoRa long-range transmission capability for about 7 euro: 2 euro for the Arduino and 5 euro for the radio module! Integration of these generic IoT becomes straightforward and the Arduino Pro Mini is available in the 3.3v & 8 MHz version for much lower power consumption, offering the possibility of running for more than a year on 4 AA regular batteries as illustrated in Fig. 4.

**Fig. 4.** Easy integration with DIY approach for maximum appropriation.

It is expected that this availability of low-cost DIY IoT will create a tremendous uptake of the technology on a large-scale, for a large variety of applications, including those from developing countries as even a limited deployment of IoT devices can have huge impacts.

## 2.3  Handling IoT Data

A complete IoT system should be able to leverage big data technique for storing, processing, and analysing data. Such a technique is Hadoop MapReduce [8]. It is a scalable data analysis and processing tool. Apache Spark [9] is a different data analytics system. With in-memory capability, it claimed to be faster than MapReduce up to a hundred times. Apache Flume [10] is a distributed, reliable service for collecting, aggregating and moving large amounts of streaming data. Apache Kafka [11] is a high-throughput, distributed, publish-subscribe messaging system. With Kafka, data can be consumed by multiple applications. Orion Context Broker [12] provides a publish-subscribe mechanism for registering context elements and managing them through updates and queries. To this end, Apache Flink [13] is a streaming data flow engine (realtime stream processing) that provides data distribution, communication and fault-tolerance.

However, there are currently several new approaches based on Platform as a Service (PaaS) offering more flexible IoT services with data processing capacity inspired from Big Data techniques and the possibility to manage storage cloud in both local and global manner. The idea of extending the PaaS approach to IoT is to propose a platform dedicated to IoT developers that can reduce the time-to-market for an application by cutting the development costs. Big Data techniques enable the processing of huge amount of data produced by sensors. These techniques allow creating actionable information and knowledge out of raw data. To this end, the local and global clouds address the intermittent connection challenge: when Internet is not available, the user can still access some IoT functionalities from the local Cloud.

Figure 5 presents a typical architecture of such an IoT platform. It shows the four main functional domains: Application Platform, IoT Platform, Security and Privacy, and Stream & Data Analytic. The Application Platform involves

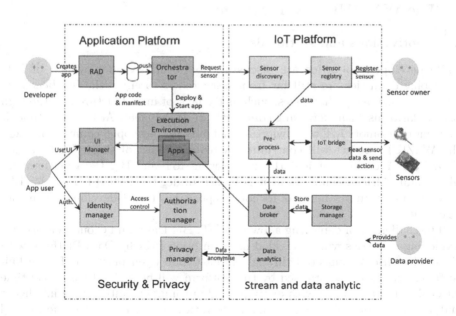

**Fig. 5.** IoT platform architecture.

the development of the application itself and its deployment in the Cloud and in the Gateway. For this purpose, a rapid application development (RAD) tool can be used, such as Node-Red. A user can provide the source code of the application, together with its manifest. The manifest file describes the application's requirements in terms of RAM, CPU, disk and also data sources (e.g. real sensors, Internet sources), big data processing engines (e.g. Flink, Hadoop), and application deployment (in the Cloud and in the IoT Gateway).

In this kind of approach and architecture, the application source code, together with the manifest, is pushed to the Cloud platform by the user. The orchestrator component will read the manifest and trigger the compilation of the application. It will then deploy the application in the Cloud Execution Environment. It will also instantiate the services needed by the application, as described in the manifest. The last task of the orchestrator is to request the sensor and data sources connections from the IoT components. The sensor discovery module will be in charge of retrieving a list of sensors that matches the manifest description. On the left side of the diagram, sensor owners can register their sensors with the platform. External data sources such as Internet APIs can also be connected directly to data broker. The sensors selected for each application will deliver their data to data broker, through the IoT bridge and pre-processor. This last component is in charge of managing the connection and configuration of the sensors. In addition, it will contain the routines for pre-processing of data, such as cleaning, extrapolating, aggregating and averaging. Historical data can be stored using the Storage manager.

## 3   The WAZIUP IoT Platform

### 3.1   Motivations and Rationals

While developed countries are discussing about massive deployment of IoT, developing countries are still far from being ready to enjoy the full benefit of IoT. They face many challenges, such as the lack of infrastructure and the high cost of platforms with increasing complexity in deployment. At the same time, it is urgent to promote IoT worldwide and not only for developed countries market. The WAZIUP project will contribute by reducing part of the technology gap. WAZIUP is focusing particularly in deploying IoT and Big Data platform for sub-saharan African countries as it is funded under the H2020 EU call for EU-Africa cooperation but many of its core propositions target developing countries is general.

The challenges of deploying a low-cost IoT, Big Data, and Cloud platform for developing countries will be tackled using an open IoT-Big Data Platform with affordable sensors connected through an Iot-Cloud open platform. The technical functionalities encompassed by the platform will be a cloud-based real-time data collection combined with analytics and automation software, an intelligent analytics of sensor and device data, an integration to third parties platforms and a Platform-as-a-Service provider.

## 3.2  Architecture Overview and Implementation

The WAZIUP IoT platform (www.waziup.io) follows the flexible IoT platform illustrated previously in Fig. 5. The open source platform has been implemented with state of the art technology and there is a GitHub repository at https://github.com/Waziup/Platform. It is the main repository for platform developers as well as application developer, being open it is accessible to everybody. The real-world WAZIUP IoT platform implementation is further illustrated in Fig. 6 which shows the WAZIUP cloud platform stack and its connection to IoT gateways through data broker (such as Orion Context Broker).

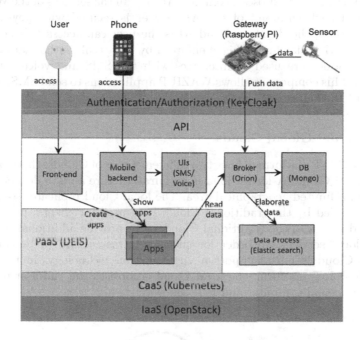

**Fig. 6.** Global overview of WAZIUP Cloud platform, and services.

The role of each component is presented, together with the technology selected in parenthesis. The WAZIUP IoT platform uses three distinct Cloud layers (in blue in the figure):

1. Infrastructure as a Service (IaaS),
2. Container as a Service (CaaS),
3. and finally Platform as a Service (PaaS).

The first layer is provided by OpenStack [14]. Its main role is to provide Virtual Machines (VMs) that run the full platform. This layer is fundamental because most of Cloud vendors (Amazon, Rackspace) use VMs as basic selling units. The second layer is provided by Kubernetes [15]. The role of this layer is to provide and serve containers, such as Docker containers, to WAZIUP services and applications. The containers provide light-weight and ultra-fast virtualization for applications and micro-services. The containers themselves are running inside the VMs. The third and final Cloud layer is provided by `Deis` [16]. It provides services to developers, such as compiling and deploying of an application. All the applications pushed by the users will be compiled with `Deis` and hosted in containers on `Kubernetes`.

Both Authentication and Authorization management is realized by `Keycloak` [17] (e.g. access the dashboard, access to the platform). Users' applications (Web, mobile) and external components (e.g. IoT gateway) need to go through an API server. The API server exposes a common API for all the services of the WAZIUP platform and each endpoint of the API server is secured with `Keycloak`. In addition, through the dashboard and APIs the user can access only to sensors that are authorized for him. This is enforced by `Keycloak` authorization layer.

Mobile phones are used to interfaces with the SMS and voice commands component. This component allows WAZIUP applications to send SMS and voice notifications to the users.

### 3.3   Local and Global Clouds

The WAZIUP IoT platform defines two different types of Clouds: the local Cloud and the global Cloud. A local Cloud is an infrastructure able to deliver services to clients in a limited geographical area. The local Cloud replicates some of the features provided by the traditional Cloud. It is used for clients that may not have a good access to the traditional Cloud, or to provide additional processing power to local services. In order for such an infrastructure to be considered as a local Cloud it must support a virtualization technology. In the case of the WAZIUP IoT platform, the local Cloud comprises the end-user or service provider's personal computer and IoT Gateway.

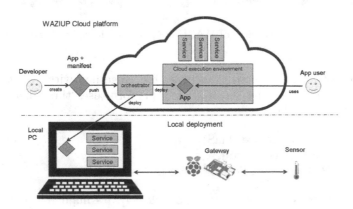

**Fig. 7.** Waziup local and global deployment.

The global Cloud, on the other end, is based on "backbone infrastructure" which increases the business opportunities for service providers and allows services to access a virtually infinite amount of computing resources. In order for such an infrastructure to be considered as a global Cloud it must support a virtualization technology and be able to host the global cloud components of the WAZIUP architecture.

One of WAZIUP innovative approach to take into account developing countries' constraints is to extend the PaaS concept to the local Cloud. On the left part of Fig. 7, the application is designed by the developer, together with the manifest file. It is pushed on the WAZIUP Cloud platform. The orchestrator then takes care of compiling and deploying the application in the various Cloud execution environments. Furthermore, the orchestrator drives the instantiation of the services in the Cloud, according to the manifest. The manifest is also describing which part of the application need to be installed locally, together with corresponding services. The local application can then connect to the gateway and collect data from the sensors.

## 3.4   Data Management and Analytics Architecture

The IoT Gateway (e.g. LoRa gateway) pushes IoT sensors' data to the data broker which can distribute further to final applications on request. The WAZIUP architecture integrates the FIWARE Orion data broker for providing current sensor values and `ElasticSearch` [18] to keep the history (time series) of sensor values. An ElasticSearch Feeder service is responsible for transferring data (current sensor values) from Orion to ElasticSearch (for historical record keeping).

ElasticSearch Feeder is written in NodeJS. It accesses Orion and Elastic-Search through their REST APIs. It allows transferring data from Orion to ElasticSearch either in a periodic manner (e.g. every 5 min) or by subscription when data are recorded in ElasticSearch only if they change in Orion. The ElasticSearch Feeder is configured by specifying a set of tasks, where each task defines the Orion's service path along with sensor' attributes and maps it to an ElasticSearch's index. A commented example of the configuration is shown below. The configuration is provided in YAML for 2 soil moisture devices (`WS_FARM1_Sensor2` and `WS_FARM1_Sensor3`) deployed in FARM1. Each device has 2 soil moisture physical sensors that provide 2 reading of soil moisture level at different depths (SM1 and SM2) and will periodically send data string formatted as follows: SM1/554/SM2/345.

```
# Defines the HTTP endpoint for subscriptions
endpoint:
  id: feeder1
  url: http://feeder
  host: 0.0.0.0
  port: 8000
# Defines the default ElasticSearch connection settings.
elasticsearch:
```

```
  host: elasticsearch
  port: 9200
# Defines the default Orion connection settings.
orion:
  uri: http://broker
# Defines (multiple) tasks.
- trigger: subscription
#   Specifies task-level Orion settings
  orion:
    service: waziup
    servicePath: /FARM1/TESTS
#   Specifies task-level Elasticsearch settings
  elasticsearch:
    index: test
#   Specifies the filter over the sensors discovered.
  filter:
#   If set, only entities listed below will be considered.
    ids:
    - WS_FARM1_Sensor2
    - WS_FARM1_Sensor3
#   If set, only attributes listed below will be considered.
    attributes:
    - SM1
    - SM2
```

### 3.5  Applications Platform Architecture

WAZIUP vision is to make it easy for IoT developers to develop new applications, dashboards and services. With WAZIUP APIs Server model, several generic proxy APIs services are developed, such as for Security (KeyCloak proxy API), Data Management (Orion proxy API), Data Analytics (ElasticSearch

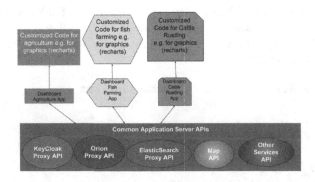

**Fig. 8.** A global view of WAZIUP Application Template platform.

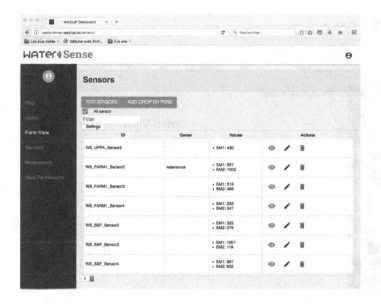

**Fig. 9.** A customized dashboard application for the soil moisture scenario.

proxy API), etc. These APIs may be developed as part of WAZIUP APIs Server, or as separate Service APIs that are just proxy APIs calling the respective service APIs. Figure 8 illustrates this concept to create application templates.

This approach is also taken at the Dashboard level where Application Development templates for IoT developers are provided to develop customized end-user applications. These APIs will be developed as a NodeJS server. For instance, instead of contacting the Orion broker in the client Dashboard, the Orion API of WAZIUP Server API is called to get the list of sensors, sensors data, subscriptions, etc. This approach will make it easier for developers to develop new dashboards having in place those that are already developed and tested on top of WAZIUP Services. Figure 9 shows the dashboard developed for the WaterSense project in Pakistan (optimization of maize crop irrigation) using the WAZIUP framework. Figure 10 shows WS_FARM1_Sensor2's historical data.

### 3.6   Service Orchestration and Resources Provisioning

The WAZIUP IoT platform offers mechanisms that autonomously analyze application requirements, user preferences and Cloud resources and accordingly decide upon the most appropriate deployment of services. The most appropriate deployment must achieve the best balance between system performance, quality of service and cost. In this context, services may be decomposed into smaller components, based on the current situation and information on data sources, in order to be migrated and executed in a local Cloud, near the data sources, following the Hadoop maxim "Moving Computation is Cheaper than Moving Data".

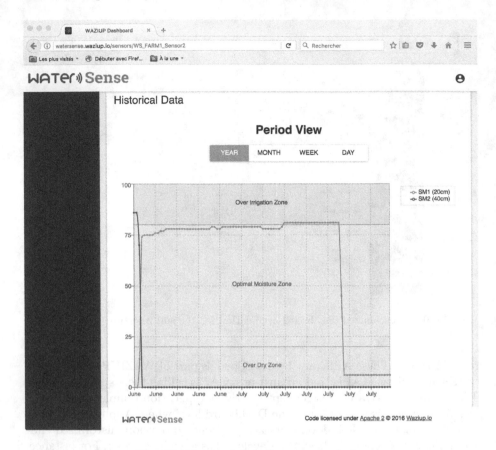

**Fig. 10.** Historical data from sensor device.

Alternatively, services may be deployed and executed in the global Cloud. Furthermore, this mechanism will facilitate the notion of "Everything as a Service", and attached gateway to host and process services on-demand, by means of service migration instead of being limited to predefined services. The local IoT Gateway may act as part of a local Cloud on an on-demand basis in coordination with the global Cloud, provided that the local Cloud has sufficient resources to process and execute the service.

### 3.7  Platform Security Architecture

Figure 11 illustrates WAZIUP services architecture in more details. The access to different WAZIUP services is performed by the WAZIUP APIs server (Dashboard API Server in Fig. 11.

The APIs server acts as a gateway placed in the demilitarized zone between the Internet and the internal network with WAZIUP services. WAZIUP APIs server provides public endpoints for the internally hosted services and proxies

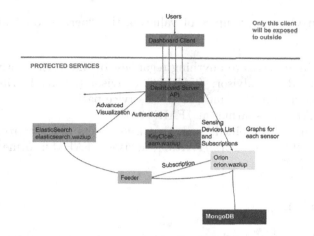

**Fig. 11.** Detailed view of WAZIUP cloud platform, and services architecture.

to them. All these services will not provide any Ingress to outside world. APIs Server can communicate with all `Kubernetes` internal services. And can respond to Client queries about different services. Thus, APIs Server will act as a proxy to provide security for WAZIUP services.

Authentication is the first requirement in implementing security. Users should be first identified by WAZIUP platform, then they can request access to different resources, i.e. authorization. WAZIUP APIs server takes care of the authentication and authorization of incoming requests from the Internet. Authentication is performed with `Keycloak` server while authorization is done directly by the WAZIUP APIs server. Depending on whether a service is accessed in an interactive manner (from a web-browser) or in a programmatic manner (directly from another service), WAZIUP APIs server provides two basic flows:

- Authentication for interactive use: A user accesses a page (e.g. through a Dashboard web client). The browser sends a request to the APIs server. The server finds out that client has not authenticated yet and redirects the client's browser to a login screen provided by `Keycloak`.
- Authentication for programmatic use (e.g. from a sensor gateway): A user generates (typically through some web-based client) an offline access refresh token. The token is given to a device (e.g. the sensor gateway) as a configuration parameter. When the device wants to make a request, it contacts `Keycloak` and requests an access token to be generated based on the refresh token.

Once the authentication is successful completed, the APIs server uses the access token to validate if the user/device has access to a particular resource. For the sake of the authorization, every user has an attribute "permissions" (which is maintained by `Keycloak`). The attribute "permissions" attaches the role of the user (admin, advisor or farmer) to resources (sensors, etc.) under a particular service path in Orion. Examples of values of the "permissions" attribute are listed below:

- "admin": admin access to anything regardless of the service path
- "advisor: /FARM1; advisor: /FARM2" - advisor (i.e. read-write access) to anything under /FARM1 and /FARM2 service paths
- "farmer: /FARM1" - farmer at /FARM1
- The roles can be combined, such that a user gets different roles at different service paths: "advisor: /FARM1; advisor: /FARM2; farmer: /FARM2; farmer: /FARM3".

## 4    Conclusion

With ICT technologies, developing countries can dramatically improve its productivity by enabling the rapid and cost-effective deployment of advanced and real-time monitoring. However, deploying an IoT platform in developing countries comes with many challenges. Among them, the most important are supporting low cost, low power, low bandwidth, and intermittent Internet. Moreover, widely accessible communication means such as SMS and voice calls need to be supported to reach the maximum users. In this article, we proposed an architecture and implementation for the IoT Big Data platform. The concepts that underpin the platform are three: PaaS approach to IoT, data processing capacity inspired from Big Data techniques and, local and global Cloud. The idea of extending the PaaS approach to IoT is to propose a platform dedicated to IoT developers that can reduce the time-to-market for an application by cutting the development costs. The Big Data techniques enable the processing of the huge amount of data produced by sensors. Those techniques allow creating actionable information and knowledge out of the raw data. Finally, the local and global Clouds address the intermittent connection challenge: when Internet is not available, the user can still access some IoT functionalities from the local Cloud.

**Acknowledgements.** This work has been carried out within the European project WAZIUP (H2020-ICT-687607).

## References

1. Sarkar, P.J., Chanagala, S.: A survey on IoT based digital agriculture monitoring system and their impact on optimal utilization of resources. J. Electron. Commun. Eng. (IOSR-JECE) 1–4 (2016)
2. ITU: Harnessing the internet of things for global development. Technical report, ITU (2015)
3. Zennaro, M., Bagula, A.: IoT for development (IoT4d). In: IoT Newsletter. 14 July 2015
4. Semtech: LoRa modulation basics. rev.2-05/2015 (2015)

5. Semtech: McKeown, J.: LoRa$^{TM}$- a communications solution for emerging LPWAN, LPHAN and industrial sensing & IoT applications. http://cwbackoffice.co.uk/docs/jeff~20mckeown.pdf. Accessed 13 Jan 2016
6. Libelium: Extreme range links: LoRa 868/915mhz sx1272 LoRa module for Arduino, Raspberry PI and Intel Galileo. http://www.cooking-hacks.com/documentation/tutorials/extreme-range-lora-sx1272-module-shield-arduino-raspberry-pi-intel-galileo. Accessed 13 Jan 2016
7. Dlodlo, N., Kalezhi, J.: The internet of things in agriculture for sustainable rural development. In: 2015 International Conference on Emerging Trends in Networks and Computer Communications (ETNCC), pp. 13–18, May 2015
8. http://hadoop.apache.org
9. http://spark.apache.org
10. https://flume.apache.org
11. http://kafka.apache.org
12. http://catalogue.fiware.org
13. http://flink.apache.org
14. https://www.openstack.org
15. http://kubernetes.io
16. http://dcis.io
17. http://www.keycloak.org
18. https://www.elastic.co

# Author Index

Printed in the United States
By Bookmasters